尾田栄一郎

It just occurred to me yesterday that "One Piece"...
is a really weird title! (explosive laugh)

-Eiichiro Oda, 2003

Eiichiro Oda began his manga career at the age of 17, when his one-shot cowboy manga **Wanted!** won second place in the coveted Tezuka manga awards. Oda went on to work as an assistant to some of the biggest manga artists in the industry, including Nobuhiro Watsuki, before winning the Hop Step Award for new artists. His pirate adventure **One Piece**, which debuted in **Weekly Shonen Jump** in 1997, quickly became one of the most popular manga in Japan.

ONE PIECE VOL. 27
SKYPIEA PART 4

SHONEN JUMP Manga Edition

STORY AND ART BY EIICHIRO ODA

English Adaptation/Lance Caselman
Translation/JN Productions
Touch-up Art & Lettering/Elena Diaz
Design/Fawn Lau
Supervising Editor/Yuki Murashige
Editor/Alexis Kirsch

VP, Production/Alvin Lu
VP, Sales & Product Marketing/Gonzalo Ferreyra
VP, Creative/Linda Espinosa
Publisher/Hyoe Narita

Published by VIZ Media, LLC
P.O. Box 77010
San Francisco, CA 94107

10 9 8 7 6 5 4 3 2 1
First printing, January 2010

PARENTAL ADVISORY
ONE PIECE is rated T for Teen and is recommended
for ages 13 and up. This volume contains fantasy
violence and tobacco usage.
ratings.viz.com

THE WORLD'S
MOST POPULAR MANGA

www.shonenjump.com

SHONEN JUMP MANGA

ONE PIECE

Vol. 27
OVERTURE

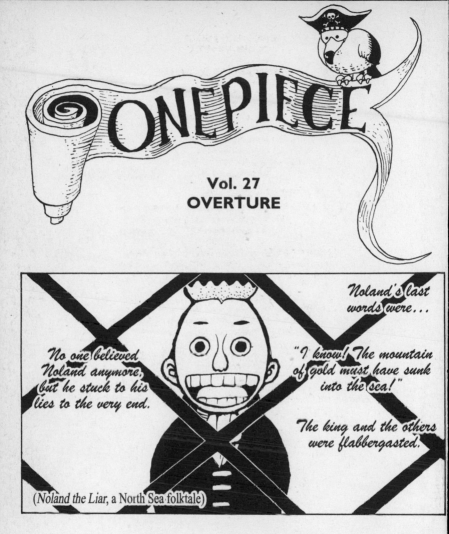

Noland's last words were...
"I know! The mountain of gold must have sunk into the sea!"
The king and the others were flabbergasted.
No one believed Noland anymore, but he stuck to his lies to the very end.
(Noland the Liar, a North Sea folktale)

STORY AND ART BY
EIICHIRO ODA

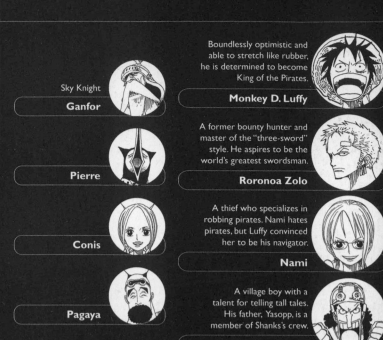

Sky Knight
Ganfor

Pierre

Conis

Pagaya

Boundlessly optimistic and able to stretch like rubber, he is determined to become King of the Pirates.
Monkey D. Luffy

A former bounty hunter and master of the "three-sword" style. He aspires to be the world's greatest swordsman.
Roronoa Zolo

A thief who specializes in robbing pirates. Nami hates pirates, but Luffy convinced her to be his navigator.
Nami

A village boy with a talent for telling tall tales. His father, Yasopp, is a member of Shanks's crew.
Usopp

The big-hearted cook (and ladies' man) whose dream is to find the legendary sea, the "All Blue."
Sanji

A blue-nosed man-reindeer and the ship's doctor.
Tony Tony Chopper

A mysterious woman in search of the Ponegliff on which true history is recorded.
Nico Robin

THE STORY OF ONE PIECE

Volume 27

Monkey D. Luffy started out as just a kid with a dream—to become the greatest pirate in history! Stirred by the tales of pirate "Red-Haired" Shanks, Luffy vowed to become a pirate himself. That was before the enchanted Devil Fruit gave Luffy the power to stretch like rubber, at the cost of being unable to swim—a serious handicap for an aspiring sea dog. Undeterred, Luffy set out to sea and recruited some crewmates—master swordsman Zolo; treasure-hunting thief Nami; lying sharpshooter Usopp; the high-kicking chef Sanji; Chopper, the walkin' talkin' reindeer doctor; and the mysterious archaeologist Robin.

On the Grand Line, Luffy and crew help Vivi, the princess of Alabasta, save her kingdom from the villainous Crocodile, one of the Seven Warlords of the Sea. After welcoming aboard a new crew member, Nico Robin, they set sail once more.

Using the compass as their guide, they continue on their course. When Robin tells them that there is an island in the sky, Luffy decides to make a detour for this new realm—Skypiea!! With a little help from Mont Blanc Cricket, the Straw Hats set sail for the sky! It isn't long before aerial attackers assault the ship. Fortunately they get a helping hand from Ganfor, the Sky Knight, but the Straw Hats aren't out of trouble yet. Apparently Skypiea is "Kami's" domain, and his followers don't take kindly to trespassers. Now Luffy and crew are considered criminals and must face the challenges of Kami's most powerful servants, the Vassals!

Skypiea Vassals

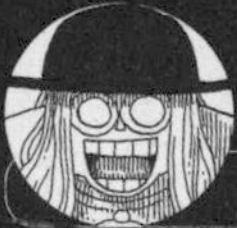

Ball Challenge

Satori of the Forest

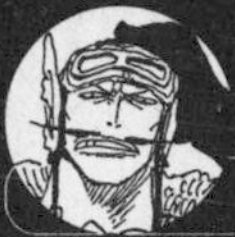

?

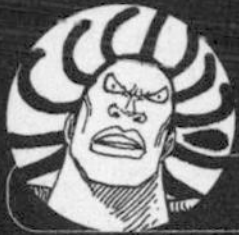

?

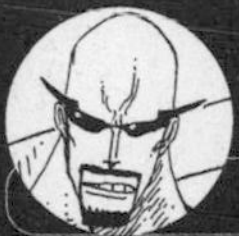

?

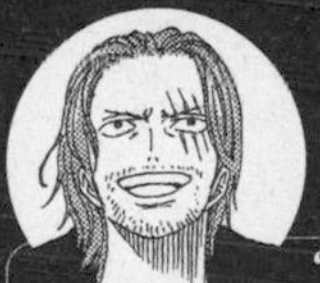

A pirate that Luffy idolizes. Shanks gave Luffy his trademark straw hat.

"Red-Haired" Shanks

SKYPIEA
ONE PIECE

Vol. 27
Overture

CONTENTS

Chapter 247:
BALL CHALLENGE

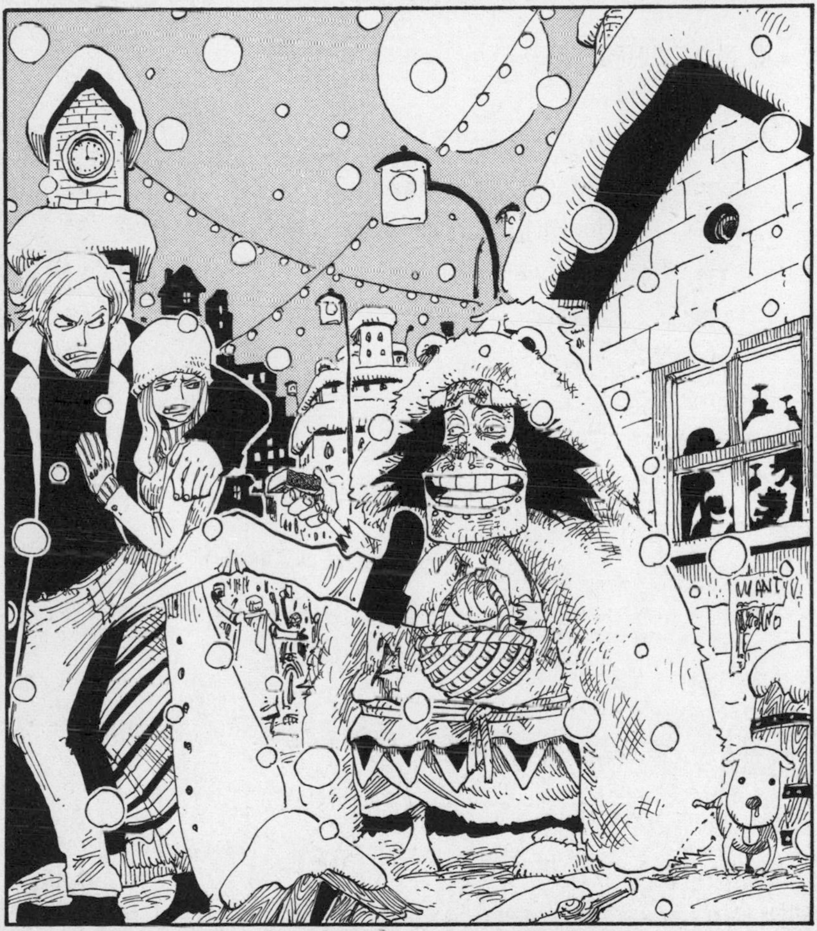

WAPOL'S OMNIVOROUS RAMPAGE, VOL. 10:
"I'M THE LITTLE MATCH GIRL!"

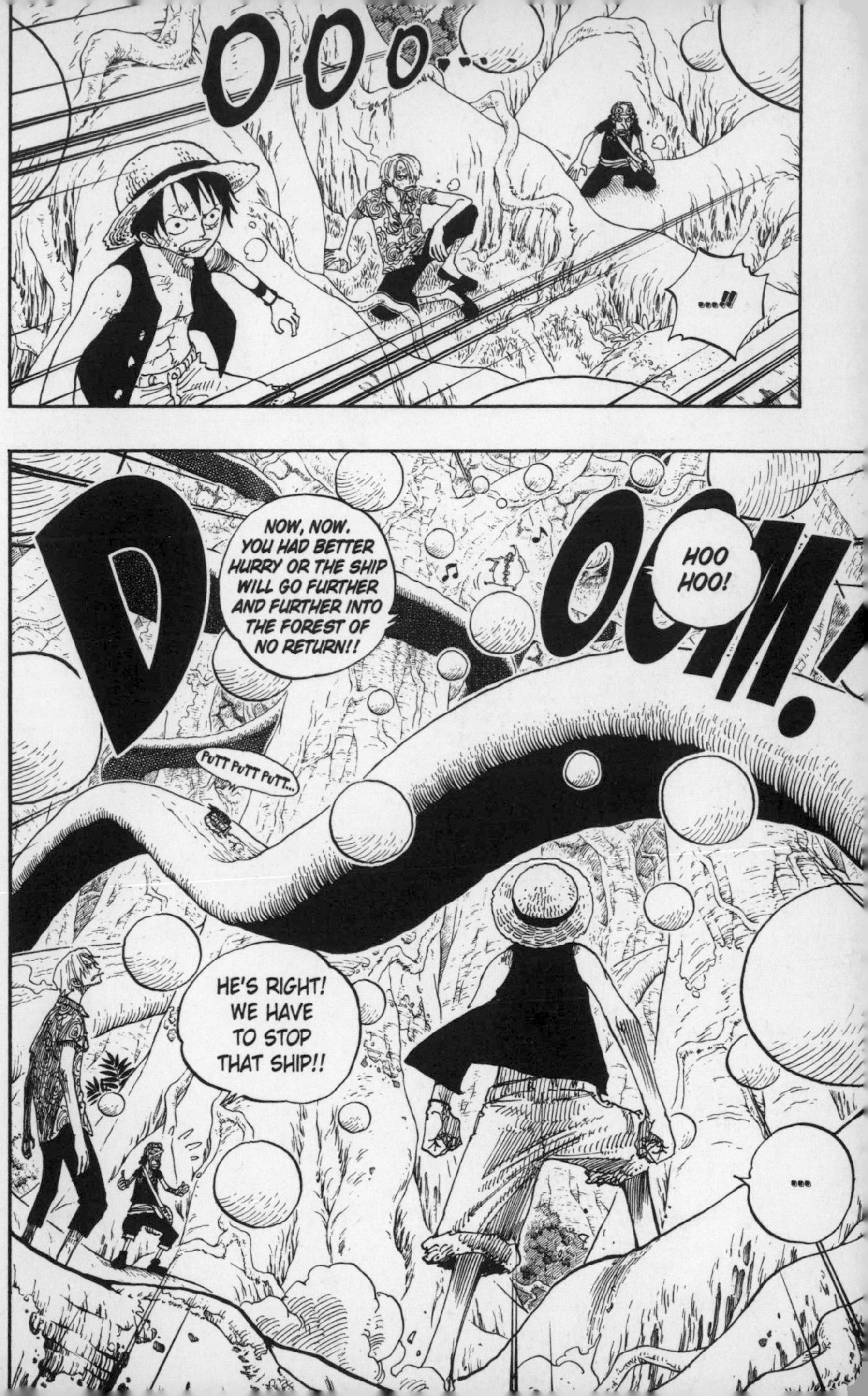
OOOO......
...!!
DOOM!!
HOO HOO!
NOW, NOW. YOU HAD BETTER HURRY OR THE SHIP WILL GO FURTHER AND FURTHER INTO THE FOREST OF NO RETURN!!
PUTT PUTT PUTT...
...
HE'S RIGHT! WE HAVE TO STOP THAT SHIP!!

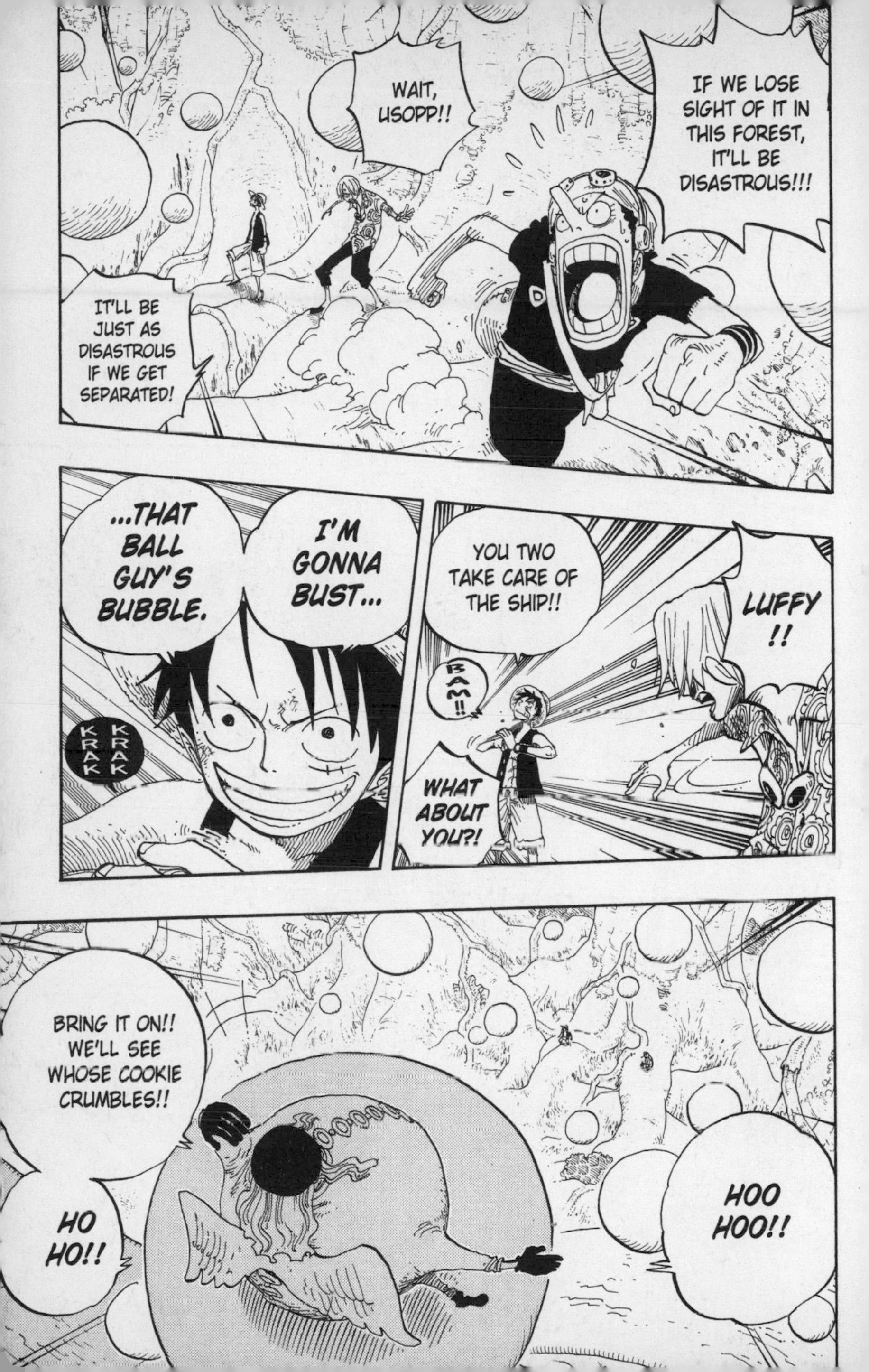
IF WE LOSE SIGHT OF IT IN THIS FOREST, IT'LL BE DISASTROUS!!!
WAIT, USOPP!!
IT'LL BE JUST AS DISASTROUS IF WE GET SEPARATED!
LUFFY!!
YOU TWO TAKE CARE OF THE SHIP!!
BAM!!
WHAT ABOUT YOU?!
I'M GONNA BUST...
...THAT BALL GUY'S BUBBLE.
KRAK KRAK
HOO HOO!!
BRING IT ON!! WE'LL SEE WHOSE COOKIE CRUMBLES!!
HO HO!!

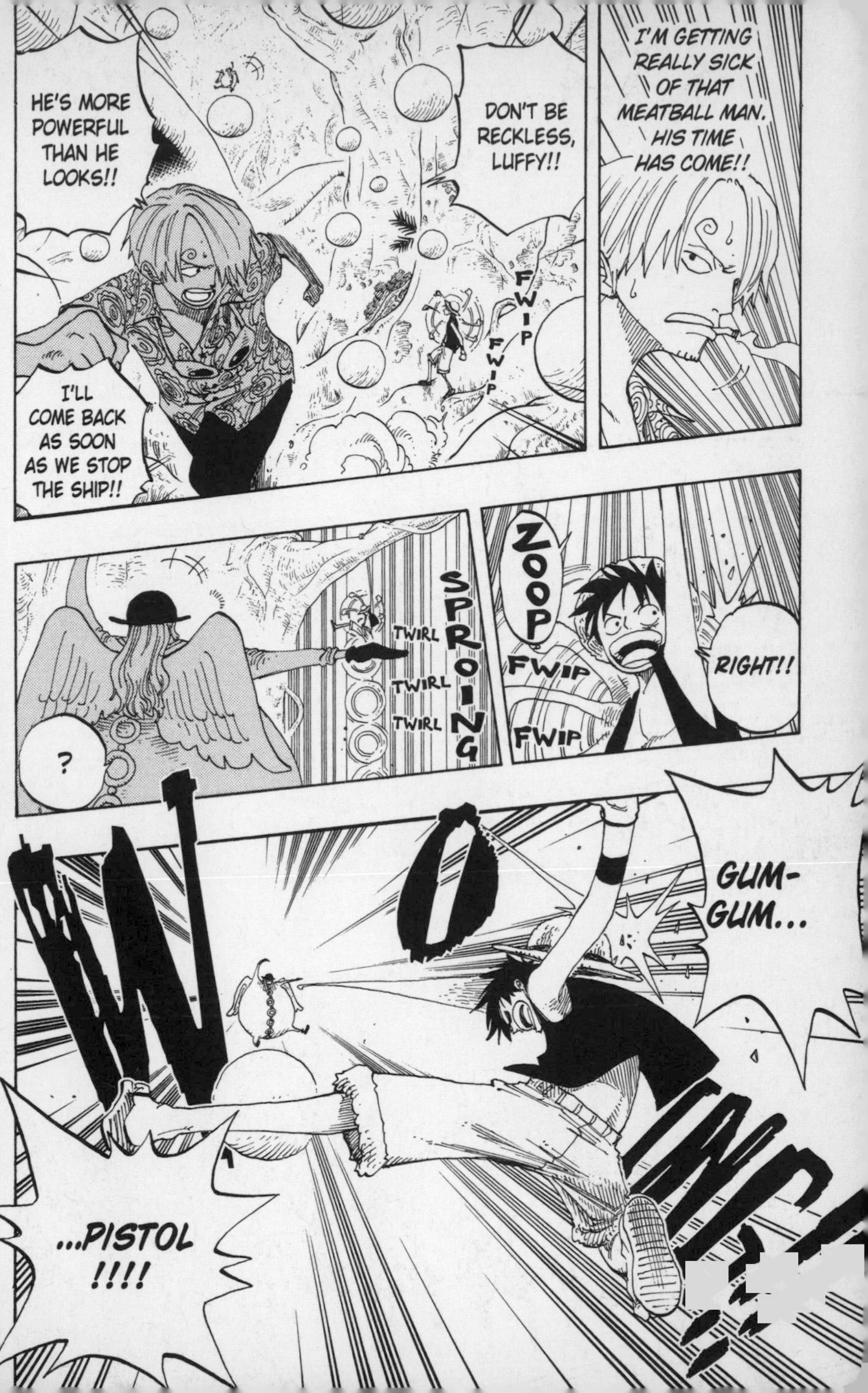
I'M GETTING REALLY SICK OF THAT MEATBALL MAN. HIS TIME HAS COME!!
DON'T BE RECKLESS, LUFFY!!
FWIP FWIP
HE'S MORE POWERFUL THAN HE LOOKS!!
I'LL COME BACK AS SOON AS WE STOP THE SHIP!!
RIGHT!!
ZOOP
FWIP FWIP
SPROING
TWIRL TWIRL TWIRL
?
GUM-GUM...
...PISTOL !!!!

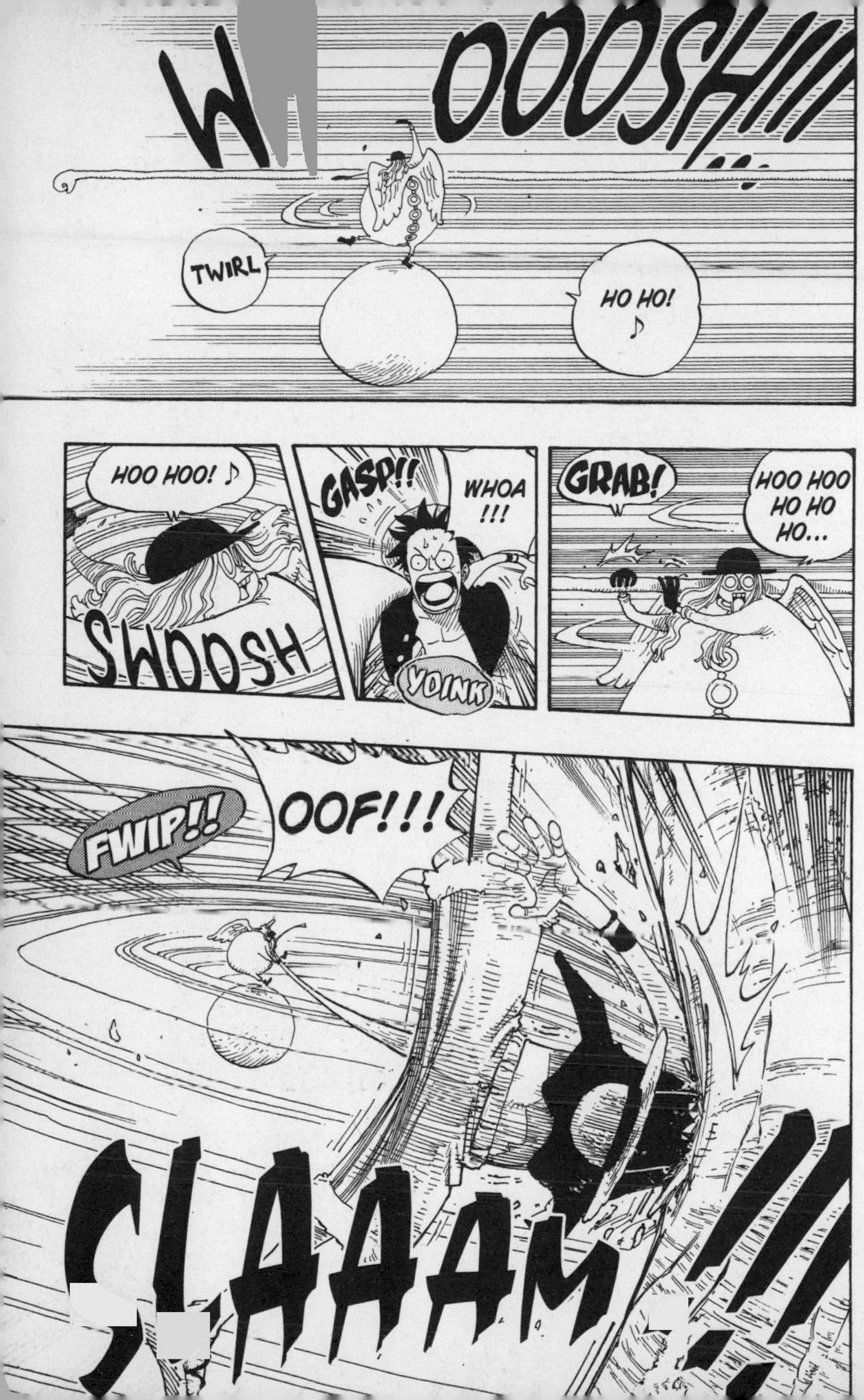
W OOOSH!!!
HO HO! ♪
TWIRL
HOO HOO HO HO HO...
GRAB!
WHOA !!!
GASP!!
YOINK
HOO HOO! ♪
SWOOSH
OOF!!!
FWIP!!
SLAAAM!!!

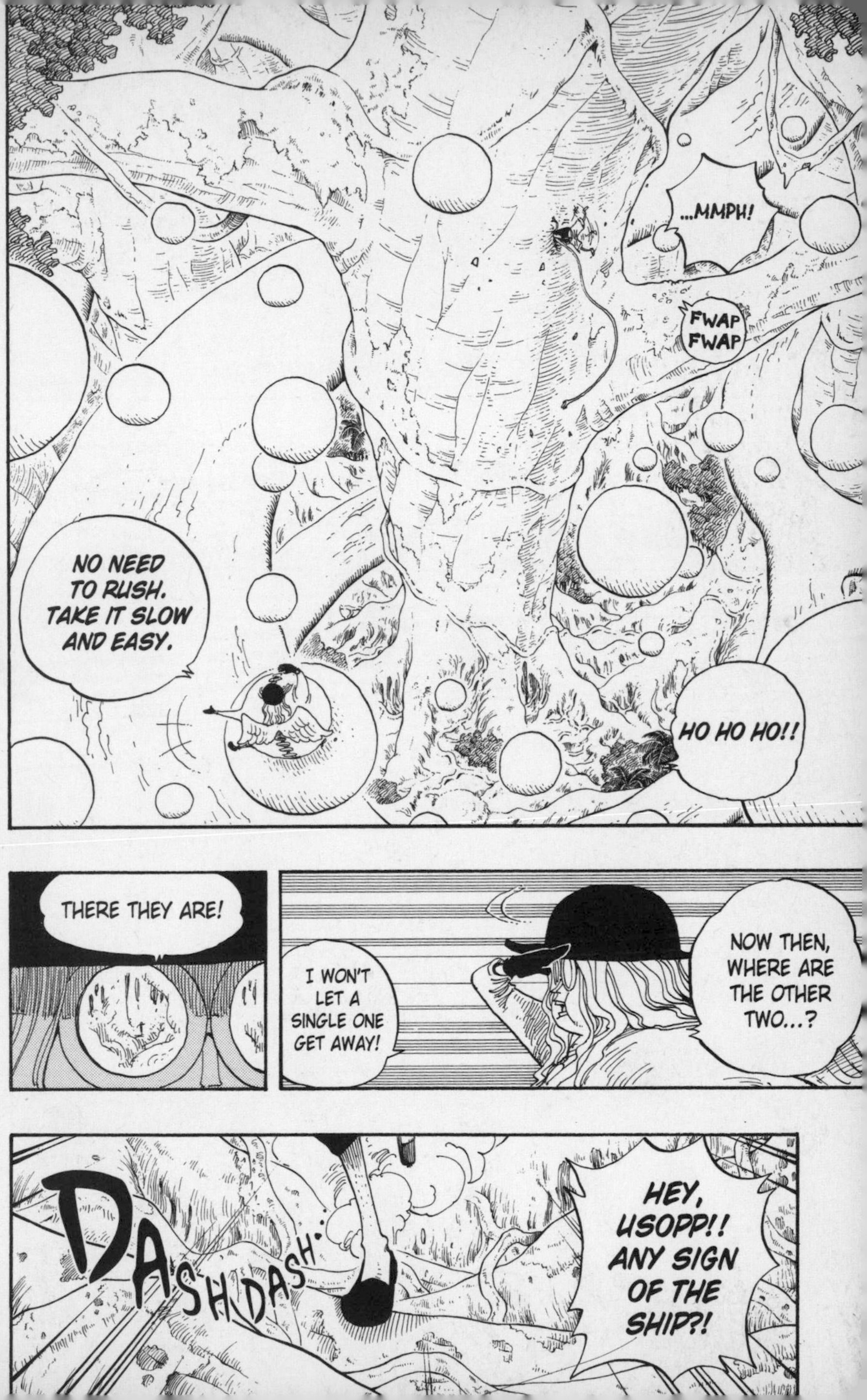
...MMPH!
FWAP FWAP
HO HO HO!!
NO NEED TO RUSH. TAKE IT SLOW AND EASY.
NOW THEN, WHERE ARE THE OTHER TWO...?
I WON'T LET A SINGLE ONE GET AWAY!
THERE THEY ARE!
HEY, USOPP!! ANY SIGN OF THE SHIP?!
DASH DASH

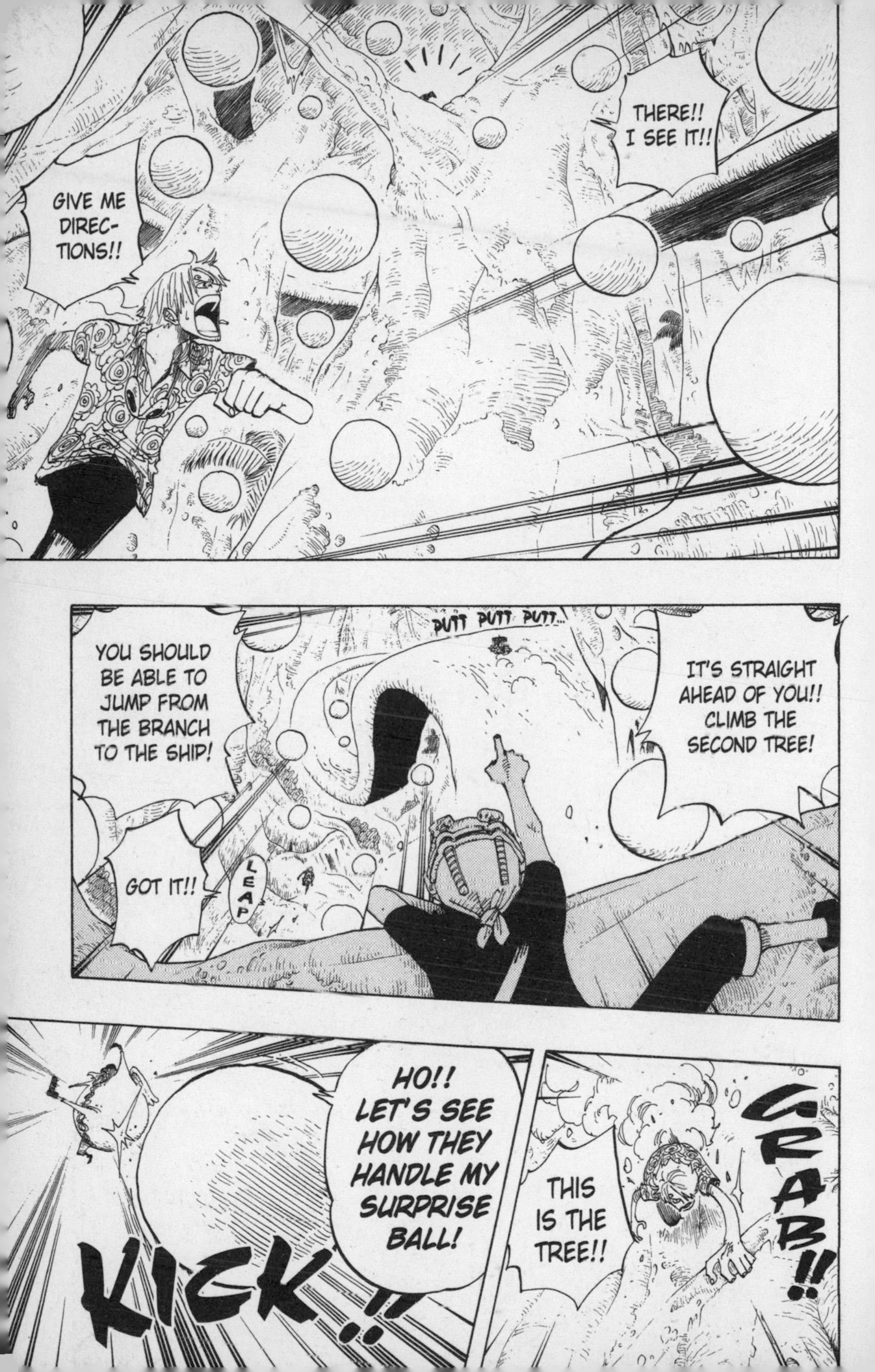
THERE!! I SEE IT!!
GIVE ME DIREC- TIONS!!
IT'S STRAIGHT AHEAD OF YOU!! CLIMB THE SECOND TREE!
PUTT PUTT PUTT...
YOU SHOULD BE ABLE TO JUMP FROM THE BRANCH TO THE SHIP!
GOT IT!!
LEAP
GRAB!!
THIS IS THE TREE!!
HO!! LET'S SEE HOW THEY HANDLE MY SURPRISE BALL!
KICK!!

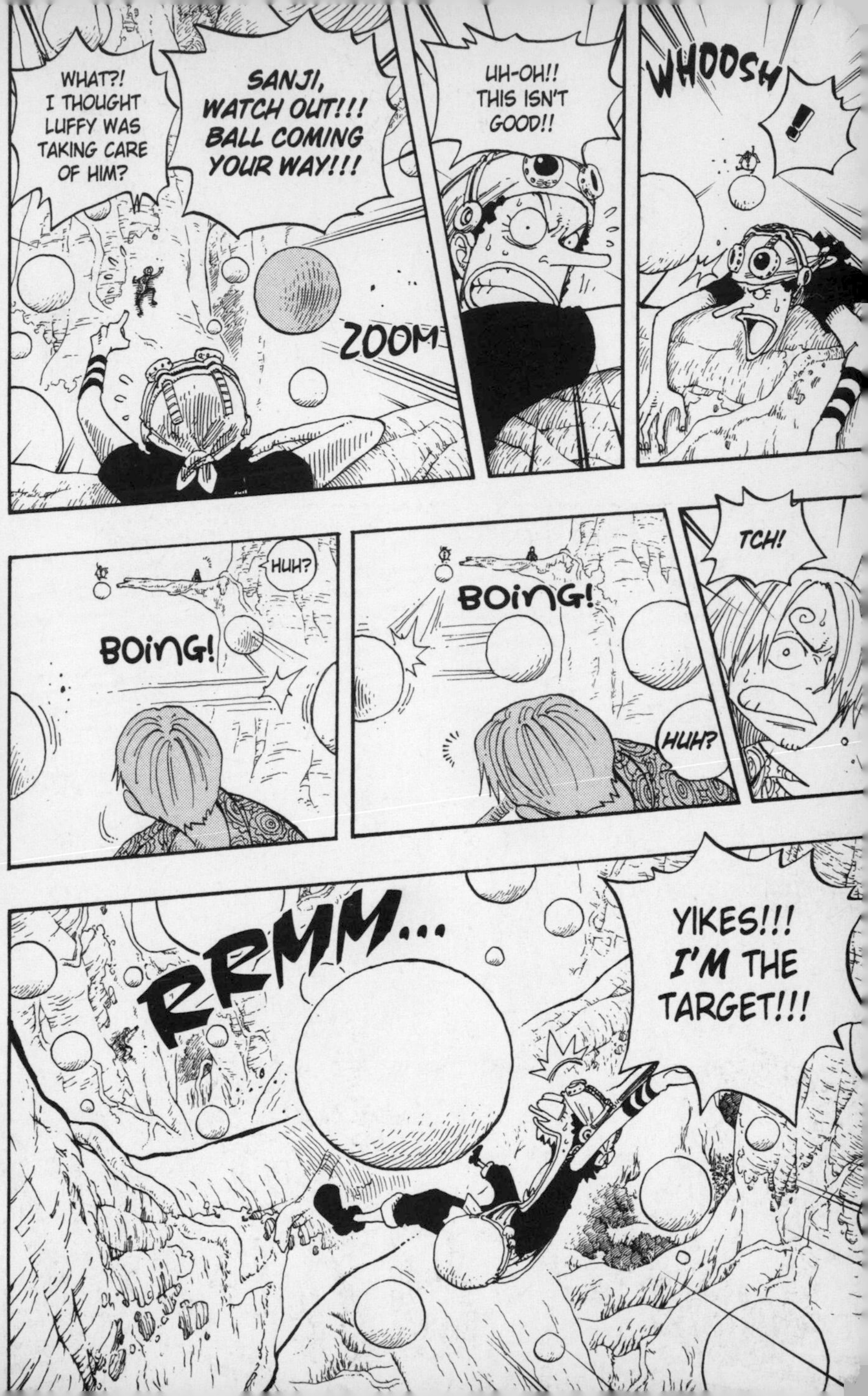
WHOOSH
!
UH-OH!! THIS ISN'T GOOD!!
SANJI, WATCH OUT!!! BALL COMING YOUR WAY!!!
WHAT?! I THOUGHT LUFFY WAS TAKING CARE OF HIM?
ZOOM
TCH!
HUH?
BOING!
HUH?
BOING!
YIKES!!! I'M THE TARGET!!!
RRMM...

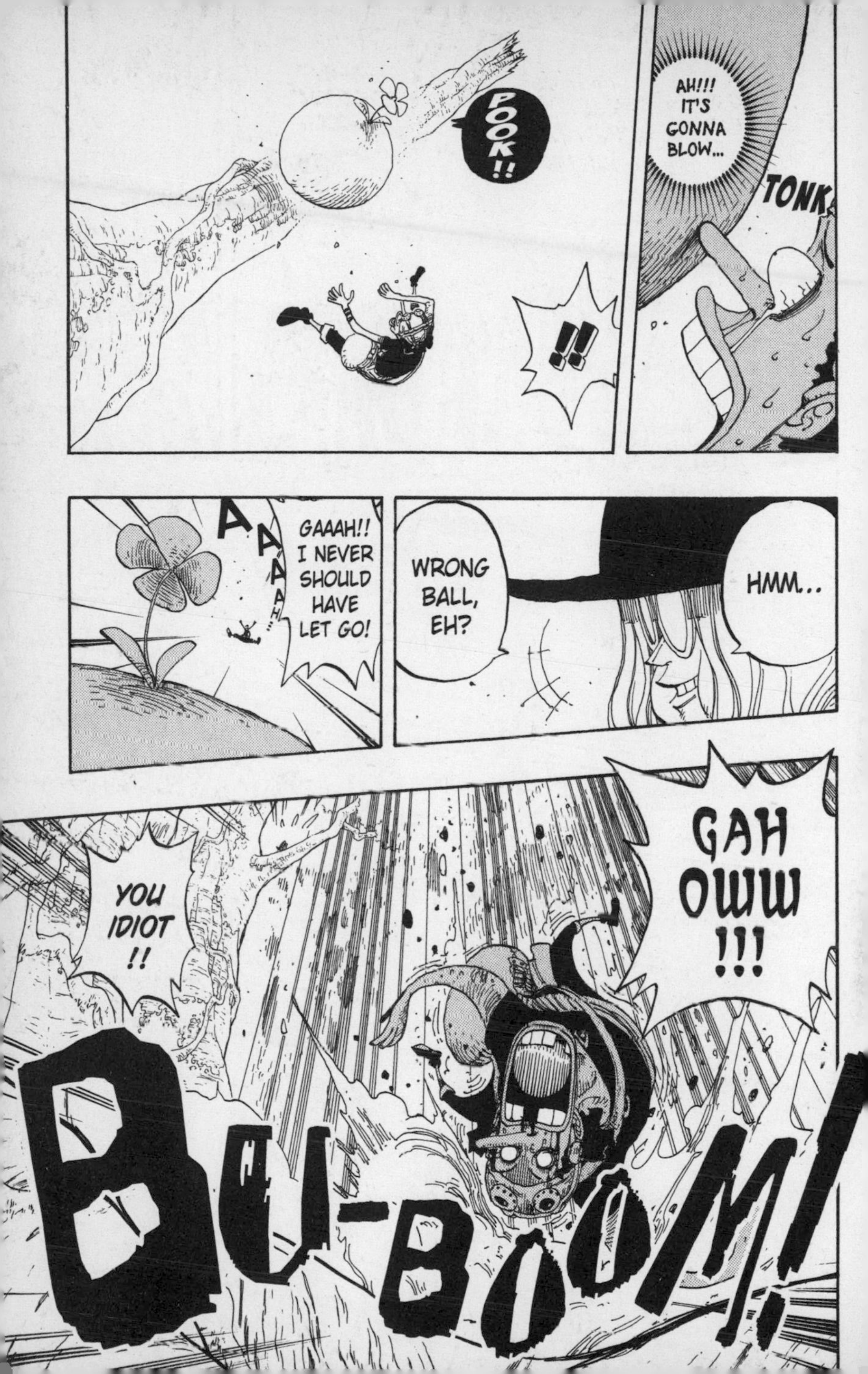
AH!!! IT'S GONNA BLOW...
TONK
POOK!!
!!
HMM...
WRONG BALL, EH?
GAAAH!! I NEVER SHOULD HAVE LET GO!
AAAAH...
GAH OWW !!!
YOU IDIOT !!
BU-BOOM!

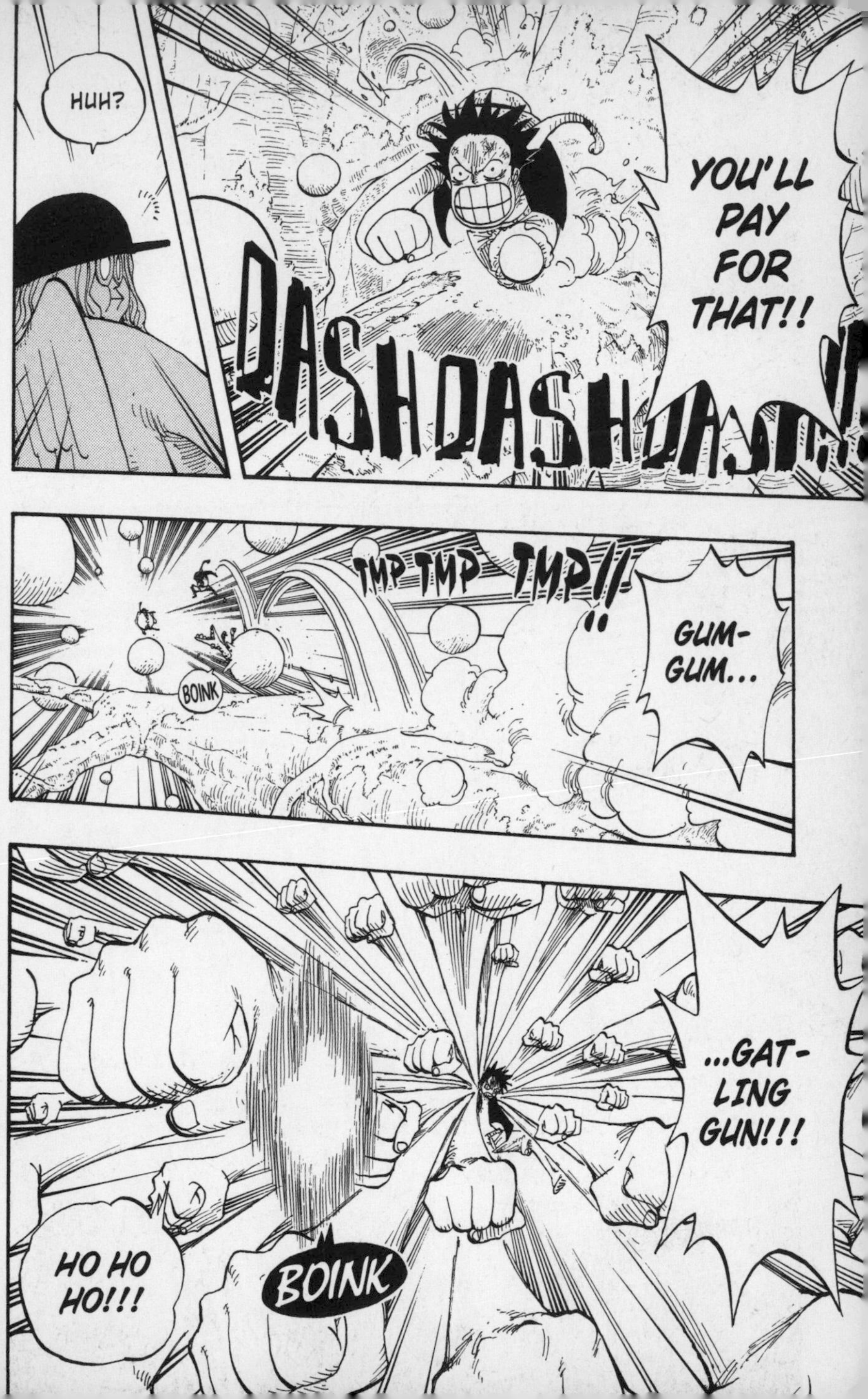
YOU'LL PAY FOR THAT!!
DASHDASHDASH!!
HUH?
GUM-GUM...
TMP TMP TMP!!
BOINK
...GAT-LING GUN!!!
BOINK
HO HO HO!!!

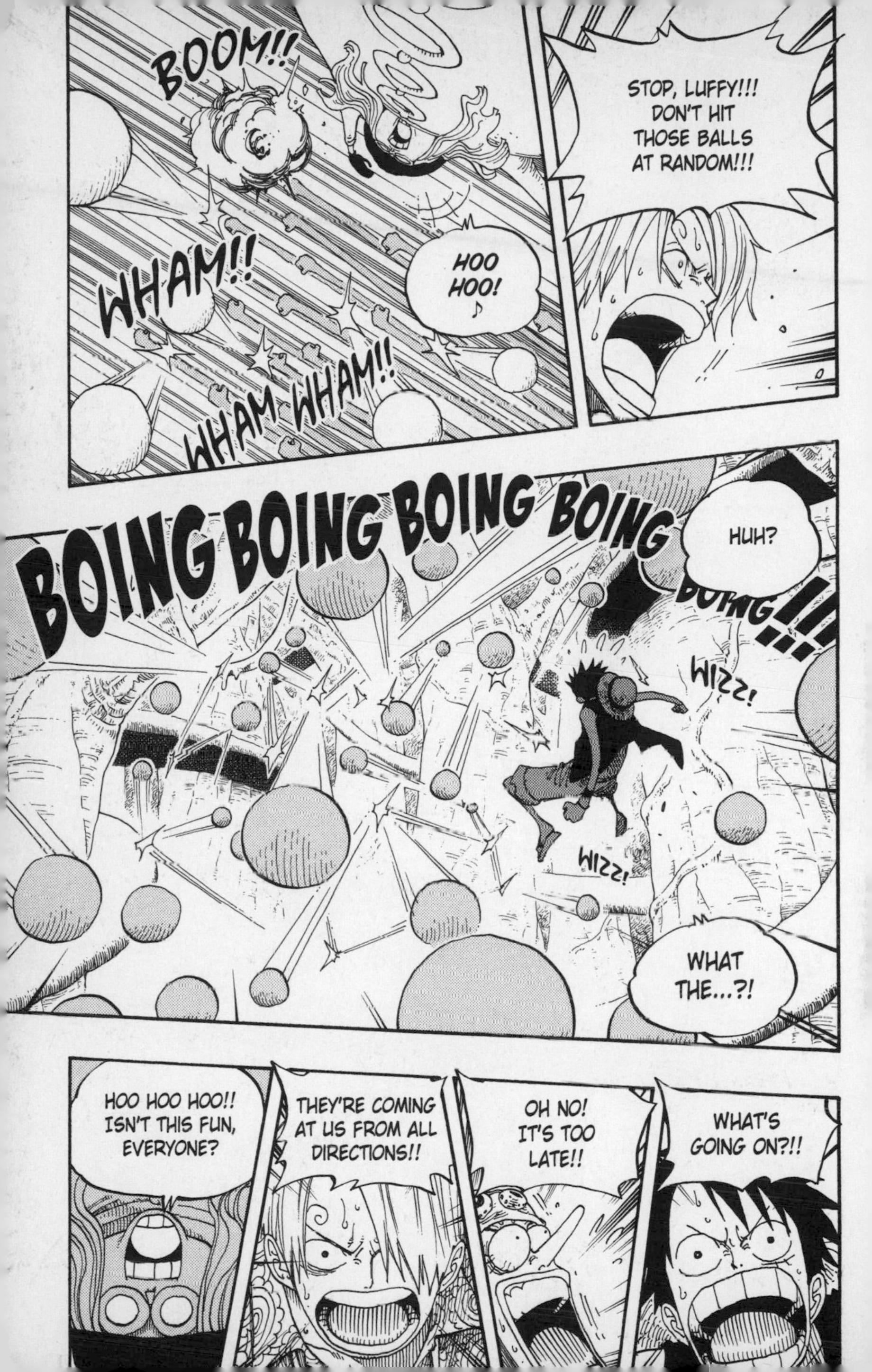
STOP, LUFFY!!! DON'T HIT THOSE BALLS AT RANDOM!!!
BOOM!!
HOO HOO! ♪
WHAM!!
WHAM WHAM!!
HUH?
BOING BOING BOING BOING
WIZZ!
WIZZ!
WHAT THE...?!
WHAT'S GOING ON?!!
OH NO! IT'S TOO LATE!!
THEY'RE COMING AT US FROM ALL DIRECTIONS!!
HOO HOO HOO!! ISN'T THIS FUN, EVERYONE?

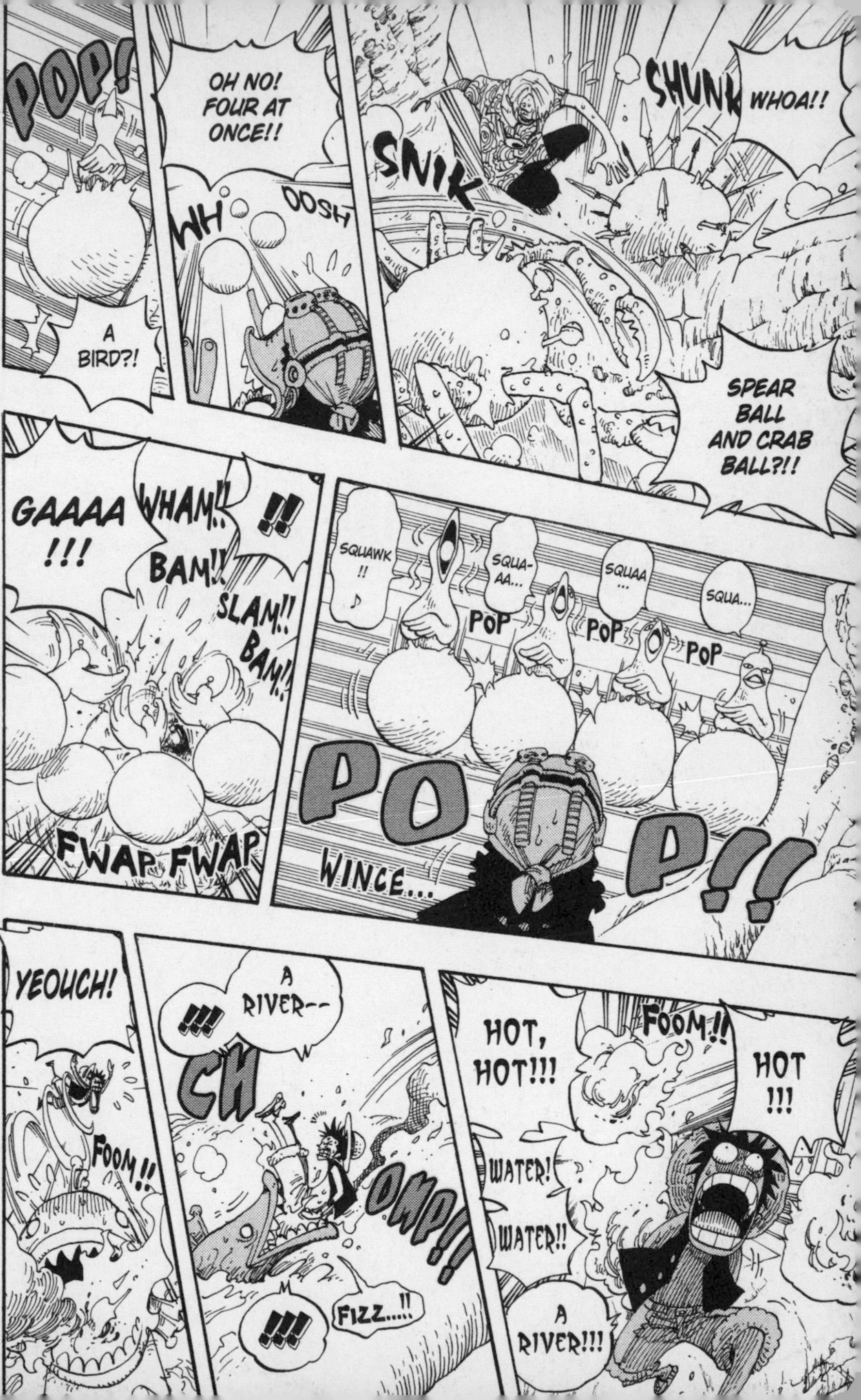
WHOA!!
SHUNK
SNIK
SPEAR BALL AND CRAB BALL?!!
OH NO! FOUR AT ONCE!!
WHOOSH
POP!
A BIRD?!
SQUA...
SQUAA...
POP
SQUA-AA...
POP
SQUAWK!! ♪
POP
POP!!
WINCE...
!!
WHAM!!
BAM!!
SLAM!!
BAM!!
GAAAA!!!
FWAP FWAP
HOT!!!
FOOM!!
HOT, HOT!!!
WATER!
WATER!!
A RIVER!!!
A RIVER--
!!!
CHOMP!!
FIZZ...!!
!!!
YEOUCH!
FOOM!!

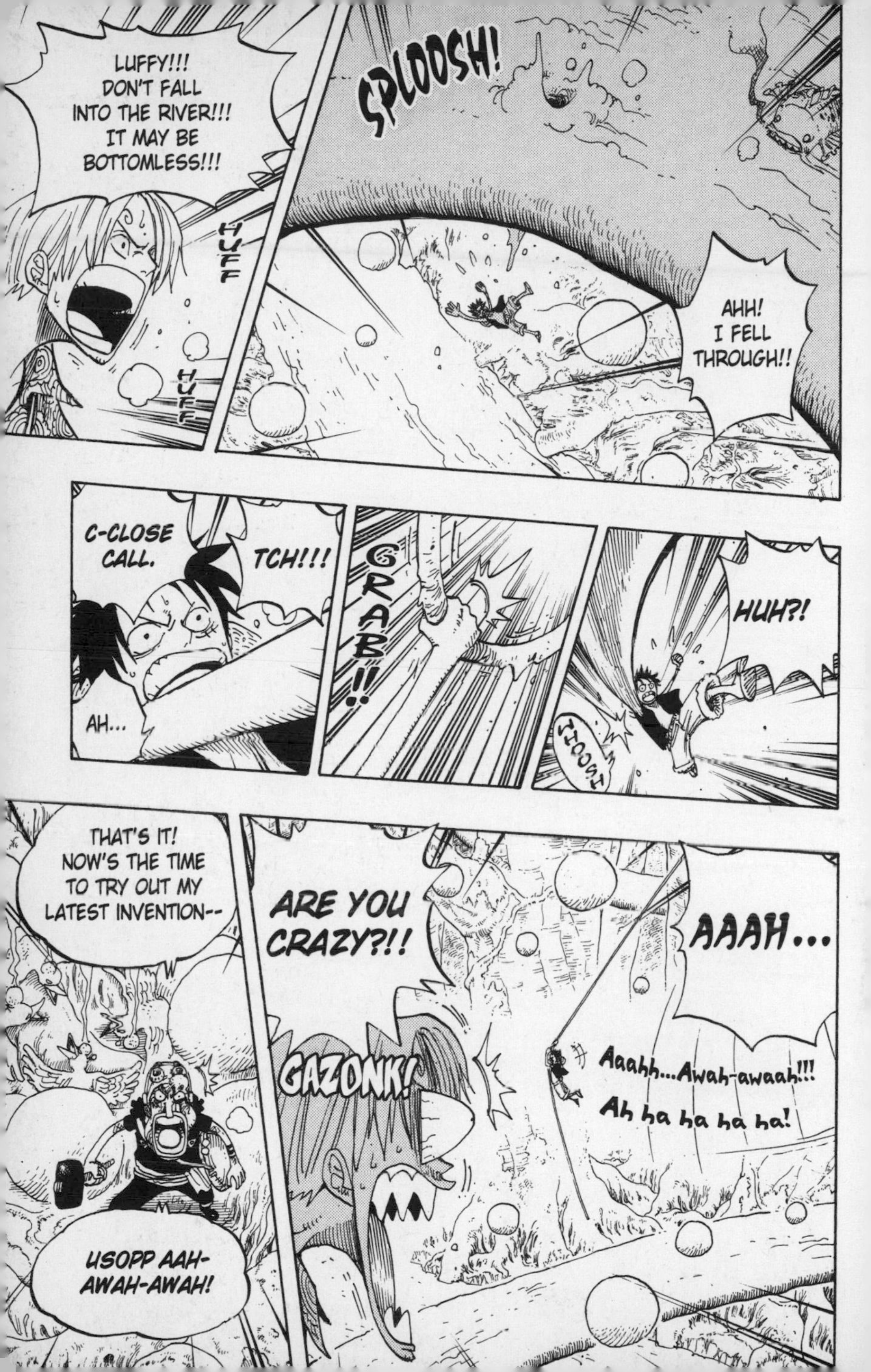
SPLOOSH!
AHH! I FELL THROUGH!!
LUFFY!!! DON'T FALL INTO THE RIVER!!! IT MAY BE BOTTOMLESS!!!
HUFF
HUFF
HUH?!
WHOOSH
GRAB!!
TCH!!!
C-CLOSE CALL.
AH...
AAAH...
ARE YOU CRAZY?!!
Aaahh...Awah-awaah!!!
Ah ha ha ha ha!
GAZONK!
THAT'S IT! NOW'S THE TIME TO TRY OUT MY LATEST INVENTION--
USOPP AAH-AWAH-AWAH!

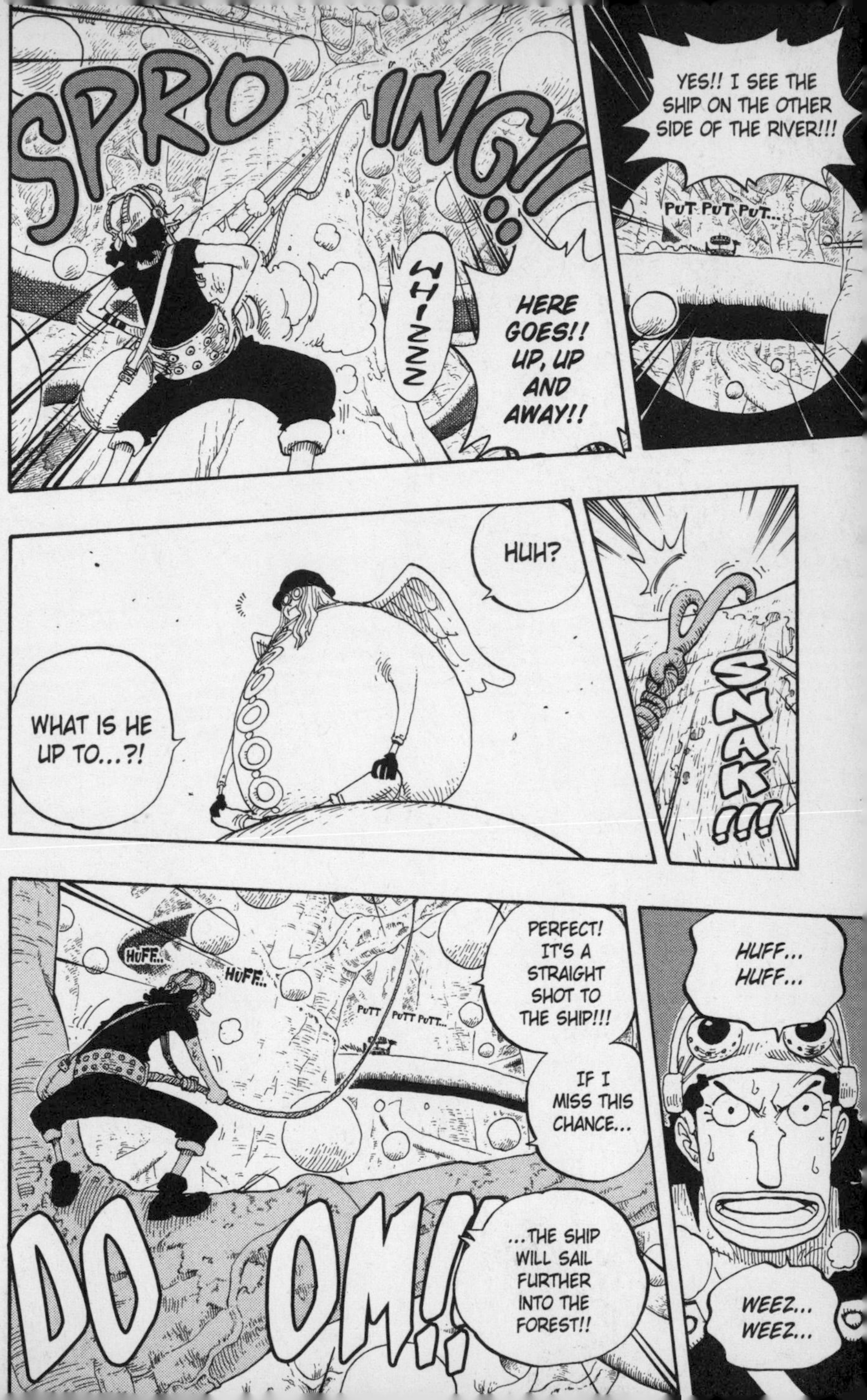
YES!! I SEE THE SHIP ON THE OTHER SIDE OF THE RIVER!!!
PUT PUT PUT...
SPRO ING!!
WHIZZZ
HERE GOES!! UP, UP AND AWAY!!
SNAK!!!
HUH?
WHAT IS HE UP TO...?!
HUFF... HUFF...
WEEZ... WEEZ...
PERFECT! IT'S A STRAIGHT SHOT TO THE SHIP!!!
IF I MISS THIS CHANCE...
...THE SHIP WILL SAIL FURTHER INTO THE FOREST!!
HUFF...
HUFF...
PUTT PUTT PUTT...
DO OM!!

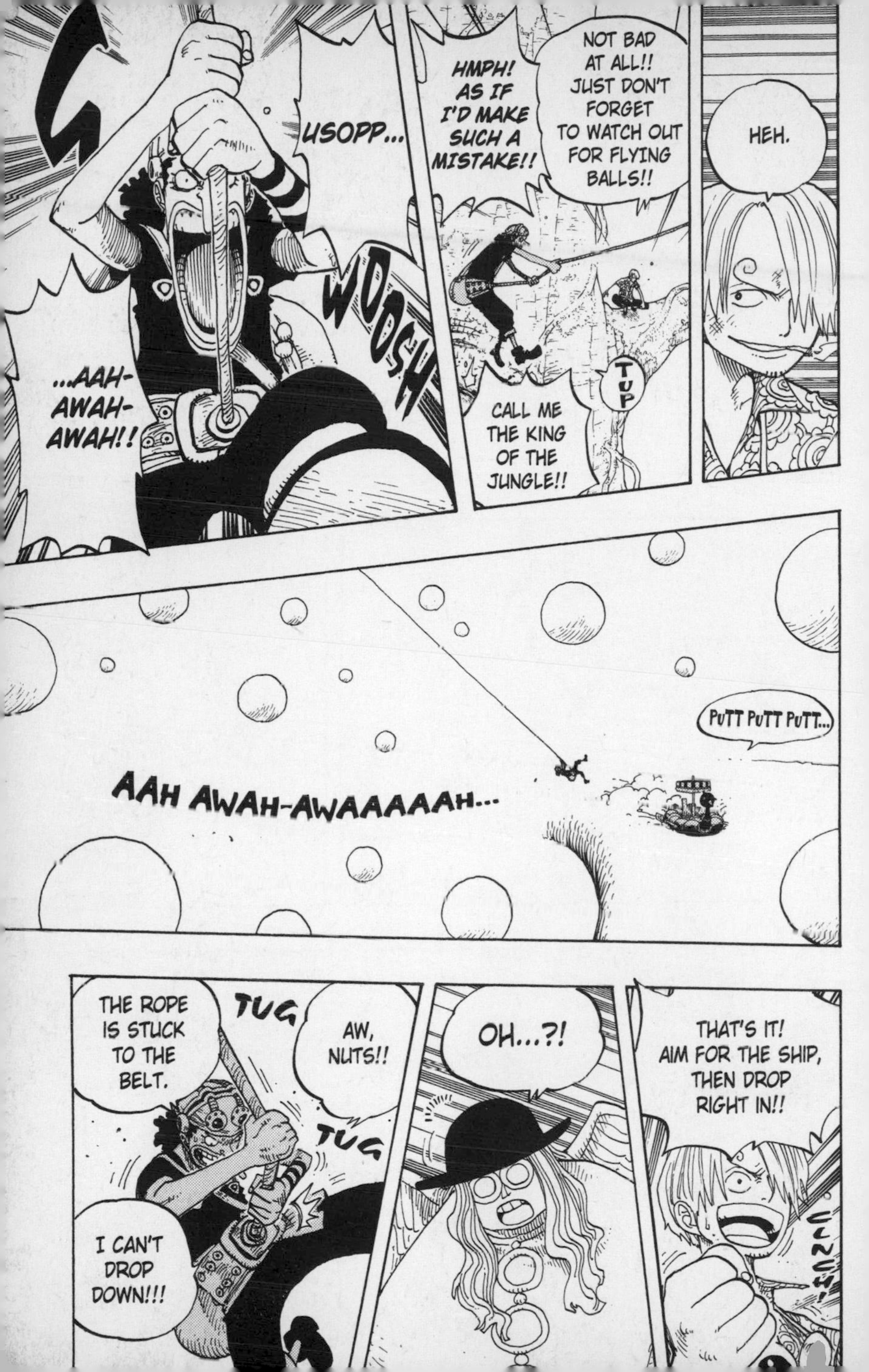
HEH.
NOT BAD AT ALL!! JUST DON'T FORGET TO WATCH OUT FOR FLYING BALLS!!
HMPH! AS IF I'D MAKE SUCH A MISTAKE!!
TUP
CALL ME THE KING OF THE JUNGLE!!
USOPP...
WOOSH
...AAH-AWAH-AWAH!!
PUTT PUTT PUTT...
AAH AWAH-AWAAAAAH...
THAT'S IT! AIM FOR THE SHIP, THEN DROP RIGHT IN!!
CLINCH!
OH...?!
AW, NUTS!!
TUG
THE ROPE IS STUCK TO THE BELT.
TUG
I CAN'T DROP DOWN!!!

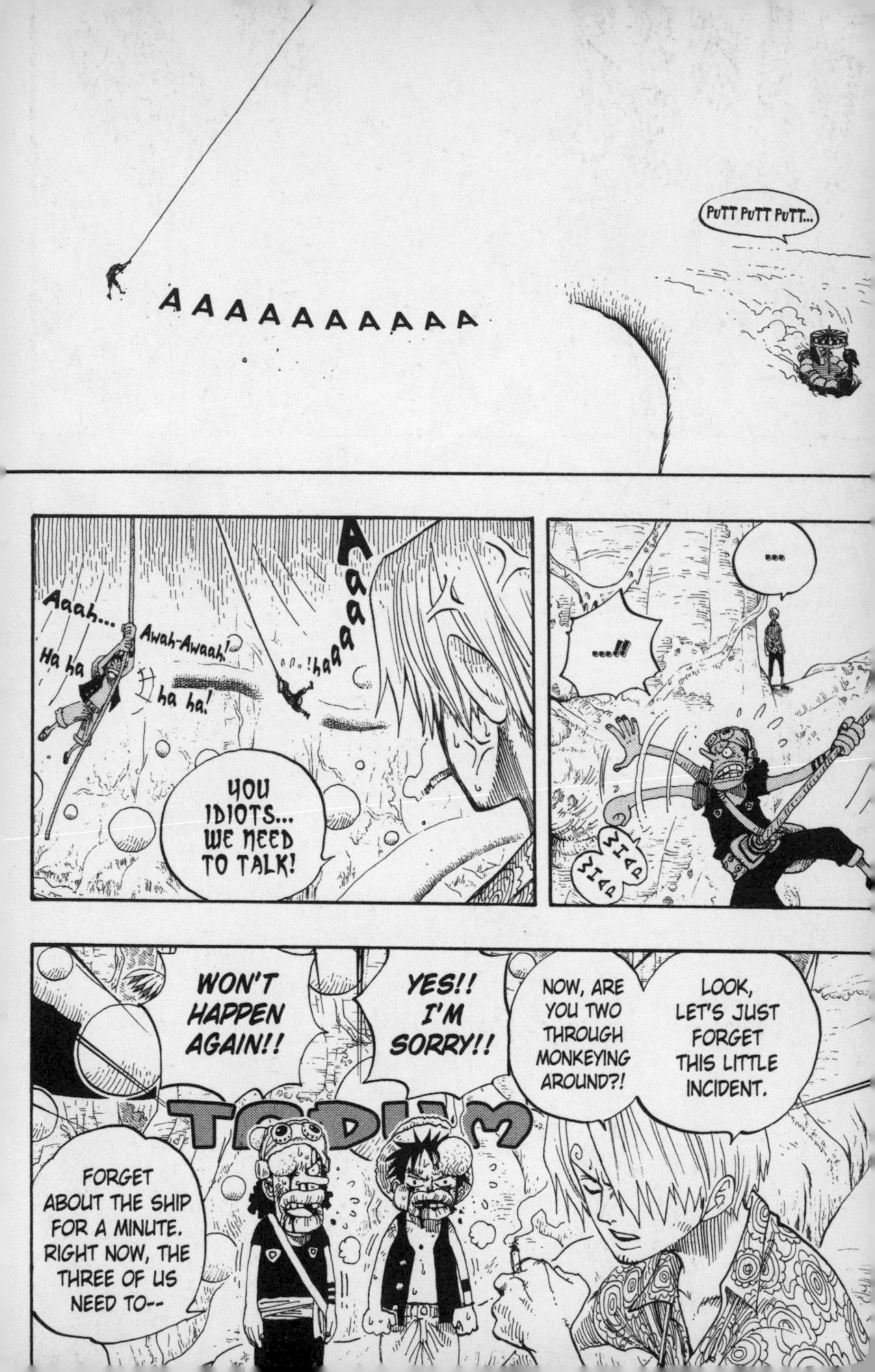

PUTT PUTT PUTT...
AAAAAAAAAA
...
...!!
Awah-Awaah!
Aaah...
Ha ha
ha ha!
YOU IDIOTS... WE NEED TO TALK!
LOOK, LET'S JUST FORGET THIS LITTLE INCIDENT.
NOW, ARE YOU TWO THROUGH MONKEYING AROUND?!
YES!! I'M SORRY!!
WON'T HAPPEN AGAIN!!
FORGET ABOUT THE SHIP FOR A MINUTE. RIGHT NOW, THE THREE OF US NEED TO--

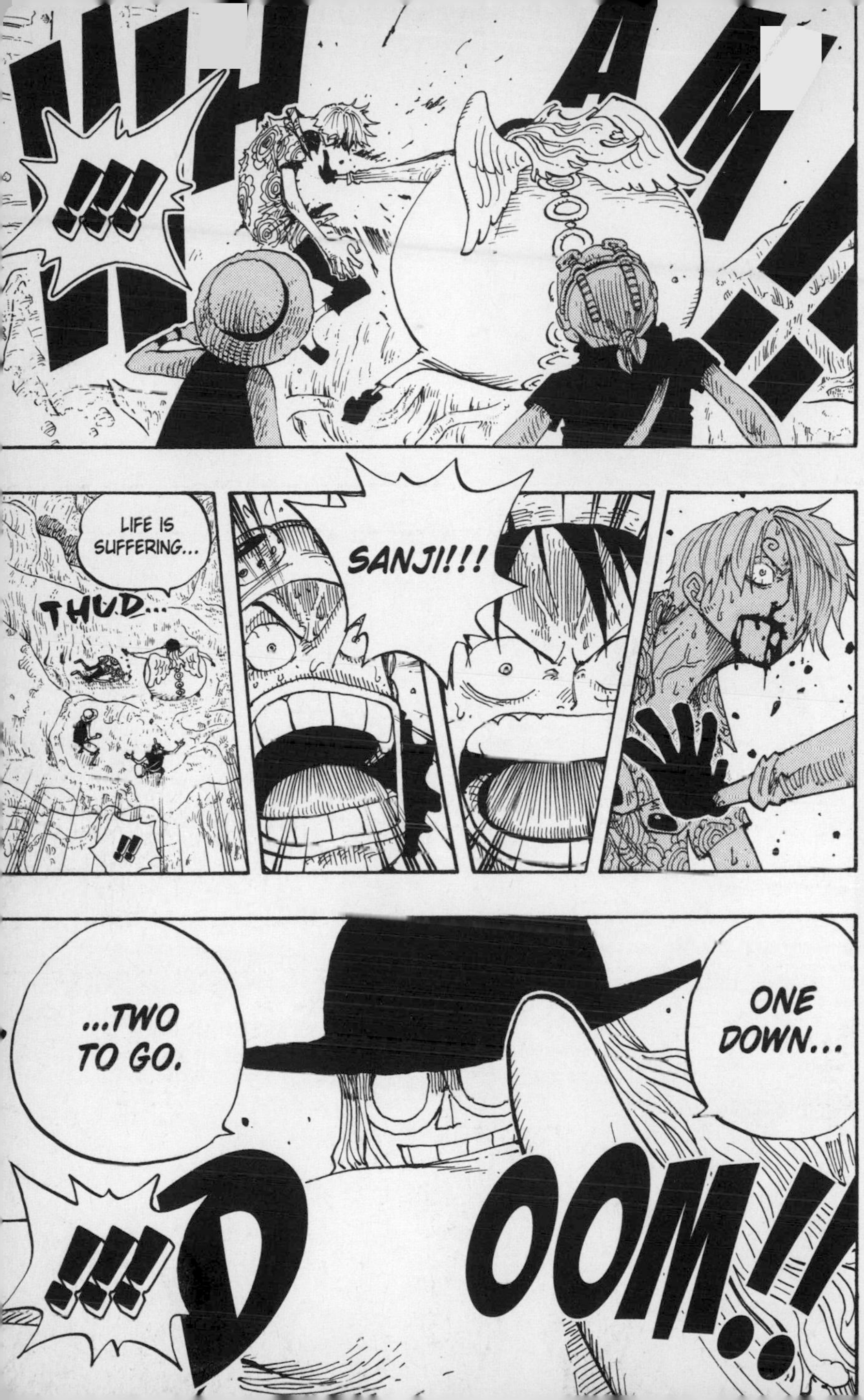
AM!!
!!!
SANJI!!!
LIFE IS SUFFERING...
THUD...
!!
ONE DOWN...
...TWO TO GO.
DOOM!!
!!!

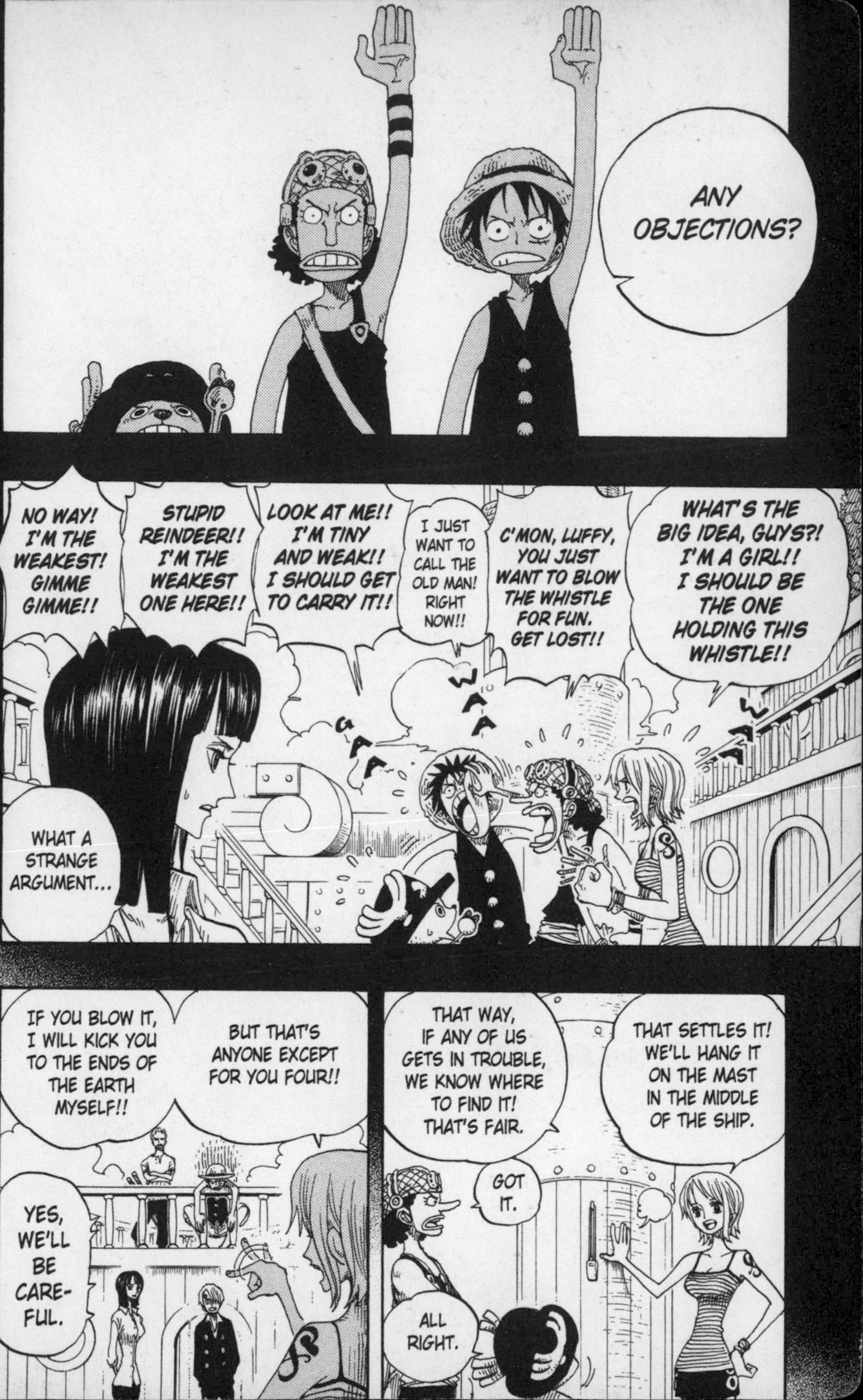
ANY OBJECTIONS?
WHAT'S THE BIG IDEA, GUYS?! I'M A GIRL!! I SHOULD BE THE ONE HOLDING THIS WHISTLE!!
C'MON, LUFFY, YOU JUST WANT TO BLOW THE WHISTLE FOR FUN. GET LOST!!
I JUST WANT TO CALL THE OLD MAN! RIGHT NOW!!
LOOK AT ME!! I'M TINY AND WEAK!! I SHOULD GET TO CARRY IT!!
STUPID REINDEER!! I'M THE WEAKEST ONE HERE!!
NO WAY! I'M THE WEAKEST! GIMME GIMME!!
WAA
WAA
GAA
WHAT A STRANGE ARGUMENT...
THAT SETTLES IT! WE'LL HANG IT ON THE MAST IN THE MIDDLE OF THE SHIP.
THAT WAY, IF ANY OF US GETS IN TROUBLE, WE KNOW WHERE TO FIND IT! THAT'S FAIR.
GOT IT.
ALL RIGHT.
BUT THAT'S ANYONE EXCEPT FOR YOU FOUR!!
IF YOU BLOW IT, I WILL KICK YOU TO THE ENDS OF THE EARTH MYSELF!!
YES, WE'LL BE CARE-FUL.

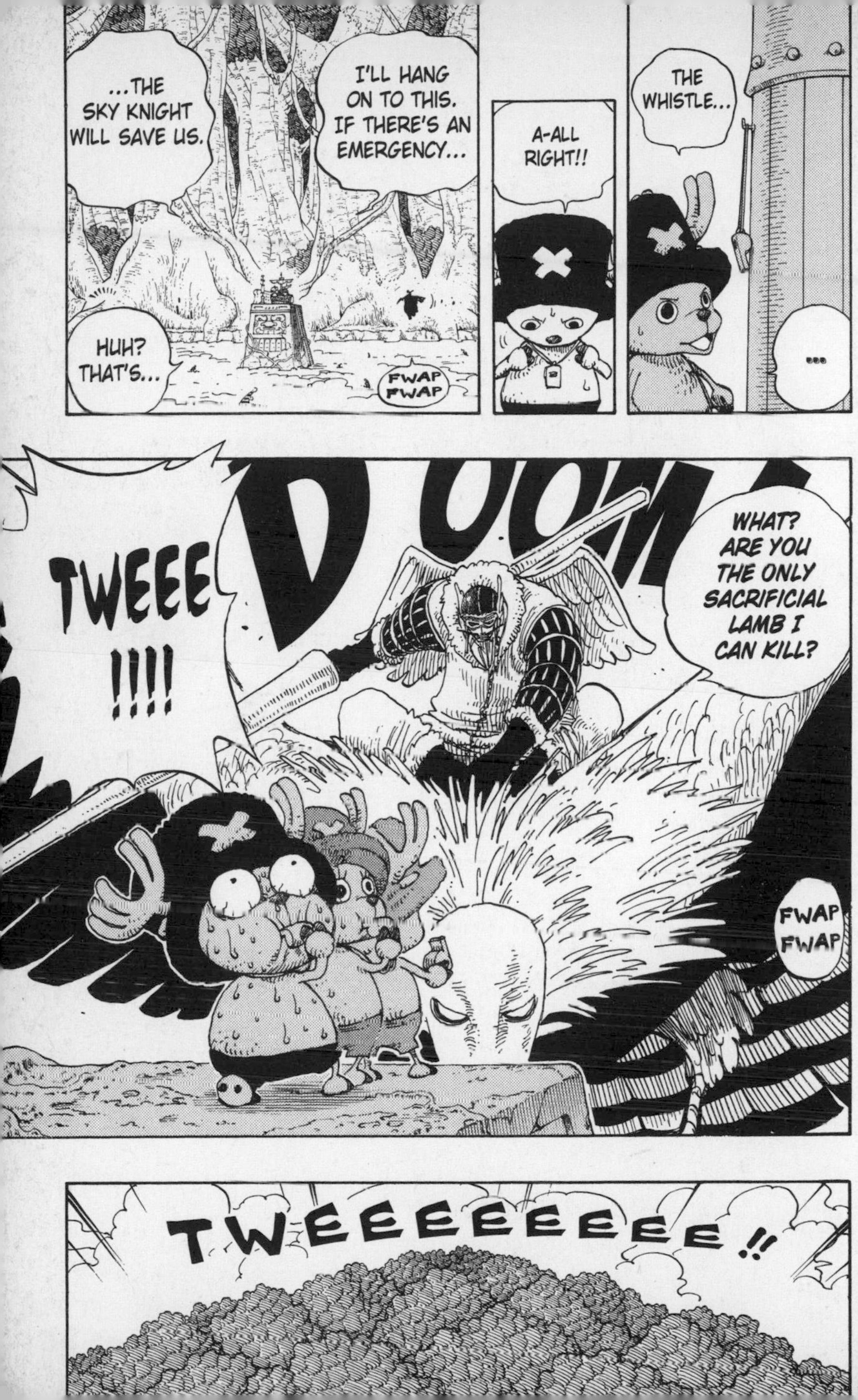
THE WHISTLE...
...
A-ALL RIGHT!!
I'LL HANG ON TO THIS. IF THERE'S AN EMERGENCY...
...THE SKY KNIGHT WILL SAVE US.
FWAP FWAP
HUH? THAT'S...
WHAT? ARE YOU THE ONLY SACRIFICIAL LAMB I CAN KILL?
DOOM
FWAP FWAP
TWEEE !!!!
TWEEEEEEEE!!

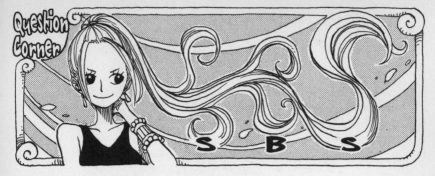

S B S

Reader: Oda Sensei! This is bad! Really bad!
         The Question Corner is about to start!
         Ah... Oh no... It's begun.
         The Question Corner has begun! (sob sob)
                    --Bara Sankaku

Oda: Don't cry. It's okay. It's just time for The Question
         Corner.

Q: Hello. I know this is sudden, but Odacchi, I just learned something
         amazing! You know those poofy moss algae balls? Apparently they
         grow at the rate of 10cm a year!! In three years, they'd be 30cm in
         diameter. Like flora on land, the more sunlight it gets, the larger it
         grows. Zolo is always sleeping on the deck. Imagine how big his
         head will grow...

A: What? Seriously...?! This is terrible! Ten centimeters
         in one year?! So in ten years, that
         would be one meter?! (→)
         Hm... Actually, It looks kind of
         cool. Moss Grows that much,
         eh? I'm looking forward
         to ten years from now so
         we can see what Zolo's...
         Oh, wait! But he's human

         Huh?!
         Hey.

Q: I want to say this to Sanji! Why do you address Nami like an adult
         while you speak to Robin like she's younger than you. Isn't it usually
         the opposite? Don't you think you're being rude to Robin, Sanji?!
                    --A Woman the Same Age as Sanji

A: Hmm... You're right. I wonder why. I Guess Nami's
         queenly personality demands it. In any case, a Guy like
         Sanji doesn't worry about age. That's just his whim.

Chapter 248:
FORMER KAMI VS. VASSAL

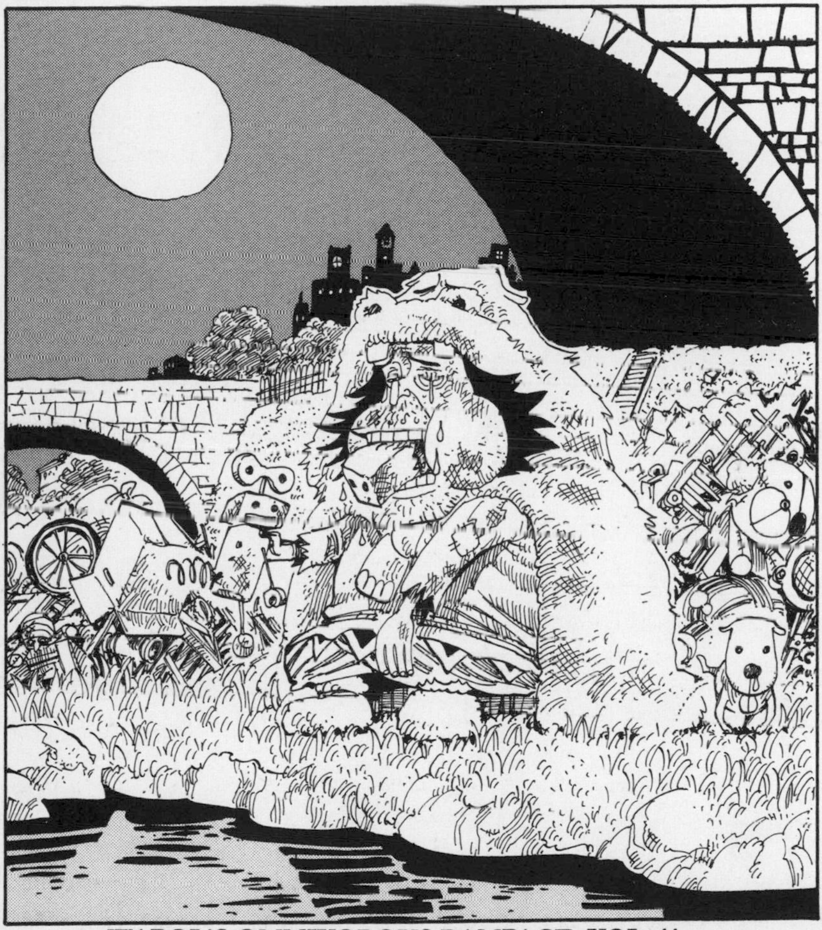

WAPOL'S OMNIVOROUS RAMPAGE, VOL. 11:
"ME UNDER THE BRIDGE"

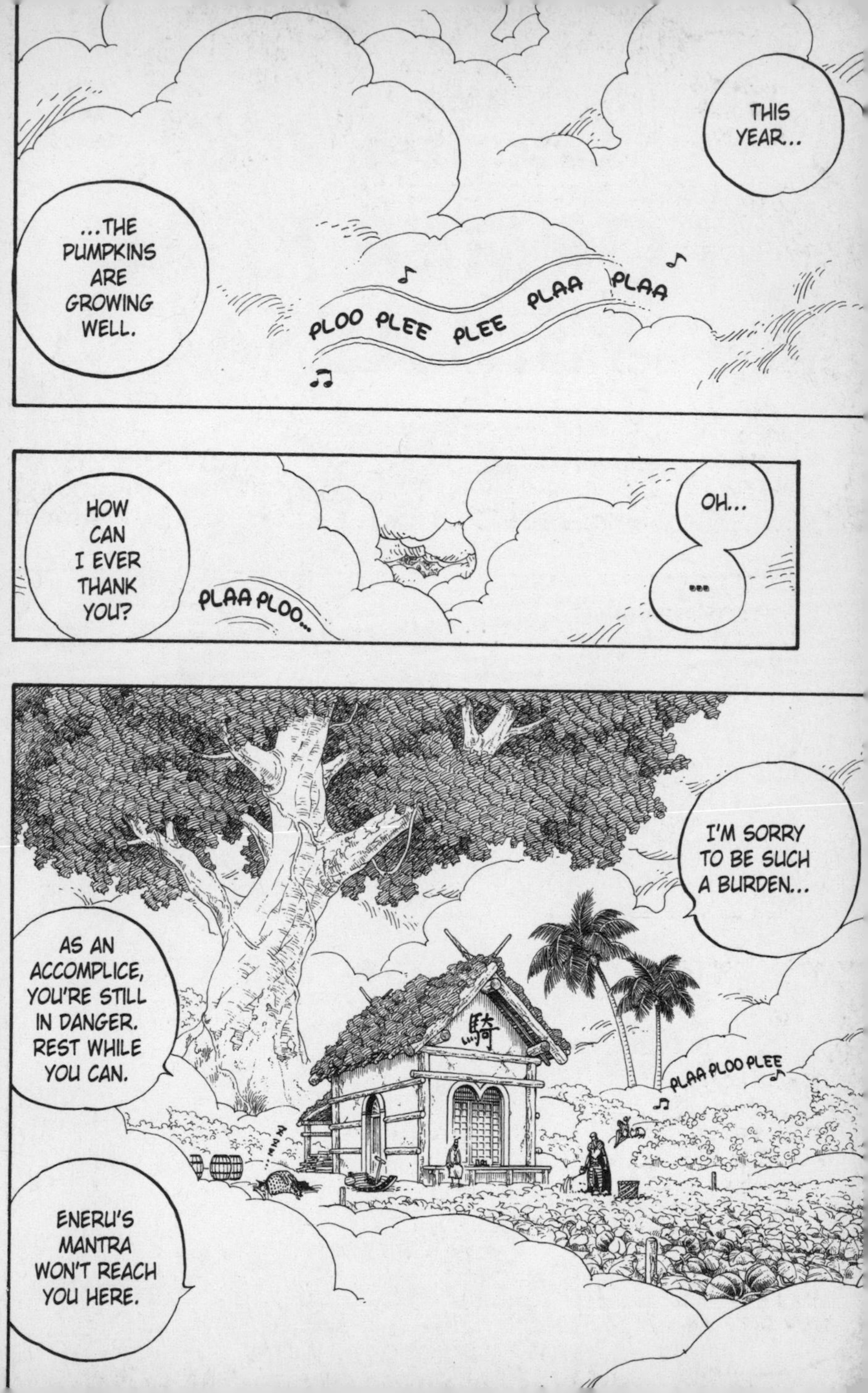
THIS YEAR...
...THE PUMPKINS ARE GROWING WELL.
PLOO PLEE PLEE PLAA PLAA
OH...
...
PLAA PLOO...
HOW CAN I EVER THANK YOU?
I'M SORRY TO BE SUCH A BURDEN...
PLAA PLOO PLEE
AS AN ACCOMPLICE, YOU'RE STILL IN DANGER. REST WHILE YOU CAN.
ENERU'S MANTRA WON'T REACH YOU HERE.

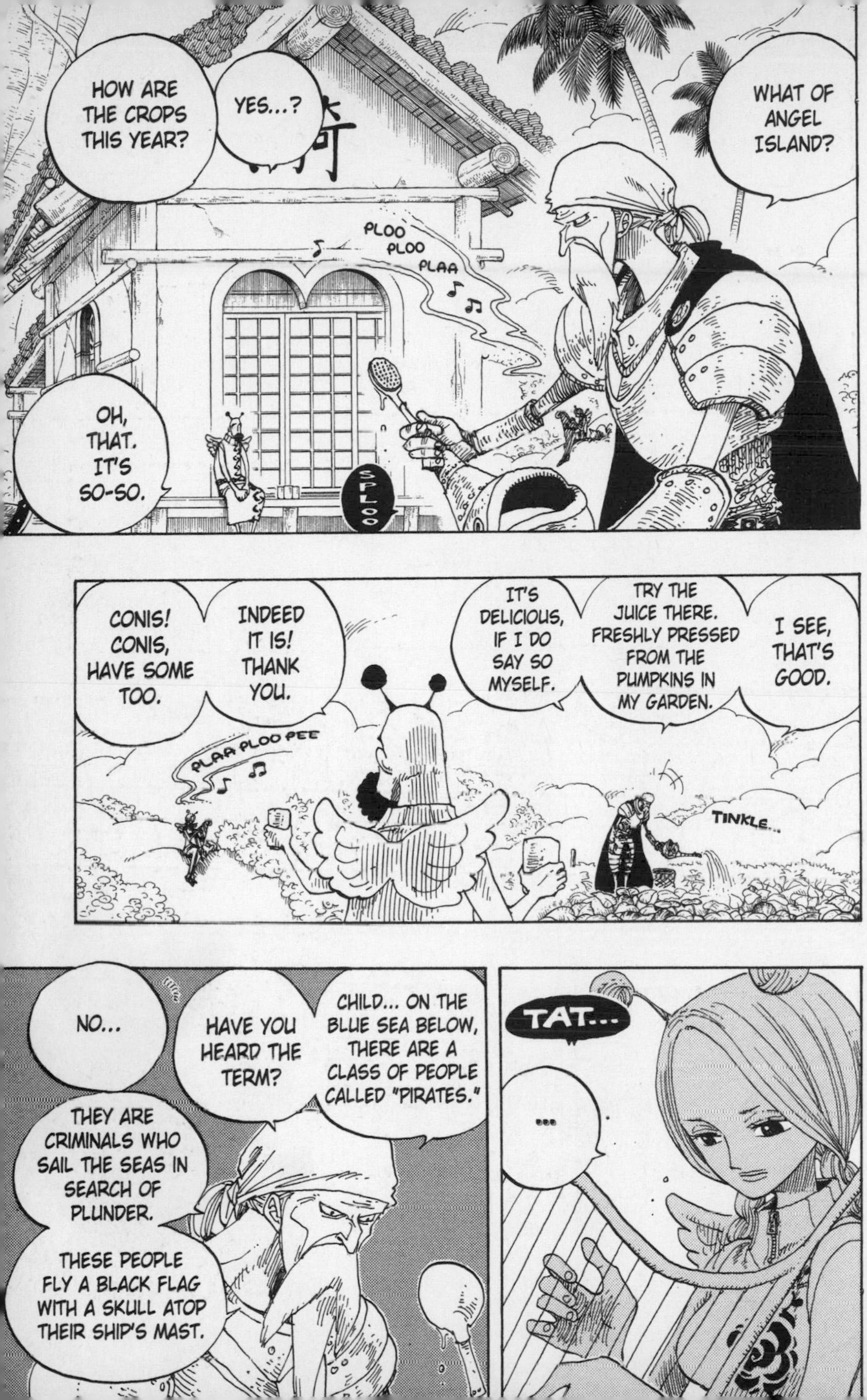
WHAT OF ANGEL ISLAND?
YES...?
HOW ARE THE CROPS THIS YEAR?
PLOO PLOO PLAA
OH, THAT. IT'S SO-SO.
SPLOO
I SEE, THAT'S GOOD.
TRY THE JUICE THERE. FRESHLY PRESSED FROM THE PUMPKINS IN MY GARDEN.
IT'S DELICIOUS, IF I DO SAY SO MYSELF.
INDEED IT IS! THANK YOU.
CONIS! CONIS, HAVE SOME TOO.
PLAA PLOO PEE
TINKLE...
TAT...
...
CHILD... ON THE BLUE SEA BELOW, THERE ARE A CLASS OF PEOPLE CALLED "PIRATES."
HAVE YOU HEARD THE TERM?
NO...
THEY ARE CRIMINALS WHO SAIL THE SEAS IN SEARCH OF PLUNDER.
THESE PEOPLE FLY A BLACK FLAG WITH A SKULL ATOP THEIR SHIP'S MAST.

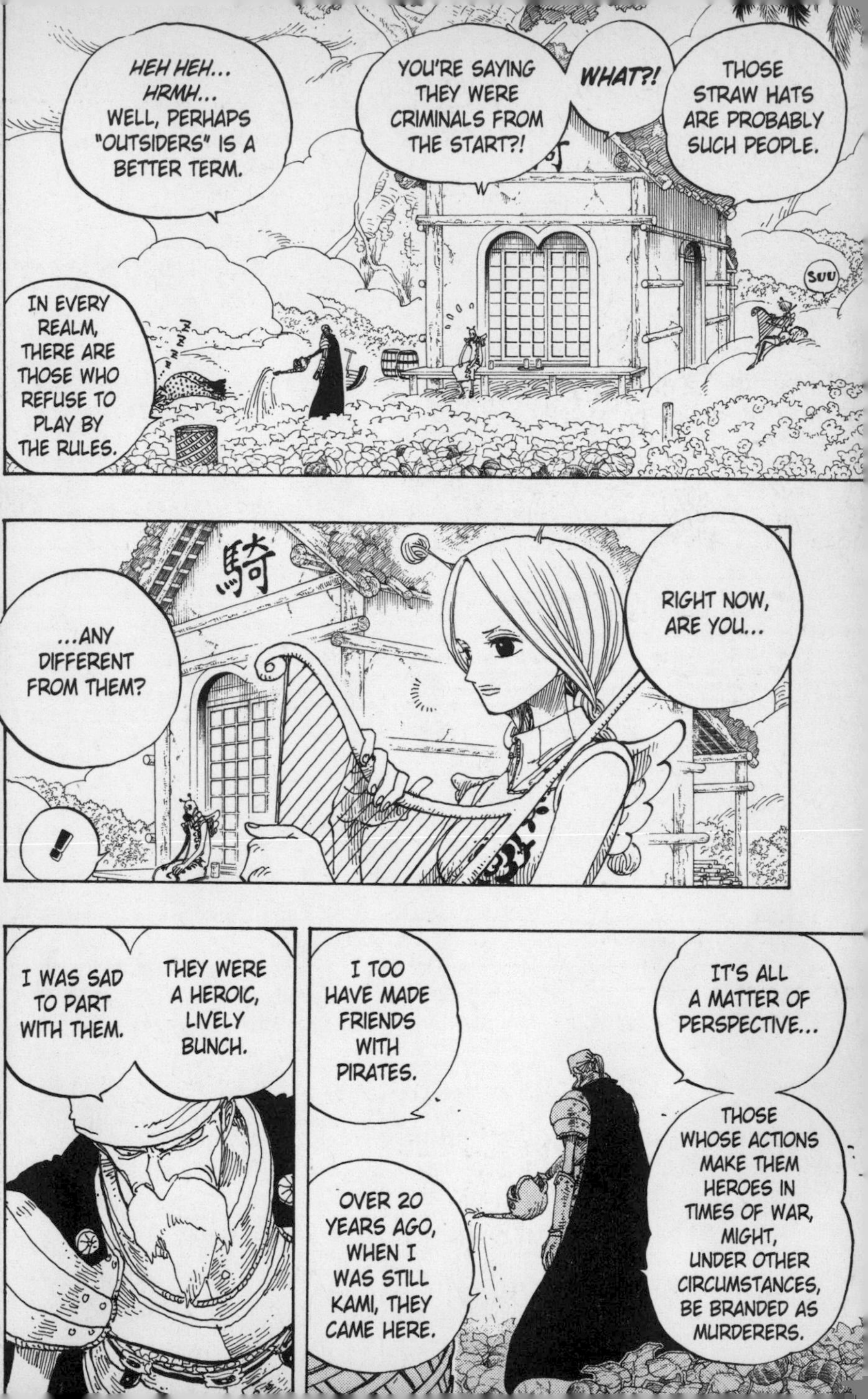
THOSE STRAW HATS ARE PROBABLY SUCH PEOPLE.
WHAT?!
YOU'RE SAYING THEY WERE CRIMINALS FROM THE START?!
HEH HEH... HRMH... WELL, PERHAPS "OUTSIDERS" IS A BETTER TERM.
SUU
IN EVERY REALM, THERE ARE THOSE WHO REFUSE TO PLAY BY THE RULES.
RIGHT NOW, ARE YOU...
騎
...ANY DIFFERENT FROM THEM?
!
IT'S ALL A MATTER OF PERSPECTIVE...
THOSE WHOSE ACTIONS MAKE THEM HEROES IN TIMES OF WAR, MIGHT, UNDER OTHER CIRCUMSTANCES, BE BRANDED AS MURDERERS.
I TOO HAVE MADE FRIENDS WITH PIRATES.
OVER 20 YEARS AGO, WHEN I WAS STILL KAMI, THEY CAME HERE.
THEY WERE A HEROIC, LIVELY BUNCH.
I WAS SAD TO PART WITH THEM.

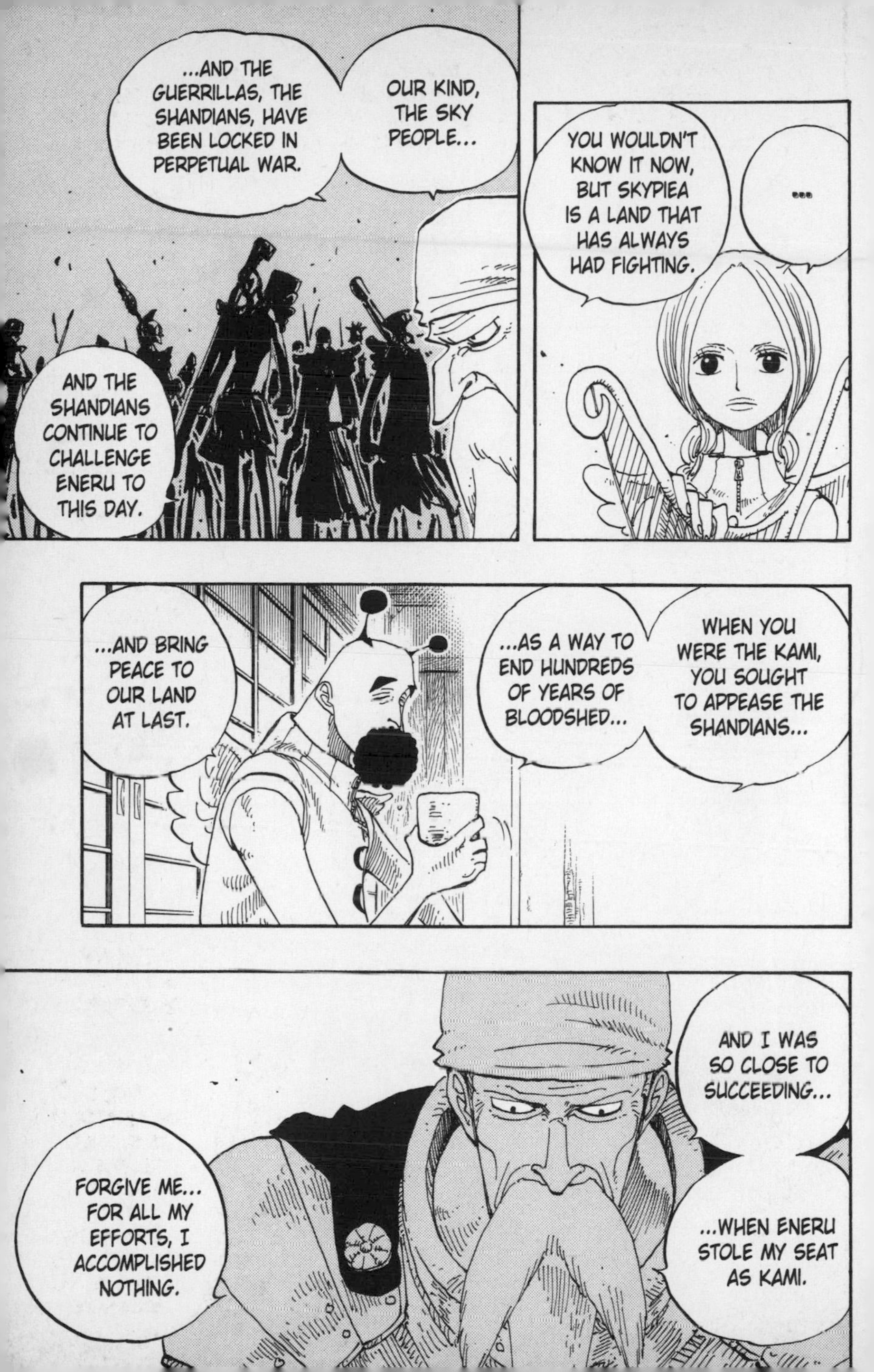
YOU WOULDN'T KNOW IT NOW, BUT SKYPIEA IS A LAND THAT HAS ALWAYS HAD FIGHTING.
...
OUR KIND, THE SKY PEOPLE...
...AND THE GUERRILLAS, THE SHANDIANS, HAVE BEEN LOCKED IN PERPETUAL WAR.
AND THE SHANDIANS CONTINUE TO CHALLENGE ENERU TO THIS DAY.
WHEN YOU WERE THE KAMI, YOU SOUGHT TO APPEASE THE SHANDIANS...
...AS A WAY TO END HUNDREDS OF YEARS OF BLOODSHED...
...AND BRING PEACE TO OUR LAND AT LAST.
AND I WAS SO CLOSE TO SUCCEEDING...
...WHEN ENERU STOLE MY SEAT AS KAMI.
FORGIVE ME... FOR ALL MY EFFORTS, I ACCOMPLISHED NOTHING.

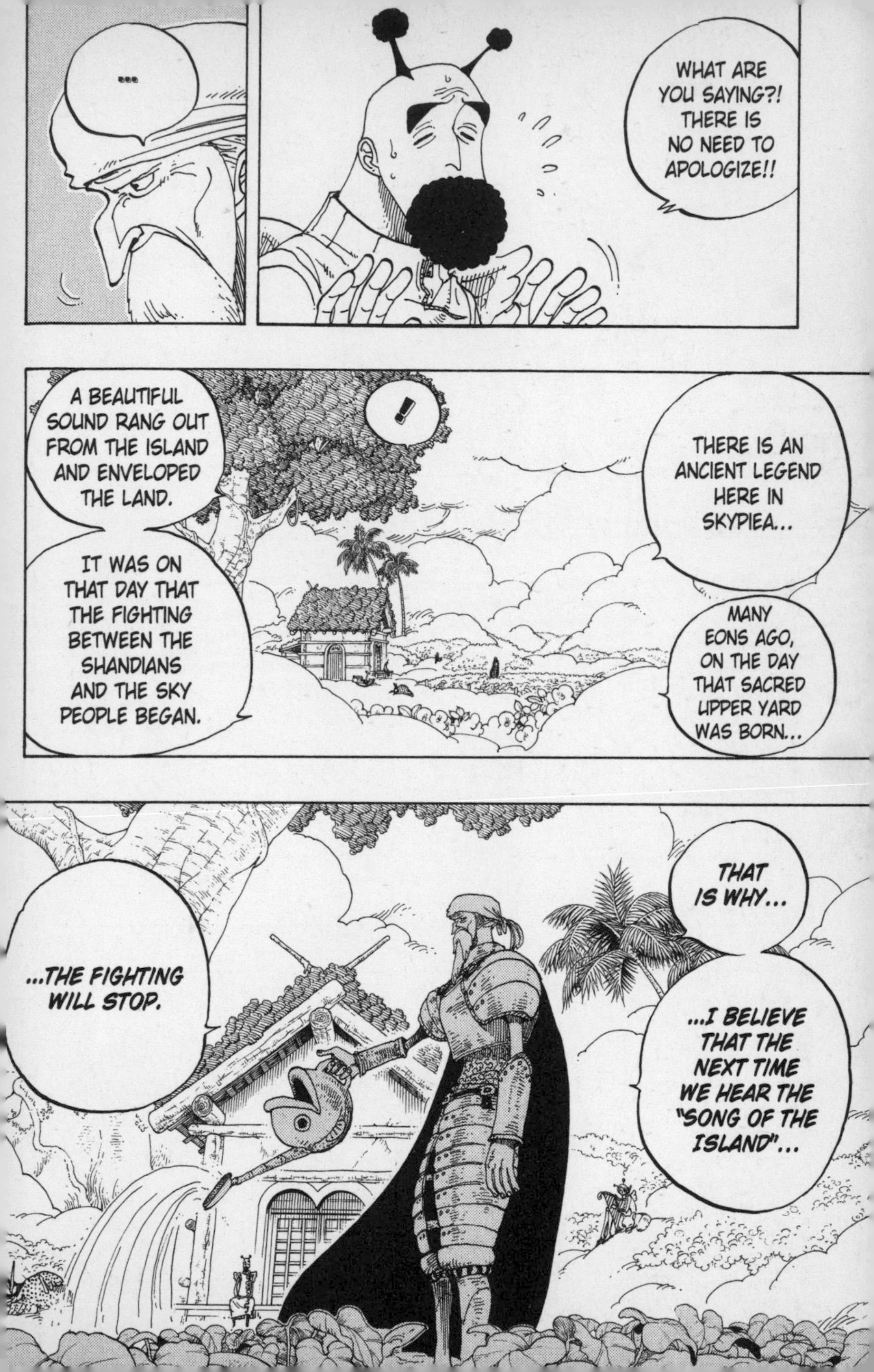
WHAT ARE YOU SAYING?! THERE IS NO NEED TO APOLOGIZE!!
...
THERE IS AN ANCIENT LEGEND HERE IN SKYPIEA...
!
MANY EONS AGO, ON THE DAY THAT SACRED UPPER YARD WAS BORN...
A BEAUTIFUL SOUND RANG OUT FROM THE ISLAND AND ENVELOPED THE LAND.
IT WAS ON THAT DAY THAT THE FIGHTING BETWEEN THE SHANDIANS AND THE SKY PEOPLE BEGAN.
THAT IS WHY...
...I BELIEVE THAT THE NEXT TIME WE HEAR THE "SONG OF THE ISLAND"...
...THE FIGHTING WILL STOP.

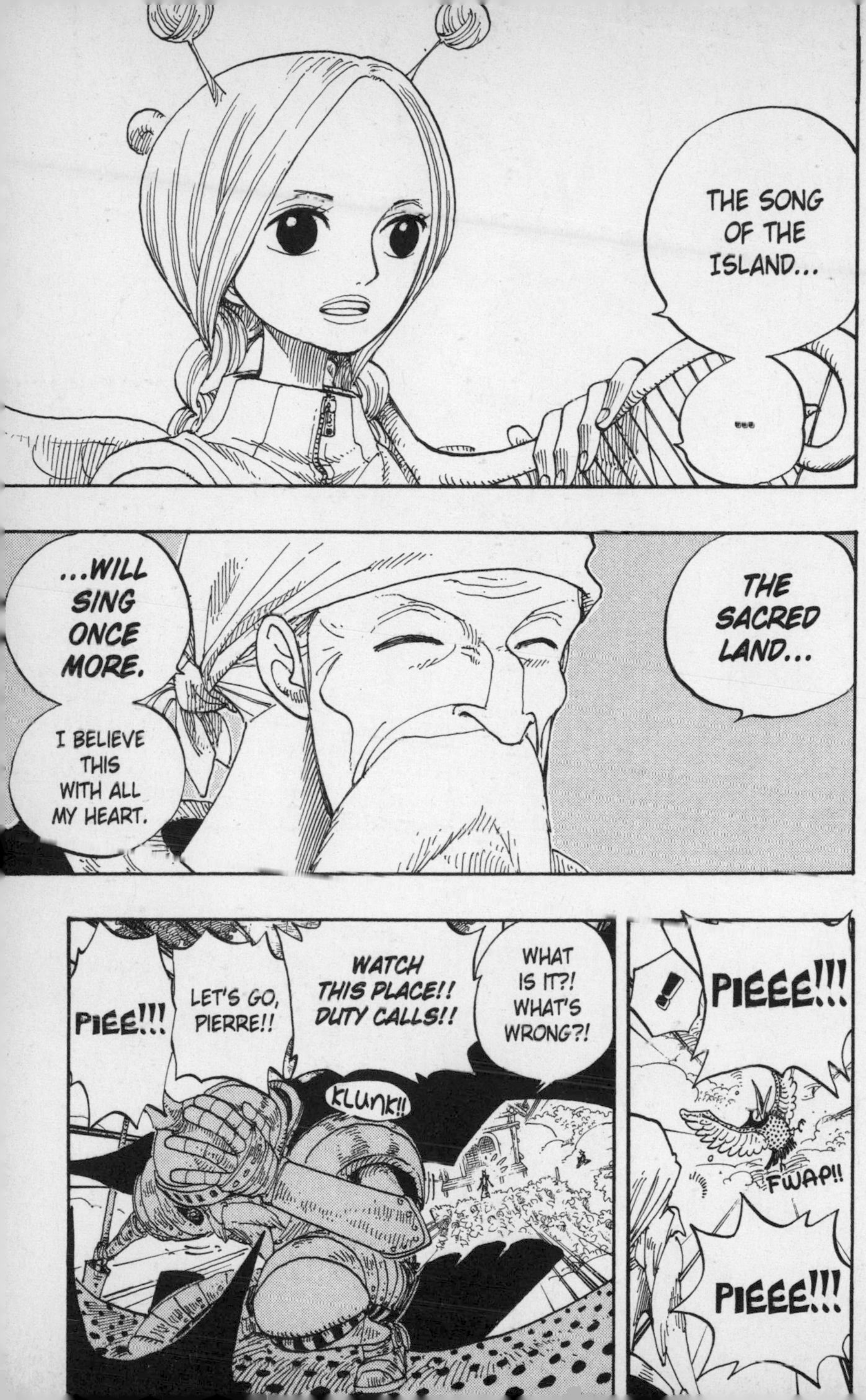
THE SONG OF THE ISLAND...
...
THE SACRED LAND...
...WILL SING ONCE MORE.
I BELIEVE THIS WITH ALL MY HEART.
!
PIEEE!!!
FWAP!!
PIEEE!!!
WHAT IS IT?! WHAT'S WRONG?!
WATCH THIS PLACE!! DUTY CALLS!!
LET'S GO, PIERRE!!
PIEE!!!
KLUNK!!

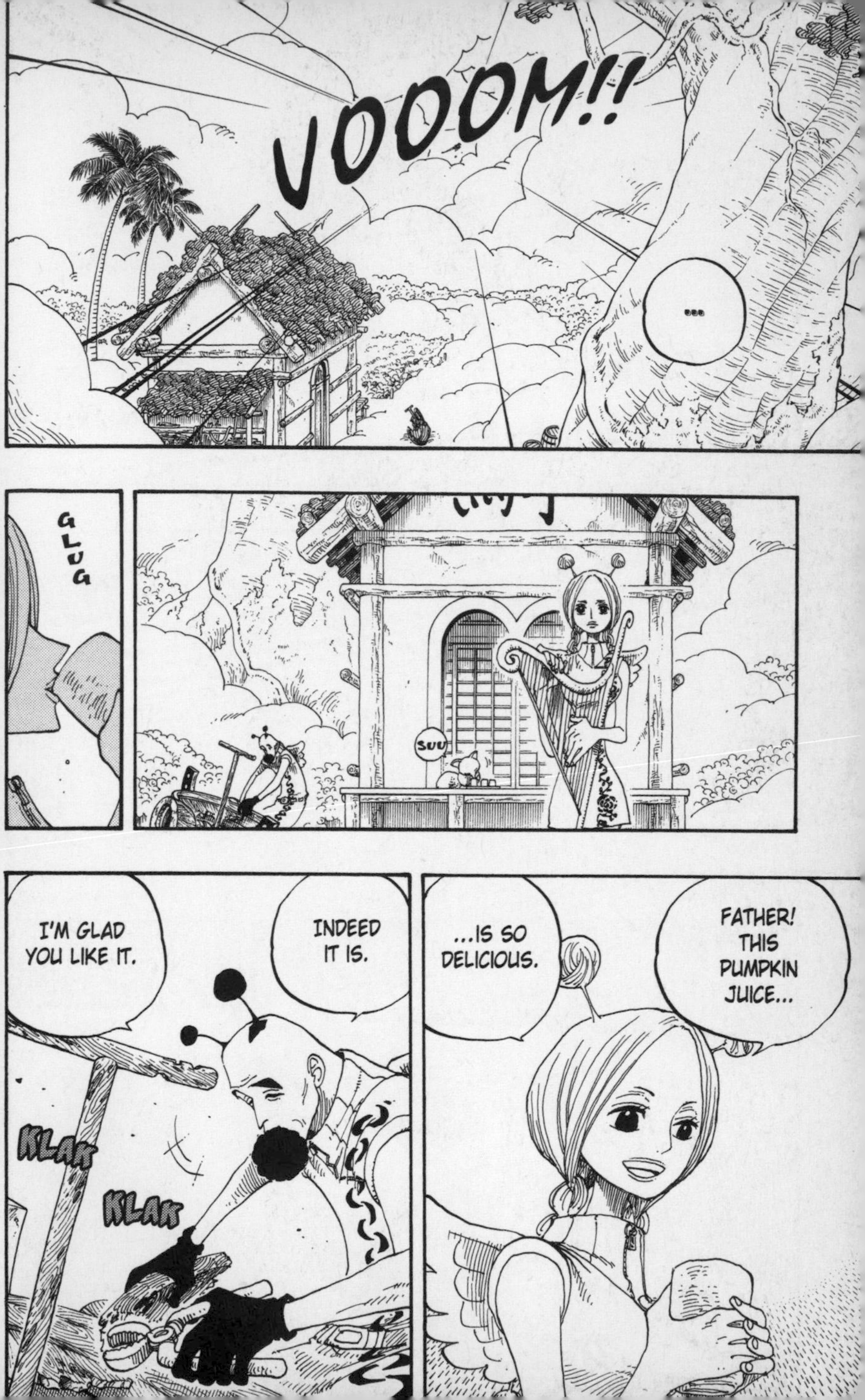
VOOOM!!
...
SUU
GLUG
FATHER! THIS PUMPKIN JUICE...
...IS SO DELICIOUS.
INDEED IT IS.
I'M GLAD YOU LIKE IT.
KLAK
KLAK

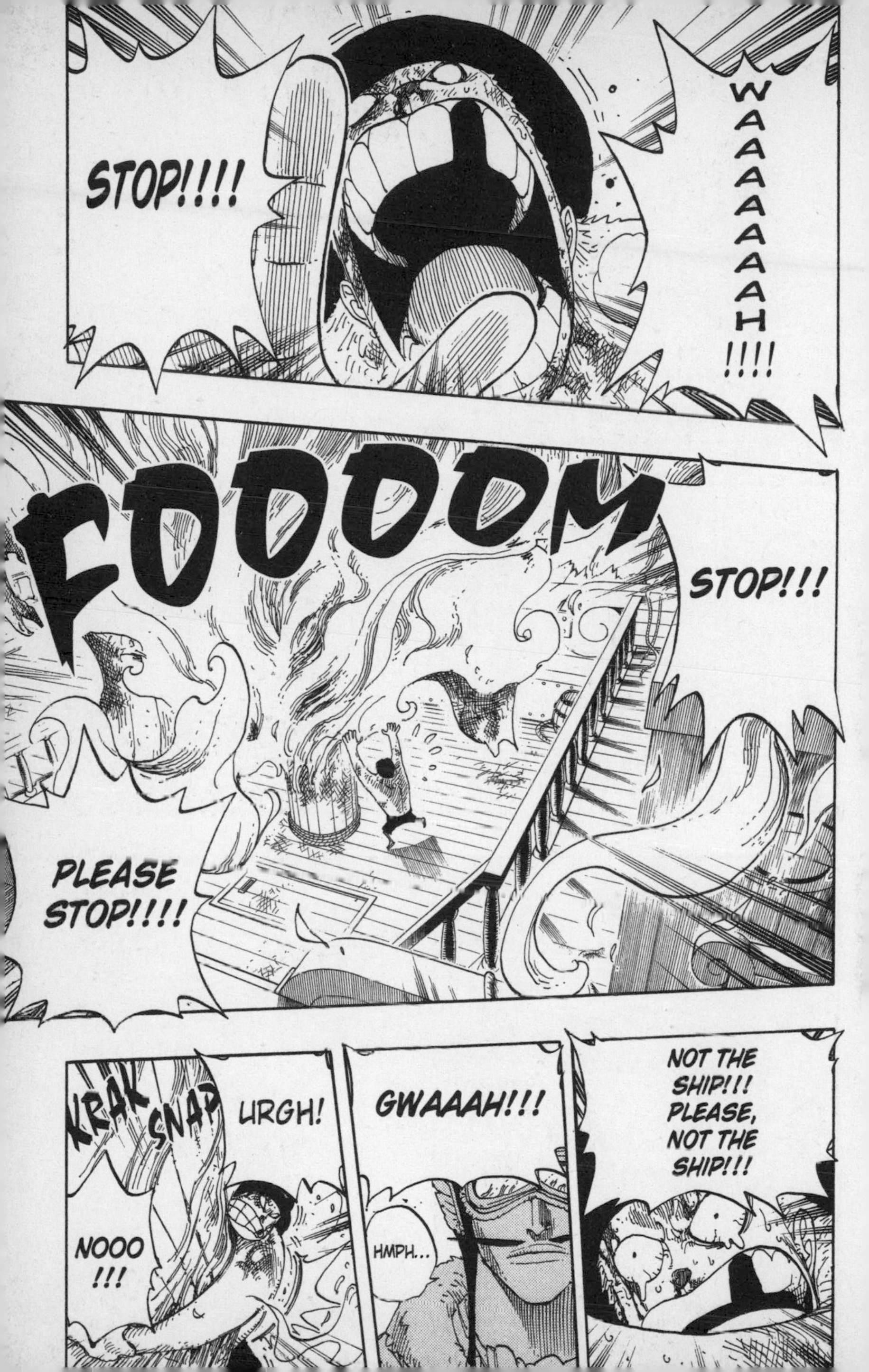
WAAAAAAAH!!!!
STOP!!!!
STOP!!!
FOOOOM
PLEASE STOP!!!!
NOT THE SHIP!!! PLEASE, NOT THE SHIP!!!
GWAAAH!!!
HMPH...
URGH!
SNAP
KRAK
NOOO!!!

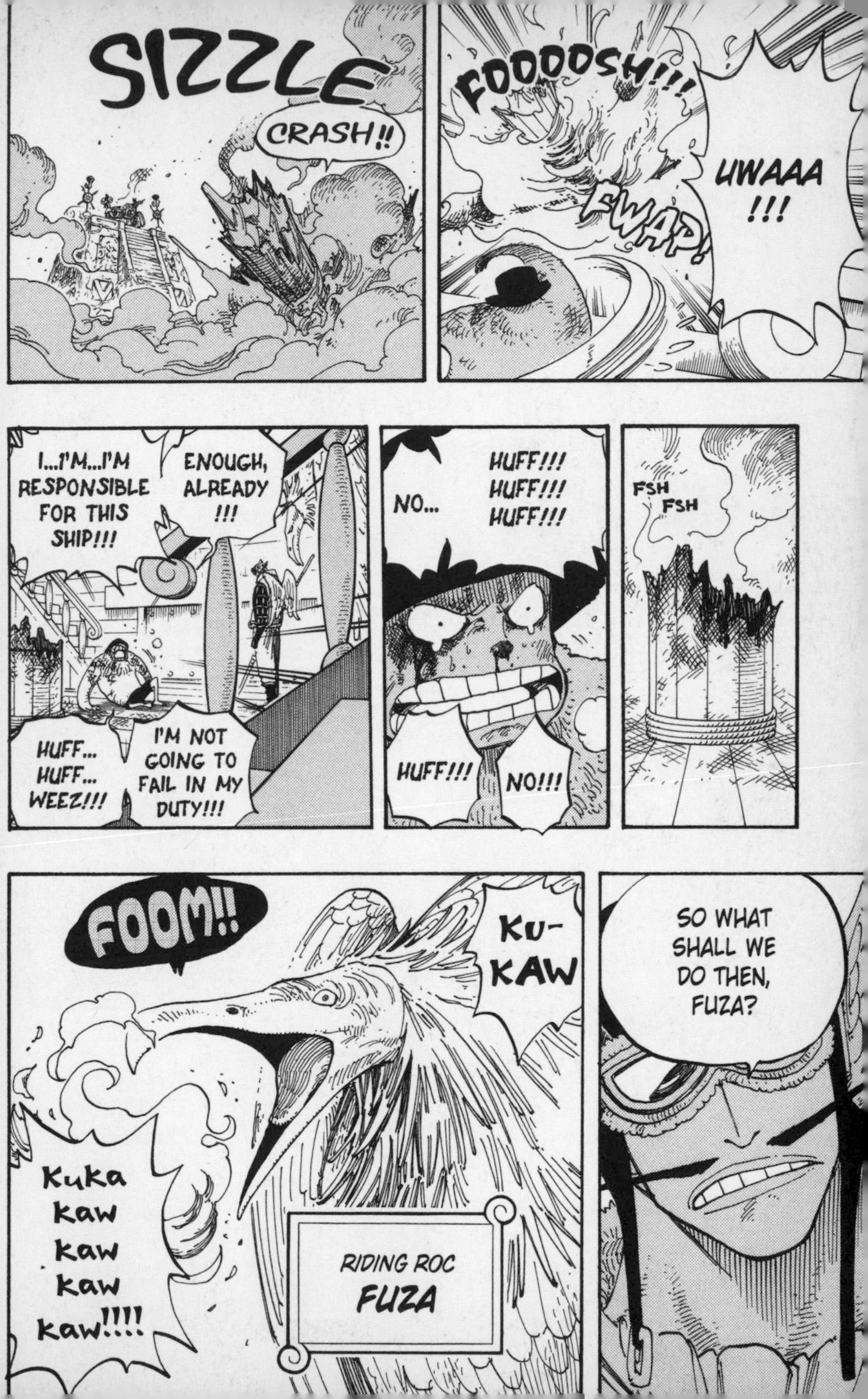
UWAAA !!!
FOOOOSH!!!
FWAP!
SIZZLE
CRASH!!
FSH FSH
HUFF!!! HUFF!!! HUFF!!!
NO...
NO!!!
HUFF!!!
ENOUGH, ALREADY !!!
I...I'M...I'M RESPONSIBLE FOR THIS SHIP!!!
I'M NOT GOING TO FAIL IN MY DUTY!!!
HUFF... HUFF... WEEZ!!!
SO WHAT SHALL WE DO THEN, FUZA?
KU-KAW
FOOM!!
RIDING ROC FUZA
Kuka kaw kaw kaw kaw!!!!

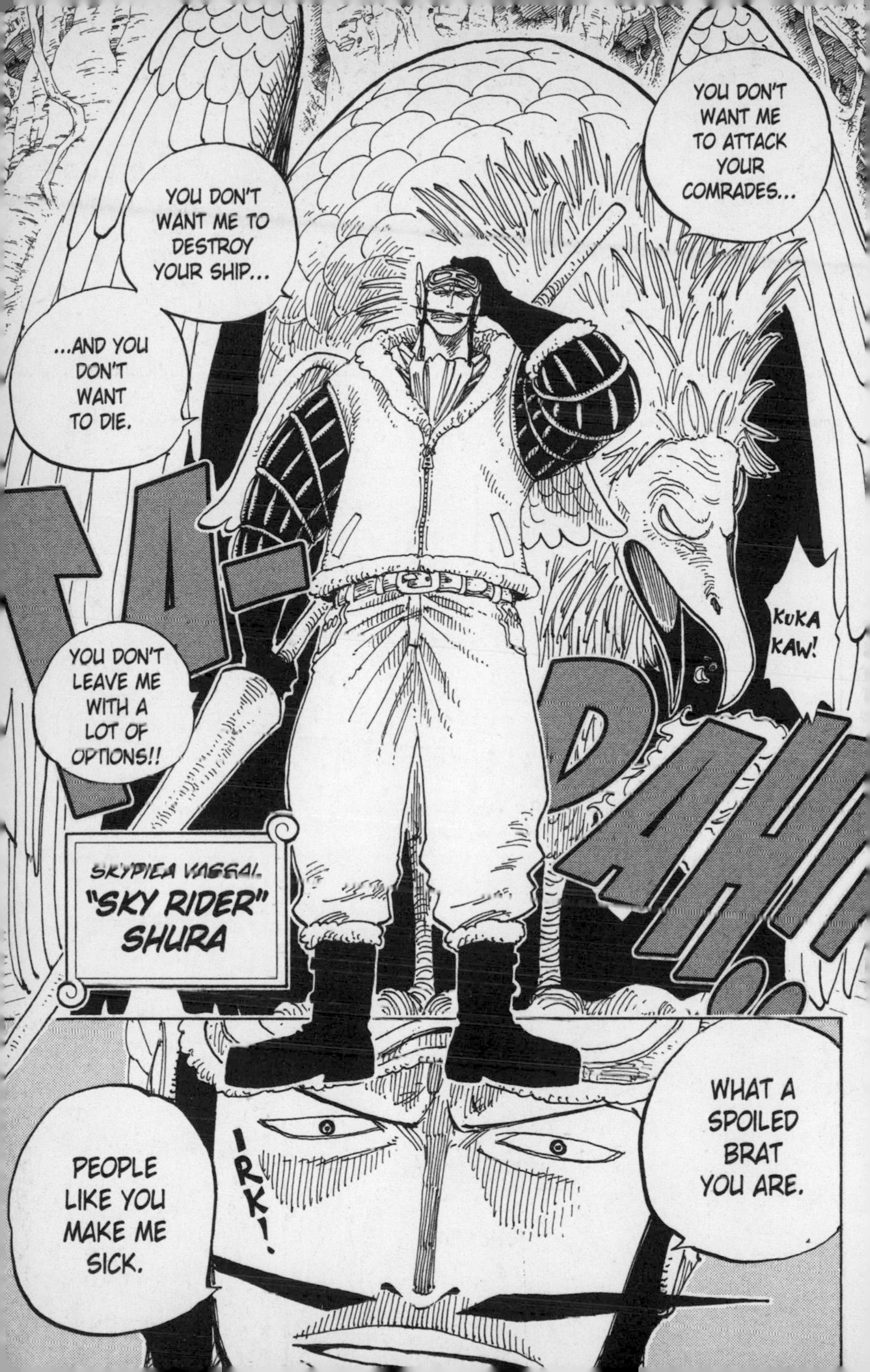
YOU DON'T WANT ME TO ATTACK YOUR COMRADES...
YOU DON'T WANT ME TO DESTROY YOUR SHIP...
...AND YOU DON'T WANT TO DIE.
KUKA KAW!
YOU DON'T LEAVE ME WITH A LOT OF OPTIONS!!
SKYPIEA VASSAL "SKY RIDER" SHURA
WHAT A SPOILED BRAT YOU ARE.
IRK!
PEOPLE LIKE YOU MAKE ME SICK.

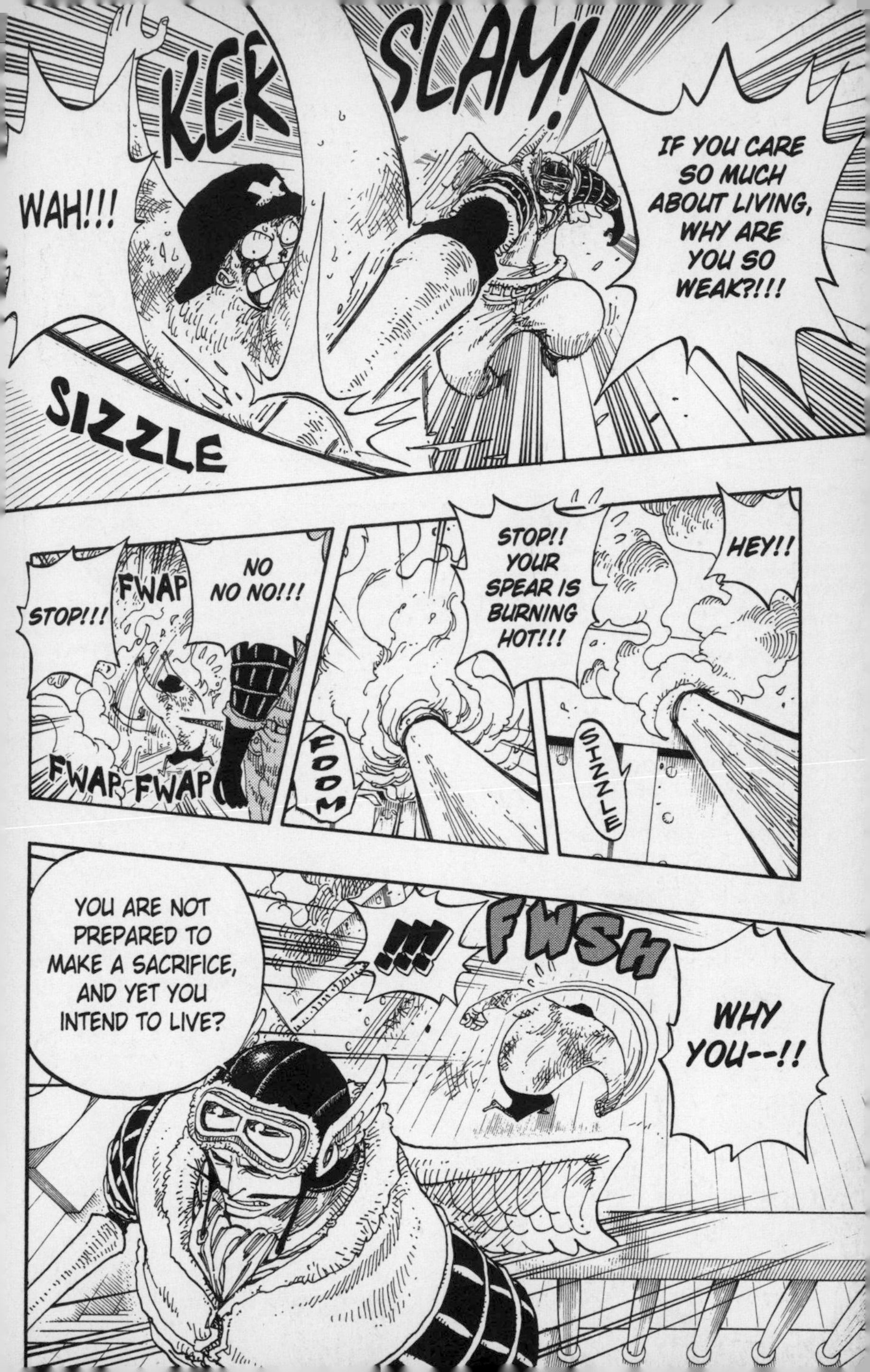
IF YOU CARE SO MUCH ABOUT LIVING, WHY ARE YOU SO WEAK?!!!
KER SLAM!
WAH!!!
SIZZLE
HEY!!
SIZZLE
STOP!! YOUR SPEAR IS BURNING HOT!!!
FOOM
NO NO NO!!!
FWAP
STOP!!!
FWAP FWAP
WHY YOU--!!
FWSH
!!!
YOU ARE NOT PREPARED TO MAKE A SACRIFICE, AND YET YOU INTEND TO LIVE?

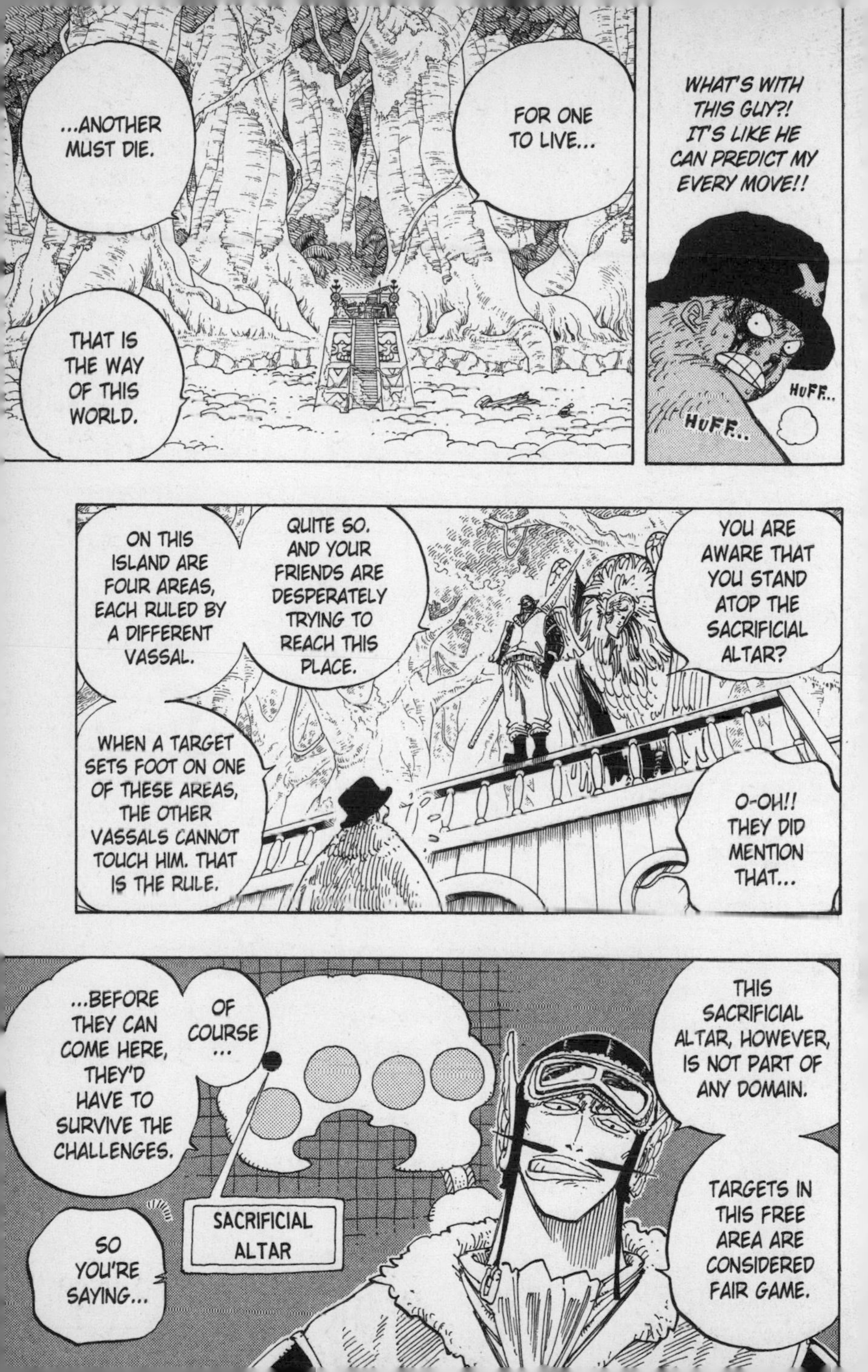
WHAT'S WITH THIS GUY?! IT'S LIKE HE CAN PREDICT MY EVERY MOVE!!
HUFF...
HUFF...
FOR ONE TO LIVE...
...ANOTHER MUST DIE.
THAT IS THE WAY OF THIS WORLD.
YOU ARE AWARE THAT YOU STAND ATOP THE SACRIFICIAL ALTAR?
O-OH!! THEY DID MENTION THAT...
QUITE SO. AND YOUR FRIENDS ARE DESPERATELY TRYING TO REACH THIS PLACE.
ON THIS ISLAND ARE FOUR AREAS, EACH RULED BY A DIFFERENT VASSAL.
WHEN A TARGET SETS FOOT ON ONE OF THESE AREAS, THE OTHER VASSALS CANNOT TOUCH HIM. THAT IS THE RULE.
THIS SACRIFICIAL ALTAR, HOWEVER, IS NOT PART OF ANY DOMAIN.
TARGETS IN THIS FREE AREA ARE CONSIDERED FAIR GAME.
OF COURSE...
...BEFORE THEY CAN COME HERE, THEY'D HAVE TO SURVIVE THE CHALLENGES.
SACRIFICIAL ALTAR
SO YOU'RE SAYING...

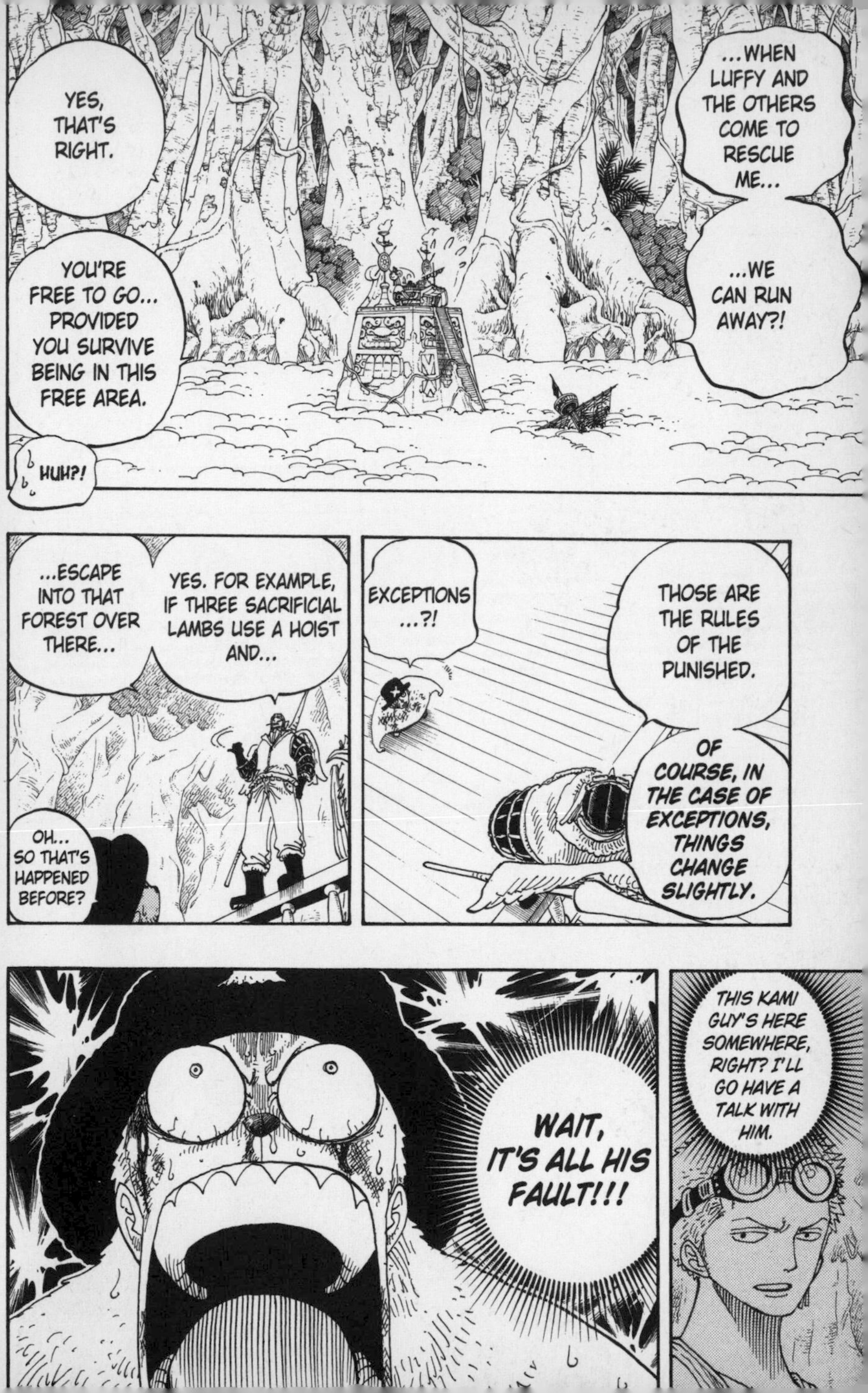
...WHEN LUFFY AND THE OTHERS COME TO RESCUE ME...
...WE CAN RUN AWAY?!
YES, THAT'S RIGHT.
YOU'RE FREE TO GO... PROVIDED YOU SURVIVE BEING IN THIS FREE AREA.
HUH?!
THOSE ARE THE RULES OF THE PUNISHED.
EXCEPTIONS ...?!
OF COURSE, IN THE CASE OF EXCEPTIONS, THINGS CHANGE SLIGHTLY.
YES. FOR EXAMPLE, IF THREE SACRIFICIAL LAMBS USE A HOIST AND...
...ESCAPE INTO THAT FOREST OVER THERE...
OH... SO THAT'S HAPPENED BEFORE?
THIS KAMI GUY'S HERE SOMEWHERE, RIGHT? I'LL GO HAVE A TALK WITH HIM.
WAIT, IT'S ALL HIS FAULT!!!

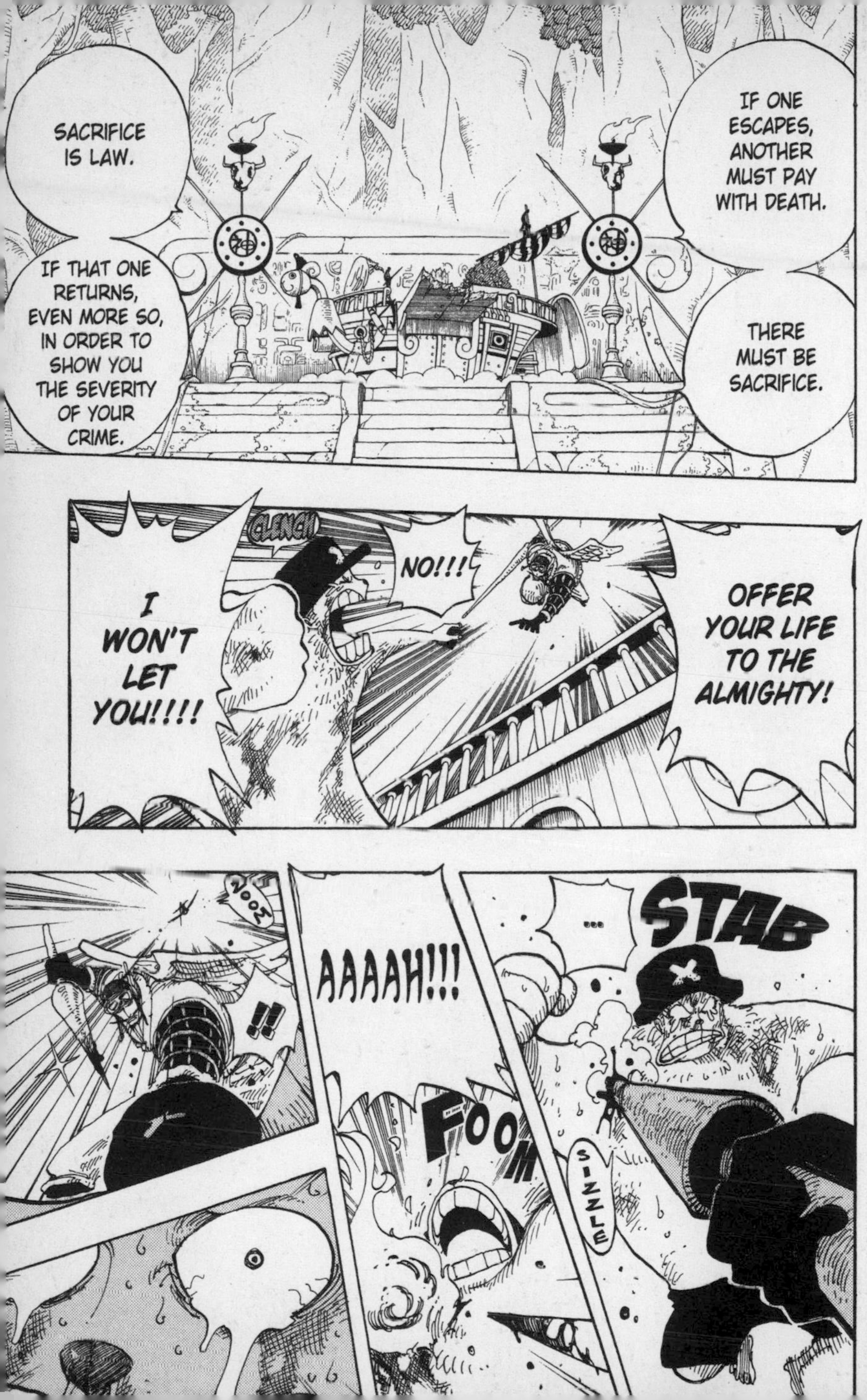
IF ONE ESCAPES, ANOTHER MUST PAY WITH DEATH.
THERE MUST BE SACRIFICE.
SACRIFICE IS LAW.
IF THAT ONE RETURNS, EVEN MORE SO, IN ORDER TO SHOW YOU THE SEVERITY OF YOUR CRIME.
OFFER YOUR LIFE TO THE ALMIGHTY!
NO!!!
CLENCH
I WON'T LET YOU!!!!
STAB
...
SIZZLE
AAAAH!!!
FOOM
ZOOM
!!

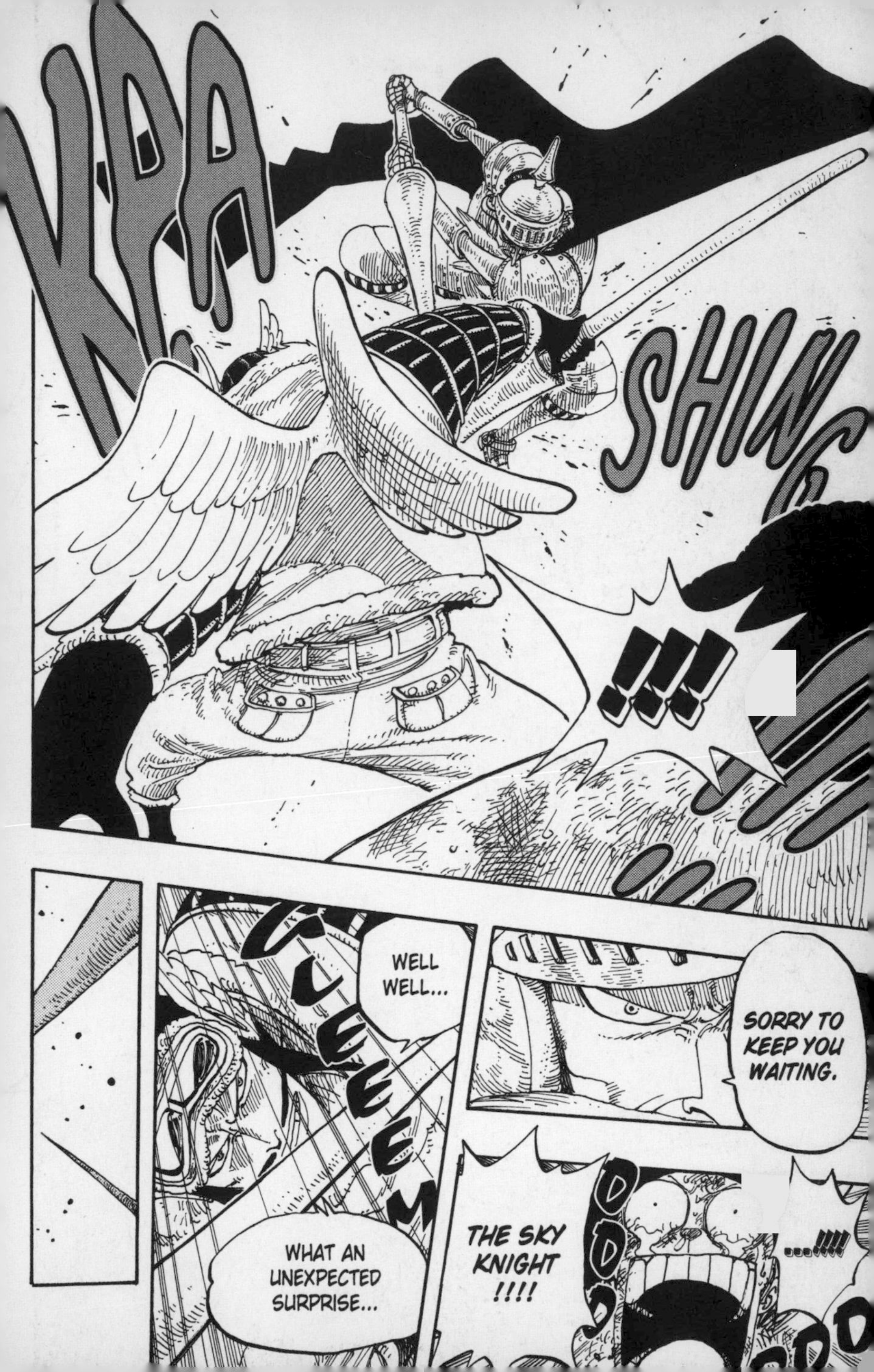
KPPA
SHING
!!!
SORRY TO KEEP YOU WAITING.
...!!!!
THE SKY KNIGHT !!!!
WELL WELL...
WHAT AN UNEXPECTED SURPRISE...

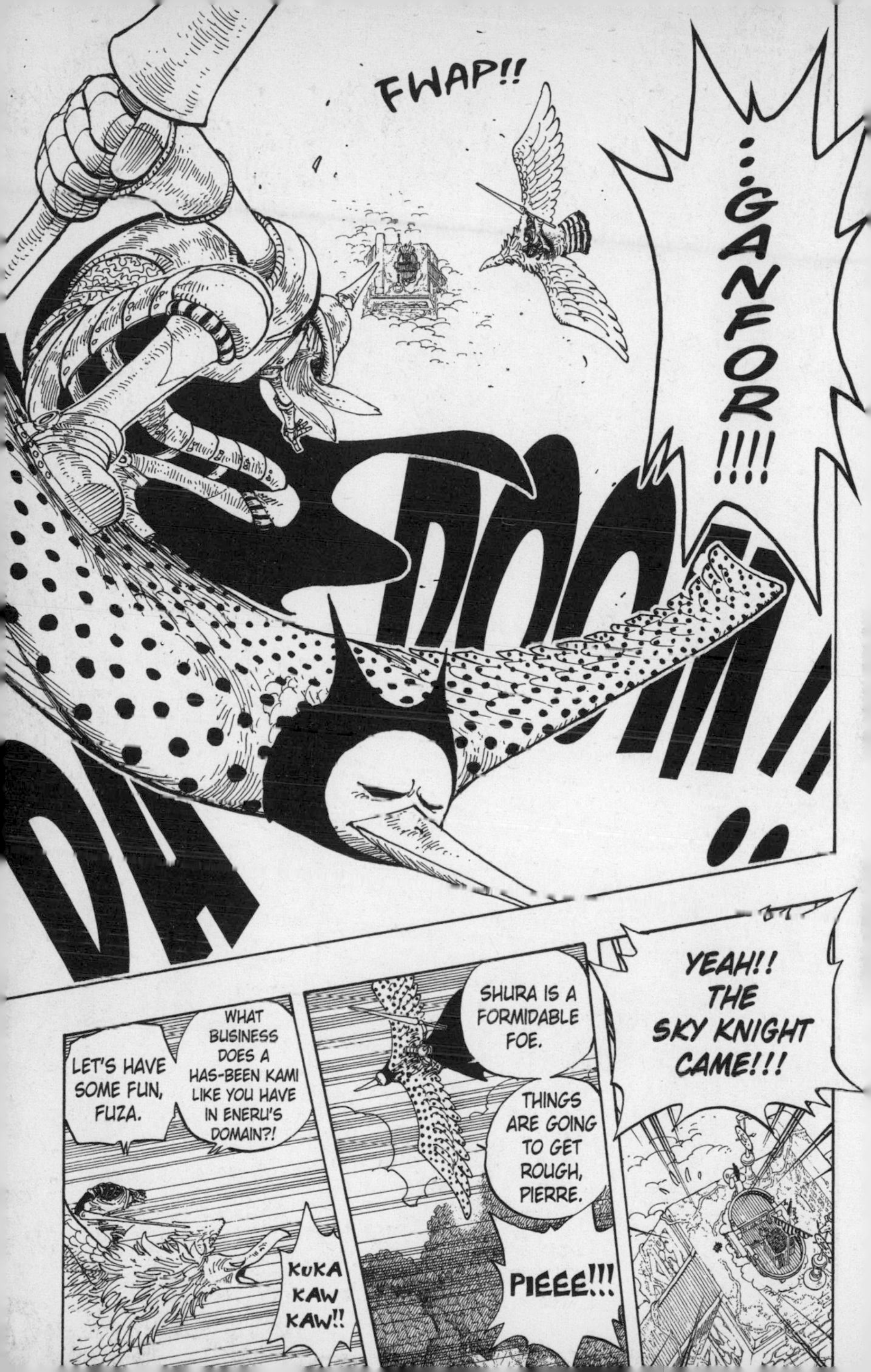
...GANFOR!!!!
FWAP!!
YEAH!! THE SKY KNIGHT CAME!!!
SHURA IS A FORMIDABLE FOE.
THINGS ARE GOING TO GET ROUGH, PIERRE.
PIEEE!!!
WHAT BUSINESS DOES A HAS-BEEN KAMI LIKE YOU HAVE IN ENERU'S DOMAIN?!
LET'S HAVE SOME FUN, FUZA.
KUKA KAW KAW!!

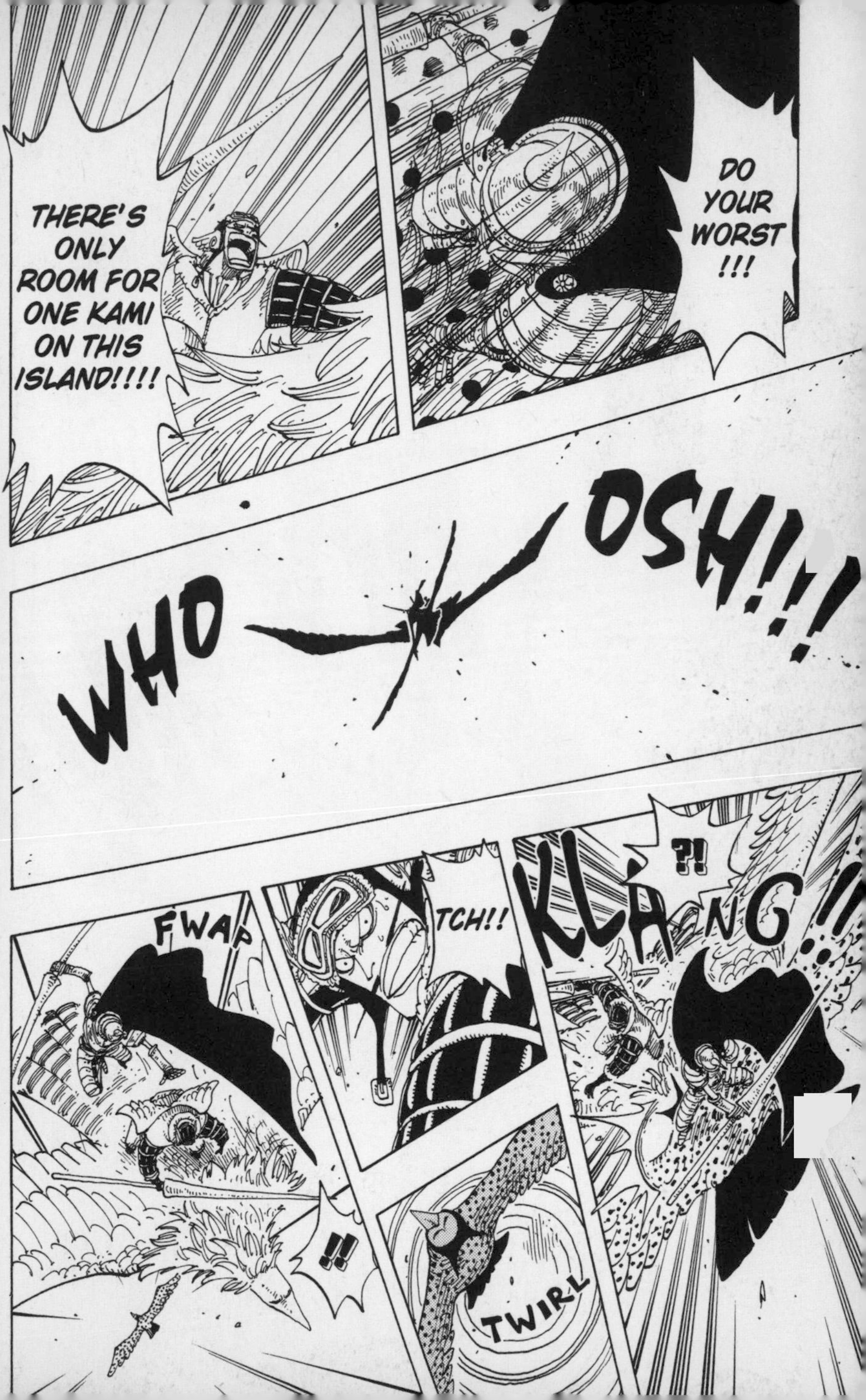
DO YOUR WORST!!!
THERE'S ONLY ROOM FOR ONE KAMI ON THIS ISLAND!!!!
WHO—OSH!!!
?!
KLANG!!!
TCH!!
TWIRL
FWAP
!!

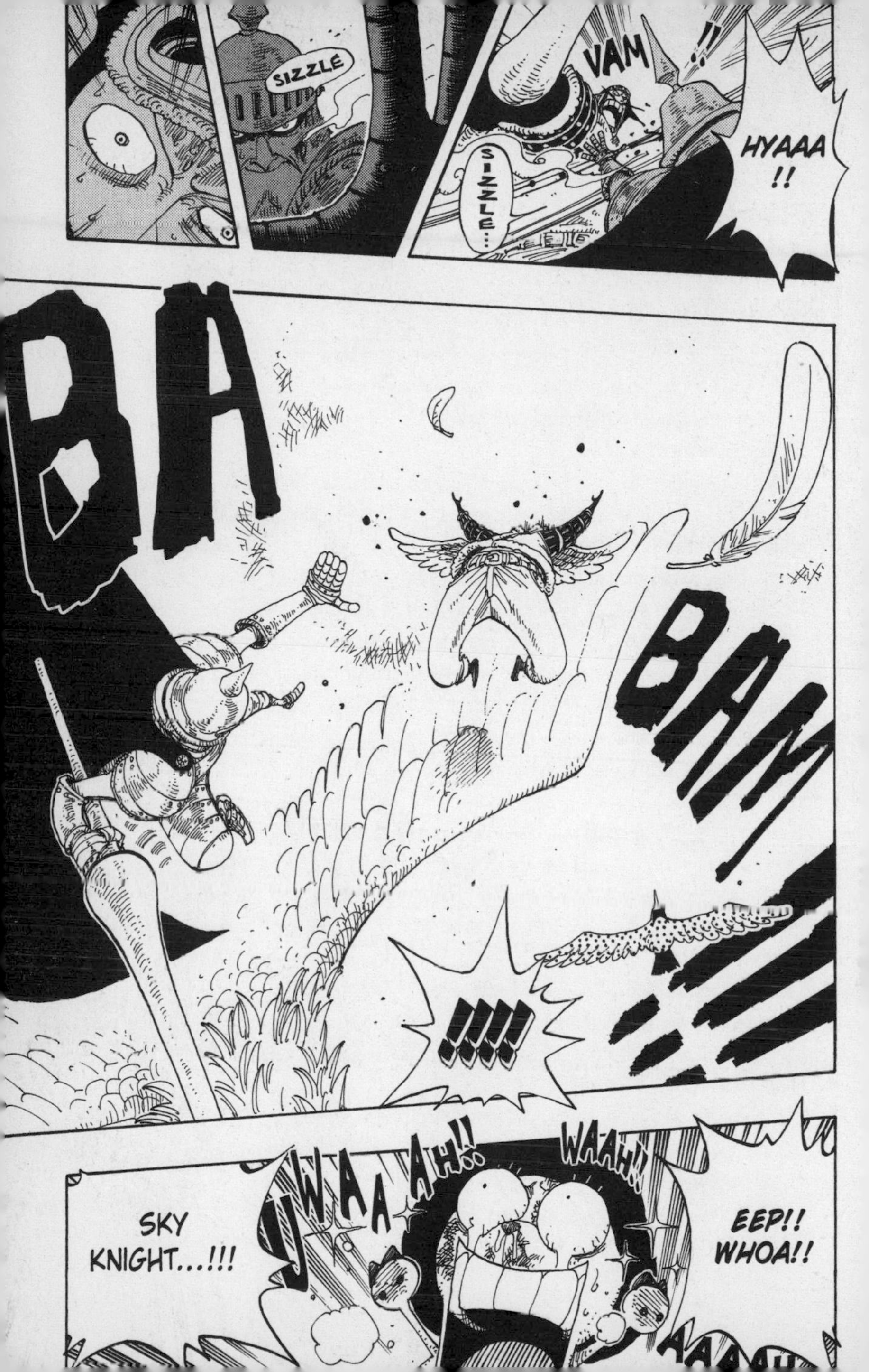
HYAAA !!
!!
VAM
SIZZLE...
SIZZLE
BA
BAM
!!!!
EEP!! WHOA!!
WAAH!!
WAAAH!!
SKY KNIGHT...!!!

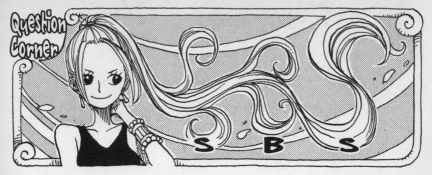

Q: Hello, Oda Sensei!! Can you give me the profiles for Captain Smoker and Hina? Are they the same captain's class and rank? Are they the same age? Or are success and age unrelated?

Q: Guten tag, Herr Oda! Please tell me, how old are Smoker and Hina? As for birthdays, how about saying that Smoker's is March 14 (White Day) and Hina's is March 3 (Girl's Day)? See ya.

A: I put the two inquiries together. Birthdays, eh? Hmm, that sounds good. As for age, Smoker is 34. And Hina is 32. They joined the Navy at the same time, and naturally, Hina was an exceptional recruit. But Smoker was a problem, never listening to his superior's orders. Call it fate or whatever, they've known each other for a long time. Smoker, who is not very adept at climbing the ladder of success, has been on the verge of discharge countless times but was saved by Hina. But in any case, they both have shown themselves to be exceptional Navy officers and were promoted to captian when still quite young.

Q: I have a question for Oda Sensei. In Chapter 212, is that thing connected to the rain-making ship a "Billower Bike"? It's supposed to be okay on the ocean, right? What kind of bike is it anyway?

A: It's actually an amphibious bike. "Billower" comes from the word "billow," as in "large wave," and that's why its tires are extra wide. I intend to use them in a story someday. Whenever "someday" is.

Chapter 249:

THE VILLAGE HIDDEN IN THE CLOUD

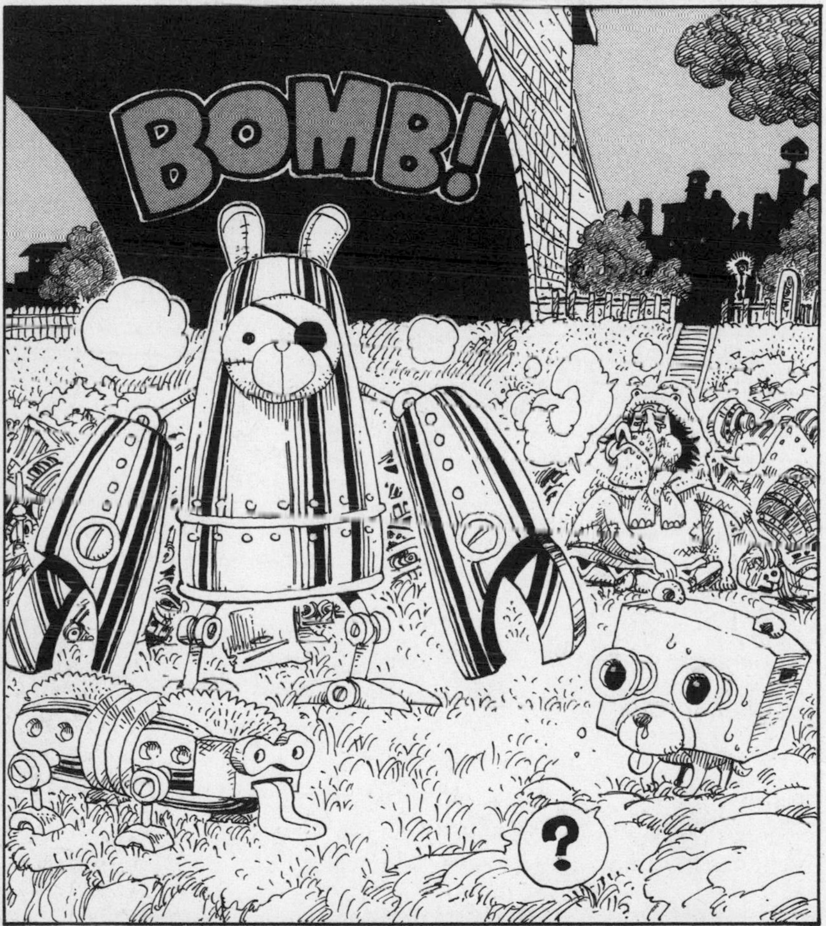

BOMB!
?

WAPOL'S OMNIVOROUS RAMPAGE, VOL. 12:
"CHOMP CHOMP FACTORY!! PLAYING ON THE DRY RIVERBED AMONG THE TRASH"

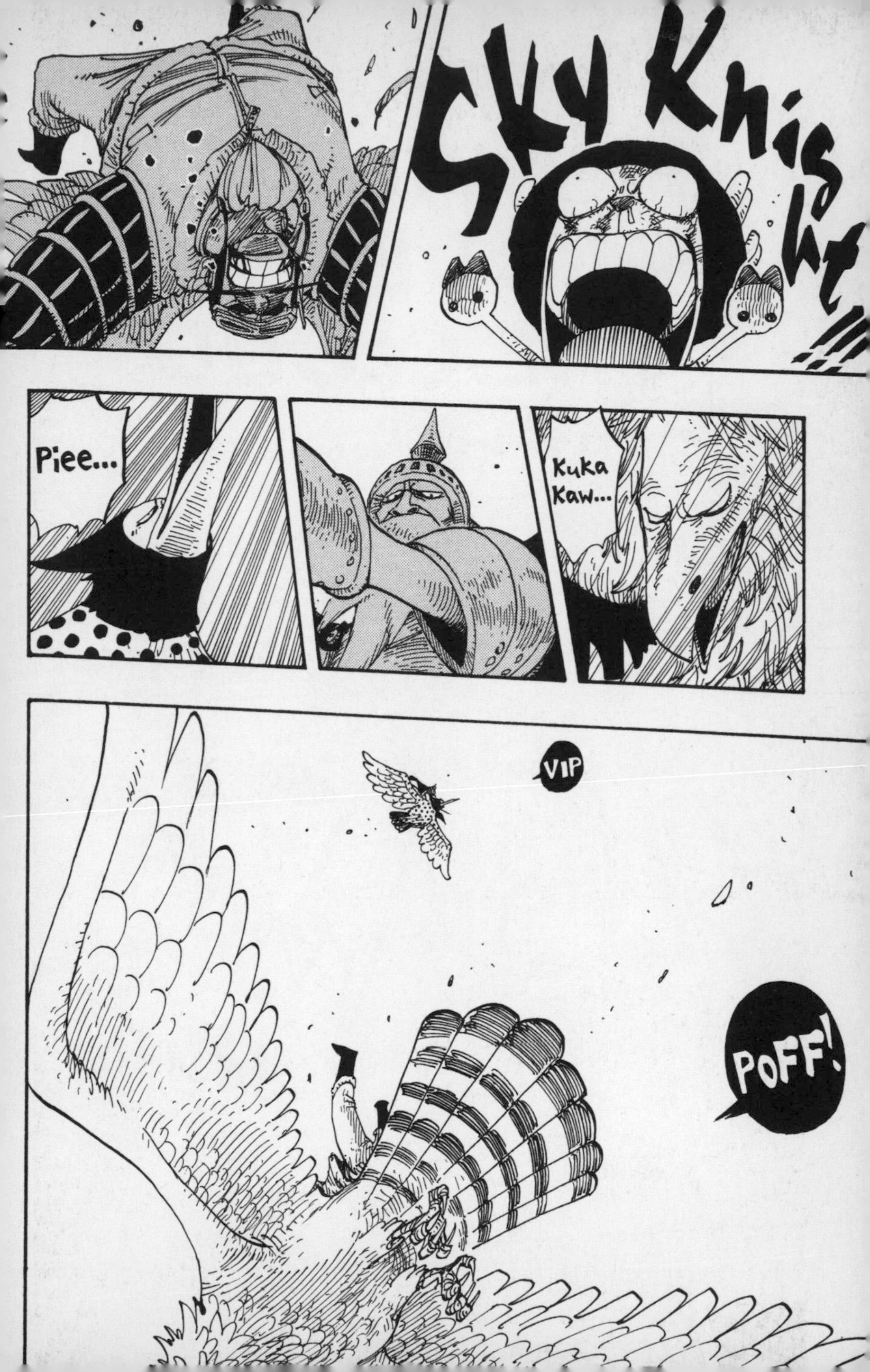
Sky Knight!!
Kuka Kaw...
Piee...
VIP
POFF!

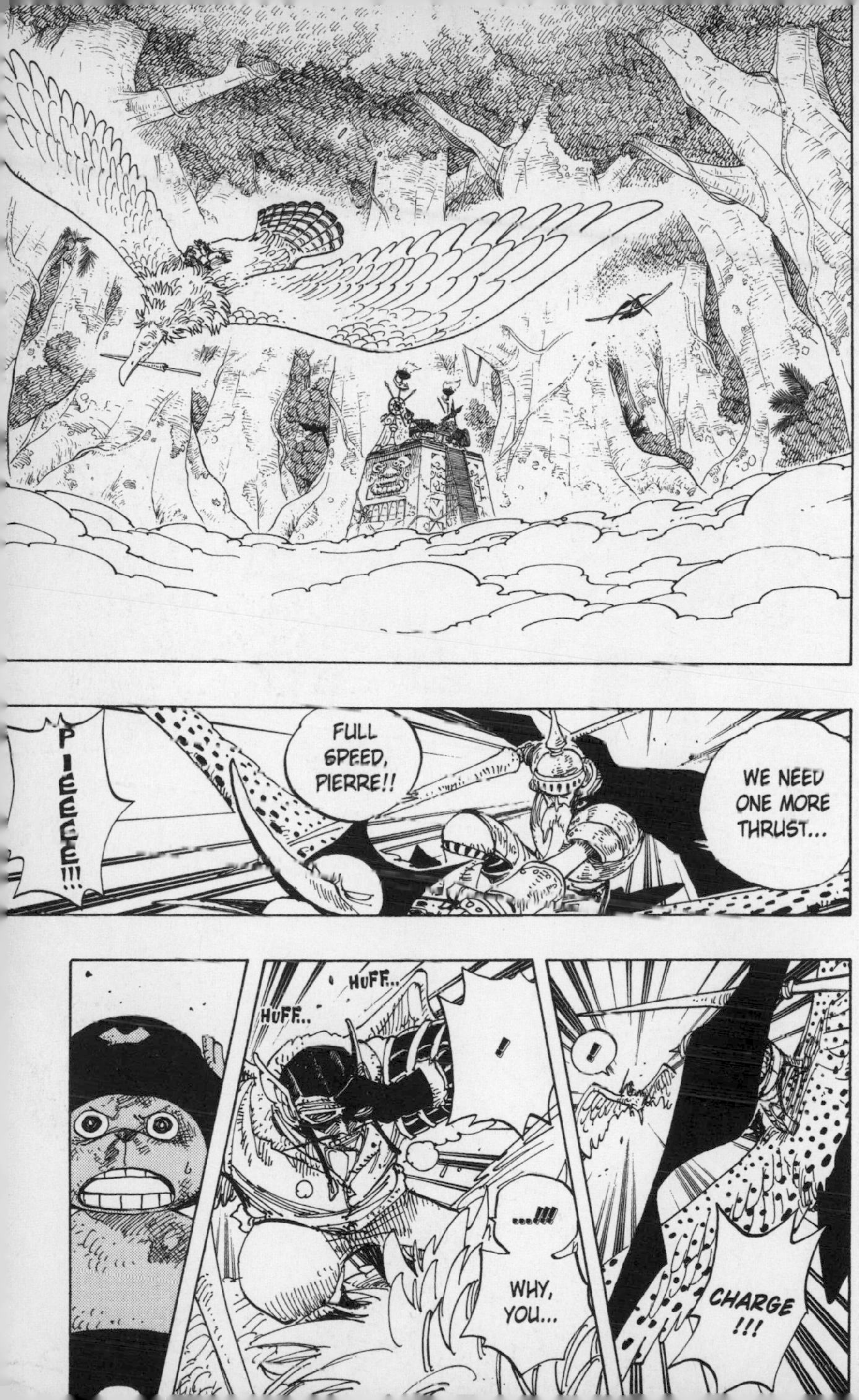
WE NEED ONE MORE THRUST...
FULL SPEED, PIERRE!!
PIEEEE!!!
!
CHARGE !!!
HUFF...
HUFF...
!
...!!!
WHY, YOU...

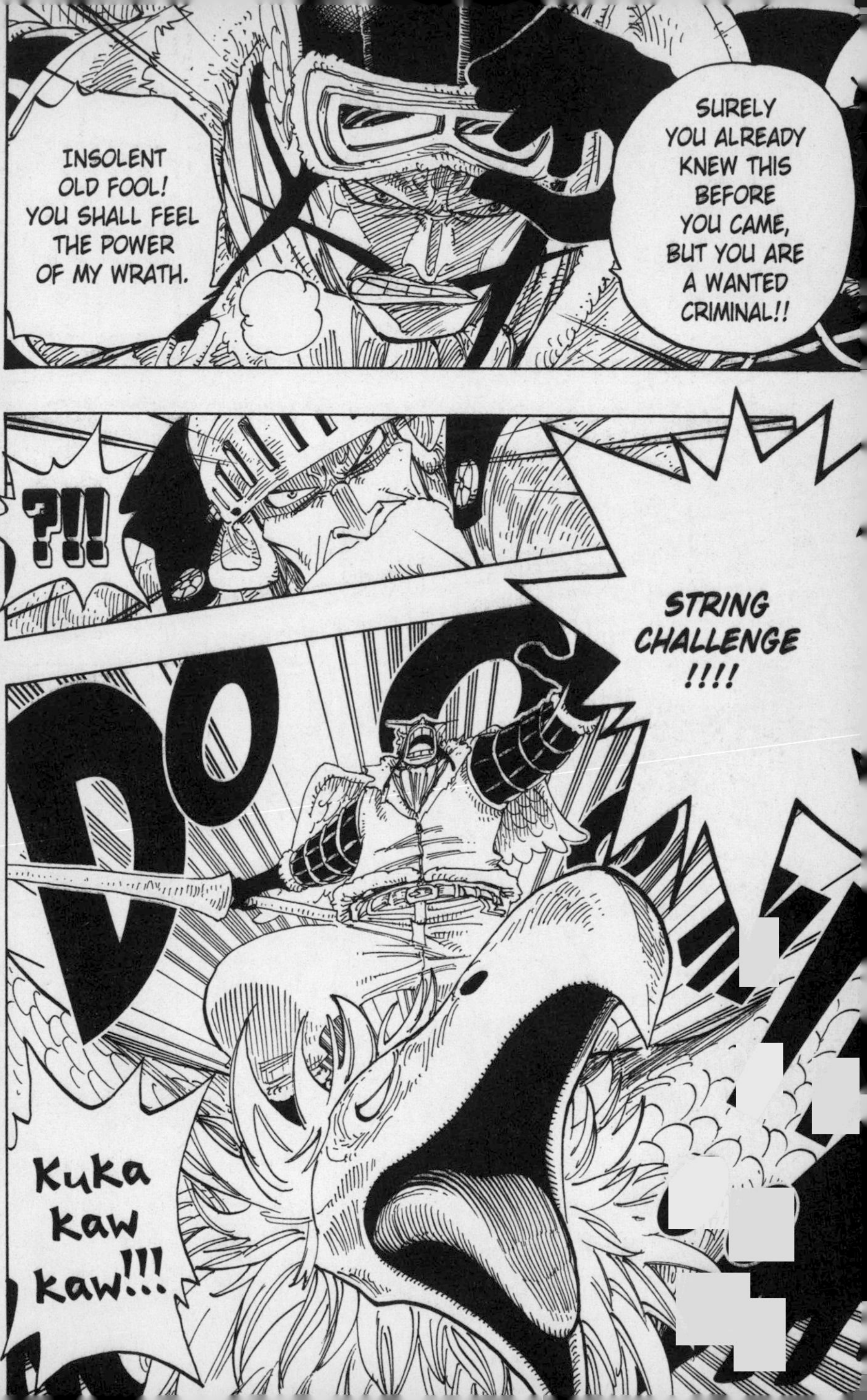
SURELY YOU ALREADY KNEW THIS BEFORE YOU CAME, BUT YOU ARE A WANTED CRIMINAL!!
INSOLENT OLD FOOL! YOU SHALL FEEL THE POWER OF MY WRATH.
?!!
STRING CHALLENGE !!!!
Kuka kaw kaw!!!...

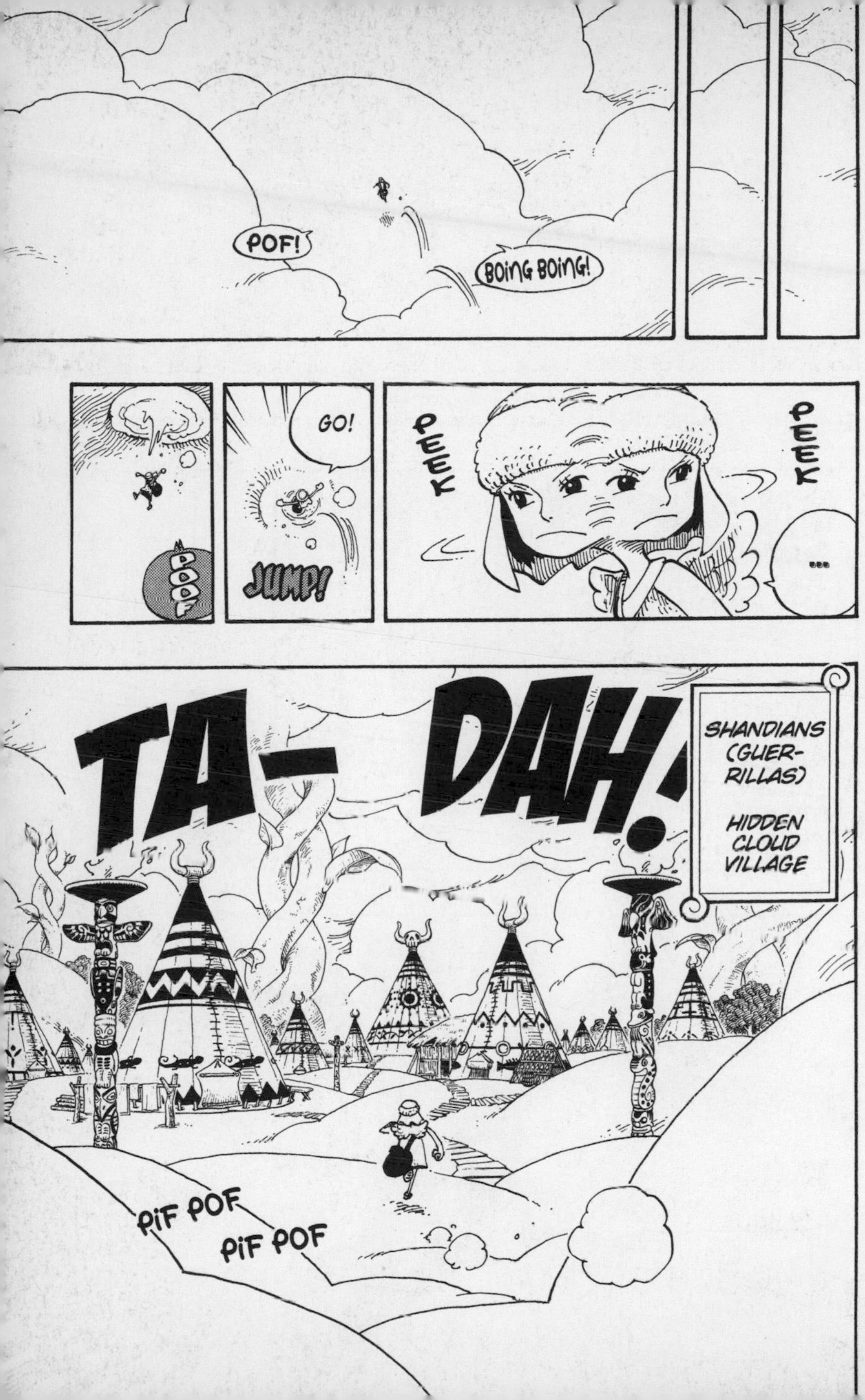
POF!
BOING BOING!
PEEK
PEEK
...
GO!
JUMP!
POOF
SHANDIANS (GUER-RILLAS)
HIDDEN CLOUD VILLAGE
TA-DAH!
PIF POF
PIF POF

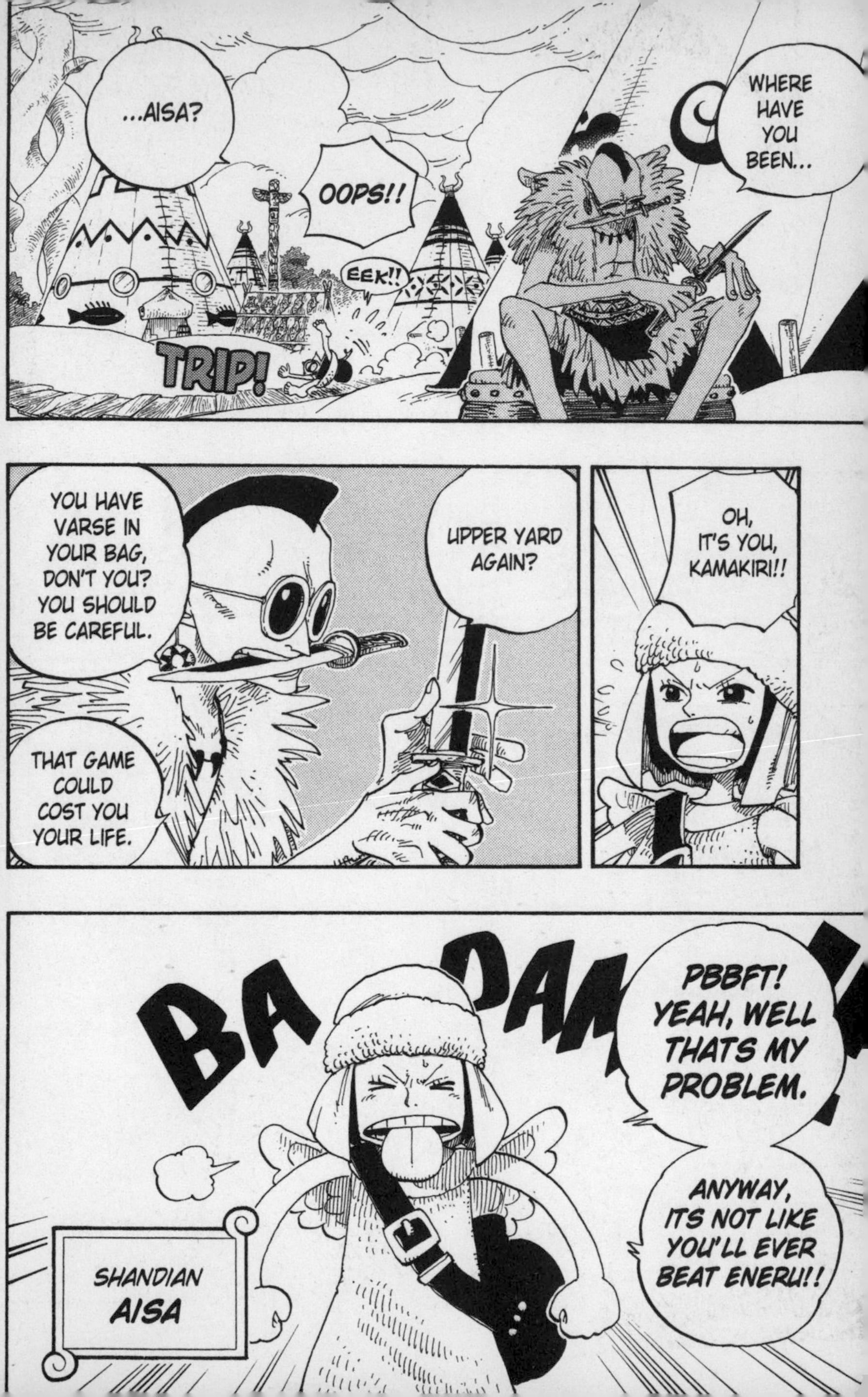
WHERE HAVE YOU BEEN...
...AISA?
OOPS!!
EEK!!
TRIP!
OH, IT'S YOU, KAMAKIRI!!
UPPER YARD AGAIN?
YOU HAVE VARSE IN YOUR BAG, DON'T YOU? YOU SHOULD BE CAREFUL.
THAT GAME COULD COST YOU YOUR LIFE.
PBBFT! YEAH, WELL THATS MY PROBLEM.
ANYWAY, ITS NOT LIKE YOU'LL EVER BEAT ENERU!!
BA DAM
SHANDIAN AISA

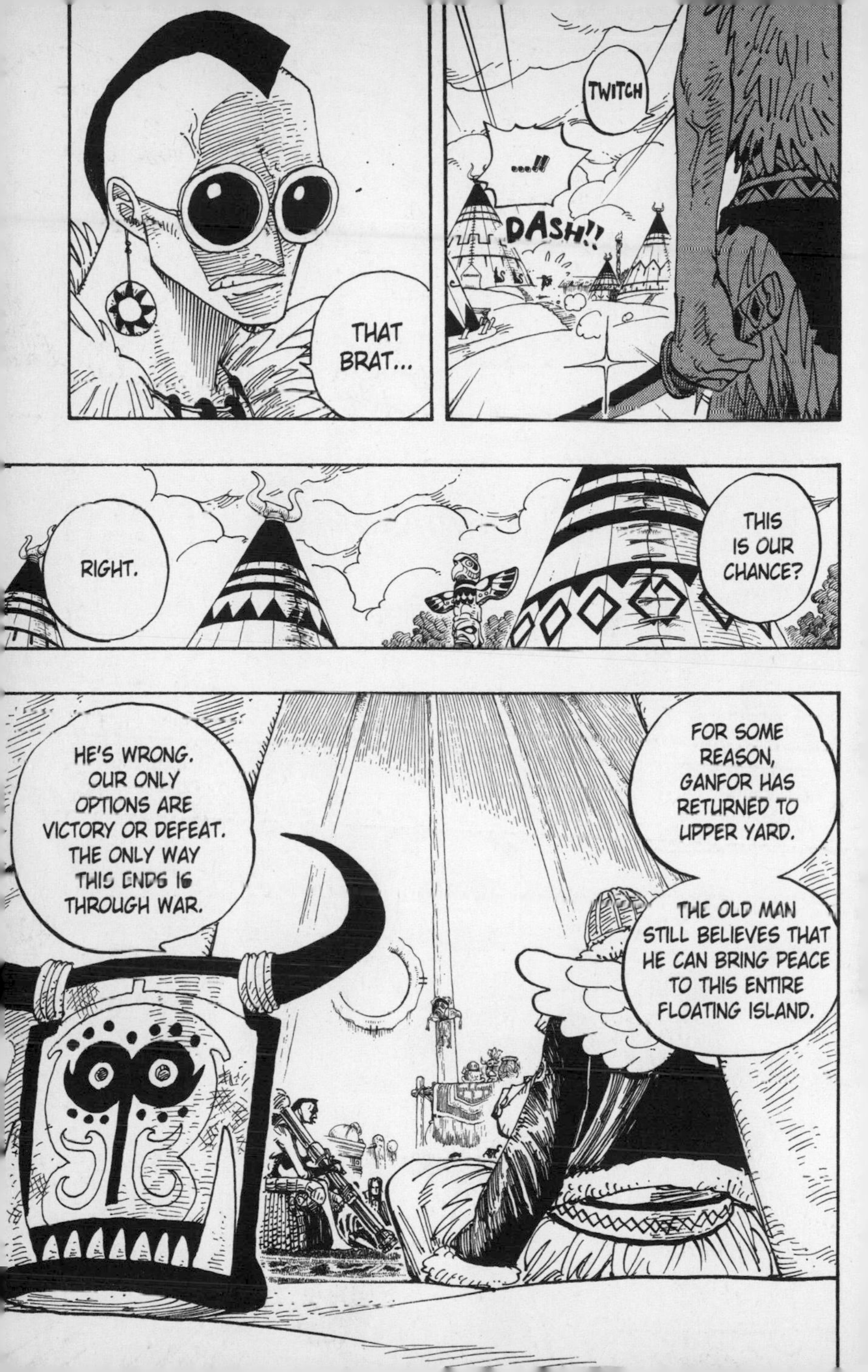
TWITCH
...!!
DASH!!
THAT BRAT...
THIS IS OUR CHANCE?
RIGHT.
FOR SOME REASON, GANFOR HAS RETURNED TO UPPER YARD.
THE OLD MAN STILL BELIEVES THAT HE CAN BRING PEACE TO THIS ENTIRE FLOATING ISLAND.
HE'S WRONG. OUR ONLY OPTIONS ARE VICTORY OR DEFEAT. THE ONLY WAY THIS ENDS IS THROUGH WAR.

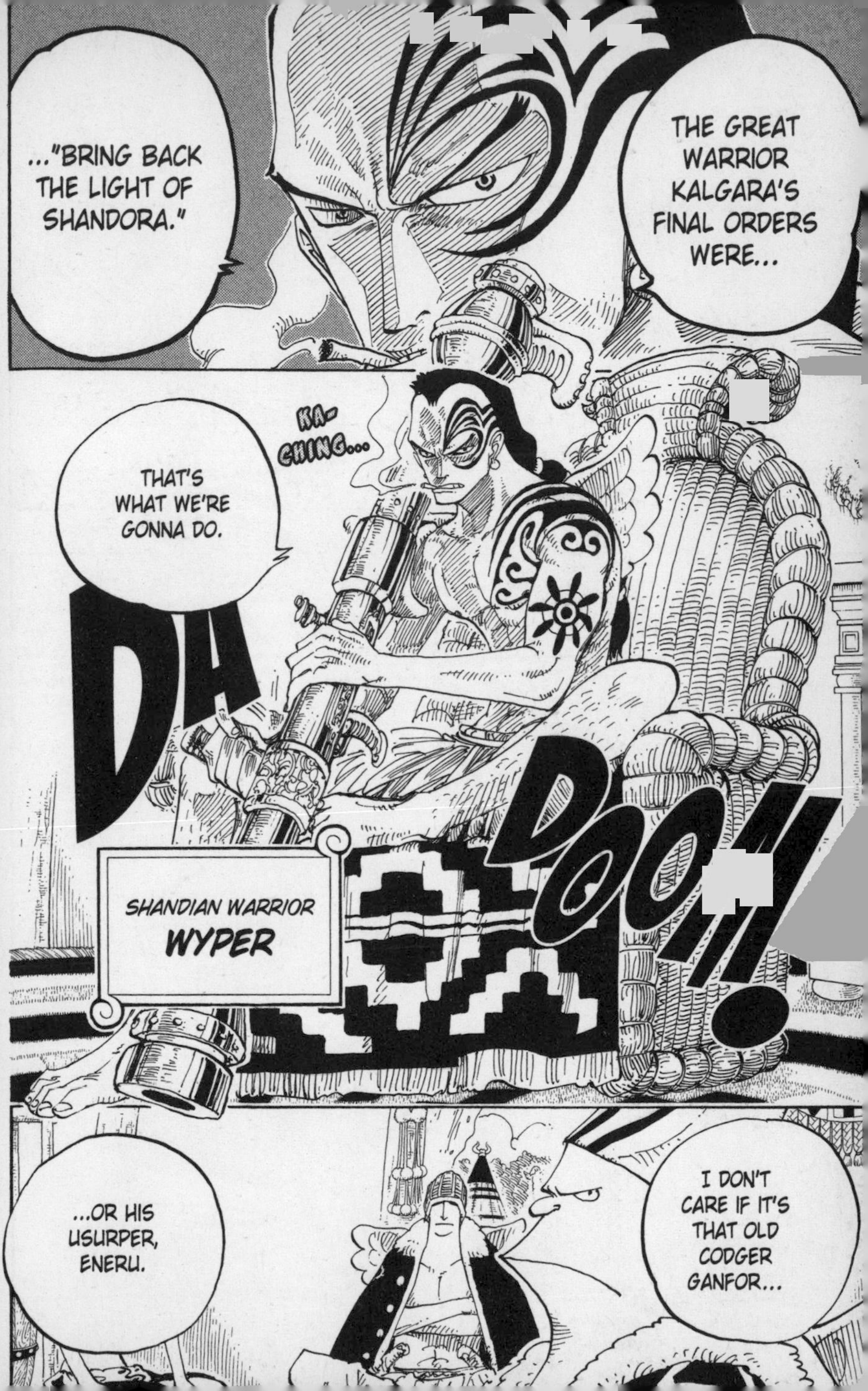
THE GREAT WARRIOR KALGARA'S FINAL ORDERS WERE...
..."BRING BACK THE LIGHT OF SHANDORA."
KA-CHING...
THAT'S WHAT WE'RE GONNA DO.
DA
DOOM!!
SHANDIAN WARRIOR
WYPER
I DON'T CARE IF IT'S THAT OLD CODGER GANFOR...
...OR HIS USURPER, ENERU.

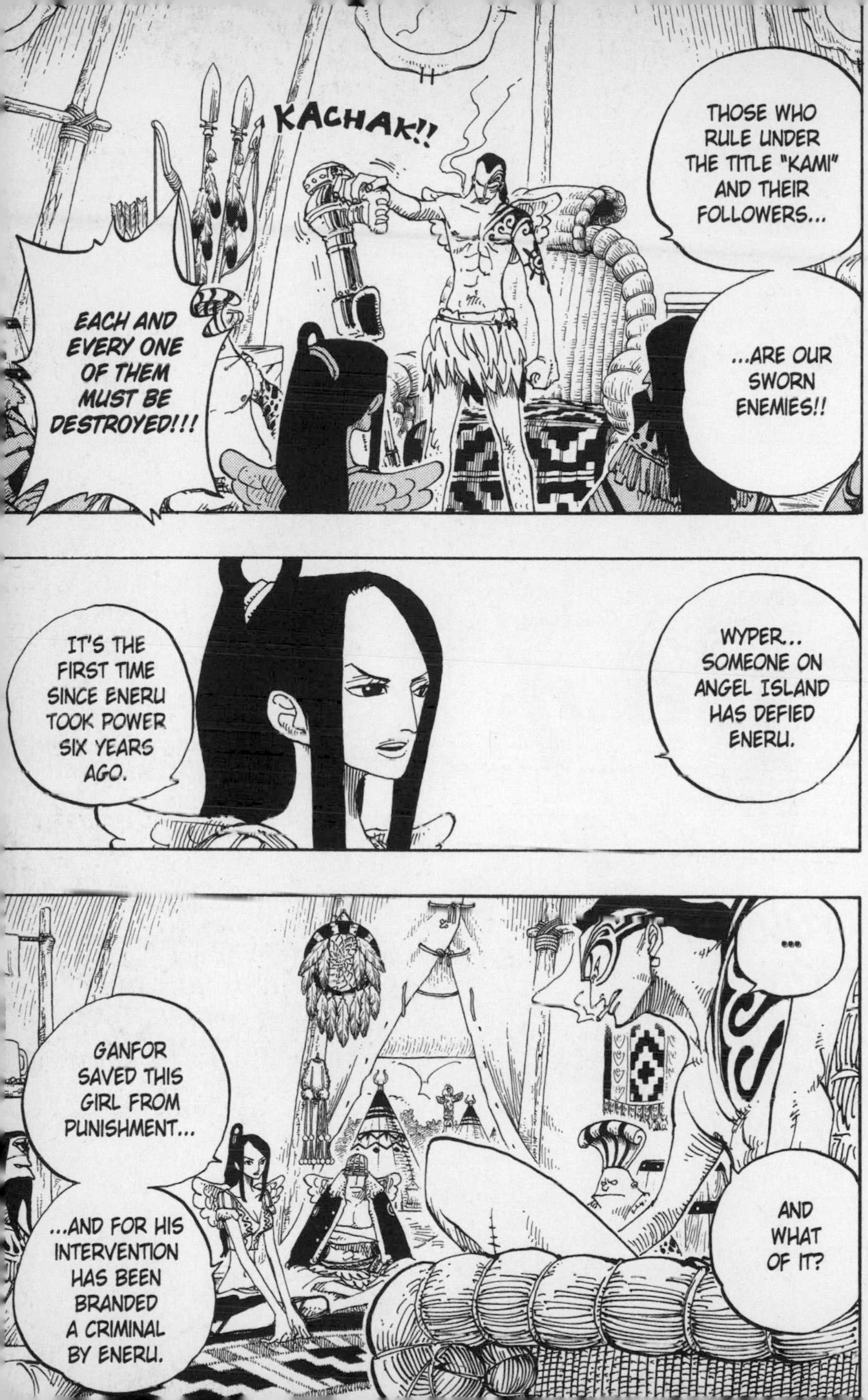
THOSE WHO RULE UNDER THE TITLE "KAMI" AND THEIR FOLLOWERS...
...ARE OUR SWORN ENEMIES!!
KACHAK!!
EACH AND EVERY ONE OF THEM MUST BE DESTROYED!!!
WYPER... SOMEONE ON ANGEL ISLAND HAS DEFIED ENERU.
IT'S THE FIRST TIME SINCE ENERU TOOK POWER SIX YEARS AGO.
...
GANFOR SAVED THIS GIRL FROM PUNISHMENT...
...AND FOR HIS INTERVENTION HAS BEEN BRANDED A CRIMINAL BY ENERU.
AND WHAT OF IT?

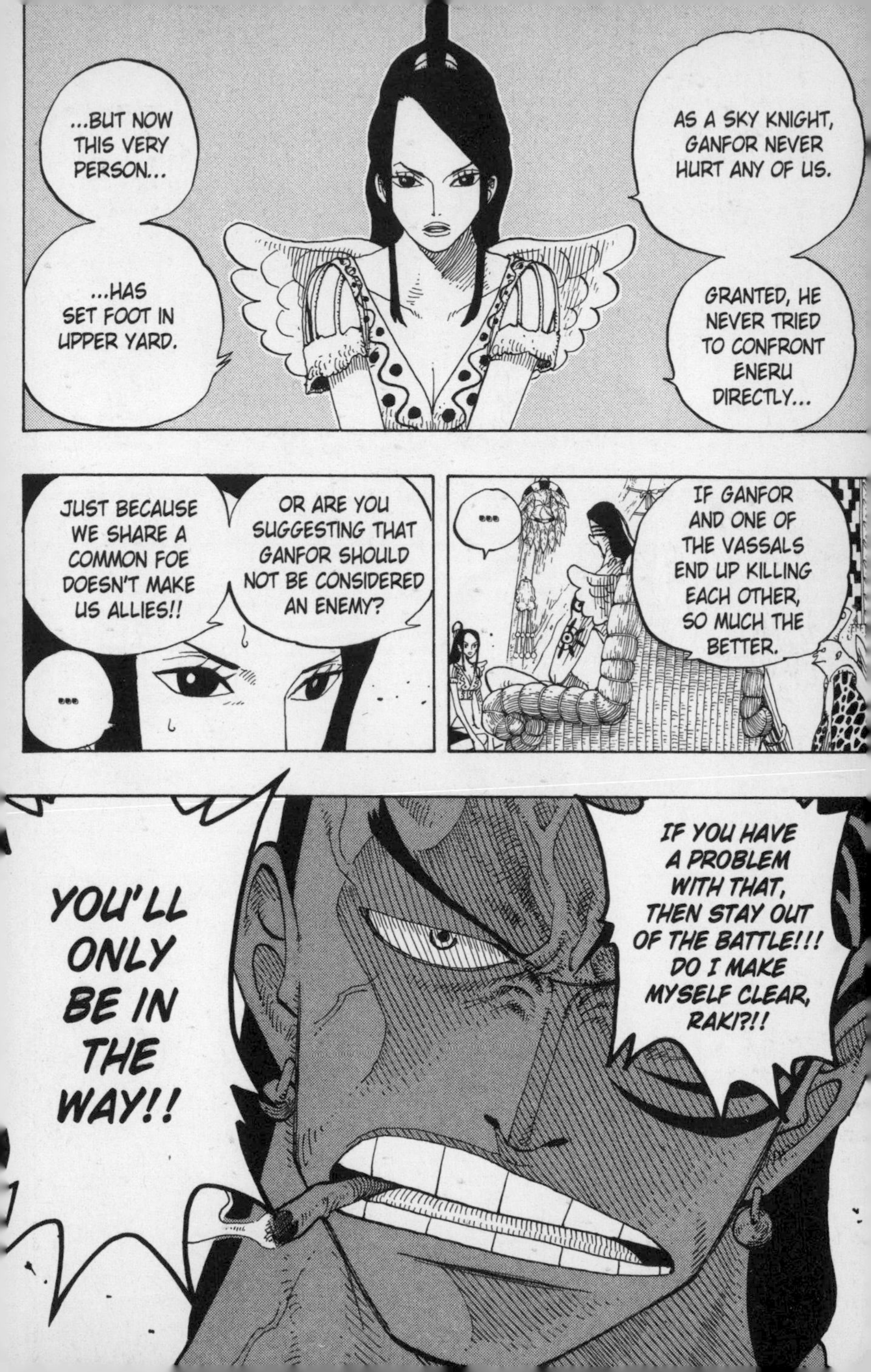
AS A SKY KNIGHT, GANFOR NEVER HURT ANY OF US.
GRANTED, HE NEVER TRIED TO CONFRONT ENERU DIRECTLY...
...BUT NOW THIS VERY PERSON...
...HAS SET FOOT IN UPPER YARD.
IF GANFOR AND ONE OF THE VASSALS END UP KILLING EACH OTHER, SO MUCH THE BETTER.
...
OR ARE YOU SUGGESTING THAT GANFOR SHOULD NOT BE CONSIDERED AN ENEMY?
JUST BECAUSE WE SHARE A COMMON FOE DOESN'T MAKE US ALLIES!!
...
IF YOU HAVE A PROBLEM WITH THAT, THEN STAY OUT OF THE BATTLE!!! DO I MAKE MYSELF CLEAR, RAKI?!!
YOU'LL ONLY BE IN THE WAY!!

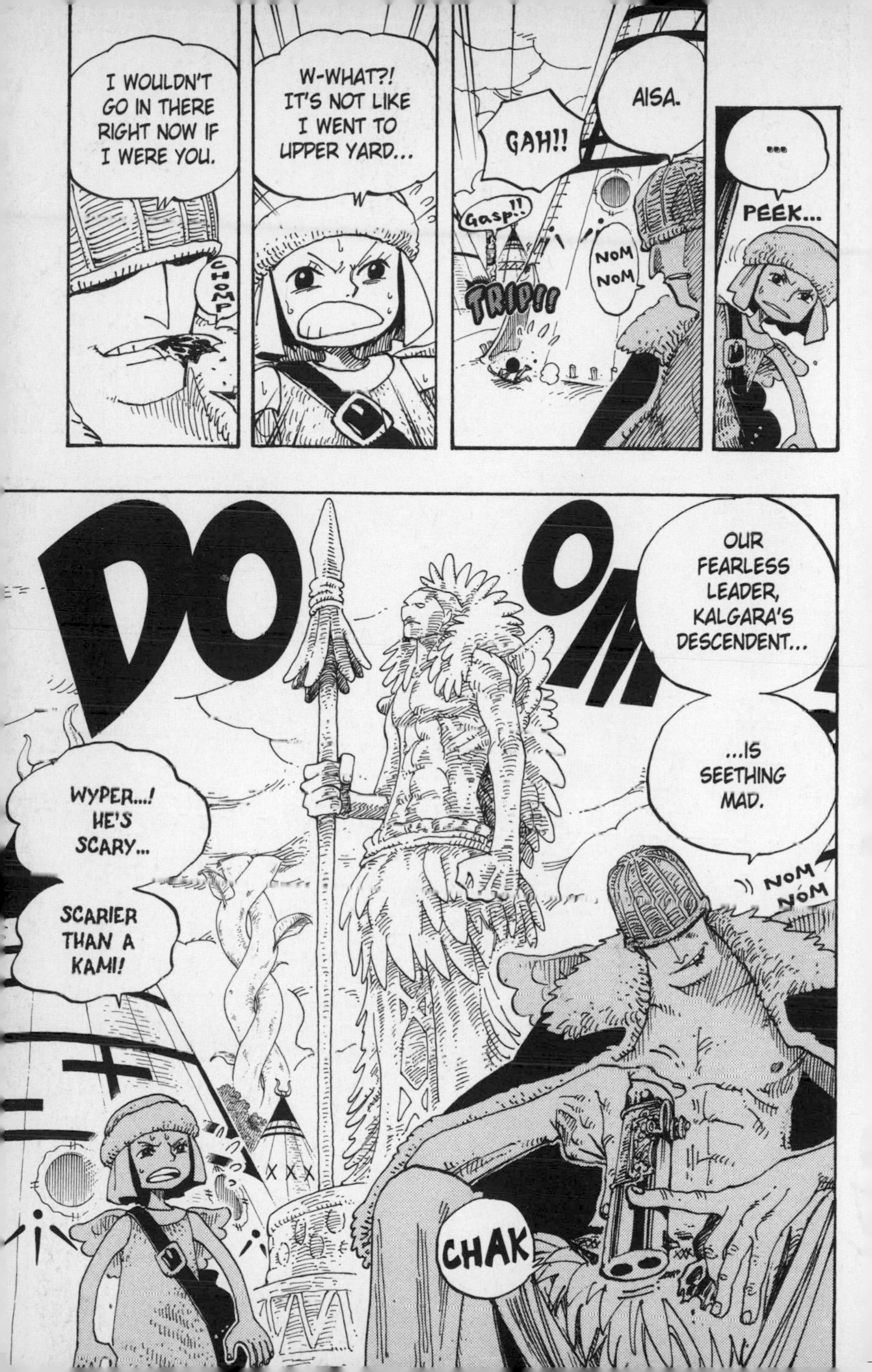
...
PEEK...
AISA.
GAH!!
Gasp!!
NOM NOM
TRIP!!
W-WHAT?! IT'S NOT LIKE I WENT TO UPPER YARD...
I WOULDN'T GO IN THERE RIGHT NOW IF I WERE YOU.
CHOMP
DOOM
OUR FEARLESS LEADER, KALGARA'S DESCENDENT...
...IS SEETHING MAD.
NOM NOM
WYPER...! HE'S SCARY...
SCARIER THAN A KAMI!
CHAK

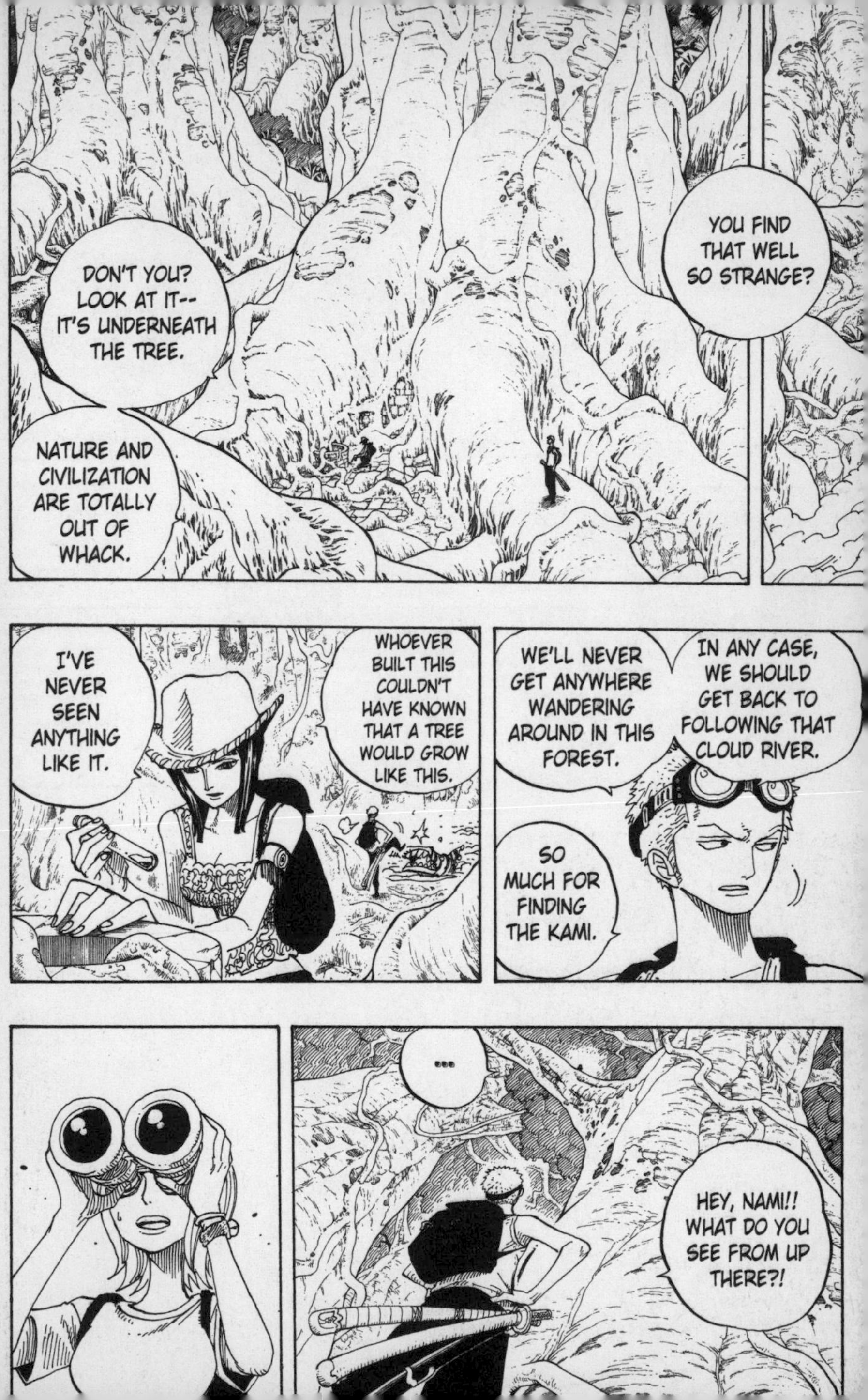
YOU FIND THAT WELL SO STRANGE?
DON'T YOU? LOOK AT IT-- IT'S UNDERNEATH THE TREE.
NATURE AND CIVILIZATION ARE TOTALLY OUT OF WHACK.
IN ANY CASE, WE SHOULD GET BACK TO FOLLOWING THAT CLOUD RIVER.
WE'LL NEVER GET ANYWHERE WANDERING AROUND IN THIS FOREST.
SO MUCH FOR FINDING THE KAMI.
WHOEVER BUILT THIS COULDN'T HAVE KNOWN THAT A TREE WOULD GROW LIKE THIS.
I'VE NEVER SEEN ANYTHING LIKE IT.
...
HEY, NAMI!! WHAT DO YOU SEE FROM UP THERE?!

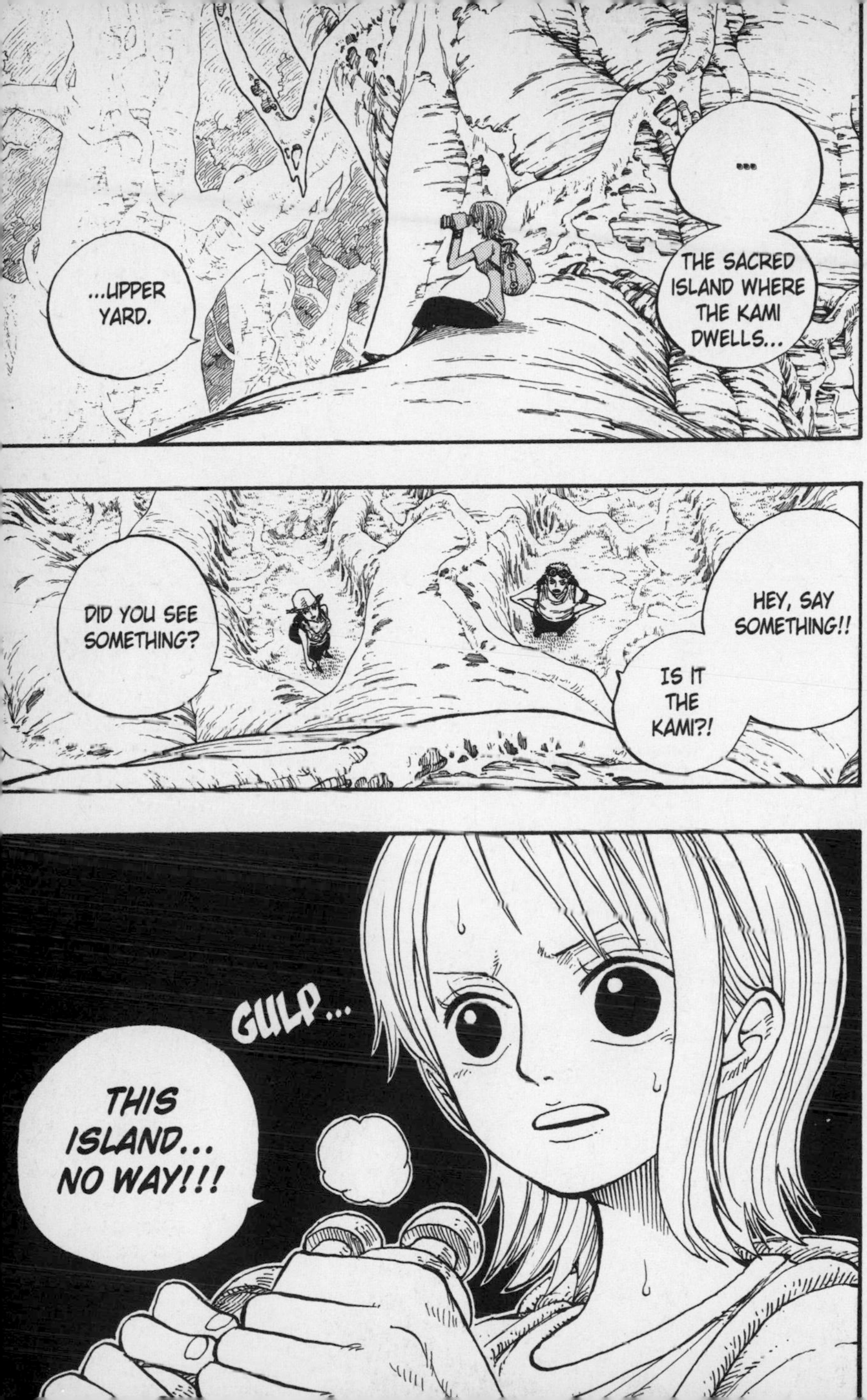
...
THE SACRED ISLAND WHERE THE KAMI DWELLS...
...UPPER YARD.
HEY, SAY SOMETHING!!
IS IT THE KAMI?!
DID YOU SEE SOMETHING?
GULP...
THIS ISLAND... NO WAY!!!

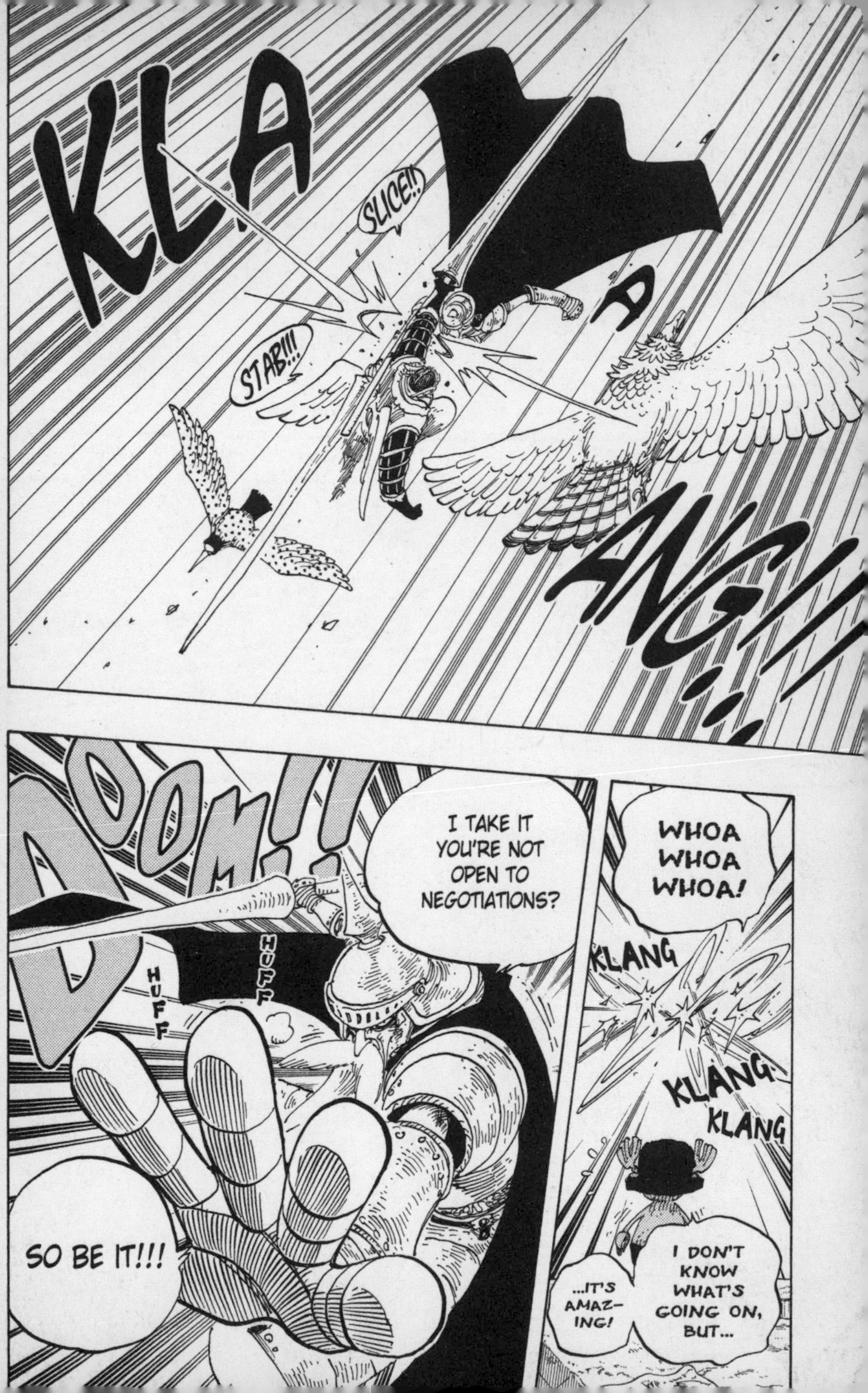
KLA
A
ANG!!
SLICE!!
STAB!!!
WHOA WHOA WHOA!
KLANG
KLANG
KLANG
KLANG
I DON'T KNOW WHAT'S GOING ON, BUT...
...IT'S AMAZ-ING!
DOOM!!
I TAKE IT YOU'RE NOT OPEN TO NEGOTIATIONS?
HUFF
HUFF
SO BE IT!!!

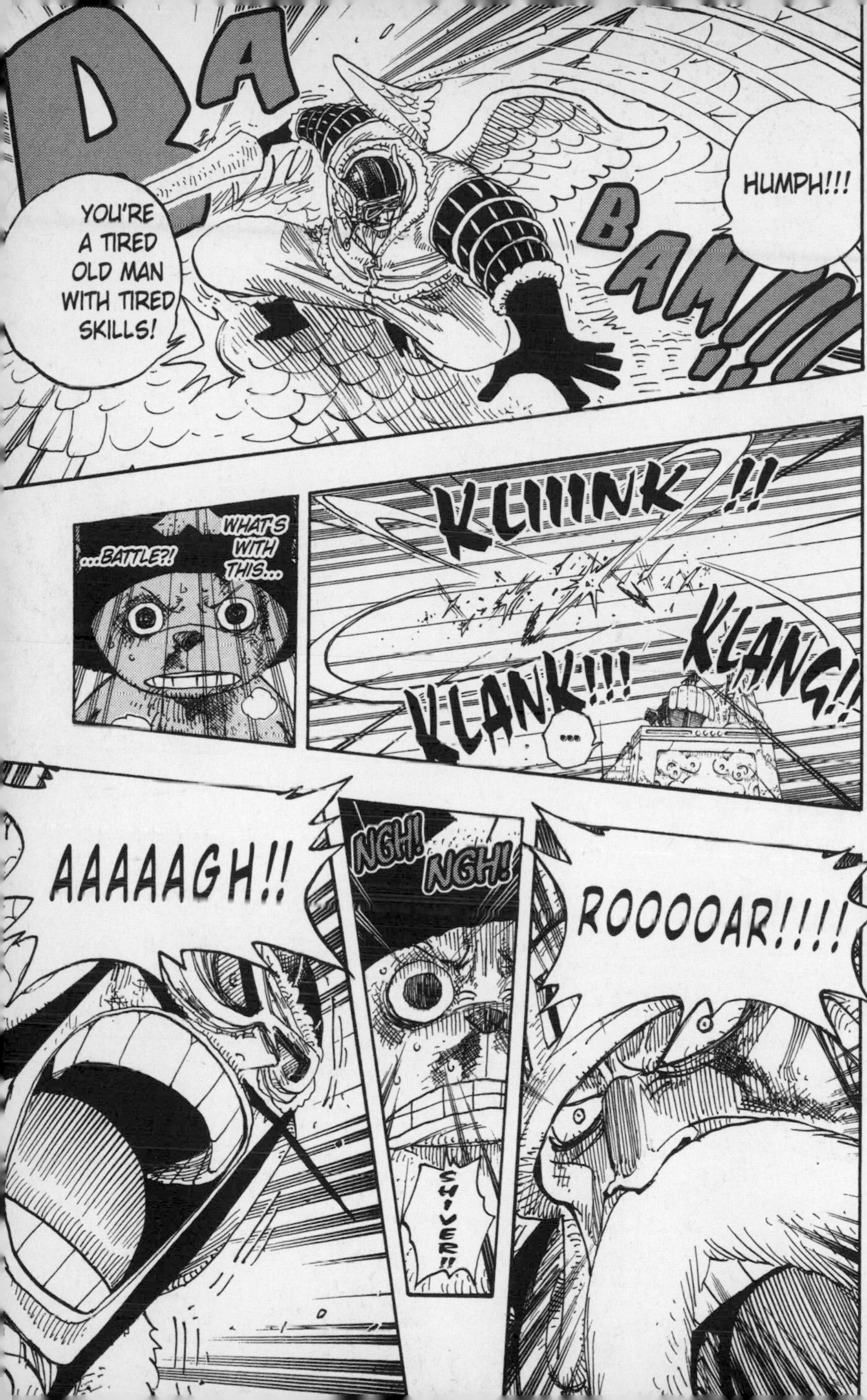
HUMPH!!!
BAM!!!!
DA
YOU'RE A TIRED OLD MAN WITH TIRED SKILLS!
KLIIIINK!!
KLANG!!
KLANK!!!
...
WHAT'S WITH THIS...
...BATTLE?!
ROOOOAR!!!!
NGH! NGH!
SHIVER!!
AAAAAGH!!

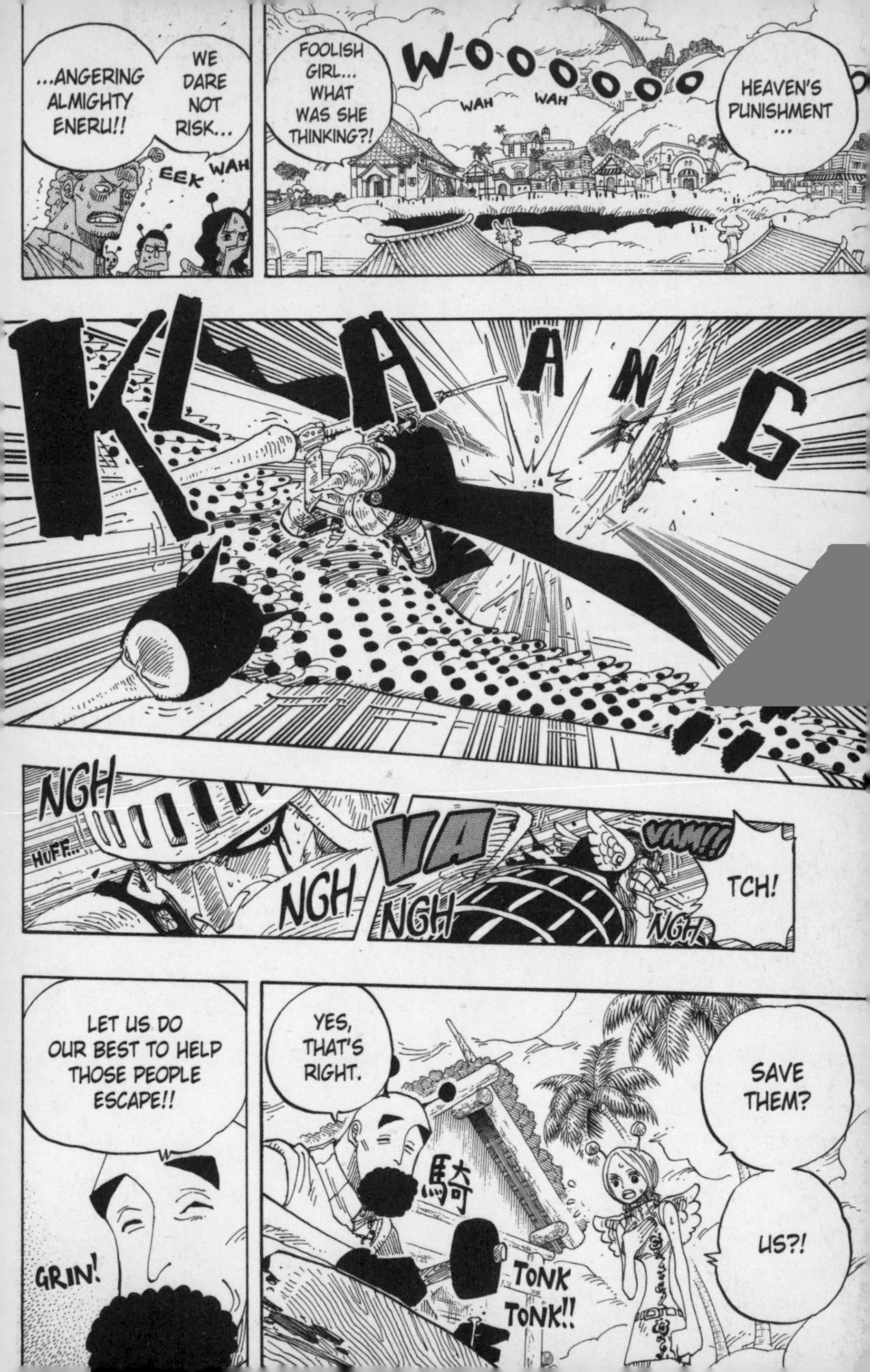
HEAVEN'S PUNISHMENT ...
WOOOOOOO
WAH
WAH
FOOLISH GIRL... WHAT WAS SHE THINKING?!
WE DARE NOT RISK...
...ANGERING ALMIGHTY ENERU!!
WAH
EEK
KLAANG
TCH!
VAM!!
NGH
VA
NGH
NGH
NGH
HUFF...
SAVE THEM?
US?!
YES, THAT'S RIGHT.
騎
TONK TONK!!
LET US DO OUR BEST TO HELP THOSE PEOPLE ESCAPE!!
GRIN!

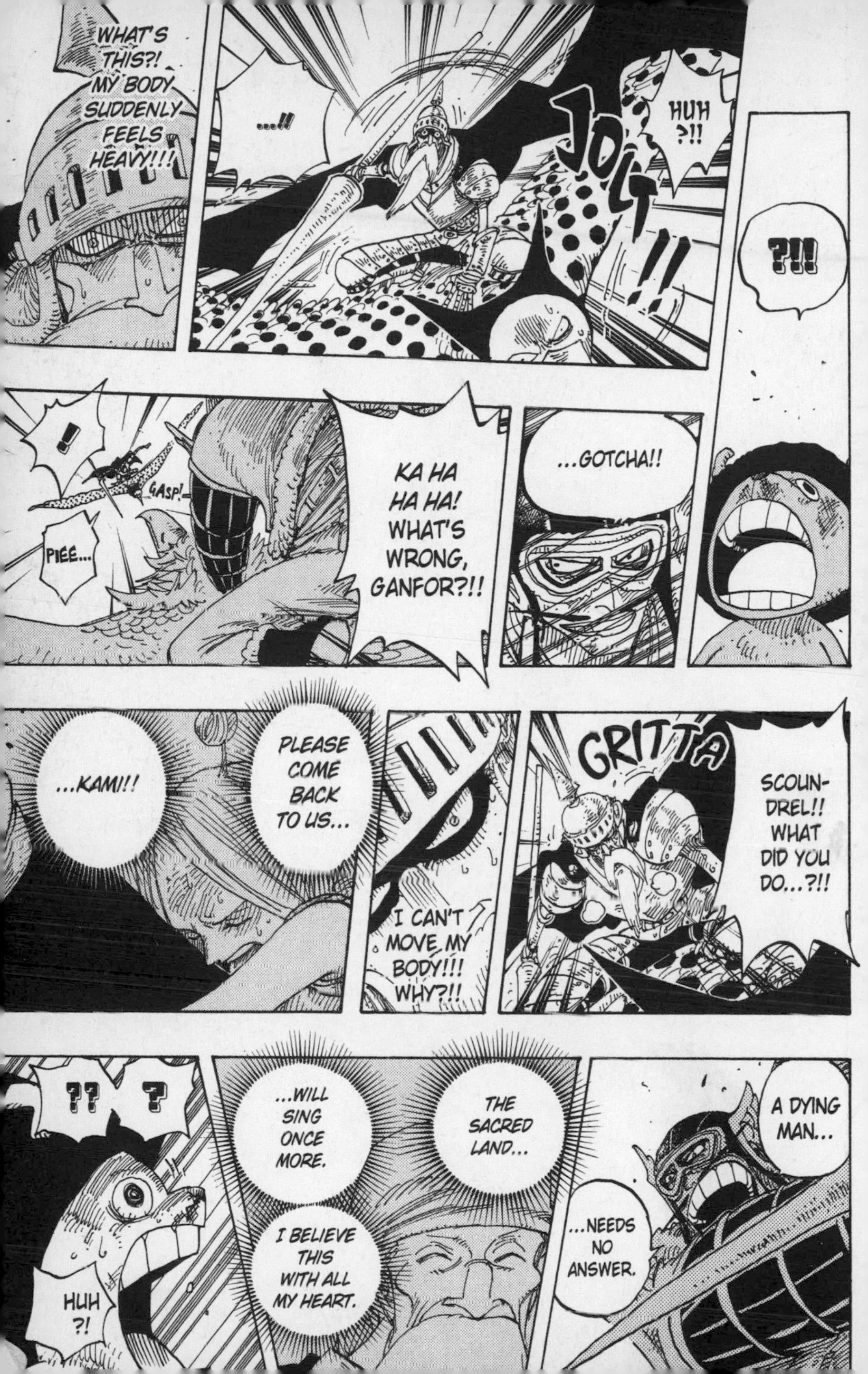
?!!
HUH ?!!
JOLT!!
...!!
WHAT'S THIS?! MY BODY SUDDENLY FEELS HEAVY!!!
...GOTCHA!!
KA HA HA HA! WHAT'S WRONG, GANFOR?!!
!
GASP!
PIEE...
GRITTA
SCOUN-DREL!! WHAT DID YOU DO...?!!
I CAN'T MOVE MY BODY!!! WHY?!!
PLEASE COME BACK TO US...
...KAMI!!
A DYING MAN...
...NEEDS NO ANSWER.
THE SACRED LAND...
...WILL SING ONCE MORE.
I BELIEVE THIS WITH ALL MY HEART.
?? ?
HUH ?!

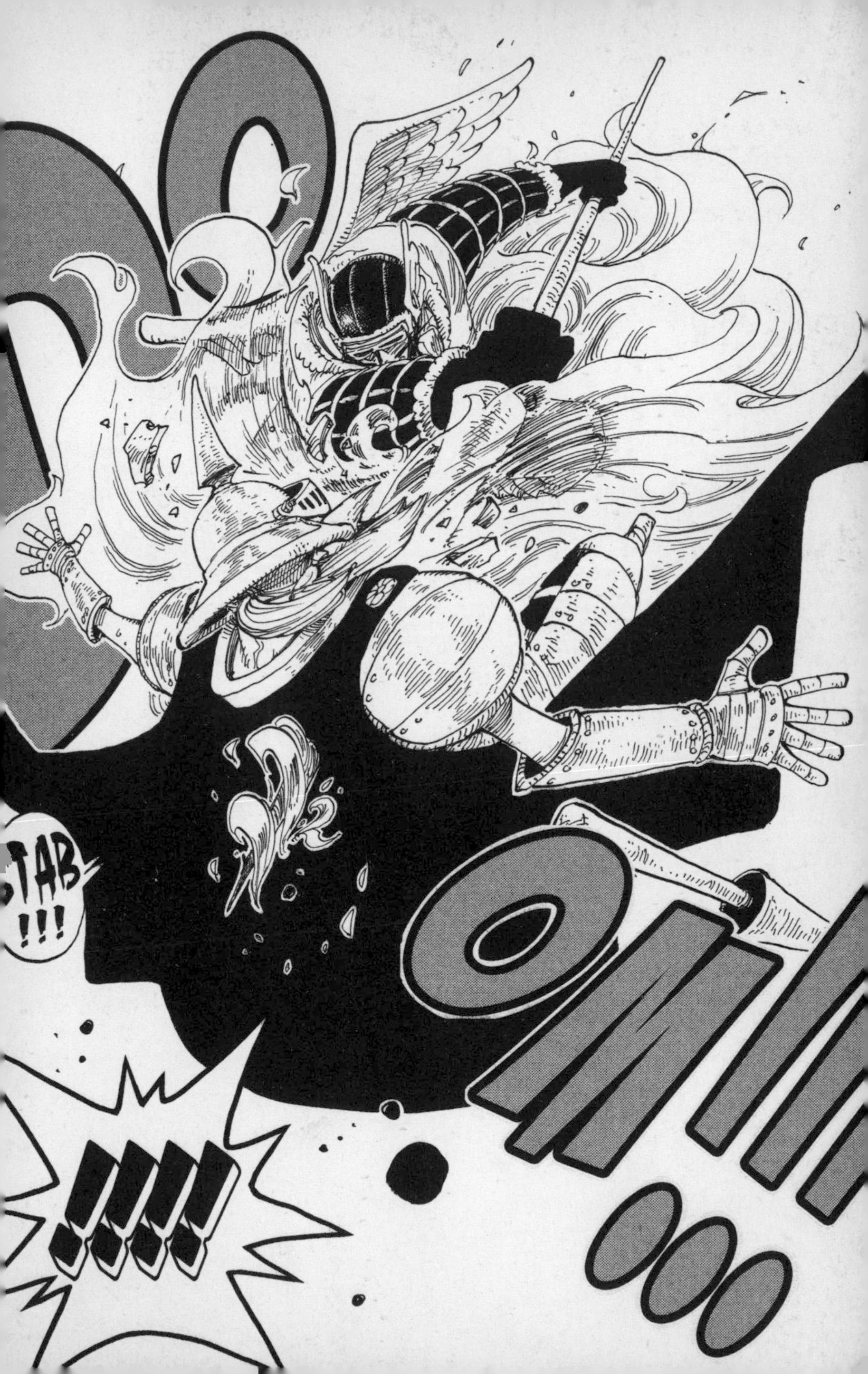
STAB !!!
!!!!

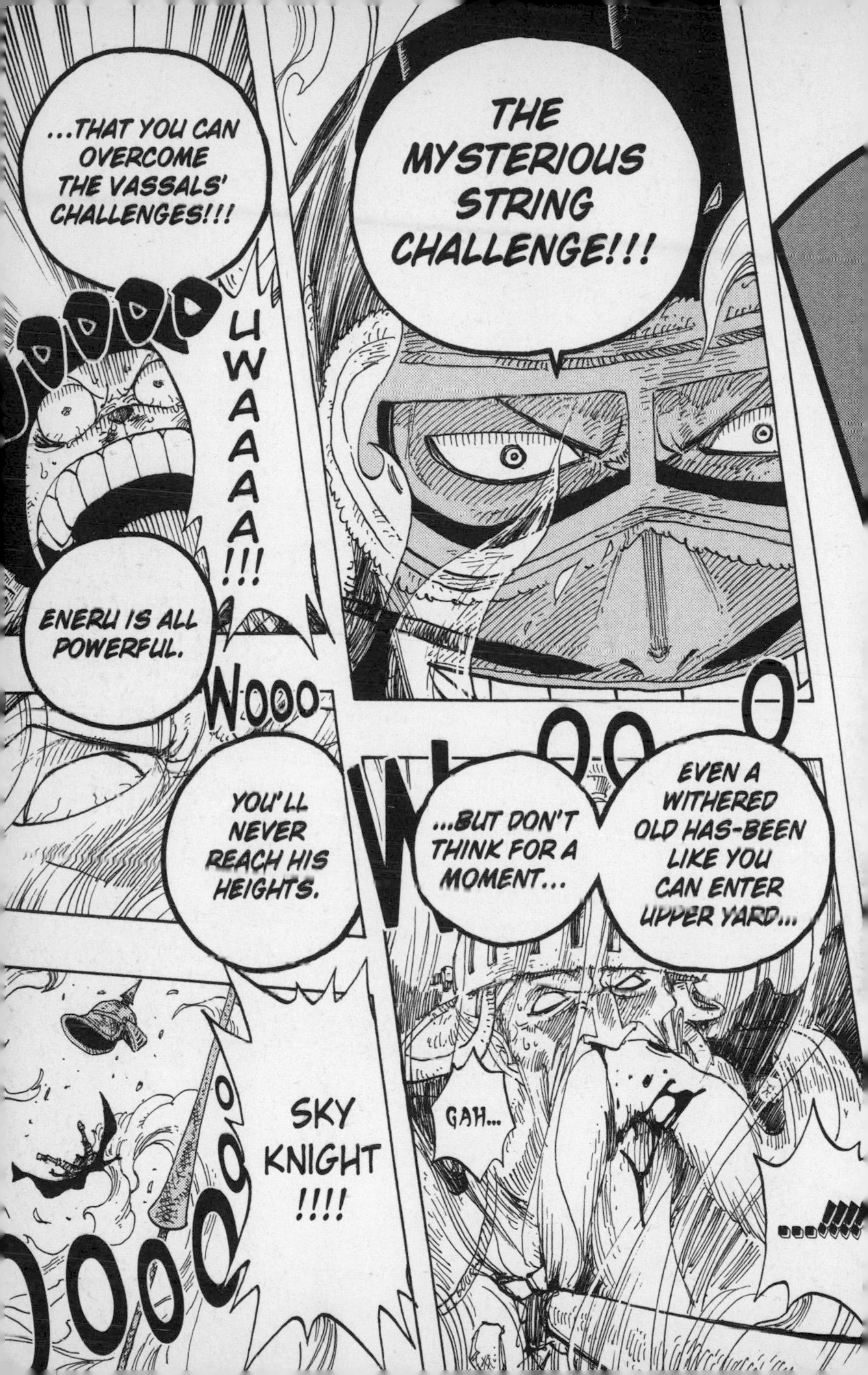
THE MYSTERIOUS STRING CHALLENGE!!!
...THAT YOU CAN OVERCOME THE VASSALS' CHALLENGES!!!
UWAAAAA!!!
ENERU IS ALL POWERFUL.
WOOOOOOO
EVEN A WITHERED OLD HAS-BEEN LIKE YOU CAN ENTER UPPER YARD...
...BUT DON'T THINK FOR A MOMENT...
YOU'LL NEVER REACH HIS HEIGHTS.
GAH...
...!!!!
SKY KNIGHT!!!!

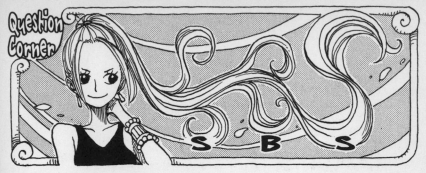

Q: I have a question for Oda Sensei. I always wonder during my Panda Man searches, who is this guy who's always near Panda Man? (→) And what is this thing that he's always carrying?

A: Huh? Who is he?

He's Tomato Gang, of course.

Yup, definitely Tomato Gang. There's no other answer. He's the collection guy, trying to collect the money Panda Man owes. He seems to be holding a pistol.

But there are rumors that it's actually a sushi roll.

Tomato Gang (38)

Q: Odacchi!! Hello! In volume 25, that guy Shoujou, who showed up after Bellamy got beat up, had a weird logo on his clothes. What's a "Cyberpanda"? Please answer through ventriloquism.

A: ×△○♡◇☆♧※ ** Yeah, right!!!

Now who's the dummy?!

Okay, enough of that.

Those clothes are, ×△○♡◇☆♧※ *...

Now who's the dummy?! Sorry for putting you through that twice.

I've been getting lectures that SBS is too haphazard lately. So I'm seriously sorry... Really!! I'm sorry.

Anyway, Cyberpanda is a knock-off of the "Dosuko 1 Panda" brand, and what's scary is that it's more expensive than the original "Dosukoi Panda." So please be careful, panda shoppers!

CYBER PANDA

Chapter 250:
BALL DRAGON

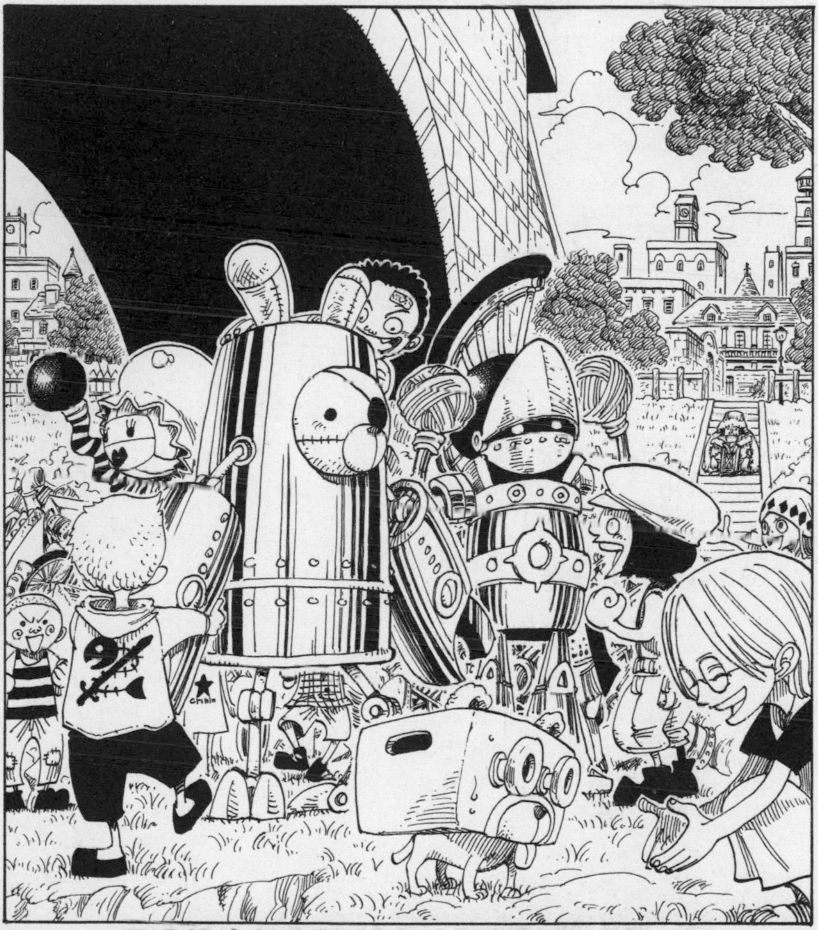

WAPOL'S OMNIVOROUS RAMPAGE, VOL. 13:
"MY TOYS CAPTURE THE HEARTS OF CHILDREN"

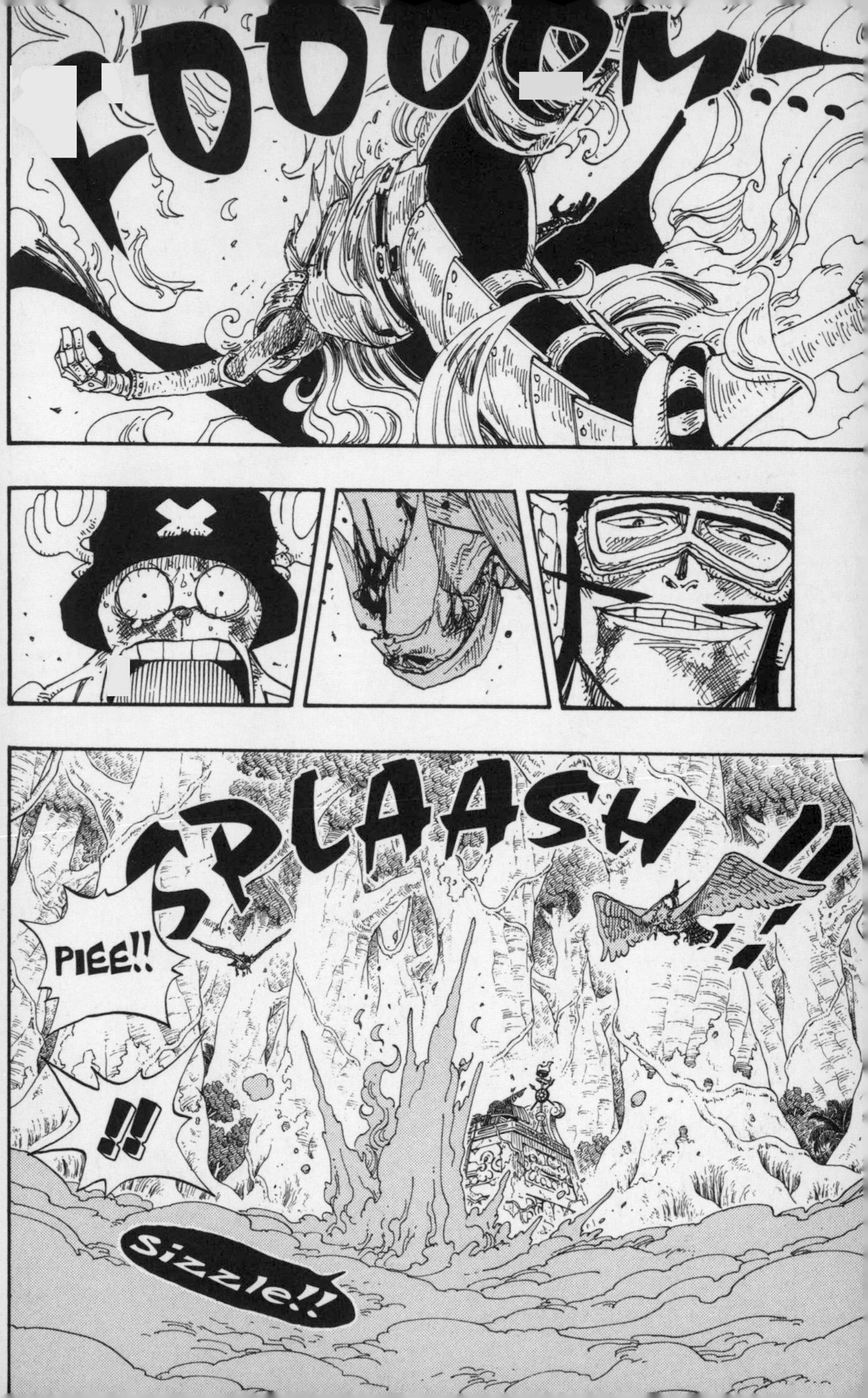
DOOM...
SPLAASH!!
PIEE!!
!!
Sizzle!!

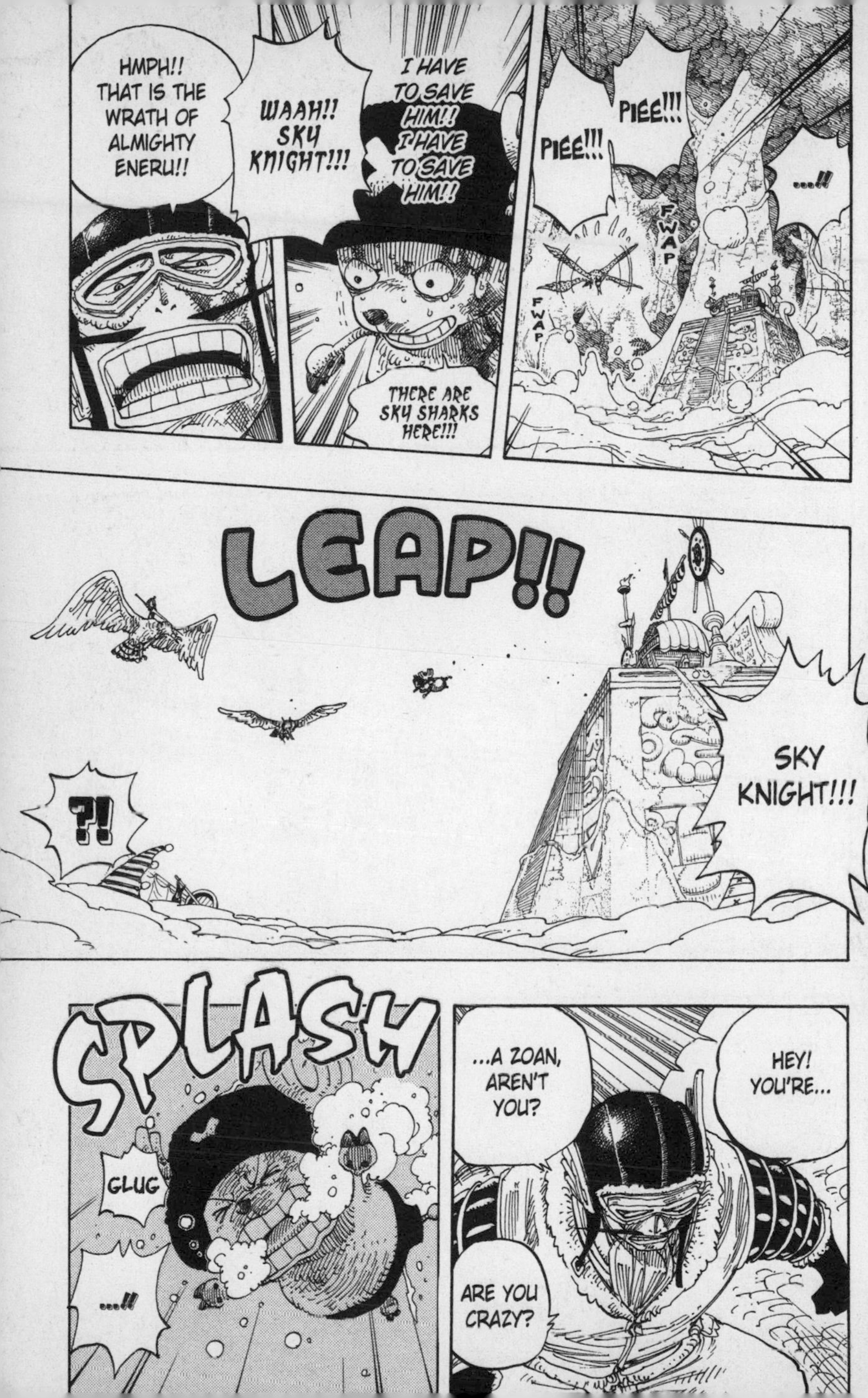
PIEE!!!
PIEE!!!
...!!
FWAP
FWAP
I HAVE TO SAVE HIM!! I HAVE TO SAVE HIM!!
WAAH!! SKY KNIGHT!!!
THERE ARE SKY SHARKS HERE!!!
HMPH!! THAT IS THE WRATH OF ALMIGHTY ENERU!!
LEAP!!
SKY KNIGHT!!!
?!
HEY! YOU'RE...
...A ZOAN, AREN'T YOU?
ARE YOU CRAZY?
SPLASH
GLUG
...!!

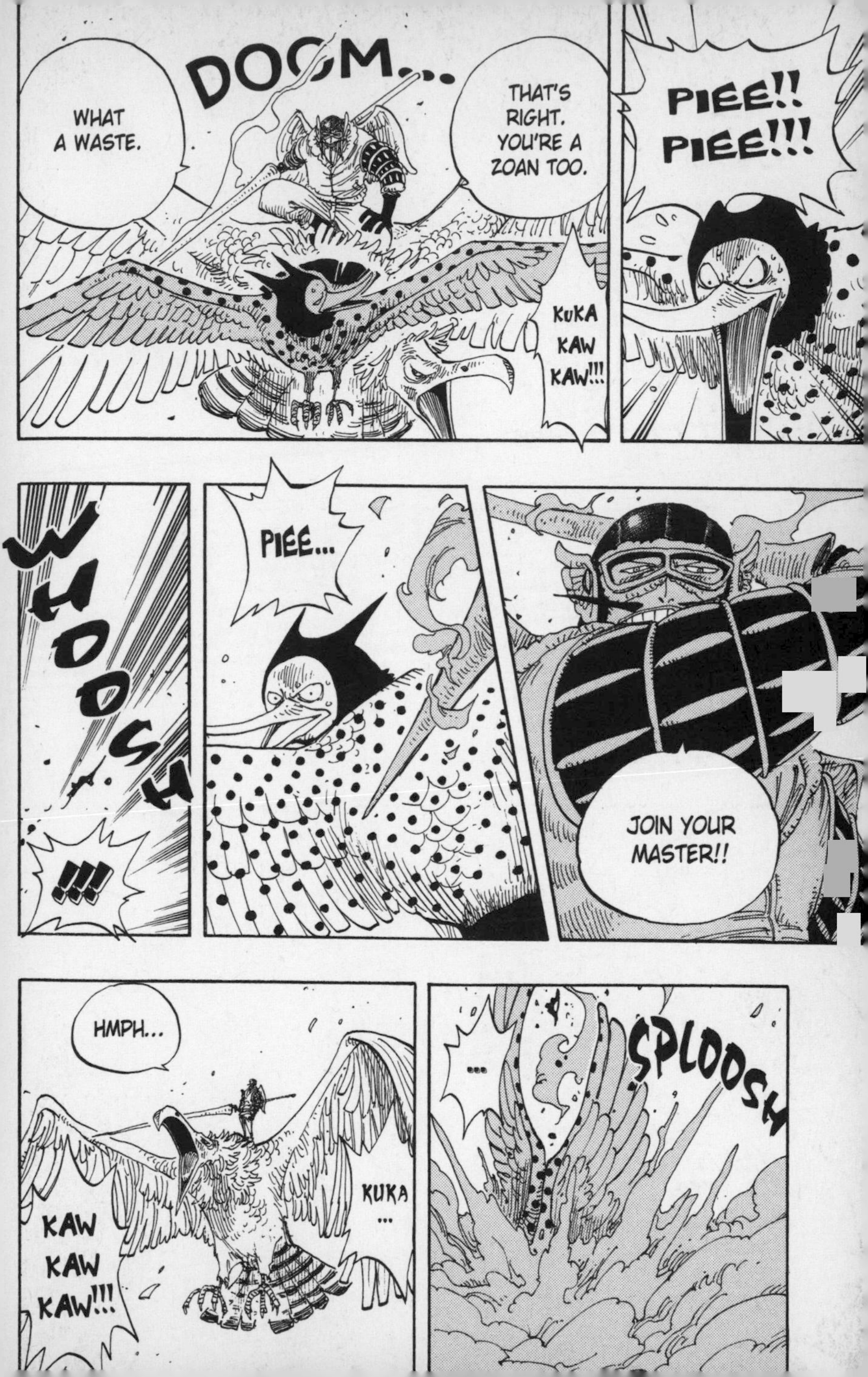
PIEE!!
PIEE!!!
THAT'S RIGHT. YOU'RE A ZOAN TOO.
DOOM...
KUKA KAW KAW!!!
WHAT A WASTE.
JOIN YOUR MASTER!!
PIEE...
WHOOSH
!!!
...
SPLOOSH
HMPH...
KUKA ...
KAW KAW KAW!!!

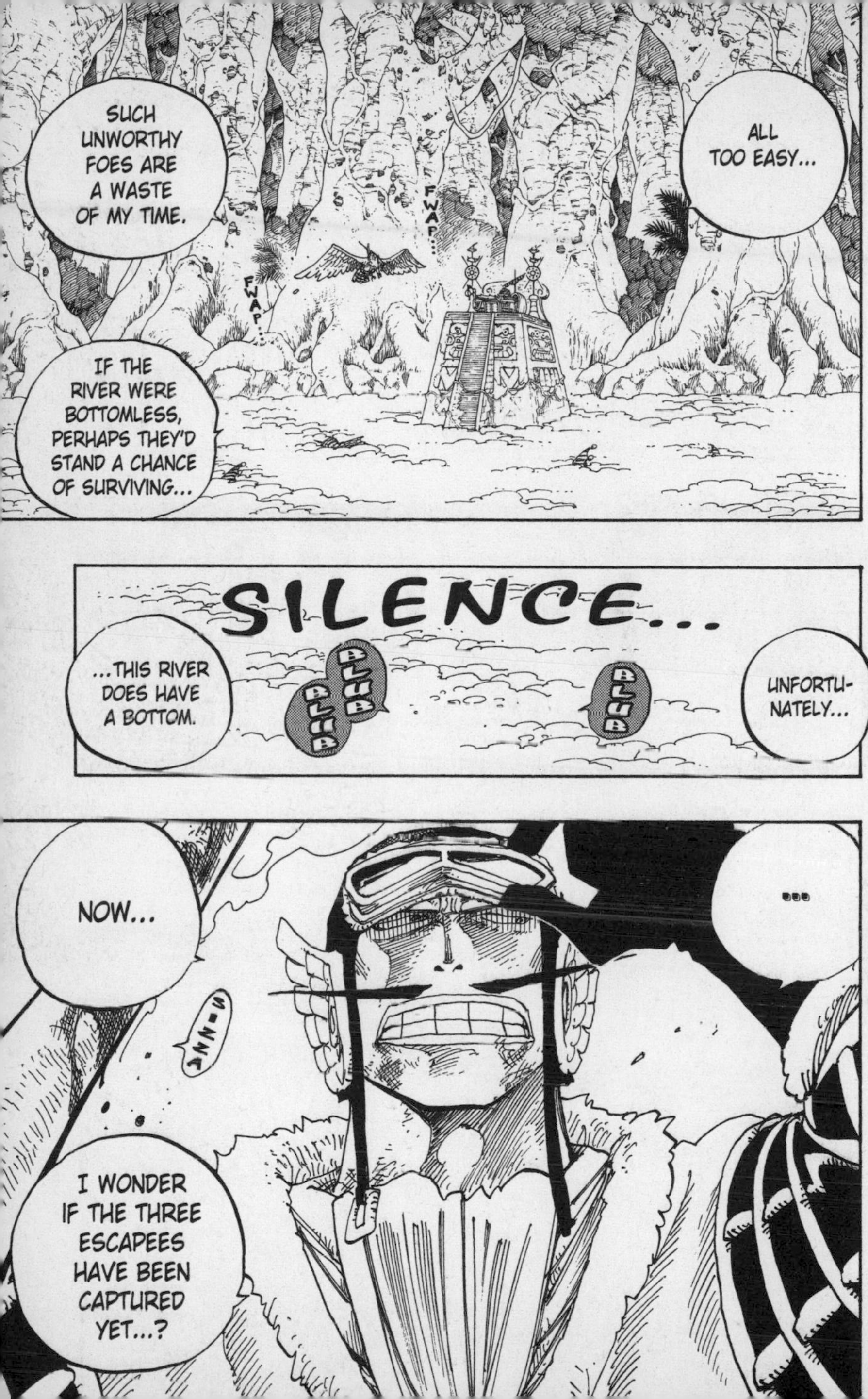
ALL TOO EASY...
SUCH UNWORTHY FOES ARE A WASTE OF MY TIME.
FWAP...
FWAP...
IF THE RIVER WERE BOTTOMLESS, PERHAPS THEY'D STAND A CHANCE OF SURVIVING...
UNFORTUNATELY...
SILENCE...
BLUB
BLUB
BLUB
...THIS RIVER DOES HAVE A BOTTOM.
...
NOW...
I WONDER IF THE THREE ESCAPEES HAVE BEEN CAPTURED YET...?

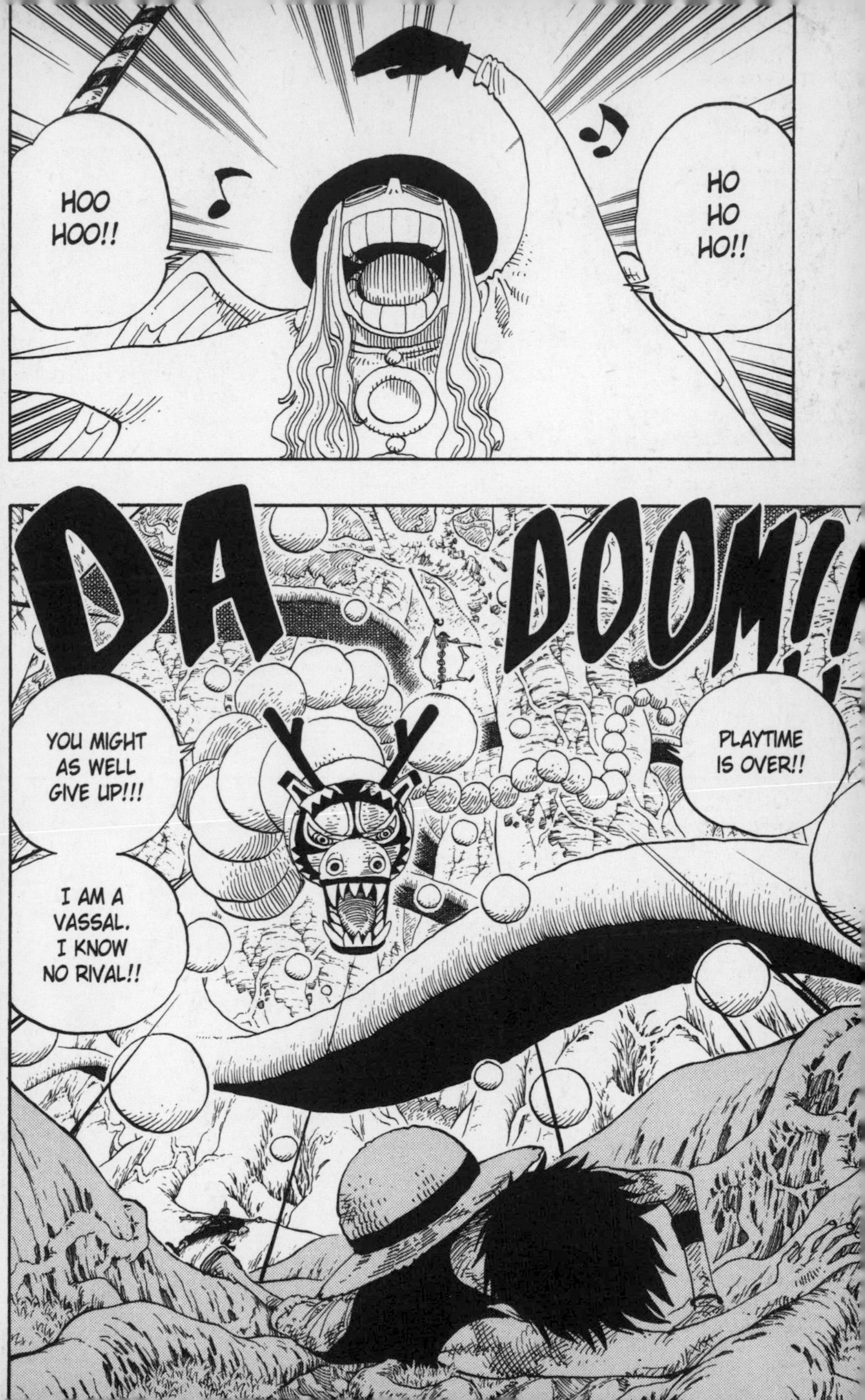
HO HO HO!!
HOO HOO!!
DA DOOM!!
PLAYTIME IS OVER!!
YOU MIGHT AS WELL GIVE UP!!!
I AM A VASSAL. I KNOW NO RIVAL!!

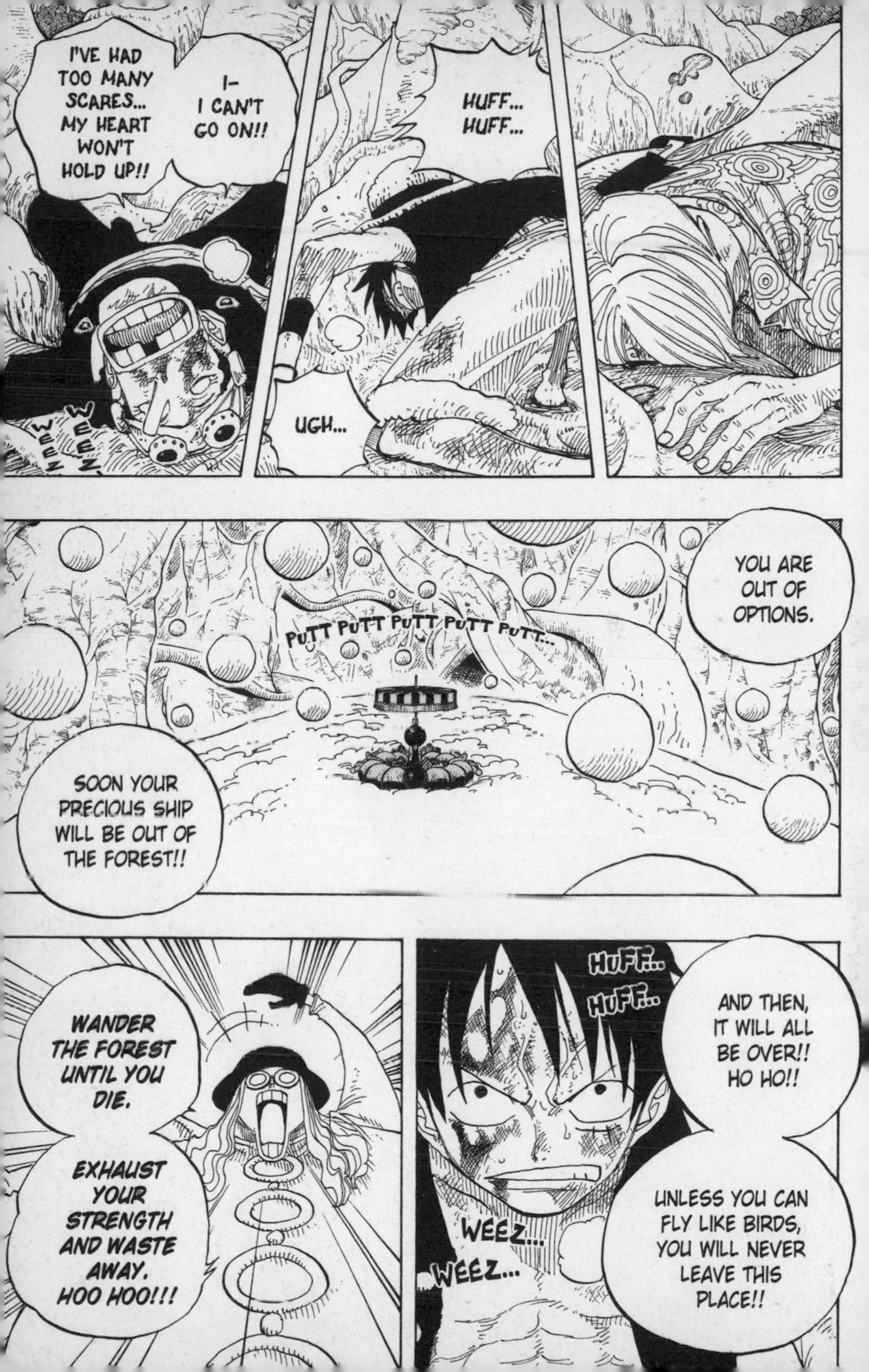
HUFF... HUFF...
UGH...
I– I CAN'T GO ON!!
I'VE HAD TOO MANY SCARES... MY HEART WON'T HOLD UP!!
WEEZ
WEEZ
YOU ARE OUT OF OPTIONS.
PUTT PUTT PUTT PUTT PUTT...
SOON YOUR PRECIOUS SHIP WILL BE OUT OF THE FOREST!!
HUFF...
HUFF...
AND THEN, IT WILL ALL BE OVER!! HO HO!!
UNLESS YOU CAN FLY LIKE BIRDS, YOU WILL NEVER LEAVE THIS PLACE!!
WEEZ...
WEEZ...
WANDER THE FOREST UNTIL YOU DIE.
EXHAUST YOUR STRENGTH AND WASTE AWAY. HOO HOO!!!

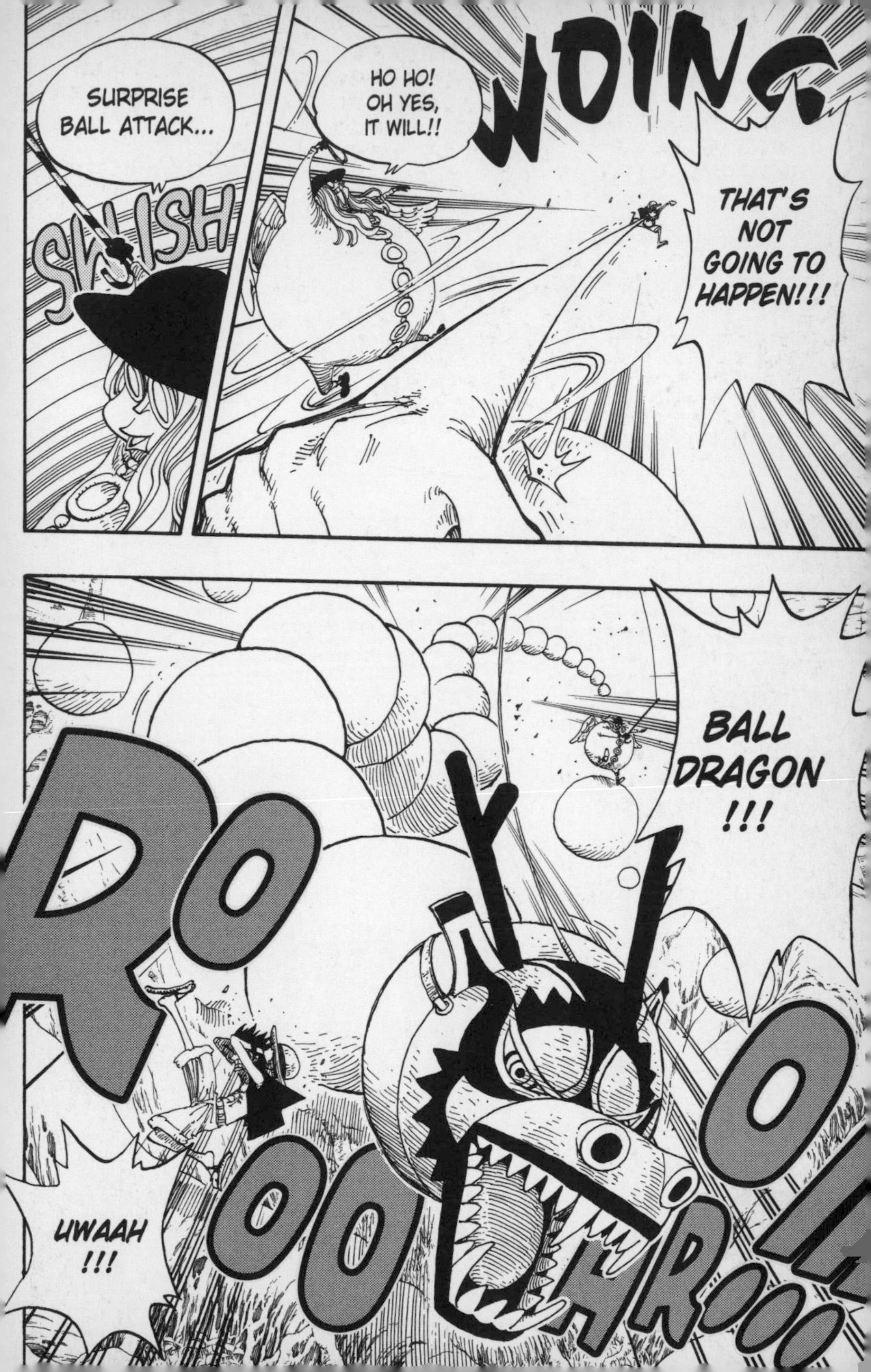
WOING
THAT'S NOT GOING TO HAPPEN!!!
HO HO! OH YES, IT WILL!!
SURPRISE BALL ATTACK...
SWISH
BALL DRAGON !!!
UWAAH !!!

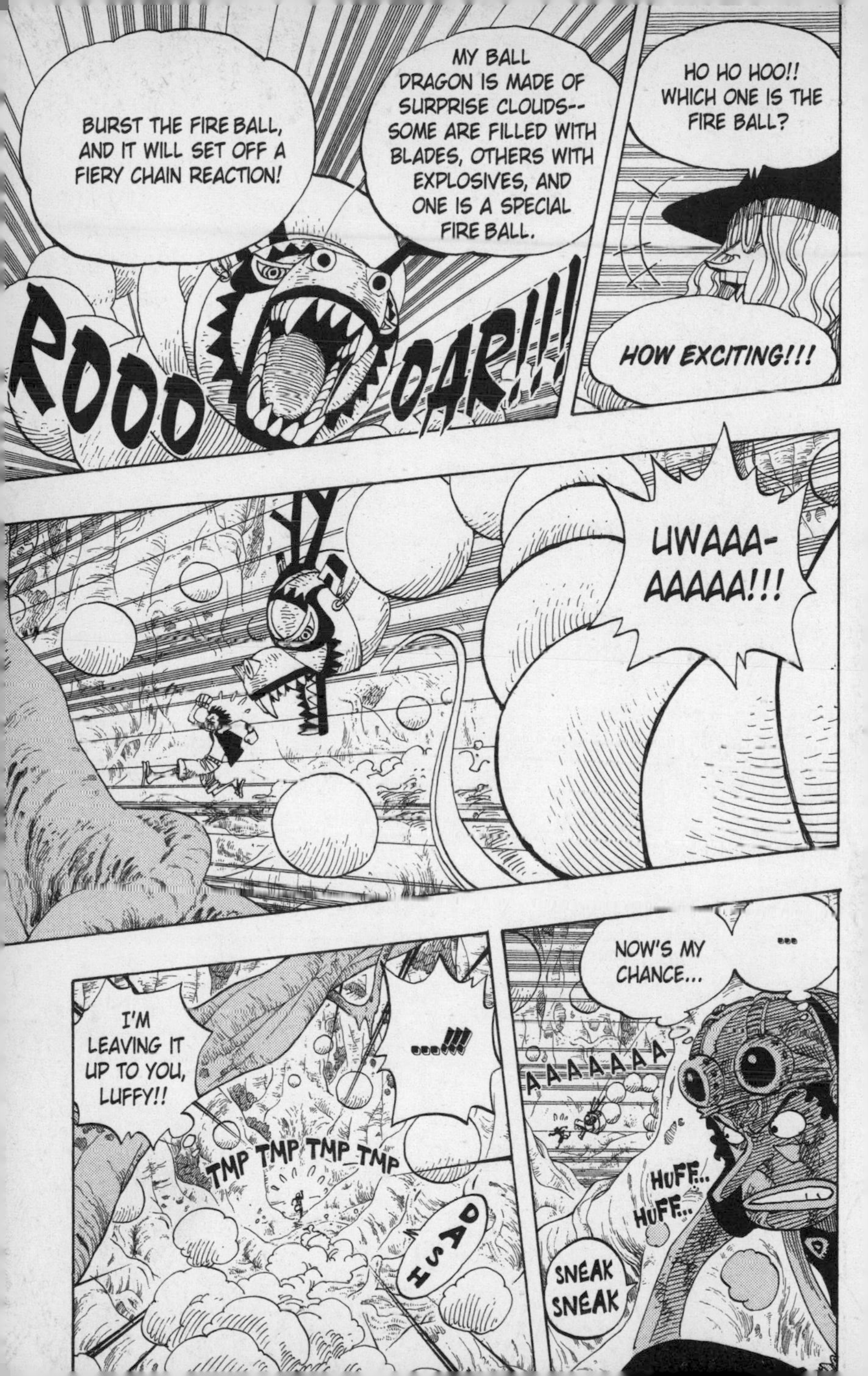
HO HO HOO!! WHICH ONE IS THE FIRE BALL?
HOW EXCITING!!!
MY BALL DRAGON IS MADE OF SURPRISE CLOUDS-- SOME ARE FILLED WITH BLADES, OTHERS WITH EXPLOSIVES, AND ONE IS A SPECIAL FIRE BALL.
BURST THE FIRE BALL, AND IT WILL SET OFF A FIERY CHAIN REACTION!
ROOOOAR!!!
UWAAA-AAAAA!!!
NOW'S MY CHANCE...
...
AAAAAAA
HUFF... HUFF...
SNEAK SNEAK
...!!!
I'M LEAVING IT UP TO YOU, LUFFY!!
TMP TMP TMP TMP
DASH

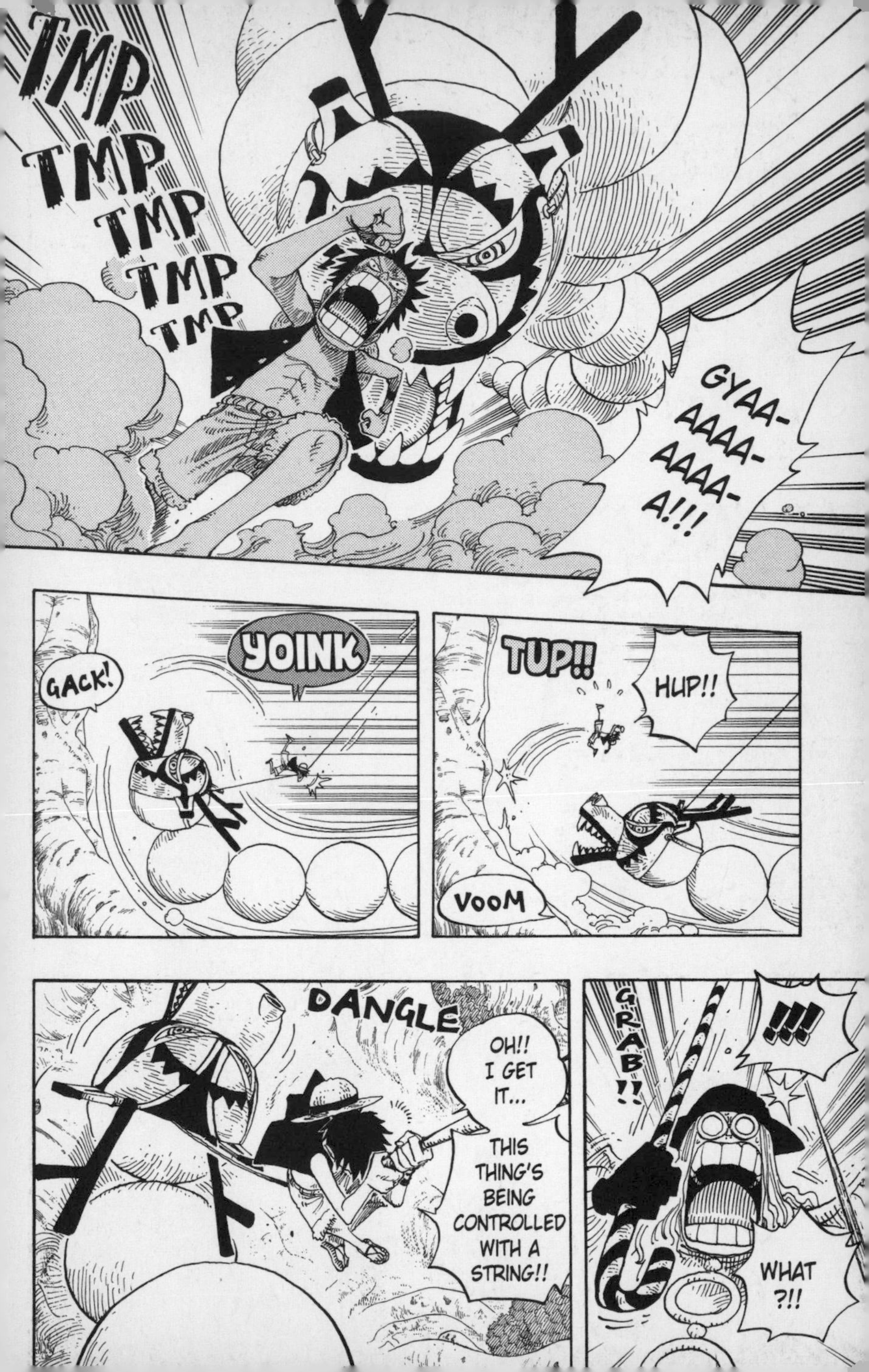
GYAA-AAAA-AAAA-A!!!
TMP TMP TMP TMP TMP
HUP!!
TUP!!
VOOM
YOINK
GACK!
!!!
GRAB!!
WHAT?!!
DANGLE
OH!! I GET IT...
THIS THING'S BEING CONTROLLED WITH A STRING!!

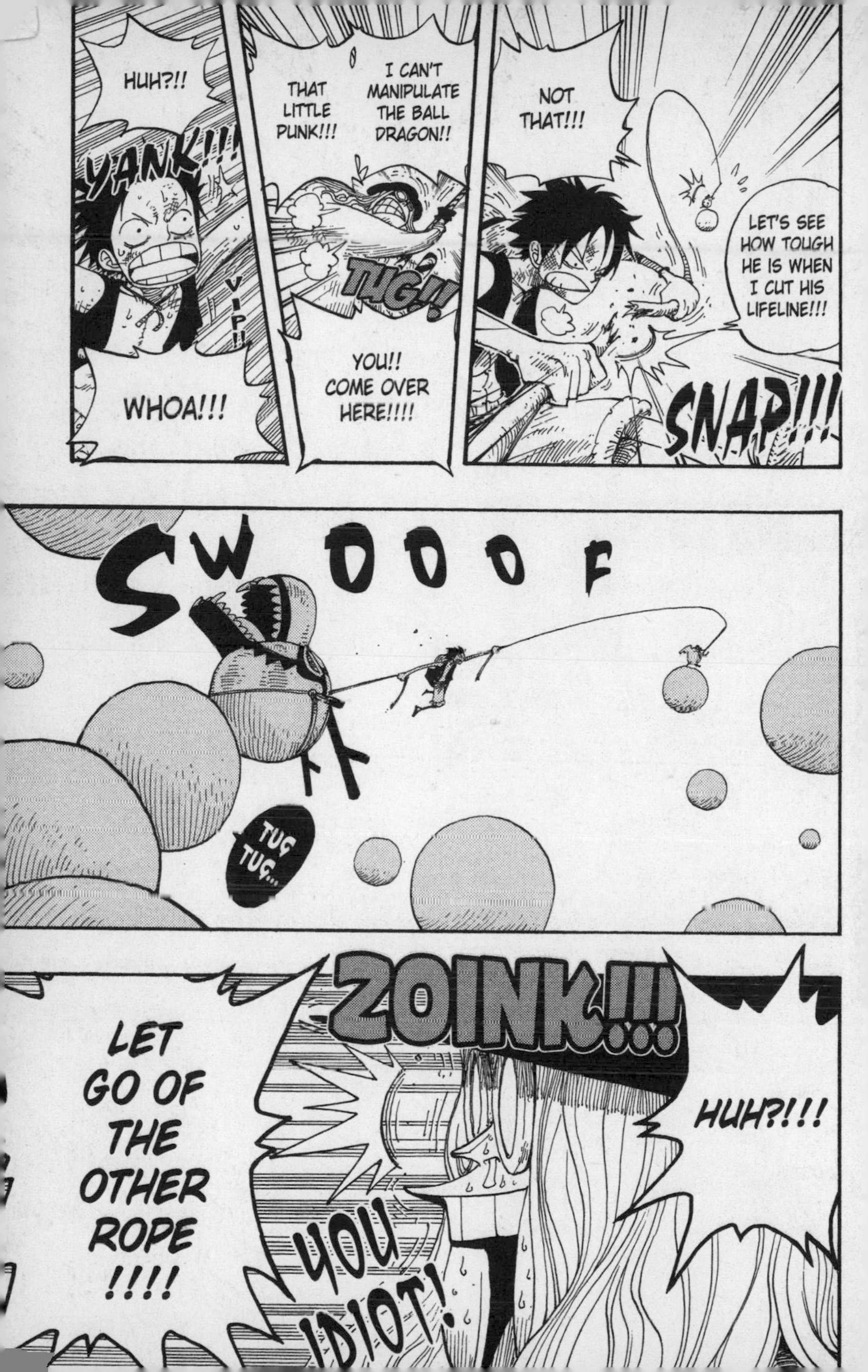
NOT THAT!!!
LET'S SEE HOW TOUGH HE IS WHEN I CUT HIS LIFELINE!!!
SNAP!!!
I CAN'T MANIPULATE THE BALL DRAGON!!
THAT LITTLE PUNK!!!
TUG!!
YOU!! COME OVER HERE!!!!
HUH?!!
YANK!!!
VIP!!
WHOA!!!
SWOOOF
TUG TUG...
ZOINK!!!
HUH?!!!
YOU IDIOT!
LET GO OF THE OTHER ROPE!!!!

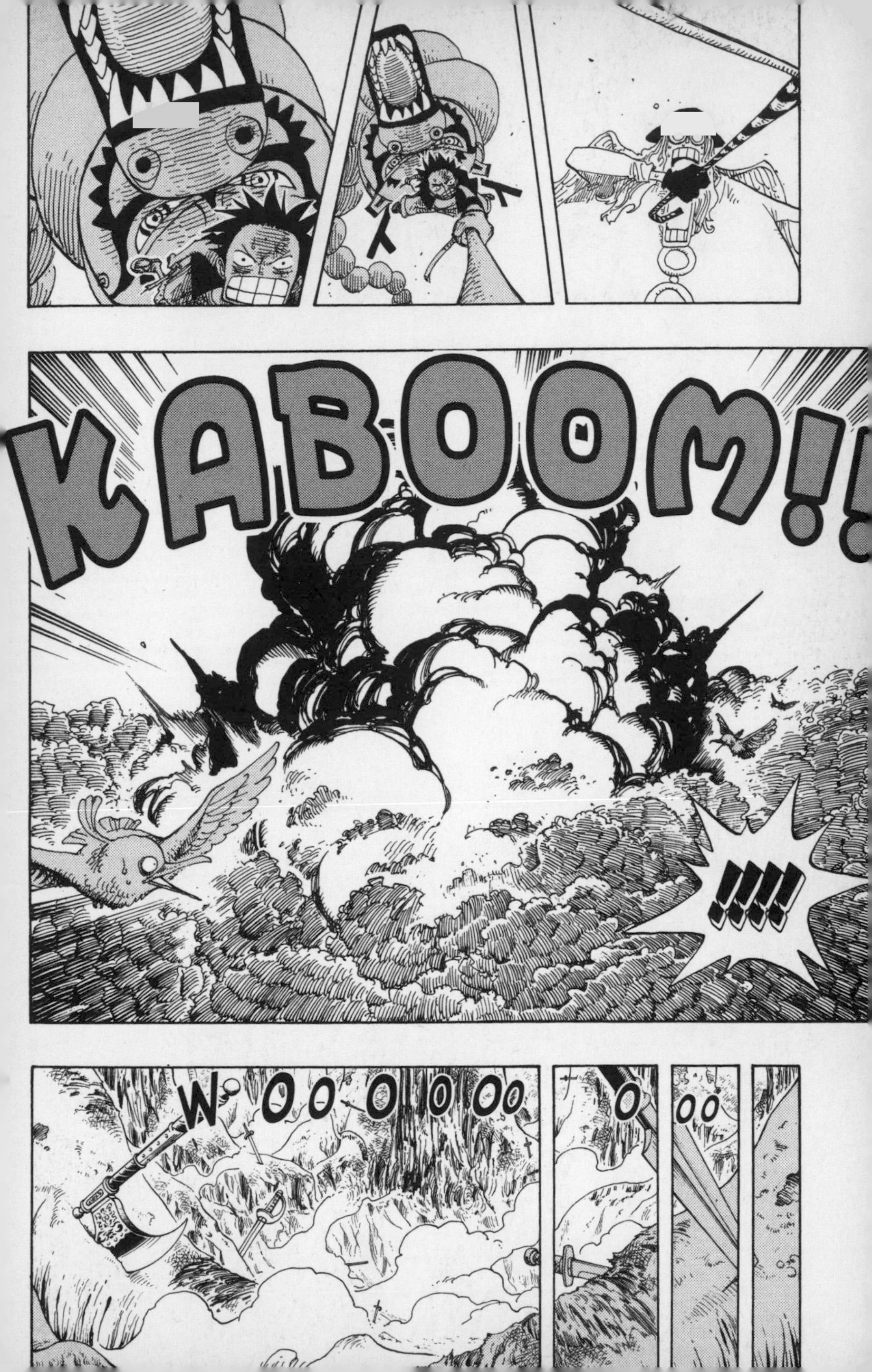
KABOOM!!
!!!!!
WOOOOOOOOO

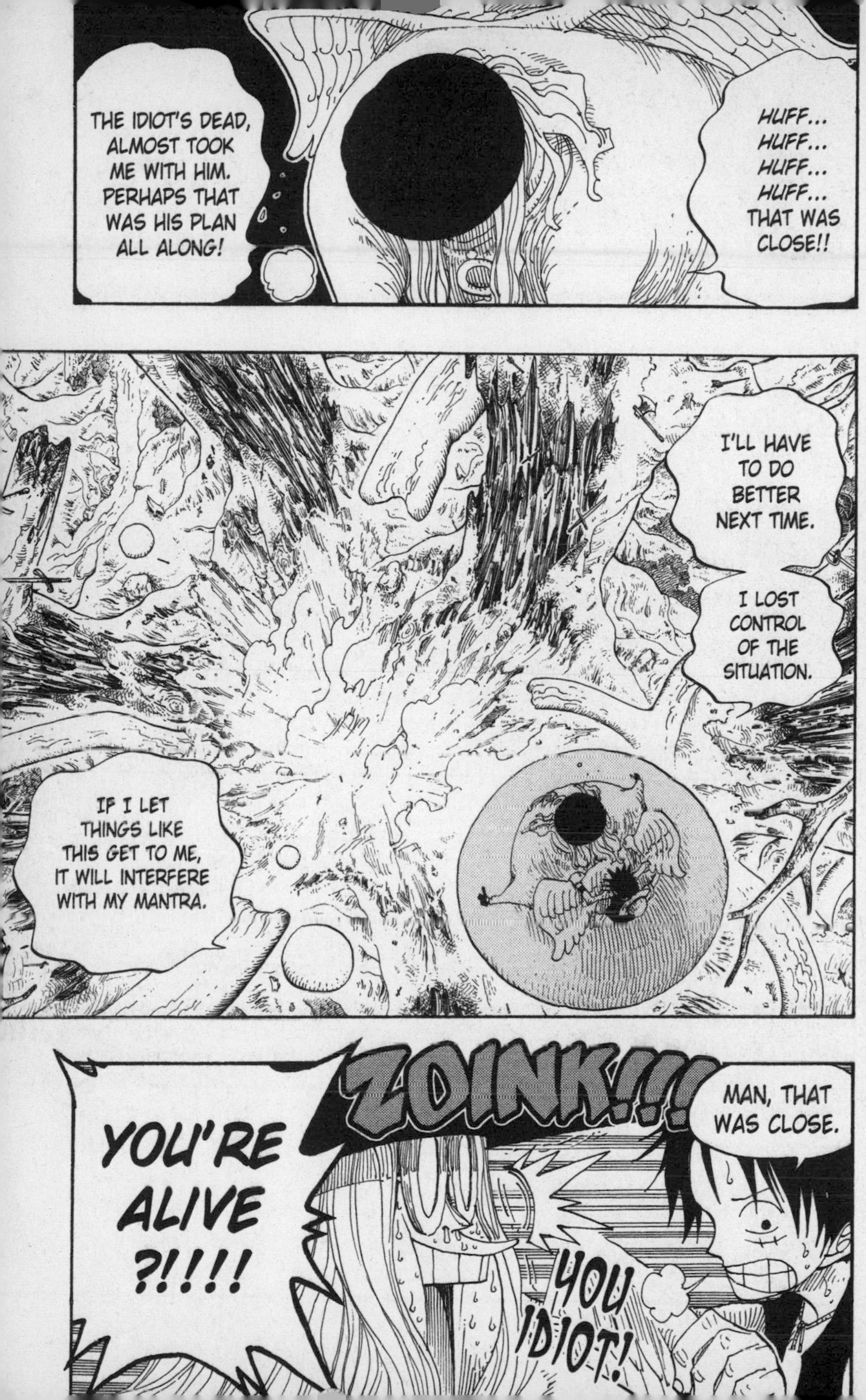
HUFF... HUFF... HUFF... HUFF... THAT WAS CLOSE!!
THE IDIOT'S DEAD, ALMOST TOOK ME WITH HIM. PERHAPS THAT WAS HIS PLAN ALL ALONG!
I'LL HAVE TO DO BETTER NEXT TIME.
I LOST CONTROL OF THE SITUATION.
IF I LET THINGS LIKE THIS GET TO ME, IT WILL INTERFERE WITH MY MANTRA.
MAN, THAT WAS CLOSE.
ZOINK!!!
YOU'RE ALIVE ?!!!!
YOU IDIOT!

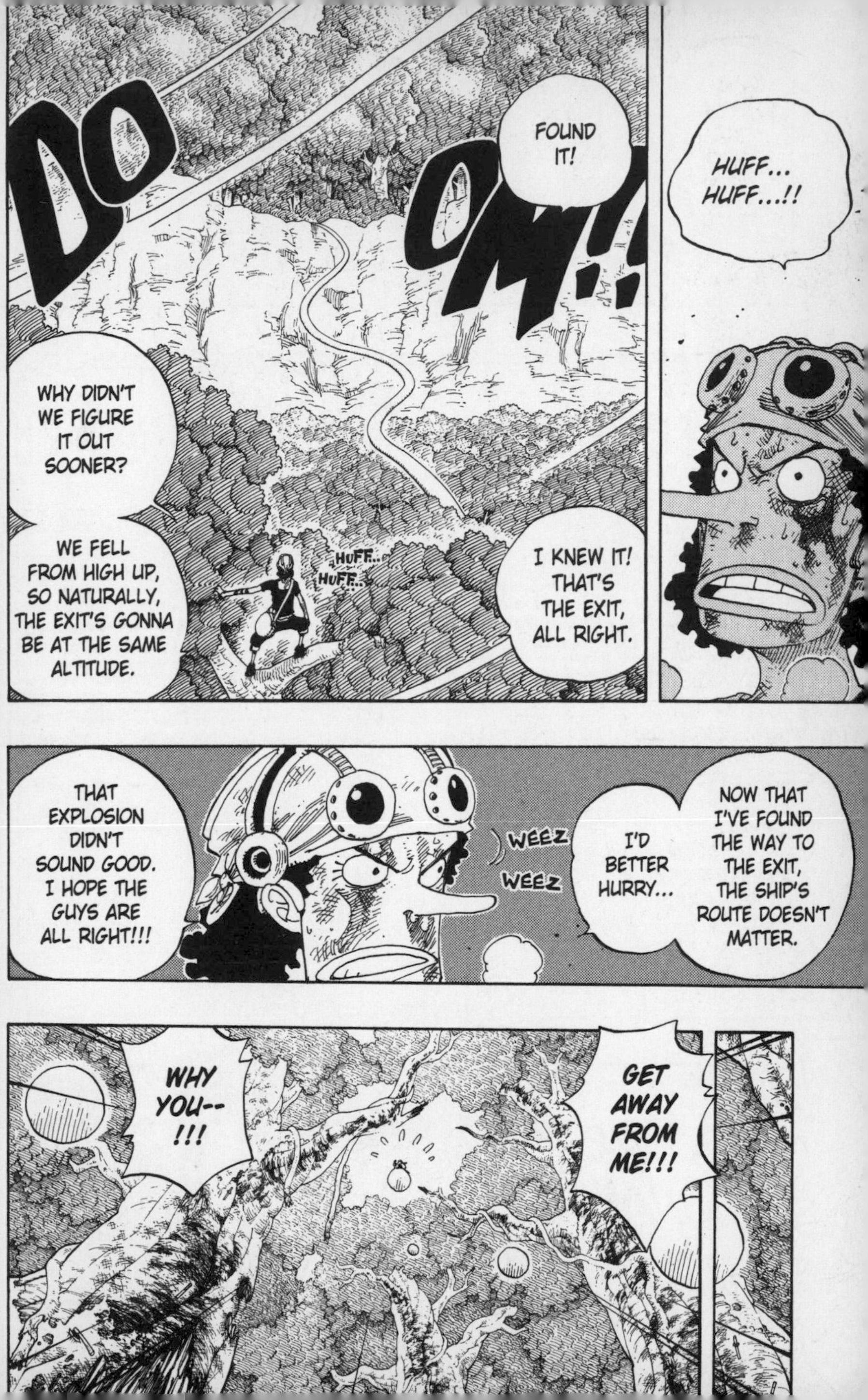
HUFF... HUFF...!!
FOUND IT!
DOOM!!
I KNEW IT! THAT'S THE EXIT, ALL RIGHT.
HUFF... HUFF...
WHY DIDN'T WE FIGURE IT OUT SOONER?
WE FELL FROM HIGH UP, SO NATURALLY, THE EXIT'S GONNA BE AT THE SAME ALTITUDE.
NOW THAT I'VE FOUND THE WAY TO THE EXIT, THE SHIP'S ROUTE DOESN'T MATTER.
I'D BETTER HURRY...
WEEZ
WEEZ
THAT EXPLOSION DIDN'T SOUND GOOD. I HOPE THE GUYS ARE ALL RIGHT!!!
GET AWAY FROM ME!!!
WHY YOU-- !!!

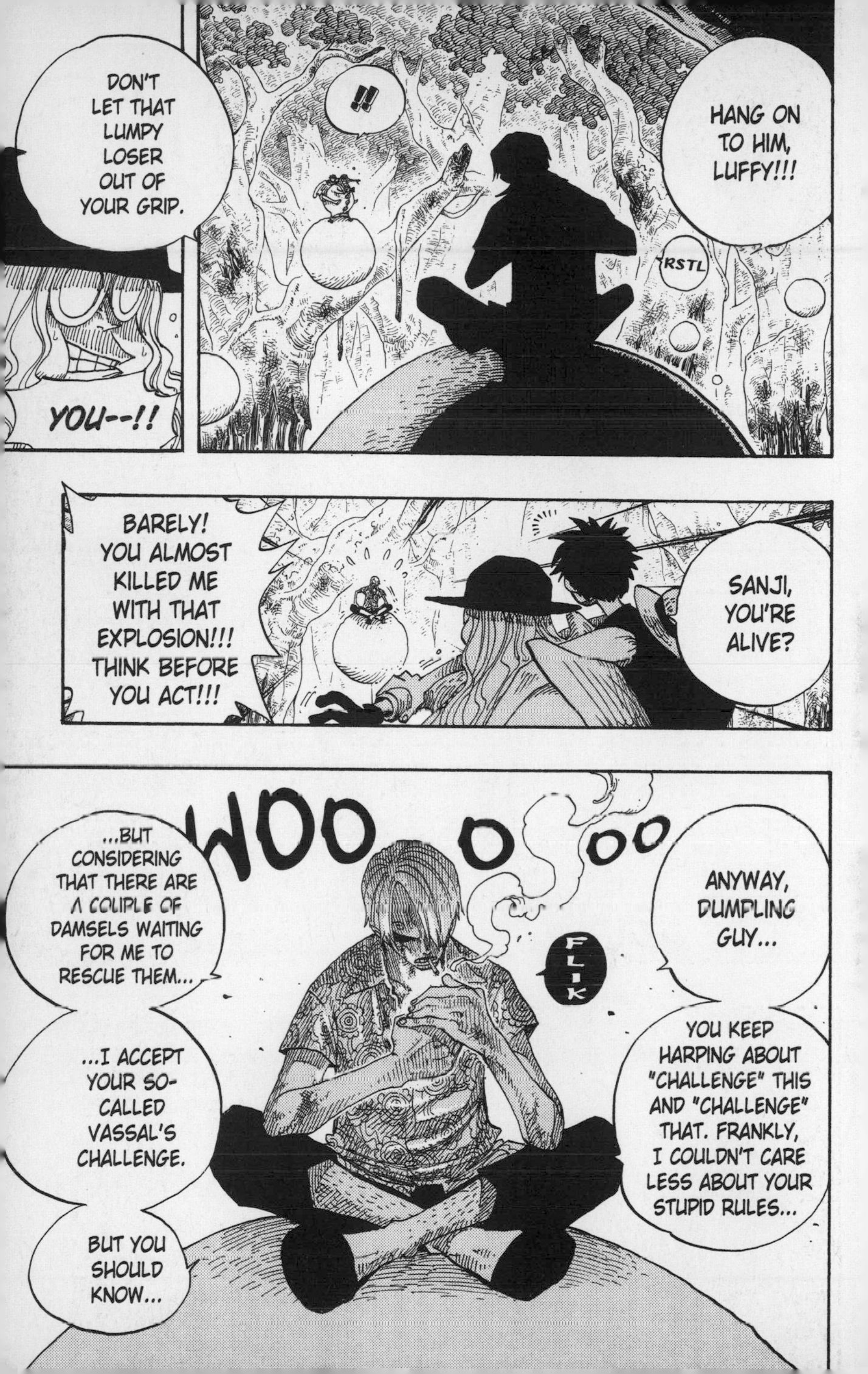
HANG ON TO HIM, LUFFY!!!
!!
RSTL
DON'T LET THAT LUMPY LOSER OUT OF YOUR GRIP.
YOU--!!
SANJI, YOU'RE ALIVE?
BARELY! YOU ALMOST KILLED ME WITH THAT EXPLOSION!!! THINK BEFORE YOU ACT!!!
ANYWAY, DUMPLING GUY...
YOU KEEP HARPING ABOUT "CHALLENGE" THIS AND "CHALLENGE" THAT. FRANKLY, I COULDN'T CARE LESS ABOUT YOUR STUPID RULES...
WOO O OO
FLIK
...BUT CONSIDERING THAT THERE ARE A COUPLE OF DAMSELS WAITING FOR ME TO RESCUE THEM...
...I ACCEPT YOUR SO-CALLED VASSAL'S CHALLENGE.
BUT YOU SHOULD KNOW...

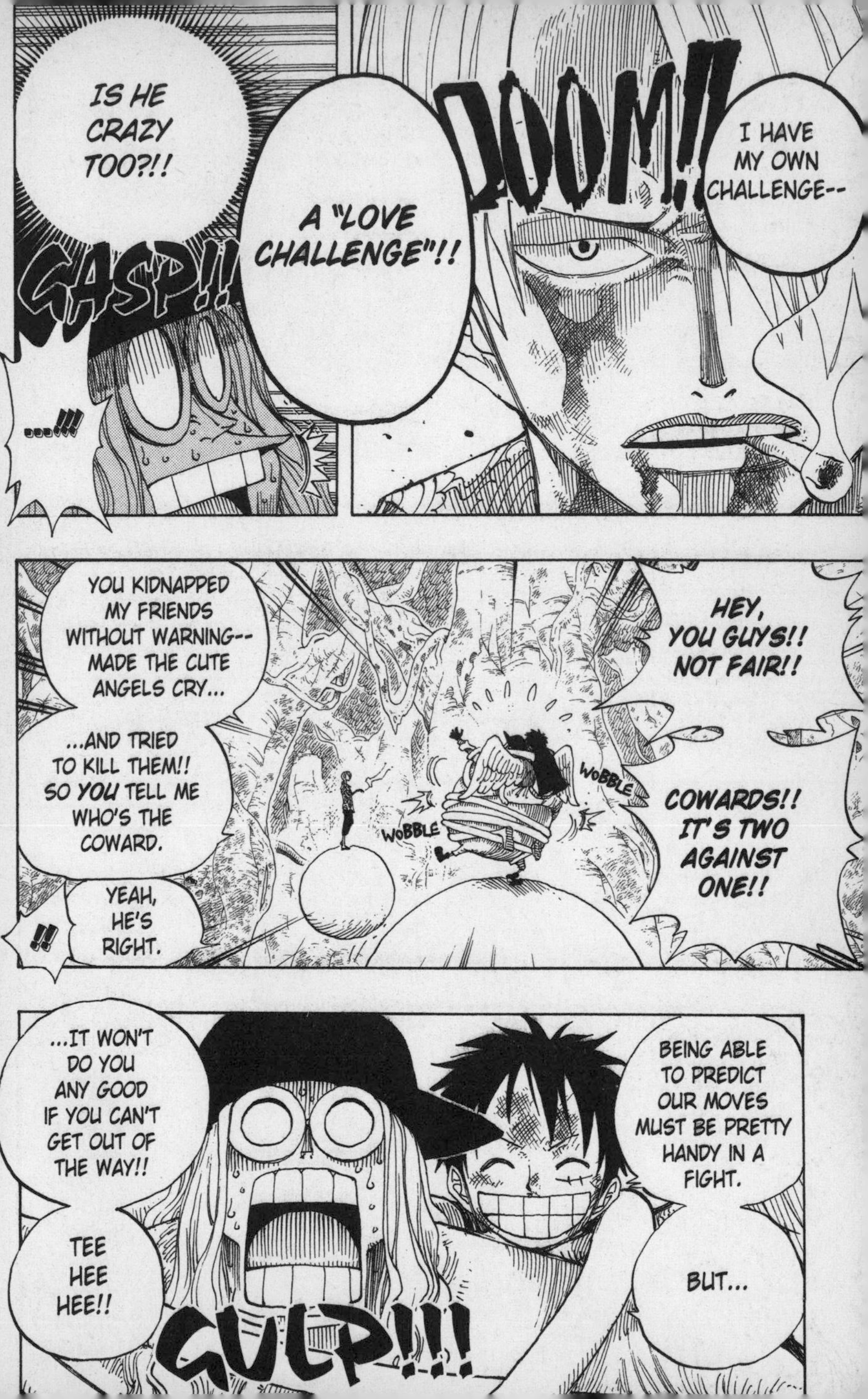
I HAVE MY OWN CHALLENGE--
DOOM!!
A "LOVE CHALLENGE"!!
IS HE CRAZY TOO?!!
GASP!!
...!!!
HEY, YOU GUYS!! NOT FAIR!!
COWARDS!! IT'S TWO AGAINST ONE!!
WOBBLE
WOBBLE
YOU KIDNAPPED MY FRIENDS WITHOUT WARNING-- MADE THE CUTE ANGELS CRY...
...AND TRIED TO KILL THEM!! SO YOU TELL ME WHO'S THE COWARD.
!!
YEAH, HE'S RIGHT.
BEING ABLE TO PREDICT OUR MOVES MUST BE PRETTY HANDY IN A FIGHT.
BUT...
...IT WON'T DO YOU ANY GOOD IF YOU CAN'T GET OUT OF THE WAY!!
TEE HEE HEE!!
GULP!!!

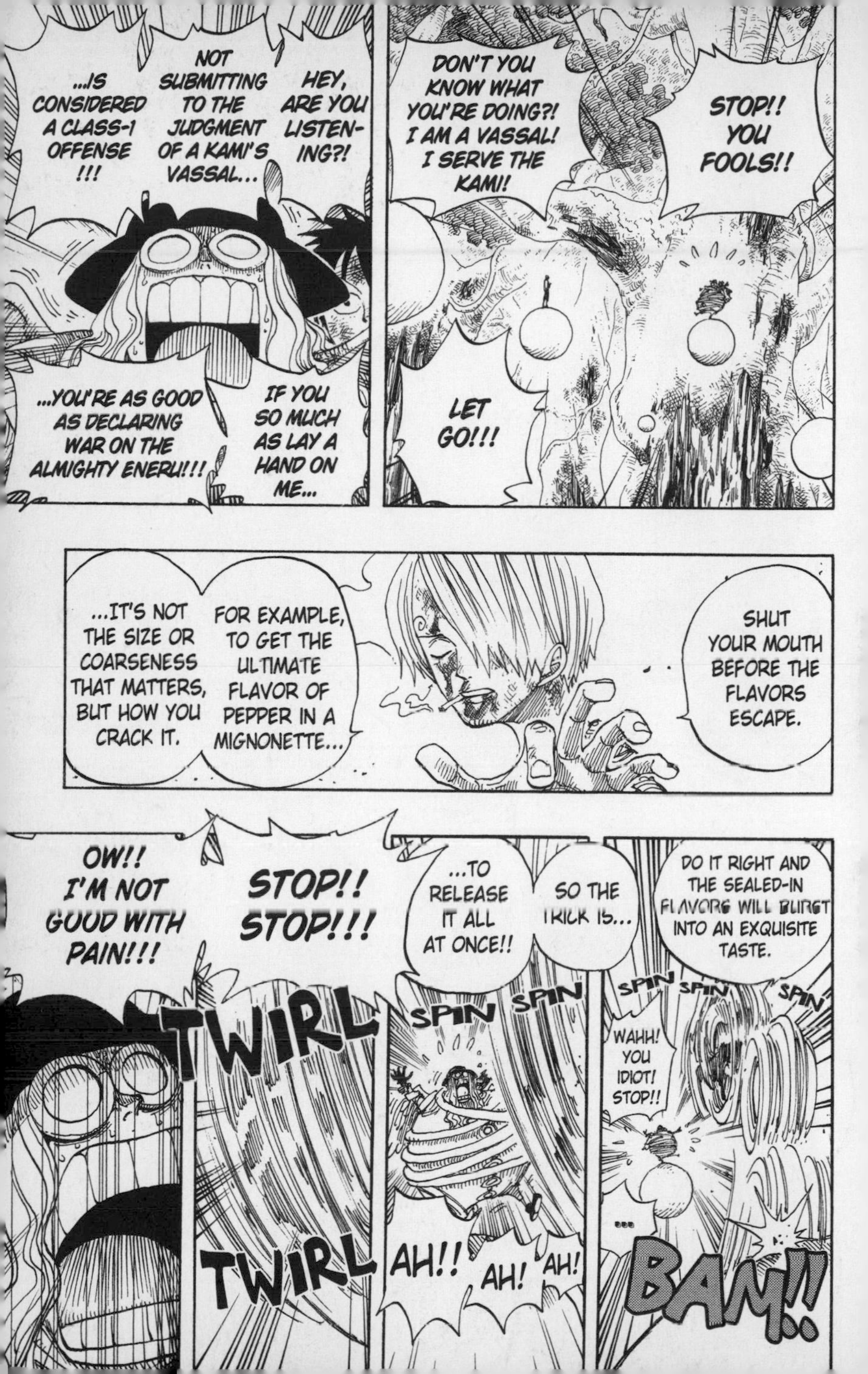
STOP!! YOU FOOLS!!
DON'T YOU KNOW WHAT YOU'RE DOING?! I AM A VASSAL! I SERVE THE KAMI!
LET GO!!!
HEY, ARE YOU LISTENING?!
NOT SUBMITTING TO THE JUDGMENT OF A KAMI'S VASSAL...
...IS CONSIDERED A CLASS-1 OFFENSE!!!
IF YOU SO MUCH AS LAY A HAND ON ME...
...YOU'RE AS GOOD AS DECLARING WAR ON THE ALMIGHTY ENERU!!!
SHUT YOUR MOUTH BEFORE THE FLAVORS ESCAPE.
FOR EXAMPLE, TO GET THE ULTIMATE FLAVOR OF PEPPER IN A MIGNONETTE...
...IT'S NOT THE SIZE OR COARSENESS THAT MATTERS, BUT HOW YOU CRACK IT.
DO IT RIGHT AND THE SEALED-IN FLAVORS WILL BURST INTO AN EXQUISITE TASTE.
SPIN SPIN SPIN
WAHH! YOU IDIOT! STOP!!
...
BAM!!
SO THE TRICK IS...
...TO RELEASE IT ALL AT ONCE!!
SPIN SPIN
AH!!
AH!
AH!
STOP!! STOP!!!
OW!! I'M NOT GOOD WITH PAIN!!!
TWIRL
TWIRL

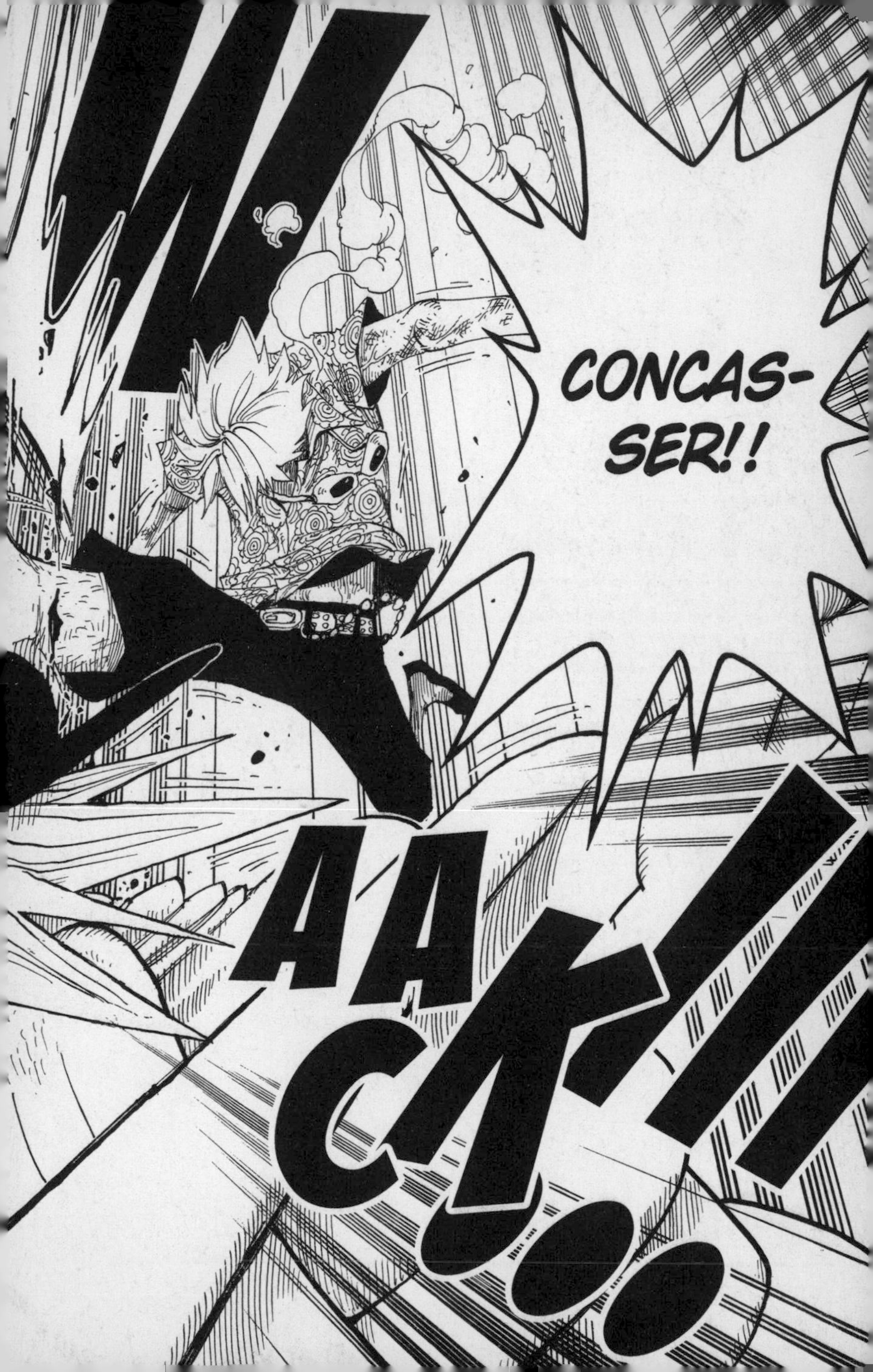
CONCAS-
SER!!

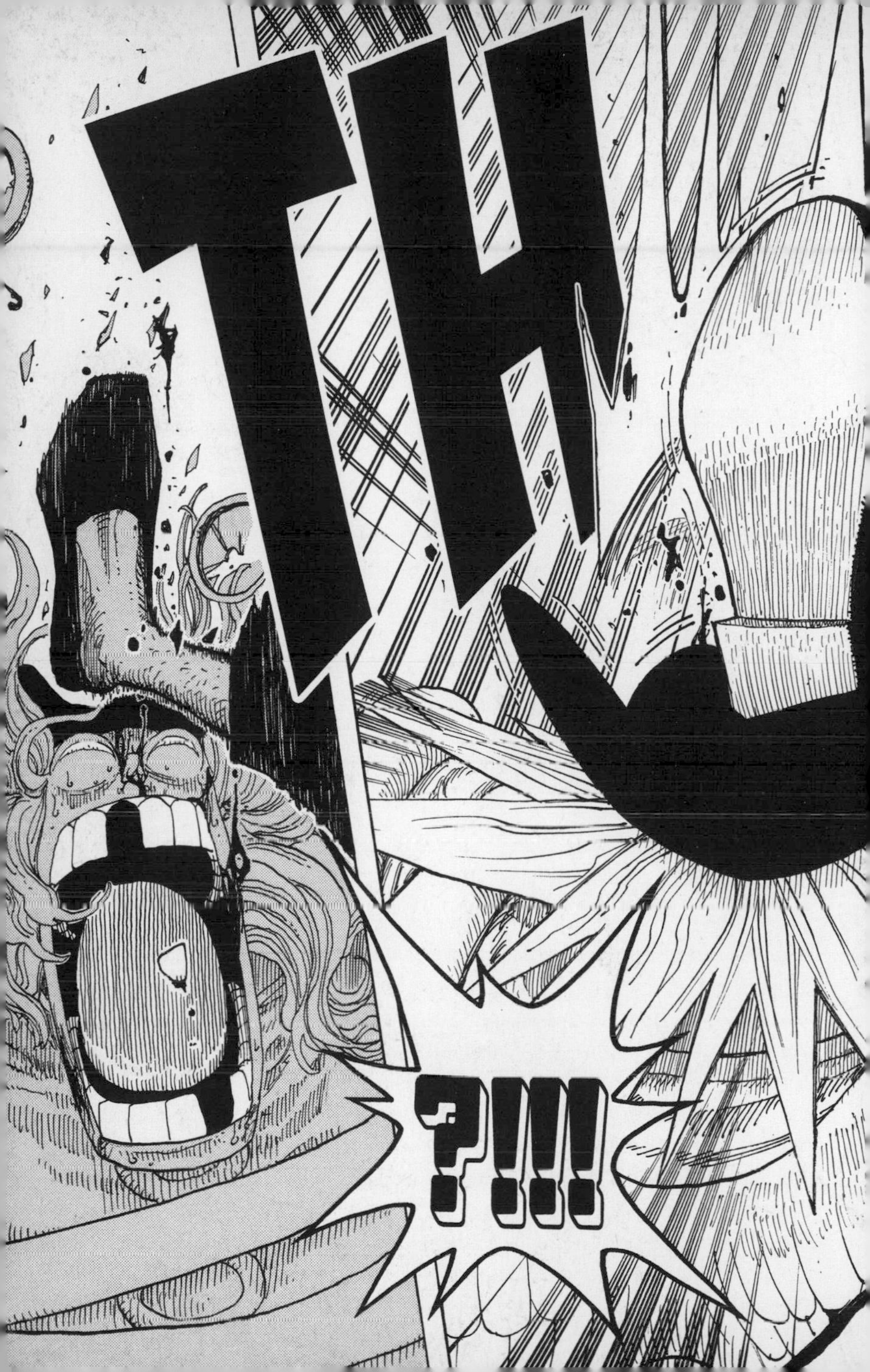
TH
?!!!

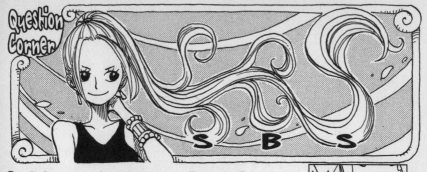
Q: Before a party, Buggy always says, "Yaraideka!"
("Let's live it up!") What's that phrase all about?
My mother says it means, "let's have a party." Is it a dialect
or something?

LET'S LIVE IT UP!!!

I SEE, AMAZING!! CAPTAIN, SHALL WE PARTY?!!

A: Hmm... I get this question often. I figured
people would grasp the meaning from the
context. Yes, it is a dialect. It's "Edo-ese," meaning it's a phrase
used in old Tokyo. There are a few old phrases like that still used
in downtown Tokyo to this day. There's "teyandei!!" which means,
"What are you saying?!" They say that "Edokko" (true Tokyo-ites)
are impatient, so the phrase, "yaraideka!" is short for "yaranai de
irareruka!" I asked my friends from the area, so I know it's right.
I've been wanting to introduce an "Edokko Pirate Crew."
It could be funny. Someday...

Q: Hi,☆Oddachi! I heard from a friend the other day that "Sokotsuya," the anime
voice of Karoo, is actually Hiroaki Hirata, who does Sanji? Huh?!
It's a lie?!

A: "Quack!" Yes. That is the voice of Hirata-san, who
does Sanji. Furthermore, Eyelashes of Alabasta is
done by Yamaguchi-san, who does Usopp. In the
anime, there are times when Sanji won't appear, or Zolo won't
appear, so the actors don't have any lines. When that happens, the
voice actors get to mess around (laugh). Like doing animal
voices. But they don't want to use their own names for such
roles, hence something like "Sokotsuya" appears in the credits.
So for important animals, please listen to the voice carefully.
If it says "Sokotsuya," it's probably one of the Straw Hats.

Chapter 251: OVERTURE

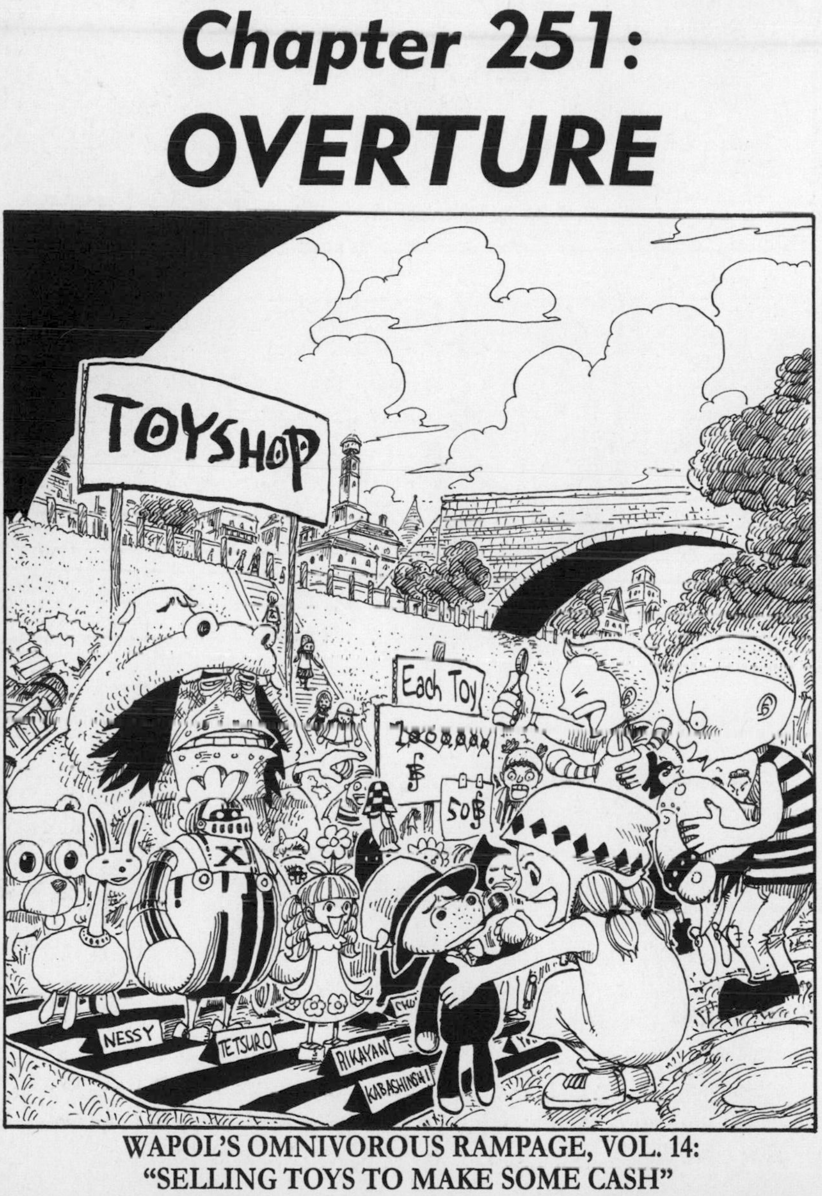
TOYSHOP
Each Toy
50$
NESSY
TETSURO
RIKAYAN
KABASHINSHI

WAPOL'S OMNIVOROUS RAMPAGE, VOL. 14:
"SELLING TOYS TO MAKE SOME CASH"

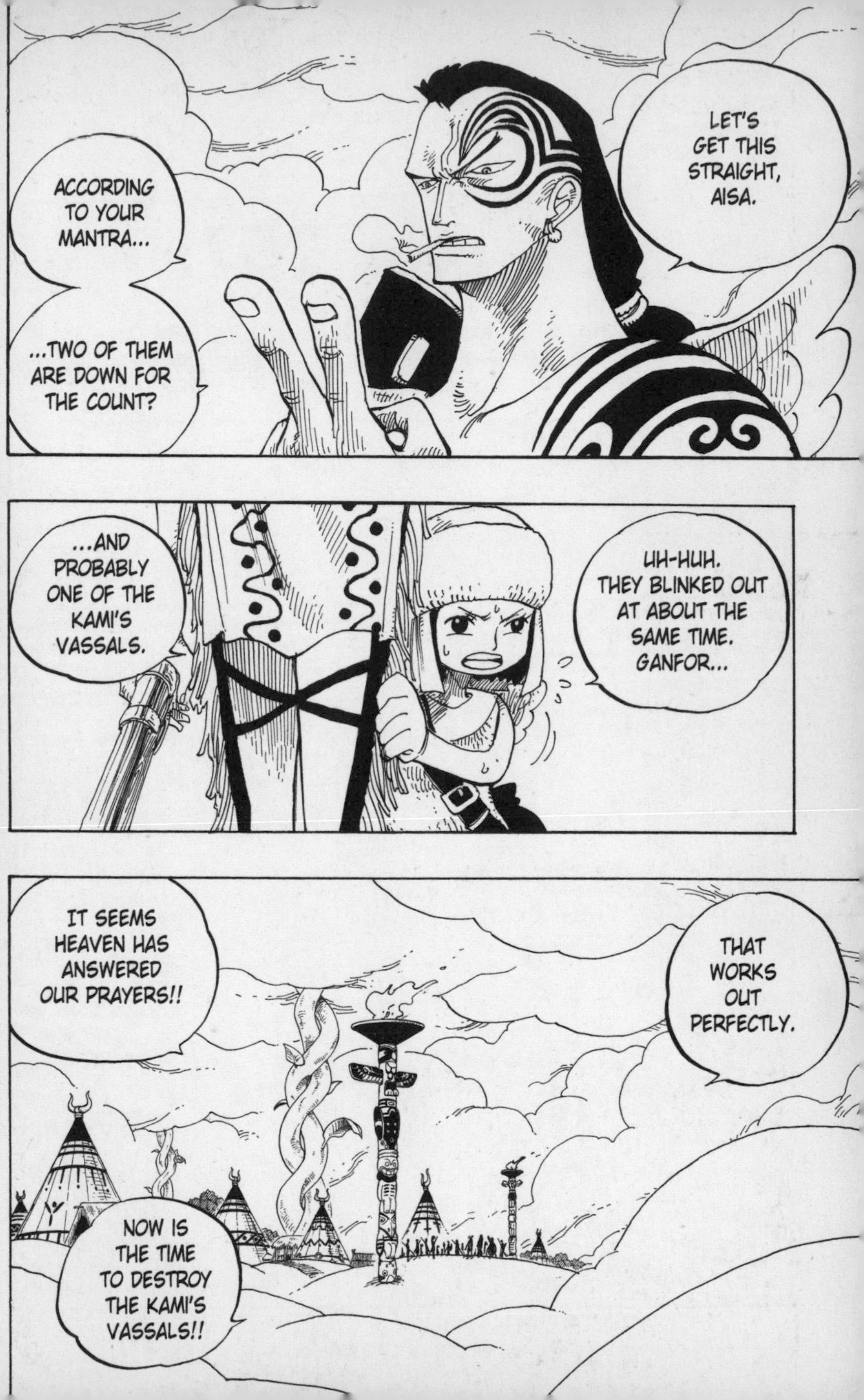
LET'S GET THIS STRAIGHT, AISA.
ACCORDING TO YOUR MANTRA...
...TWO OF THEM ARE DOWN FOR THE COUNT?
...AND PROBABLY ONE OF THE KAMI'S VASSALS.
UH-HUH. THEY BLINKED OUT AT ABOUT THE SAME TIME. GANFOR...
THAT WORKS OUT PERFECTLY.
IT SEEMS HEAVEN HAS ANSWERED OUR PRAYERS!!
NOW IS THE TIME TO DESTROY THE KAMI'S VASSALS!!

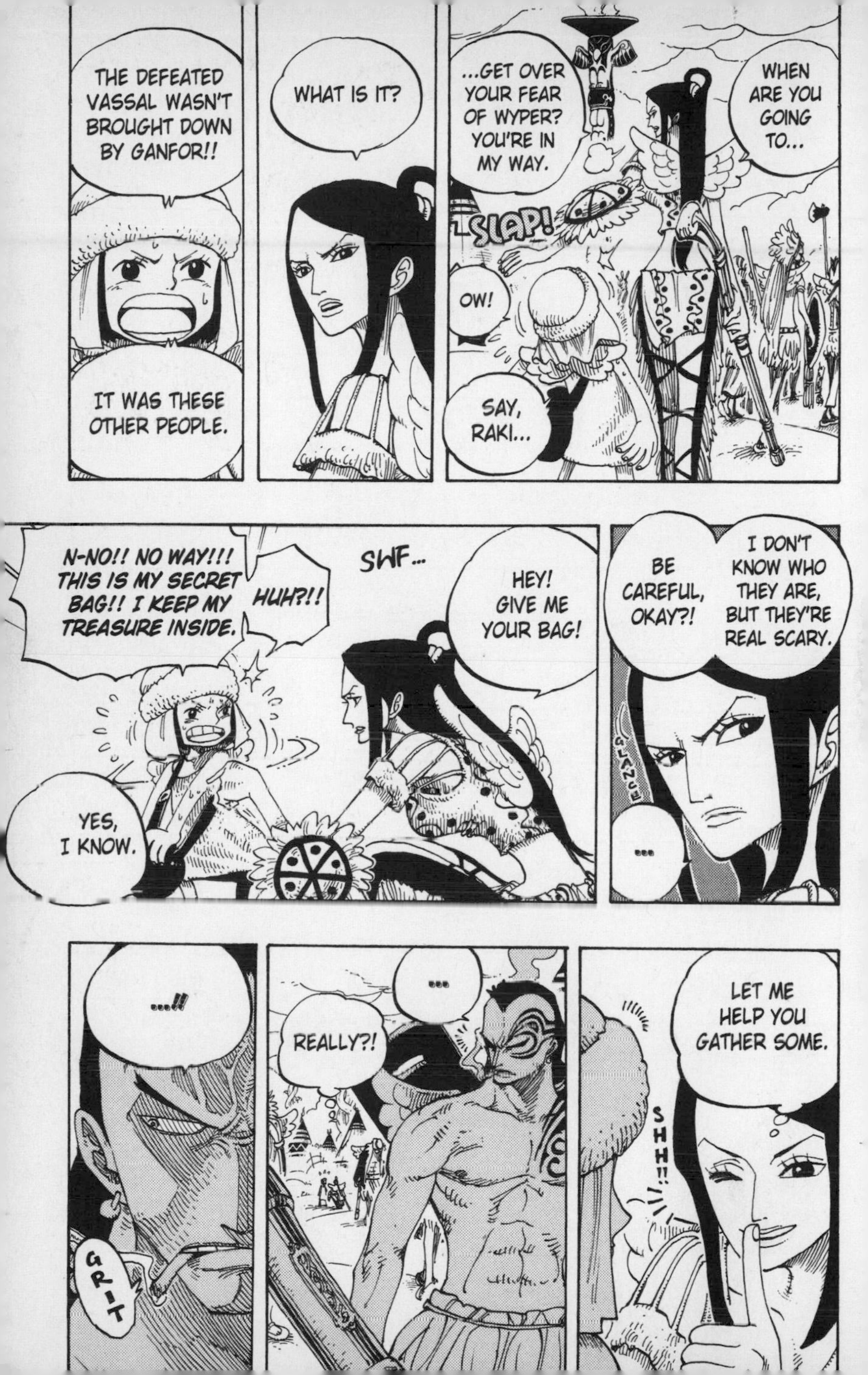
WHEN ARE YOU GOING TO...
...GET OVER YOUR FEAR OF WYPER? YOU'RE IN MY WAY.
SLAP!
OW!
SAY, RAKI...
WHAT IS IT?
THE DEFEATED VASSAL WASN'T BROUGHT DOWN BY GANFOR!!
IT WAS THESE OTHER PEOPLE.
I DON'T KNOW WHO THEY ARE, BUT THEY'RE REAL SCARY.
BE CAREFUL, OKAY?!
GLANCE
...
HEY! GIVE ME YOUR BAG!
SWF...
HUH?!!
N-NO!! NO WAY!!! THIS IS MY SECRET BAG!! I KEEP MY TREASURE INSIDE.
YES, I KNOW.
LET ME HELP YOU GATHER SOME.
SHH!!
...
REALLY?!
...!!
GRIT

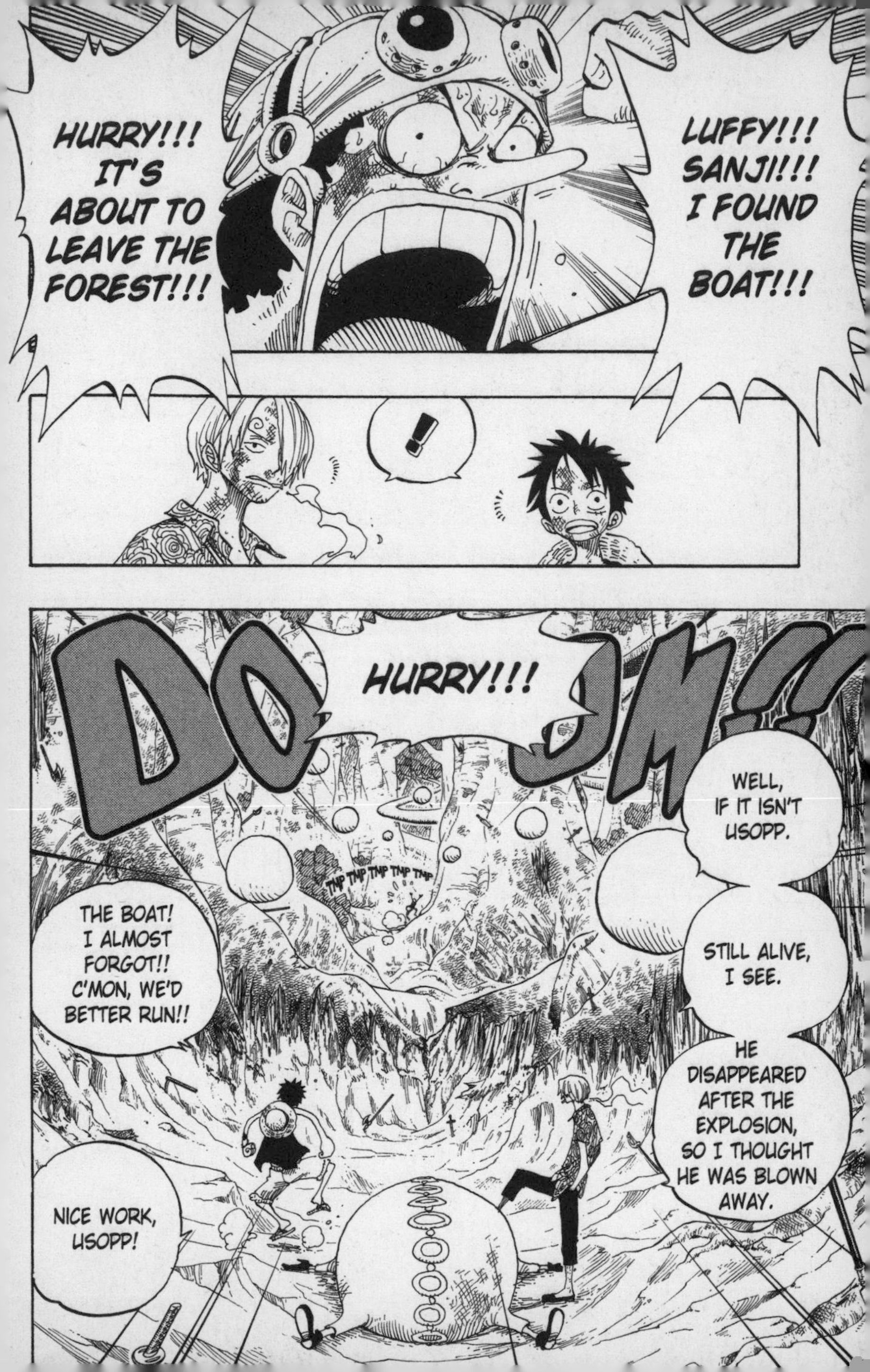
LUFFY!!! SANJI!!! I FOUND THE BOAT!!!
HURRY!!! IT'S ABOUT TO LEAVE THE FOREST!!!
!
HURRY!!!
TMP TMP TMP TMP TMP
WELL, IF IT ISN'T USOPP.
STILL ALIVE, I SEE.
HE DISAPPEARED AFTER THE EXPLOSION, SO I THOUGHT HE WAS BLOWN AWAY.
THE BOAT! I ALMOST FORGOT!! C'MON, WE'D BETTER RUN!!
NICE WORK, USOPP!

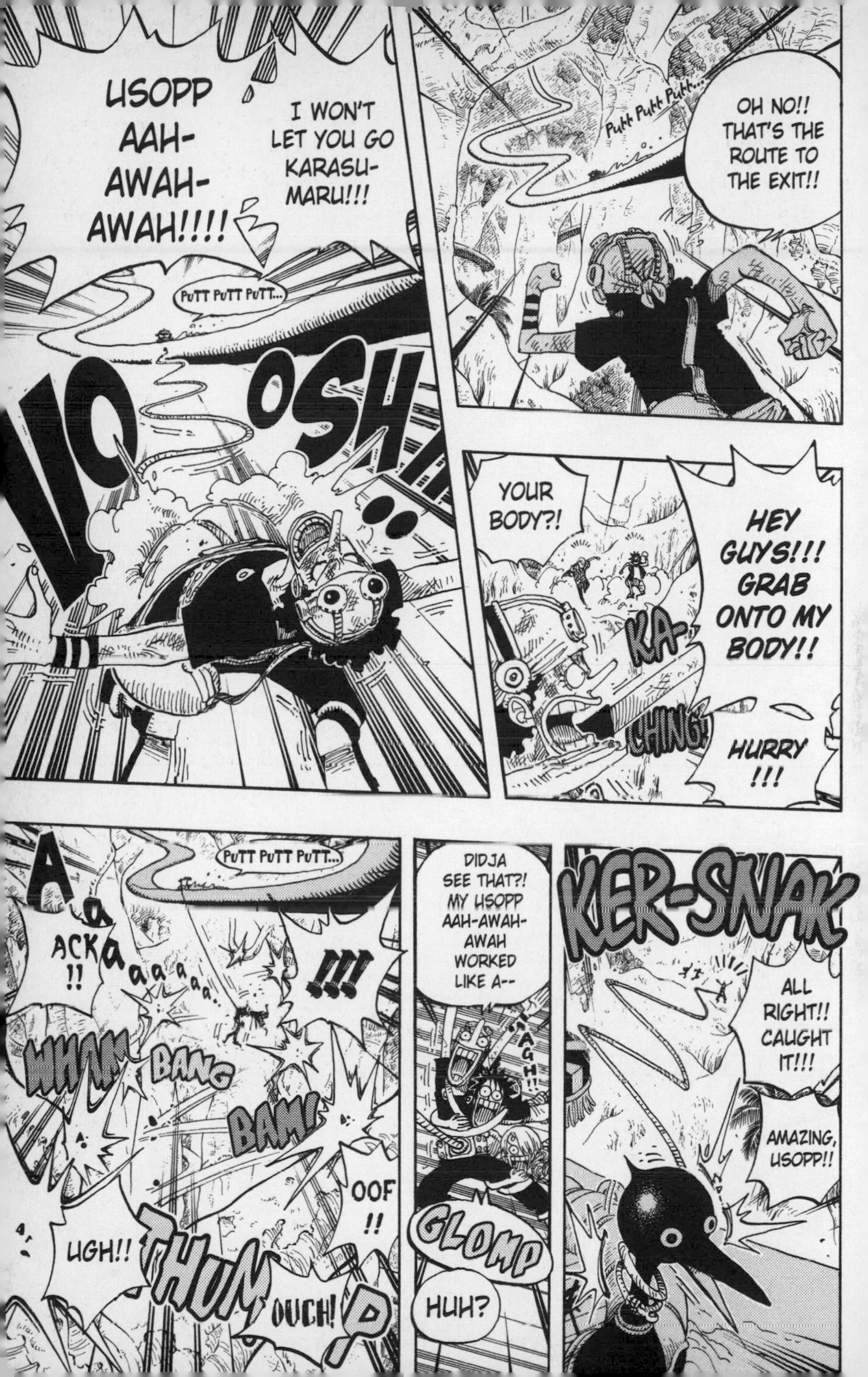
Putt Putt Putt...
OH NO!! THAT'S THE ROUTE TO THE EXIT!!
HEY GUYS!!! GRAB ONTO MY BODY!!
YOUR BODY?!
KA-CHING!
HURRY!!!
I WON'T LET YOU GO KARASU-MARU!!!
USOPP AAH-AWAH-AWAH!!!!
PUTT PUTT PUTT...
VOOSH
KER-SNAK
ALL RIGHT!! CAUGHT IT!!!
AMAZING, USOPP!!
DIDJA SEE THAT?! MY USOPP AAH-AWAH-AWAH WORKED LIKE A--
AAGH!!
GLOMP
HUH?
PUTT PUTT PUTT...
!!!
Aaaaaaa...
ACKA !!
WHAM
BANG
BAM!
OOF!!
UGH!!
THUMP
OUCH!

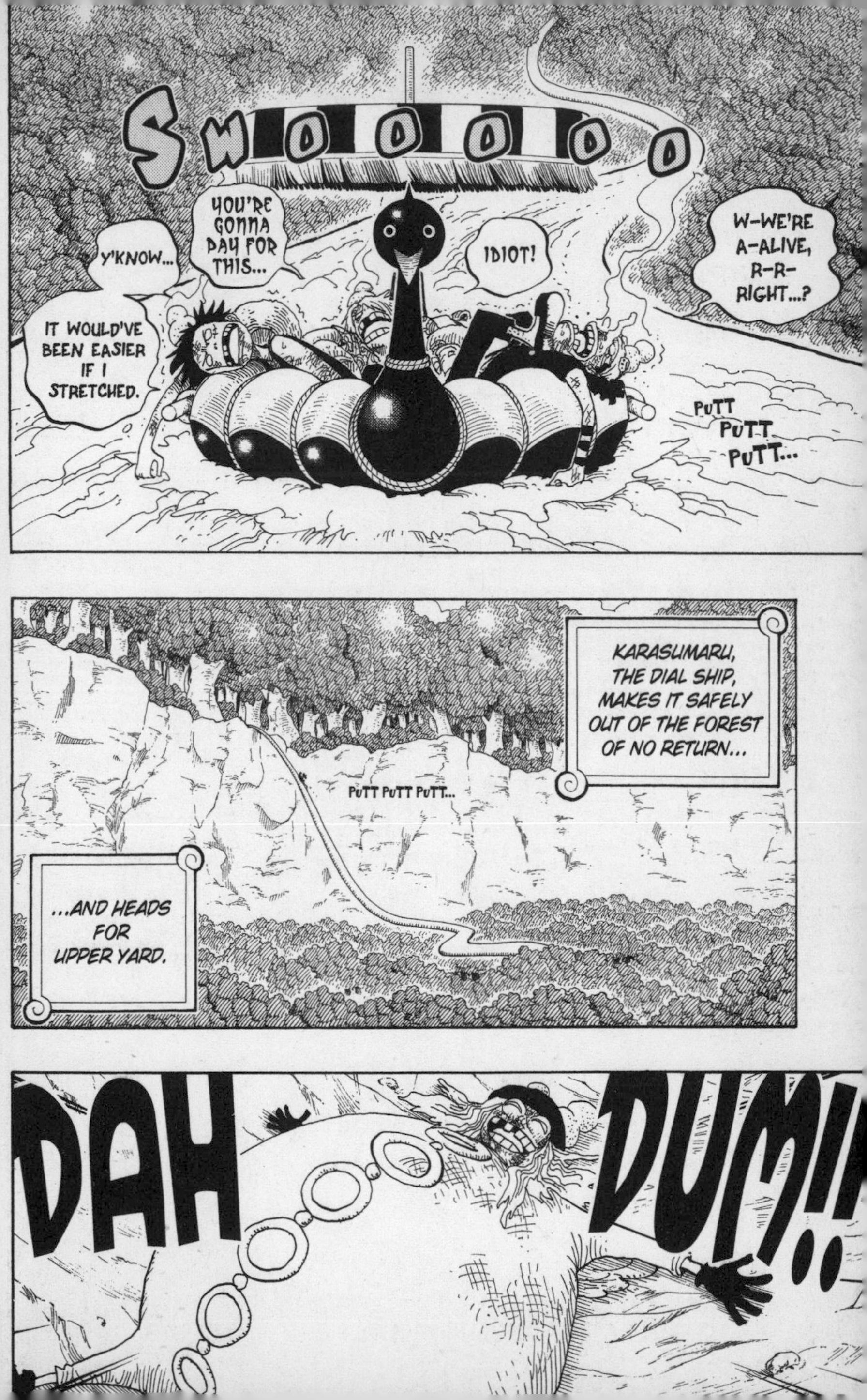
SWOOOOO
W-WE'RE A-ALIVE, R-R-RIGHT...?
IDIOT!
YOU'RE GONNA PAY FOR THIS...
Y'KNOW...
IT WOULD'VE BEEN EASIER IF I STRETCHED.
PUTT PUTT PUTT...
KARASUMARU, THE DIAL SHIP, MAKES IT SAFELY OUT OF THE FOREST OF NO RETURN...
PUTT PUTT PUTT...
...AND HEADS FOR UPPER YARD.
DAH DUM!!

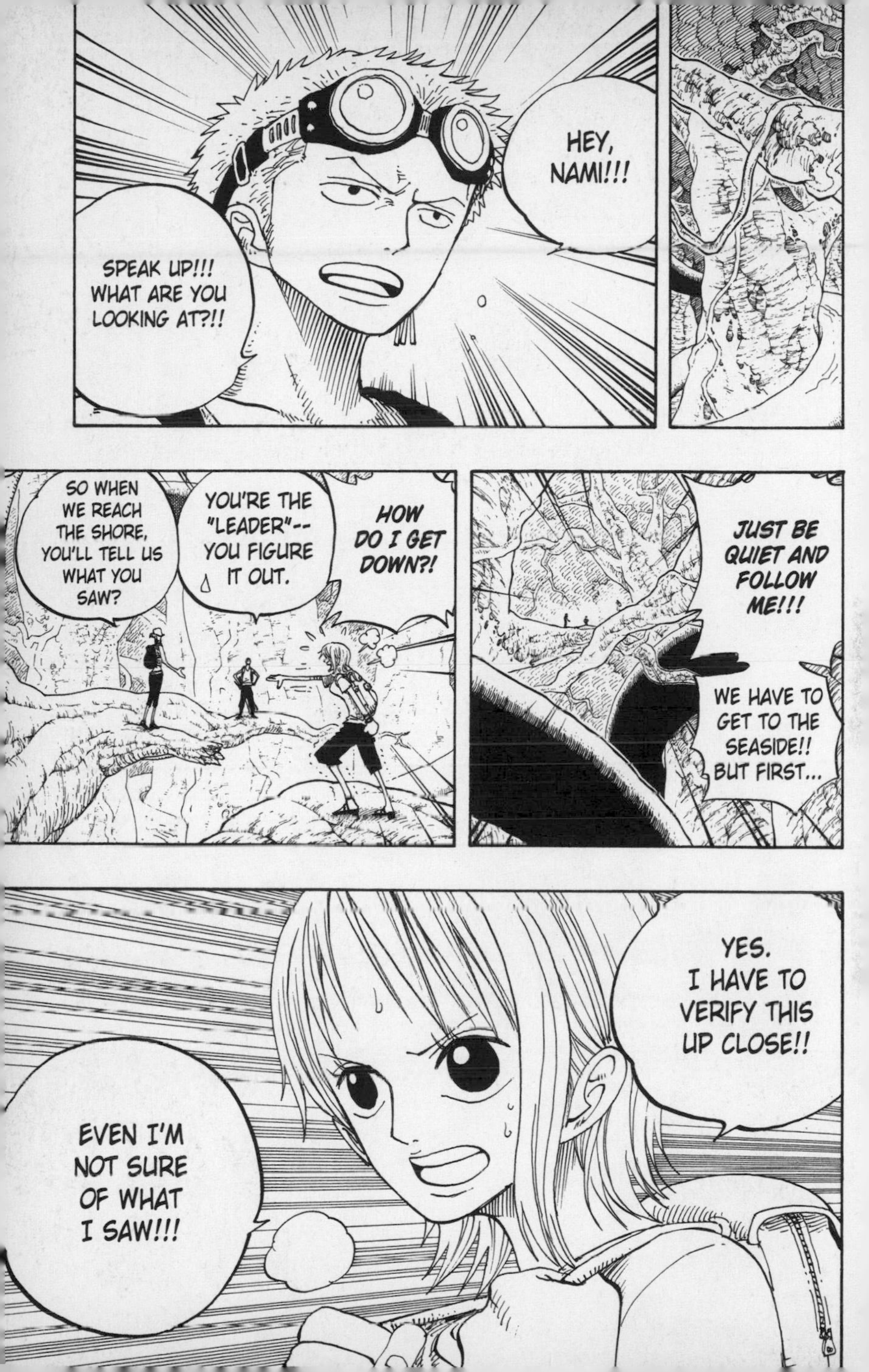
HEY, NAMI!!!
SPEAK UP!!! WHAT ARE YOU LOOKING AT?!!
JUST BE QUIET AND FOLLOW ME!!!
WE HAVE TO GET TO THE SEASIDE!! BUT FIRST...
HOW DO I GET DOWN?!
YOU'RE THE "LEADER"-- YOU FIGURE IT OUT.
SO WHEN WE REACH THE SHORE, YOU'LL TELL US WHAT YOU SAW?
YES. I HAVE TO VERIFY THIS UP CLOSE!!
EVEN I'M NOT SURE OF WHAT I SAW!!!

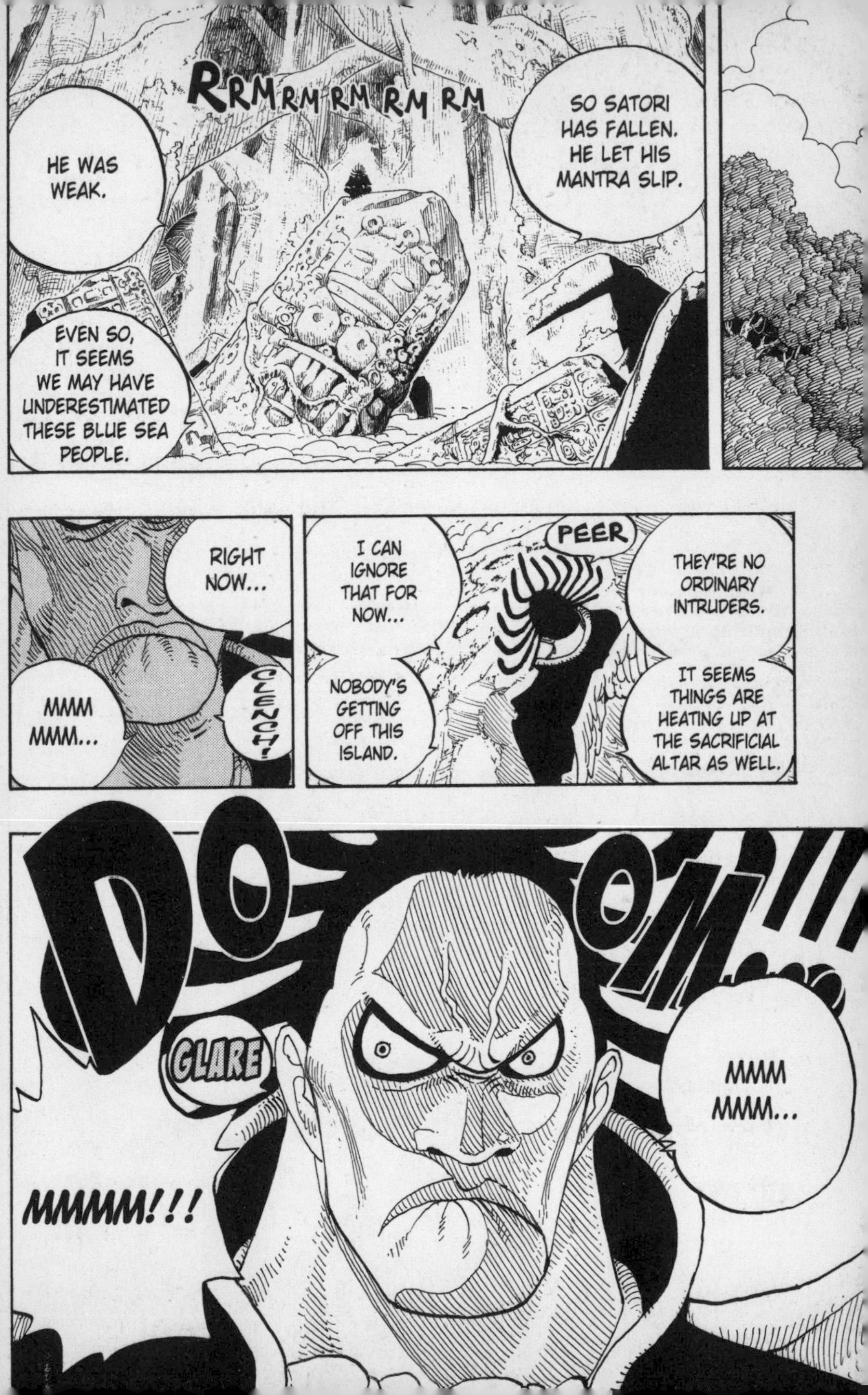
SO SATORI HAS FALLEN. HE LET HIS MANTRA SLIP.
RRMRM RM RM RM RM
HE WAS WEAK.
EVEN SO, IT SEEMS WE MAY HAVE UNDERESTIMATED THESE BLUE SEA PEOPLE.
PEER
THEY'RE NO ORDINARY INTRUDERS.
IT SEEMS THINGS ARE HEATING UP AT THE SACRIFICIAL ALTAR AS WELL.
I CAN IGNORE THAT FOR NOW...
NOBODY'S GETTING OFF THIS ISLAND.
RIGHT NOW...
CLENCH!
MMM MMM...
DO-OM!!!
MMM MMM...
GLARE
MMMM!!!

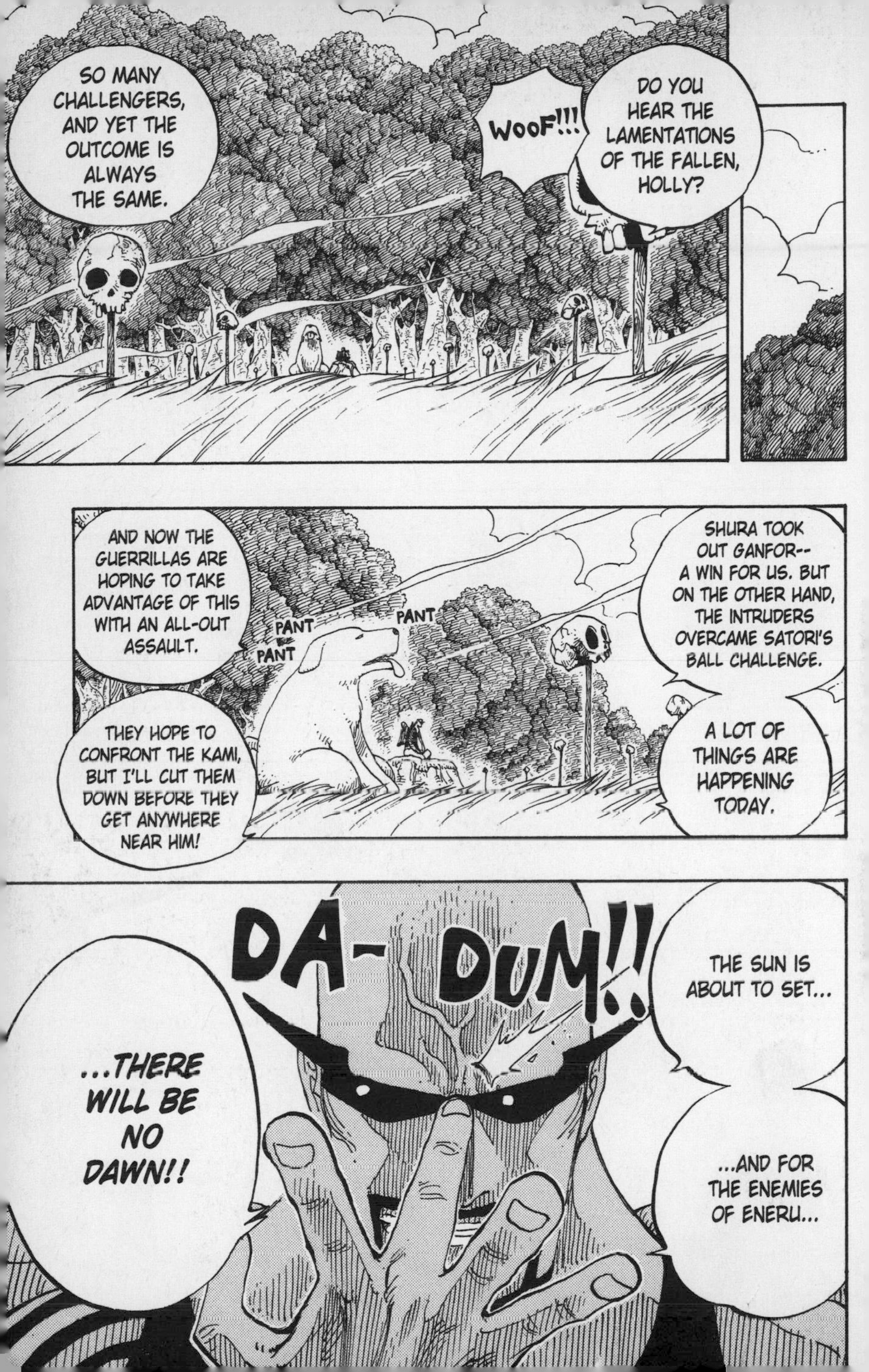
DO YOU HEAR THE LAMENTATIONS OF THE FALLEN, HOLLY?
WOOF!!!
SO MANY CHALLENGERS, AND YET THE OUTCOME IS ALWAYS THE SAME.
SHURA TOOK OUT GANFOR-- A WIN FOR US. BUT ON THE OTHER HAND, THE INTRUDERS OVERCAME SATORI'S BALL CHALLENGE.
A LOT OF THINGS ARE HAPPENING TODAY.
PANT
PANT
PANT
AND NOW THE GUERRILLAS ARE HOPING TO TAKE ADVANTAGE OF THIS WITH AN ALL-OUT ASSAULT.
THEY HOPE TO CONFRONT THE KAMI, BUT I'LL CUT THEM DOWN BEFORE THEY GET ANYWHERE NEAR HIM!
THE SUN IS ABOUT TO SET...
...AND FOR THE ENEMIES OF ENERU...
DA-DUM!!
...THERE WILL BE NO DAWN!!

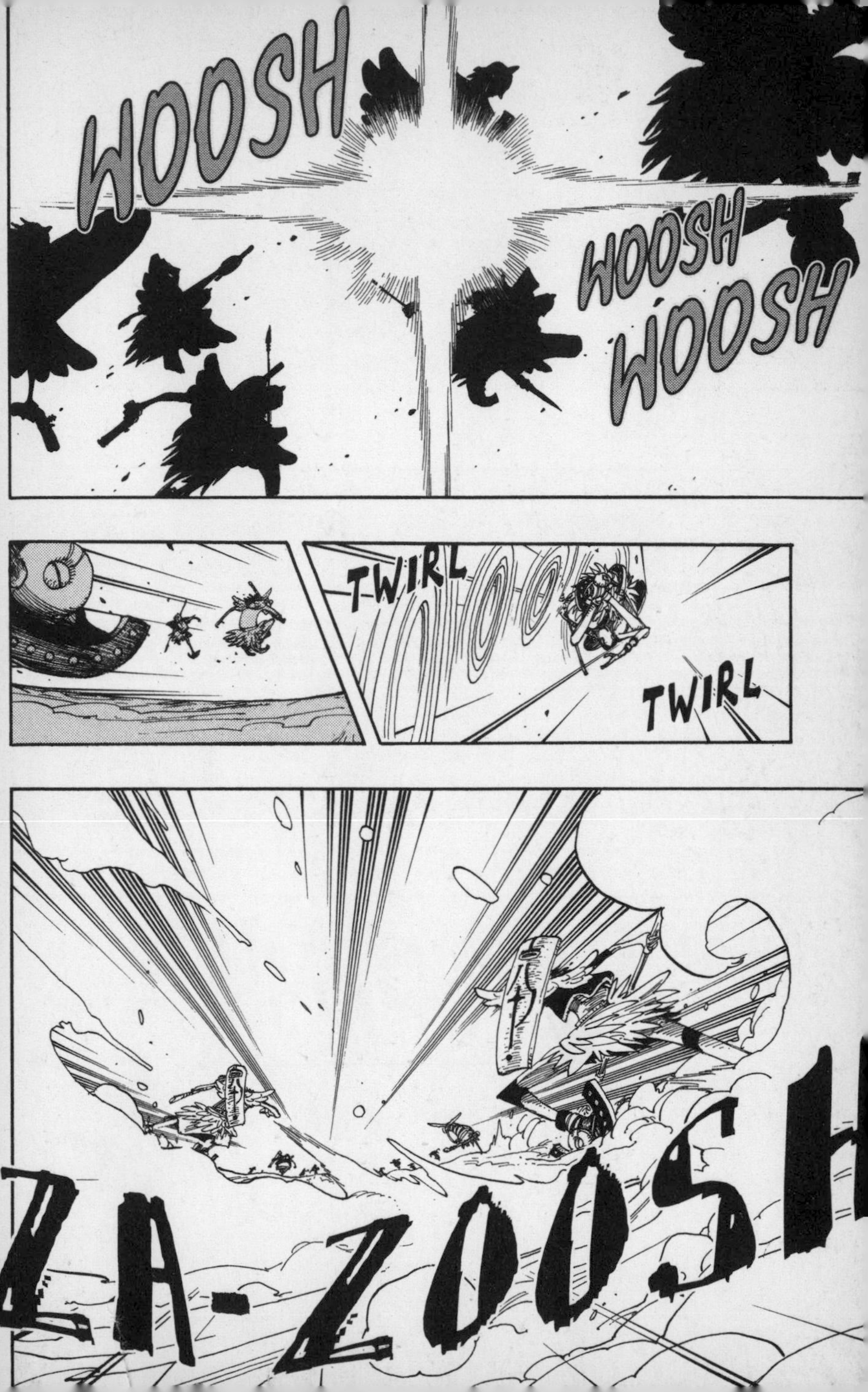
WOOSH WOOSH
WOOSH
TWIRL
TWIRL
ZA-ZOOSH

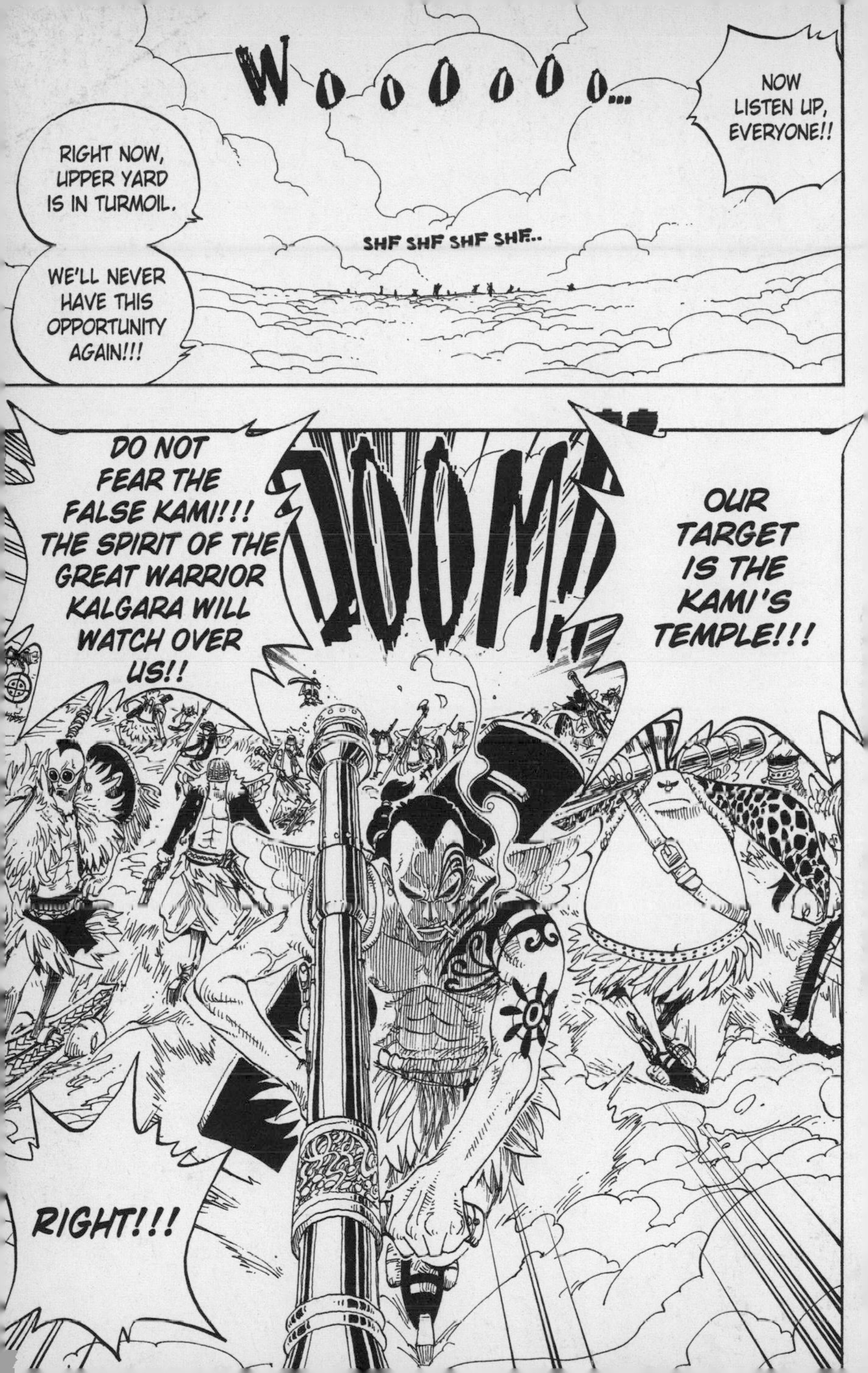
NOW LISTEN UP, EVERYONE!!
WOOOOOO...
RIGHT NOW, UPPER YARD IS IN TURMOIL.
WE'LL NEVER HAVE THIS OPPORTUNITY AGAIN!!!
SHF SHF SHF SHF..
OUR TARGET IS THE KAMI'S TEMPLE!!!
DOOM!!
DO NOT FEAR THE FALSE KAMI!!! THE SPIRIT OF THE GREAT WARRIOR KALGARA WILL WATCH OVER US!!
RIGHT!!!

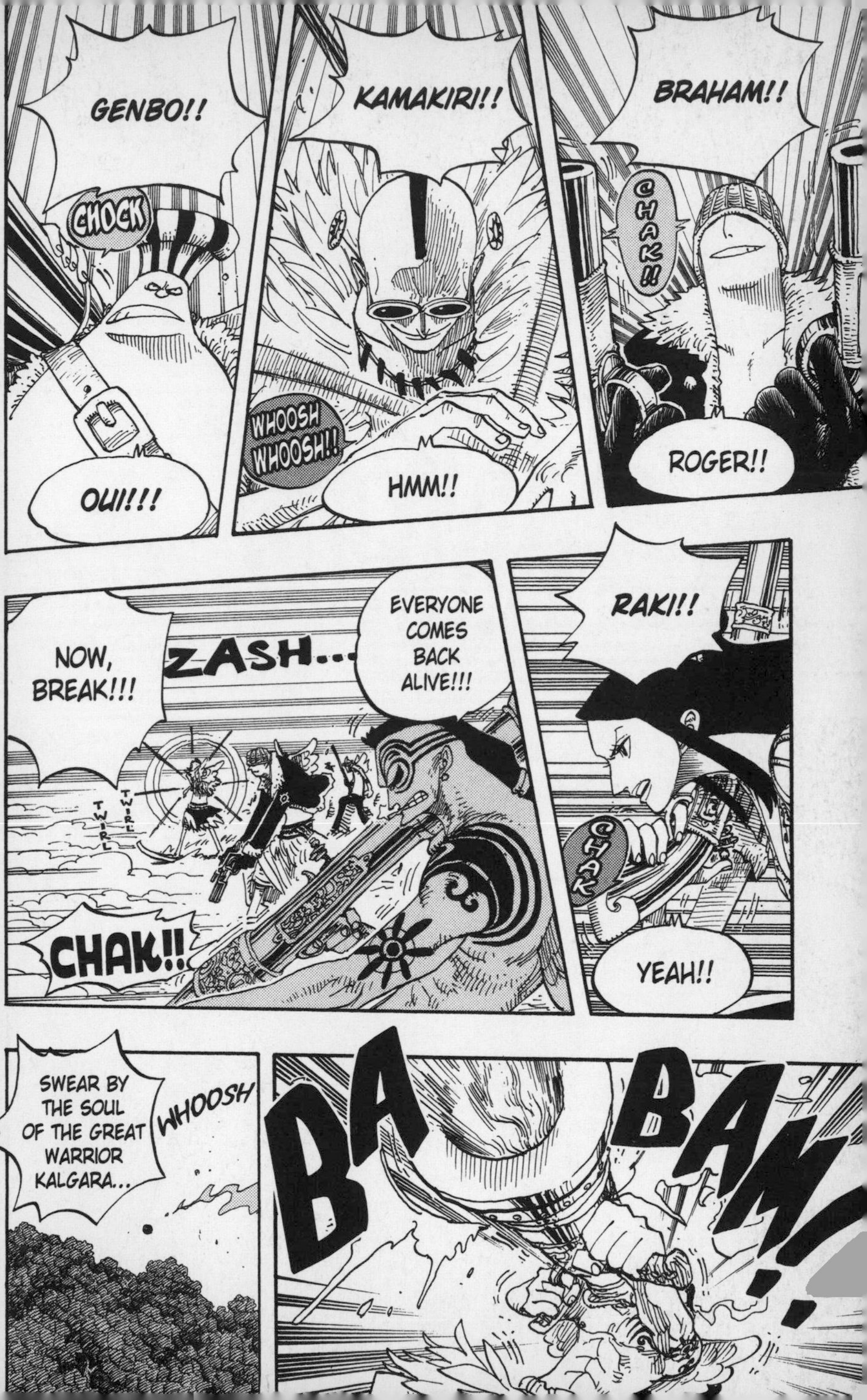
BRAHAM!!
CHAK!!
ROGER!!
KAMAKIRI!!
WHOOSH WHOOSH!!
HMM!!
GENBO!!
CHOCK
OUI!!!
RAKI!!
CHAK
YEAH!!
EVERYONE COMES BACK ALIVE!!!
NOW, BREAK!!!
ZASH...
TWIRL
TWIRL
CHAK!!
BA BAM!!
SWEAR BY THE SOUL OF THE GREAT WARRIOR KALGARA...
WHOOSH

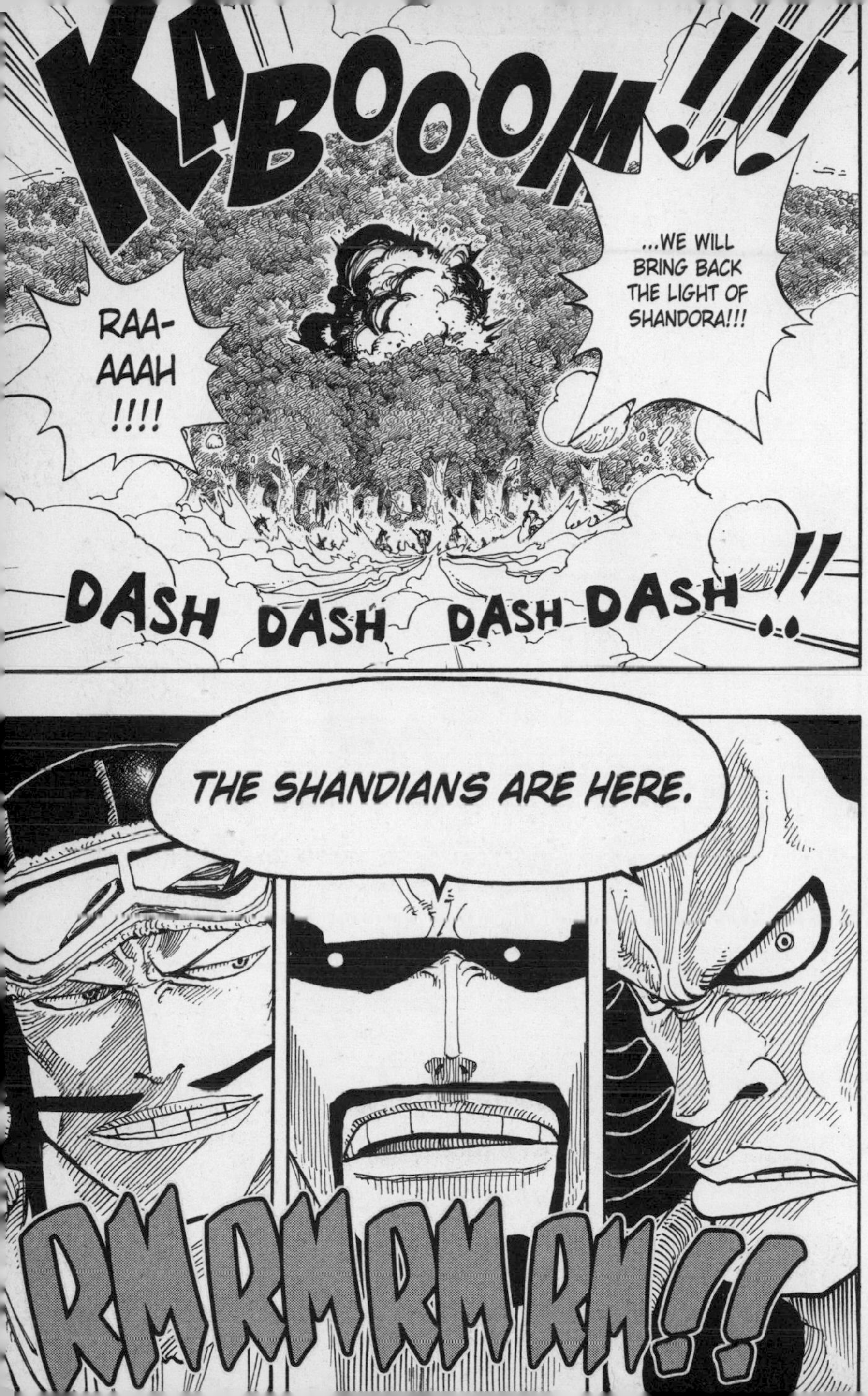
KABOOOM!!!
...WE WILL BRING BACK THE LIGHT OF SHANDORA!!!
RAA-AAAH!!!!
DASH DASH DASH DASH!!
THE SHANDIANS ARE HERE.
RMRMRMRM!!

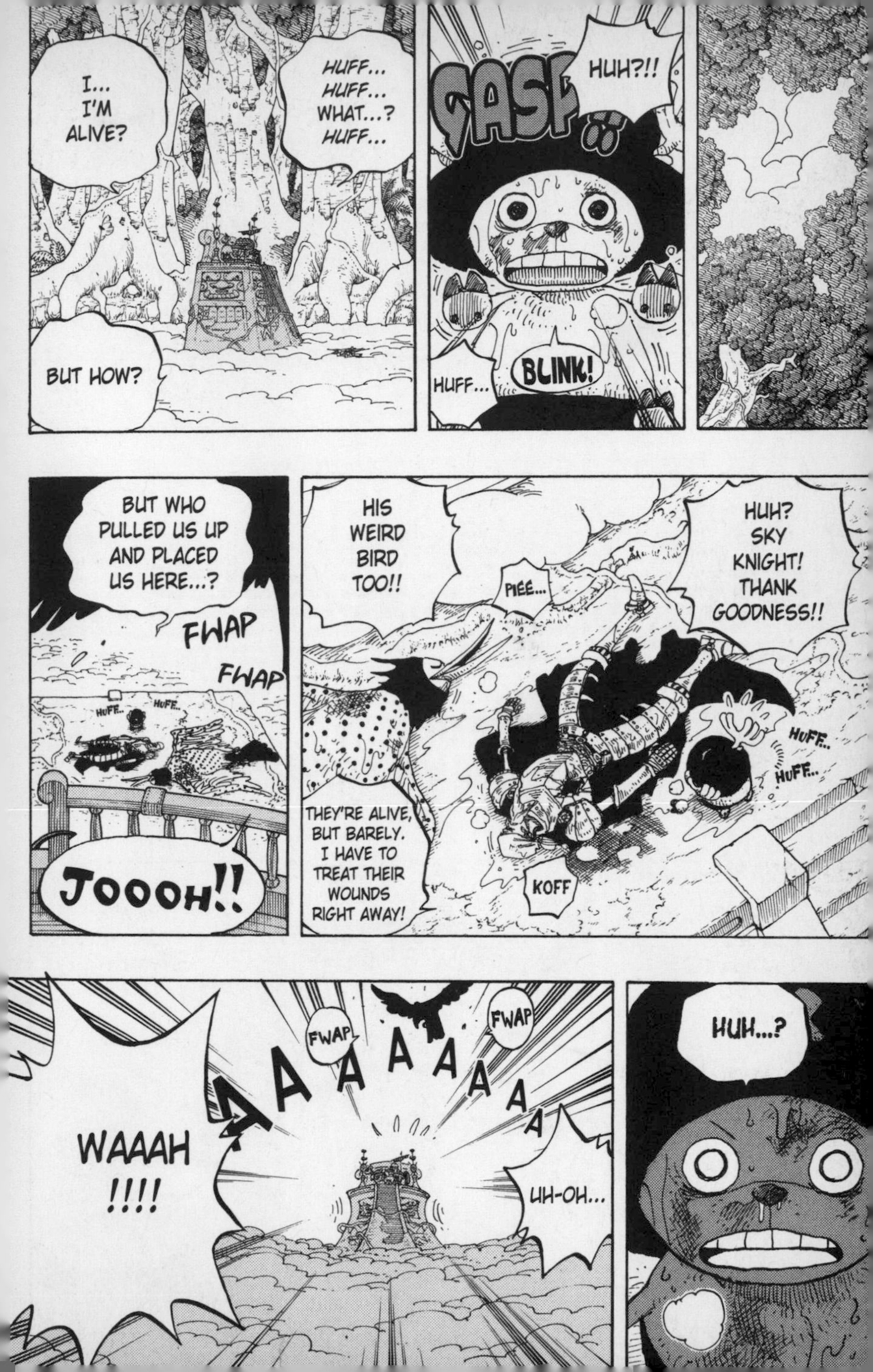
HUH?!!
GASP
BLINK!
HUFF...
HUFF... HUFF... WHAT...? HUFF...
I... I'M ALIVE?
BUT HOW?
HUH? SKY KNIGHT! THANK GOODNESS!!
HIS WEIRD BIRD TOO!!
PIEE...
HUFF.. HUFF..
THEY'RE ALIVE, BUT BARELY. I HAVE TO TREAT THEIR WOUNDS RIGHT AWAY!
KOFF
BUT WHO PULLED US UP AND PLACED US HERE...?
FWAP
FWAP
HUFF.. HUFF..
JOOOH!!
HUH...?
FWAP
FWAP
AAAAAAAAA
WAAAH !!!!
UH-OH...

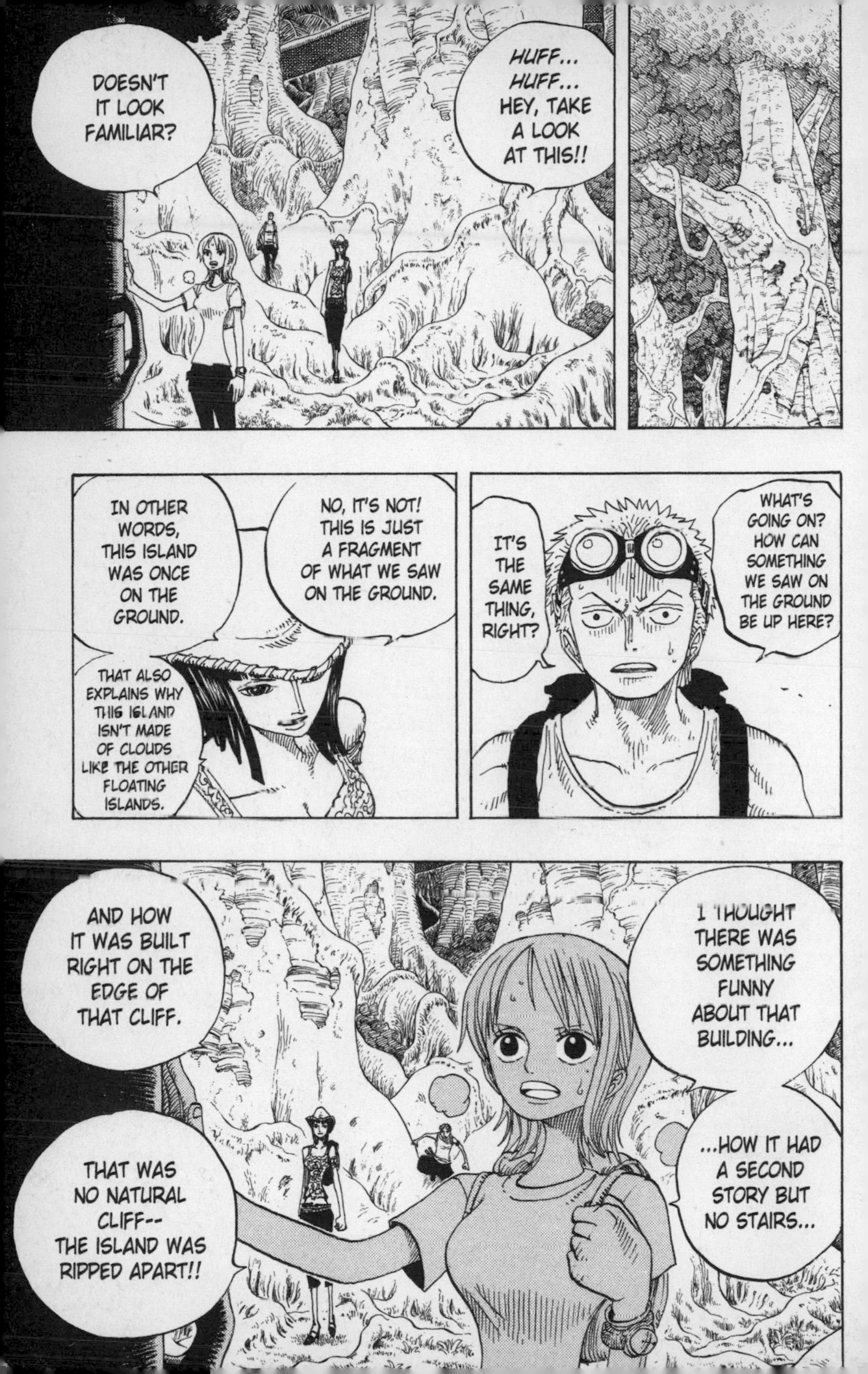
HUFF... HUFF... HEY, TAKE A LOOK AT THIS!!
DOESN'T IT LOOK FAMILIAR?
WHAT'S GOING ON? HOW CAN SOMETHING WE SAW ON THE GROUND BE UP HERE?
IT'S THE SAME THING, RIGHT?
NO, IT'S NOT! THIS IS JUST A FRAGMENT OF WHAT WE SAW ON THE GROUND.
IN OTHER WORDS, THIS ISLAND WAS ONCE ON THE GROUND.
THAT ALSO EXPLAINS WHY THIS ISLAND ISN'T MADE OF CLOUDS LIKE THE OTHER FLOATING ISLANDS.
I THOUGHT THERE WAS SOMETHING FUNNY ABOUT THAT BUILDING...
...HOW IT HAD A SECOND STORY BUT NO STAIRS...
AND HOW IT WAS BUILT RIGHT ON THE EDGE OF THAT CLIFF.
THAT WAS NO NATURAL CLIFF-- THE ISLAND WAS RIPPED APART!!

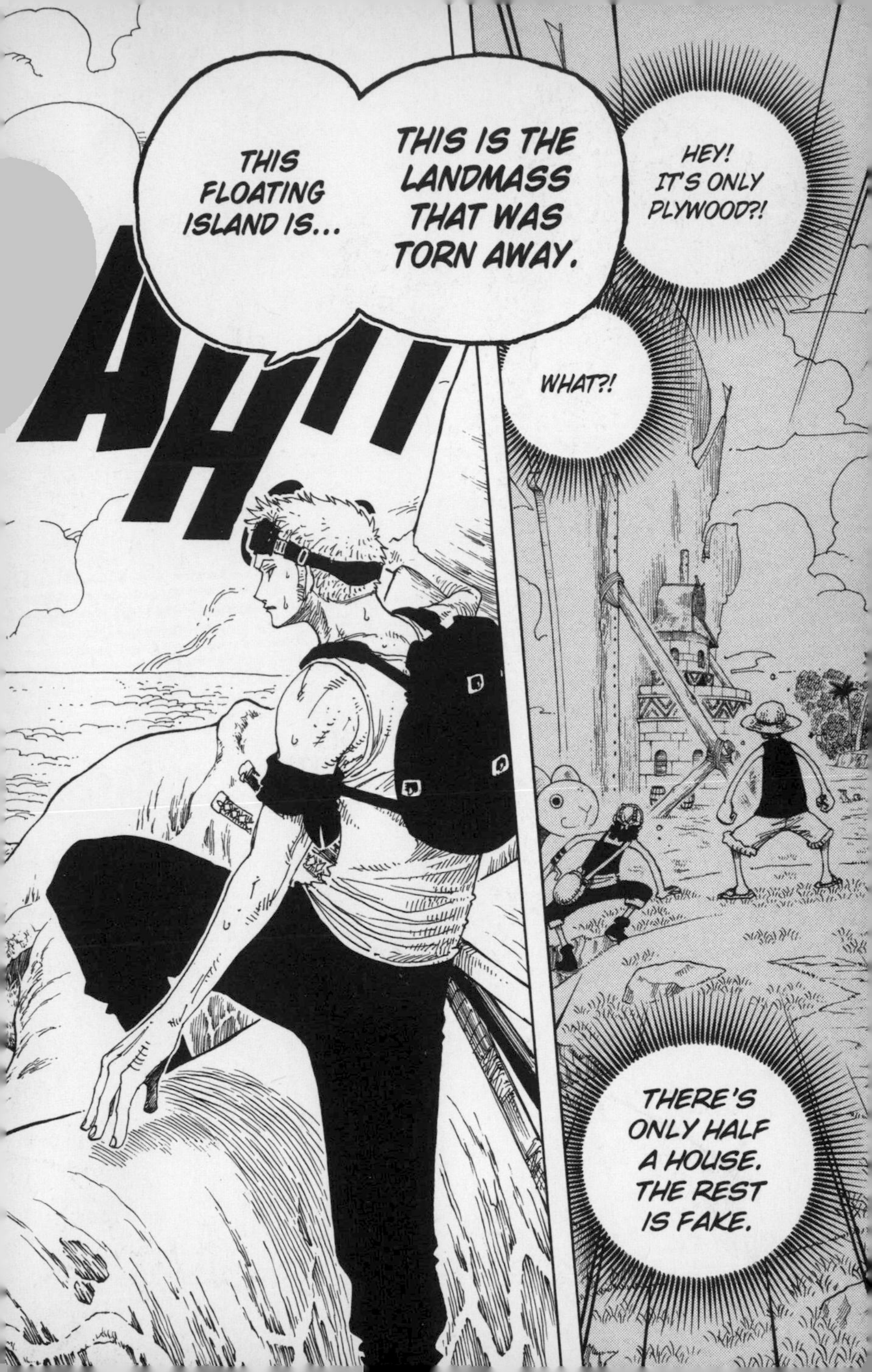
HEY! IT'S ONLY PLYWOOD?!
WHAT?!
THERE'S ONLY HALF A HOUSE. THE REST IS FAKE.
THIS FLOATING ISLAND IS... THIS IS THE LANDMASS THAT WAS TORN AWAY.
AH!!

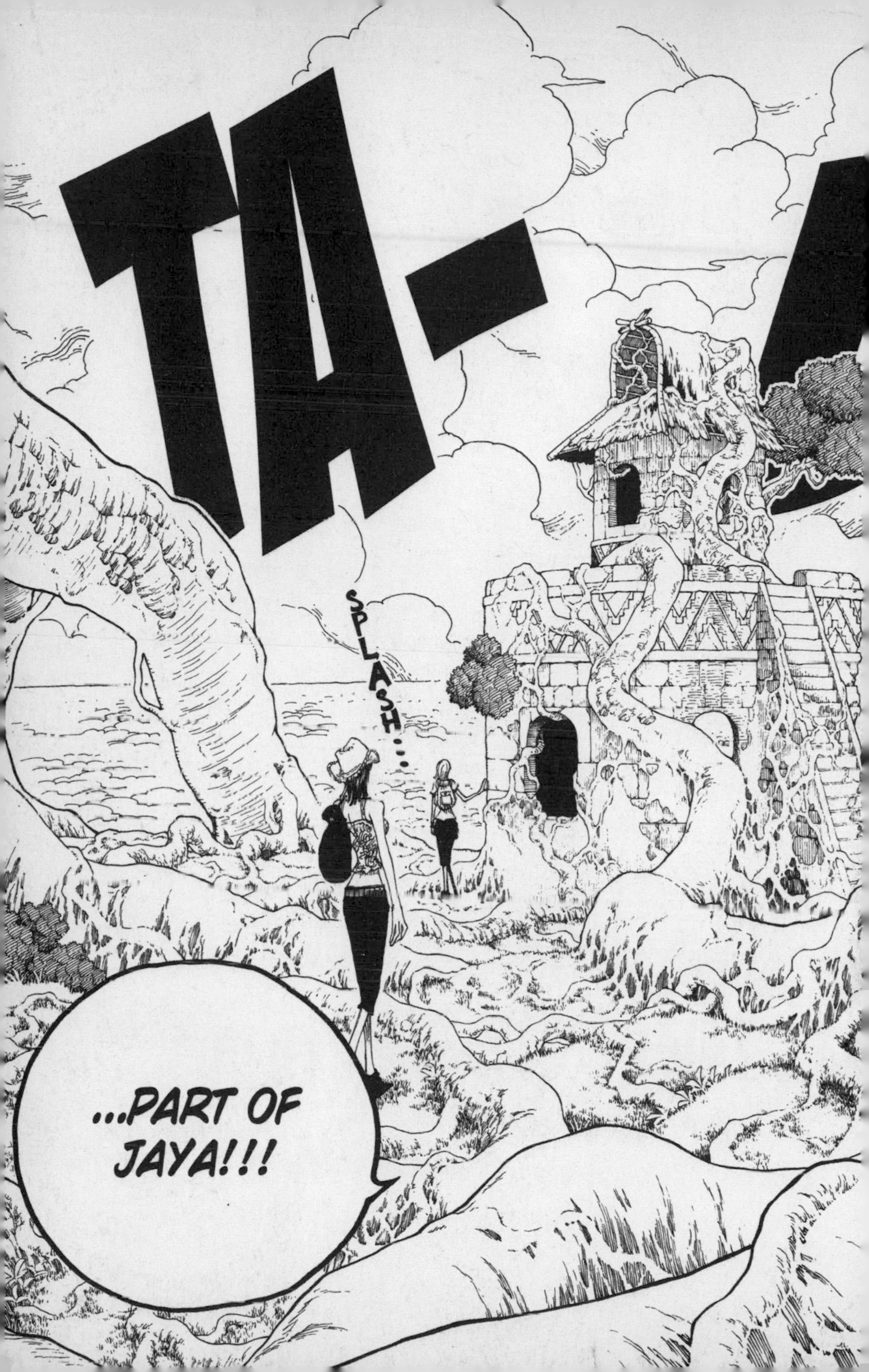
TA-
SPLASH...
...PART OF JAYA!!!

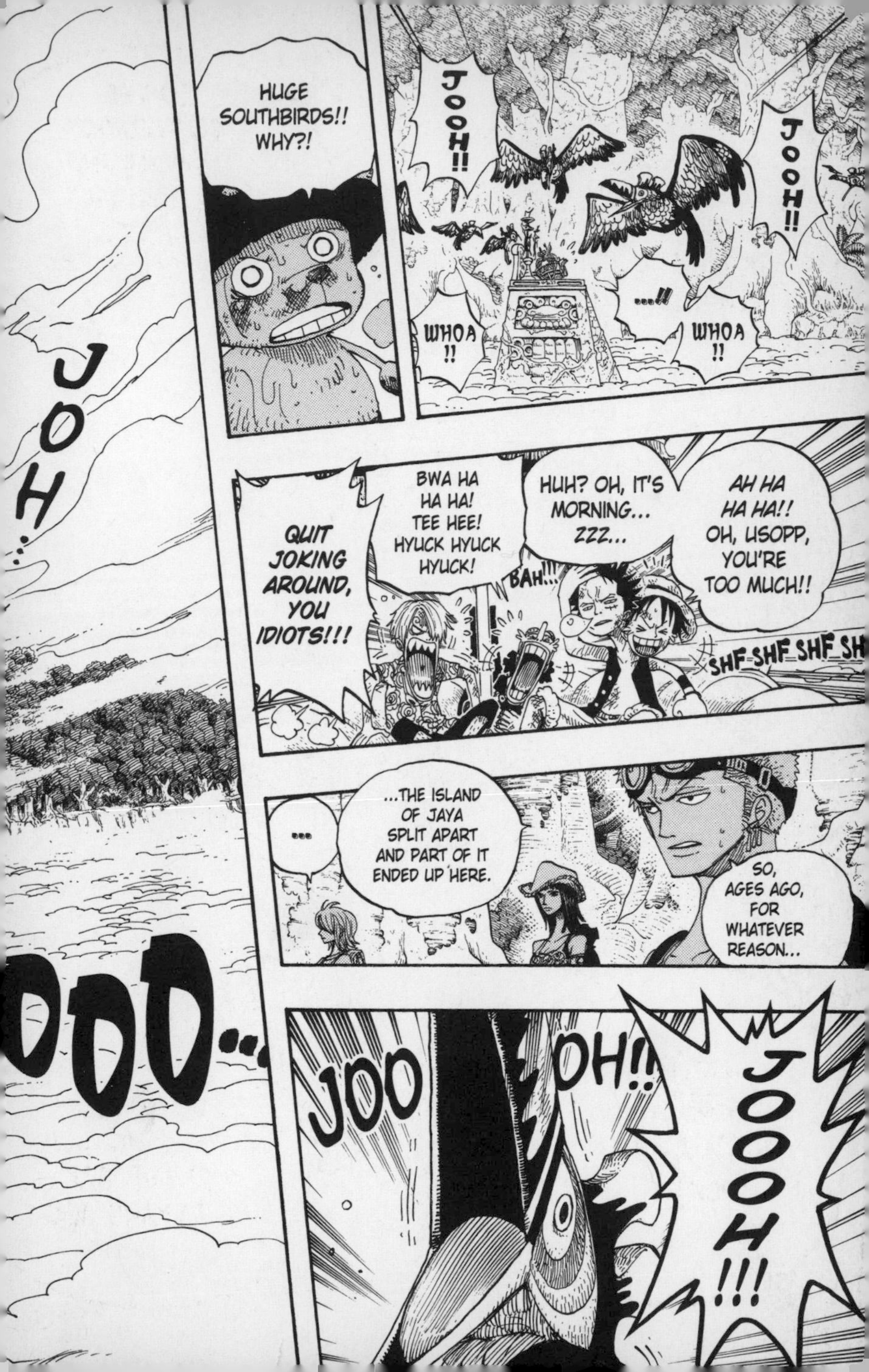
JOOH!!
JOOH!!
...!!
WHOA !!
WHOA !!
HUGE SOUTHBIRDS!! WHY?!
AH HA HA HA!! OH, USOPP, YOU'RE TOO MUCH!!
HUH? OH, IT'S MORNING... ZZZ...
BWA HA HA HA! TEE HEE! HYUCK HYUCK HYUCK!
BAH!!
SHF SHF SHF SH
QUIT JOKING AROUND, YOU IDIOTS!!!
SO, AGES AGO, FOR WHATEVER REASON...
...THE ISLAND OF JAYA SPLIT APART AND PART OF IT ENDED UP HERE.
...
JOOOOH!!!
JOO OH!!
JOH...
ODDD...

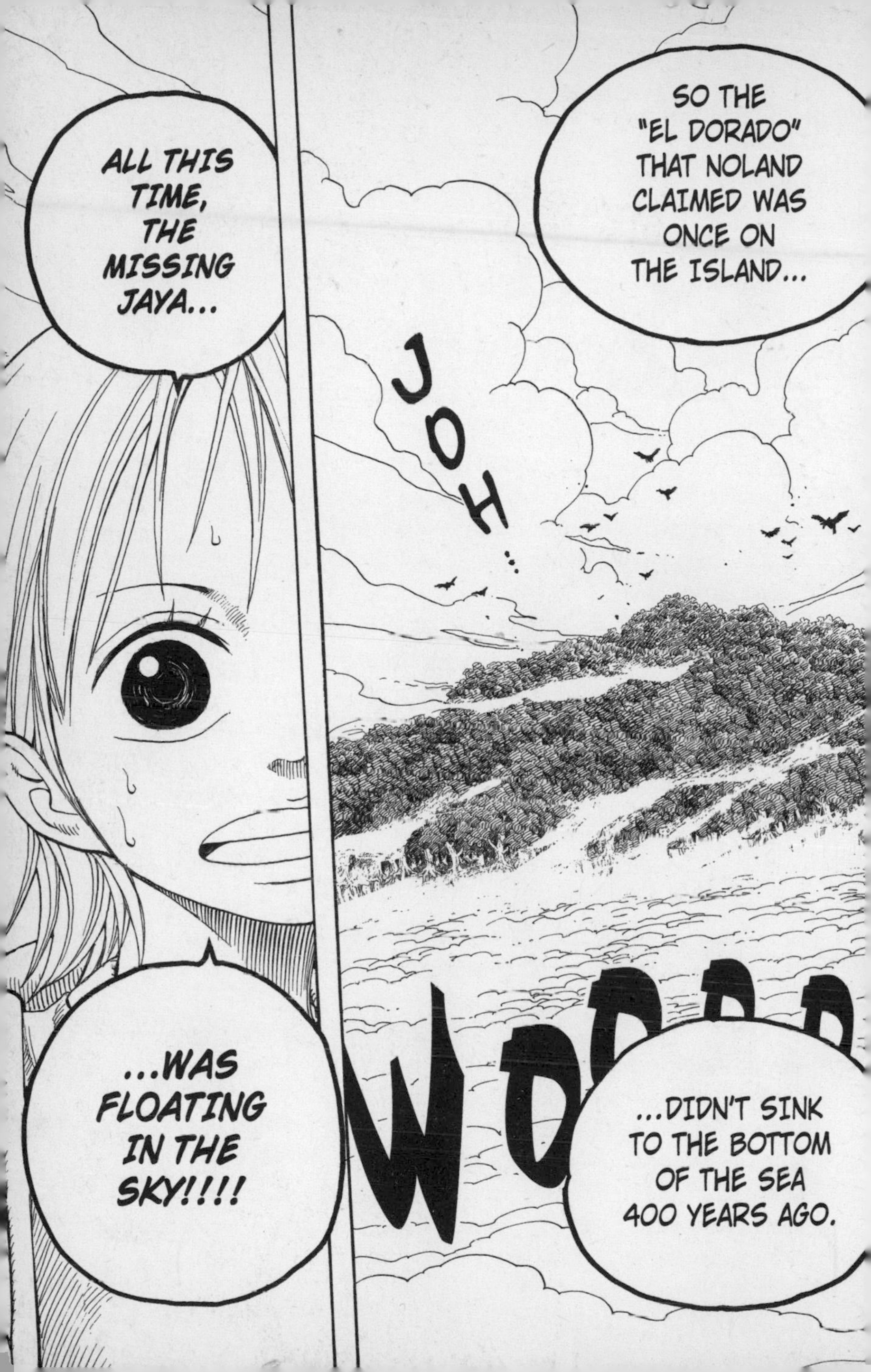
SO THE "EL DORADO" THAT NOLAND CLAIMED WAS ONCE ON THE ISLAND...
JOH...
...DIDN'T SINK TO THE BOTTOM OF THE SEA 400 YEARS AGO.
ALL THIS TIME, THE MISSING JAYA...
...WAS FLOATING IN THE SKY!!!!

Question Corner
SBS

...A GREAT ADVENTURE!!

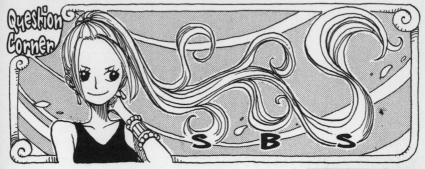

Q: Good morning. Err… In volume 25, chapter 235, page 174, I accidentally read the word "Roman!!!" (Adventure) as "marron!!!!" (chestnut). I'm sure many other readers saw this as well. (Cricket's head is shaped like a chestnut, after all.) Would you consider changing it to Marron?

--Mari Yaguchi Fan Club Captain, Bocchin

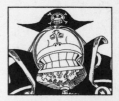

A: No. What are you saying? Cripes. You understand the theme of the Jaya arc, don't you? It's all about "a man's adventure"!!! Geez!! He's cool, that man. How can you even think of marron? It's totally different. Plus, in that arc, not one mention was made of marron or chestnuts. Let me make that clear. The Jaya arc is about "a marr--" I mean, "a man's adventure"!!!

Q: Hello, Oda Sensei! I was reading a book on mythology at the library recently, and I saw a Chinese monkey monster named "Shoujou." Is that where you got the name for your Shoujou? I got so excited. What's the story?

--Fujiko

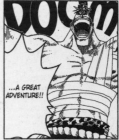

A: Hmm. That's originally the source, but in Japan, the kanji is different. Although it can refer to that same mythological beast, more commonly "shoujou" refers to an orangutan. So that's why I used the name. That's also how I got the name "Masira." In Japan, monkeys were once called "masira." So I used that for a name as well.

Chapter 252:
JUNCTION

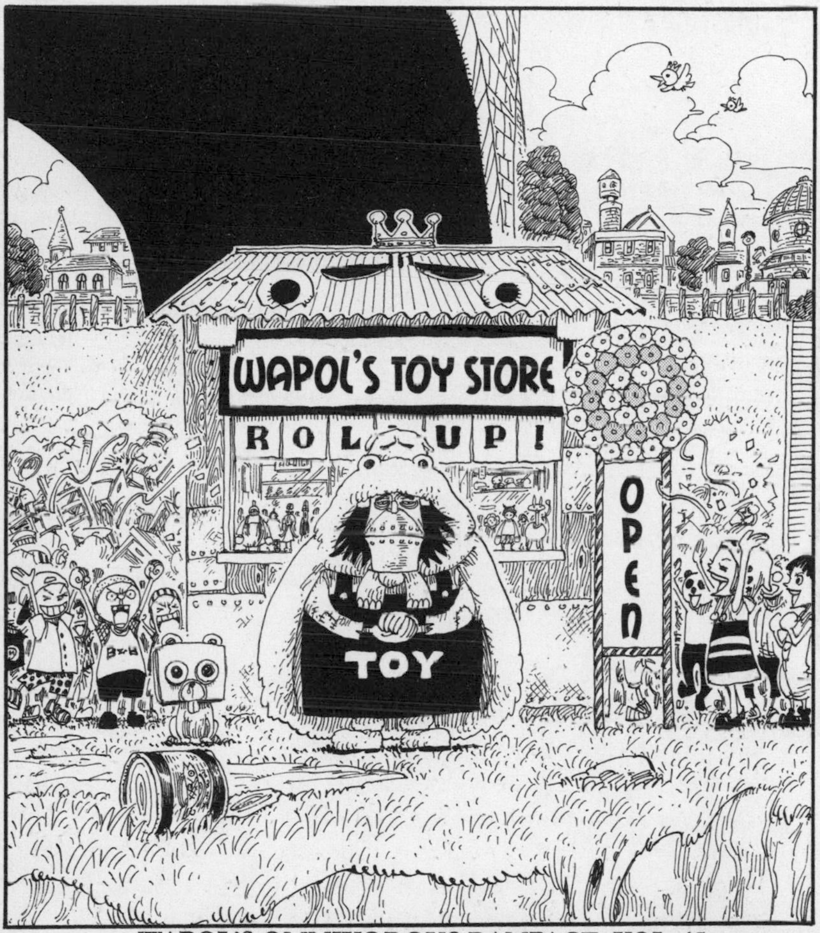
WAPOL'S TOY STORE
ROLL UP!
OPEN
TOY

WAPOL'S OMNIVOROUS RAMPAGE, VOL. 15:
"WAPOL'S TOY STORE IS OFFICIALLY OPEN
FOR BUSINESS!"

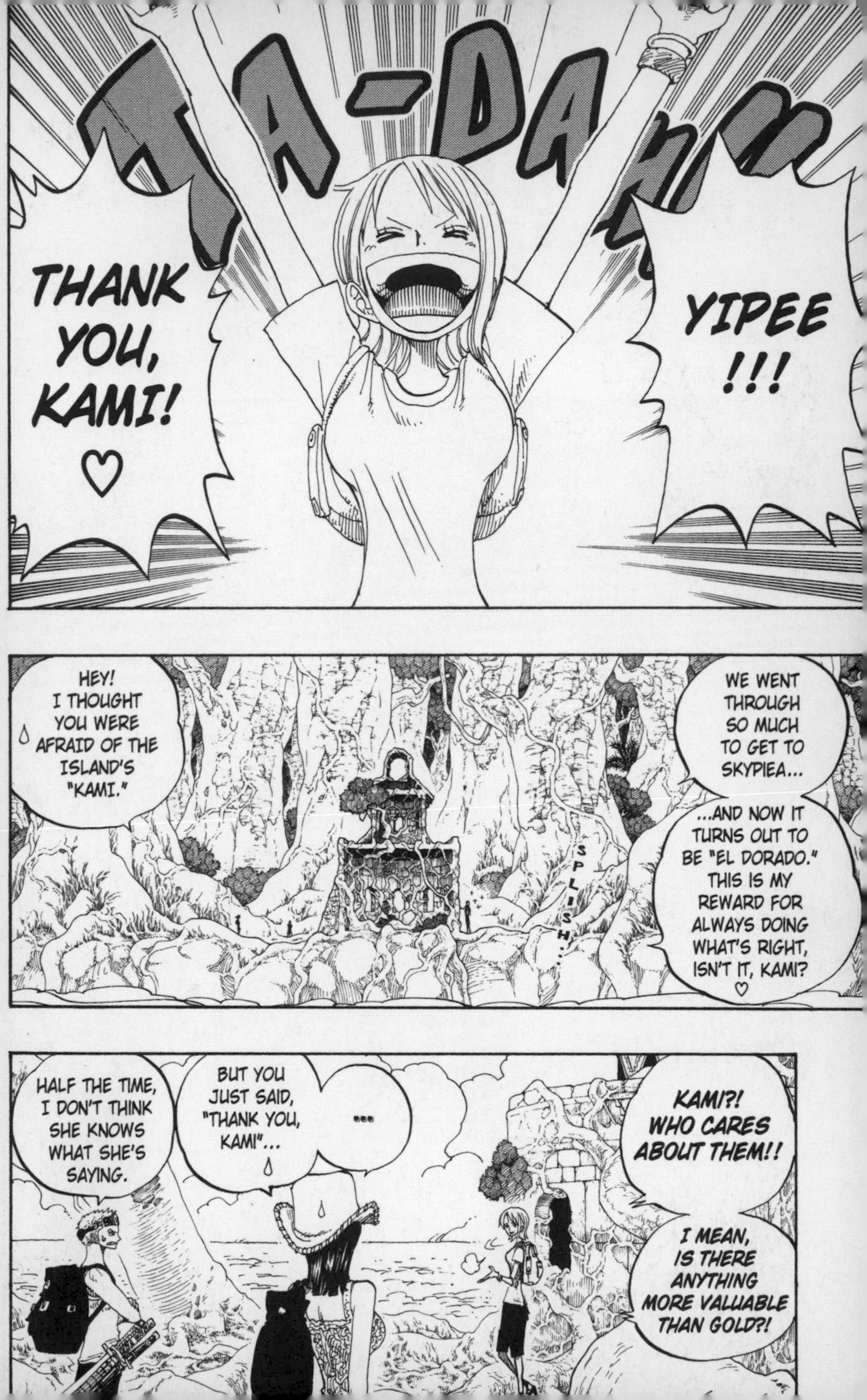
TA-DAMM
YIPEE !!!
THANK YOU, KAMI! ♡
WE WENT THROUGH SO MUCH TO GET TO SKYPIEA...
...AND NOW IT TURNS OUT TO BE "EL DORADO." THIS IS MY REWARD FOR ALWAYS DOING WHAT'S RIGHT, ISN'T IT, KAMI? ♡
SPLISH...
HEY! I THOUGHT YOU WERE AFRAID OF THE ISLAND'S "KAMI."
KAMI?! WHO CARES ABOUT THEM!!
I MEAN, IS THERE ANYTHING MORE VALUABLE THAN GOLD?!
...
BUT YOU JUST SAID, "THANK YOU, KAMI"...
HALF THE TIME, I DON'T THINK SHE KNOWS WHAT SHE'S SAYING.

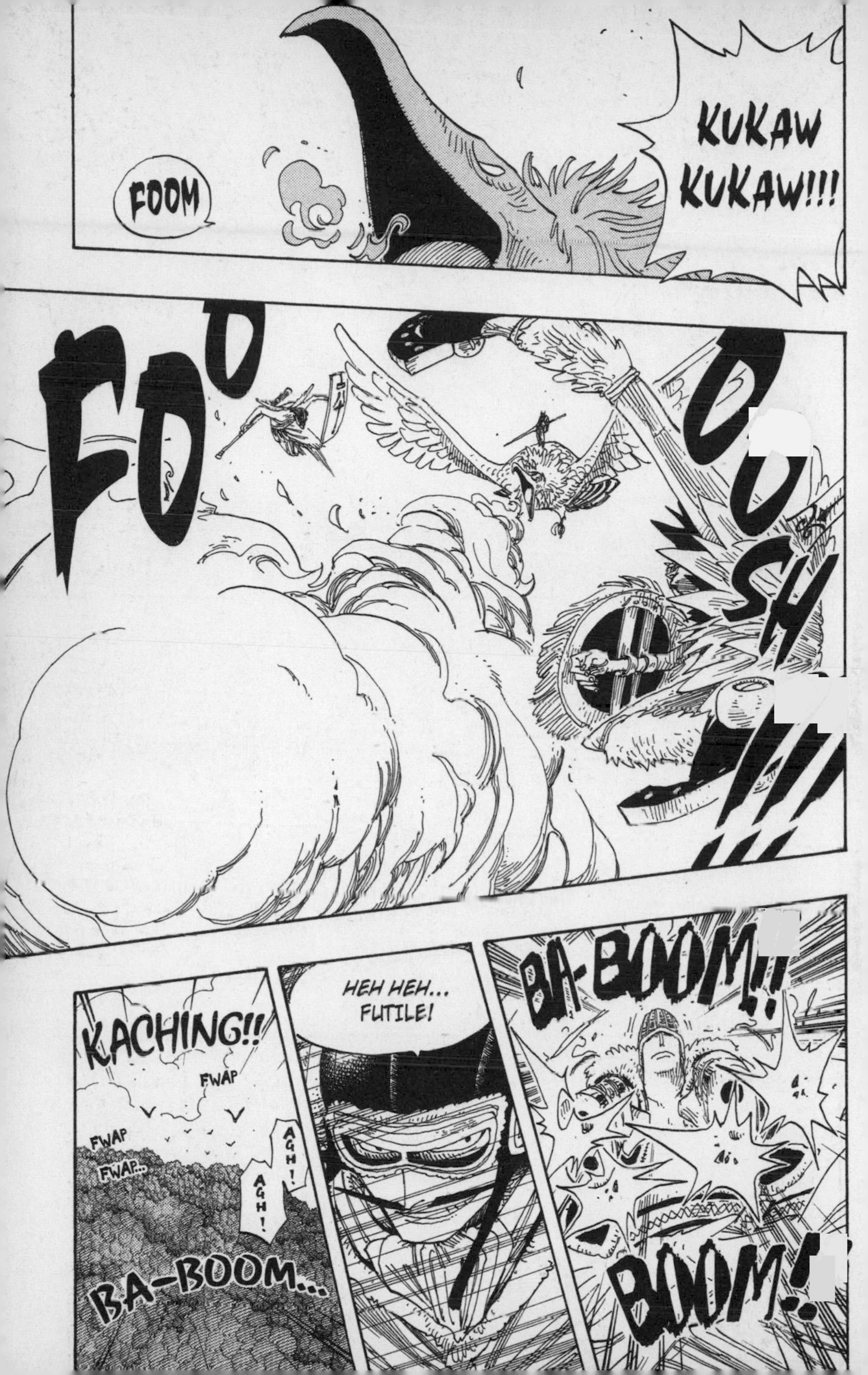
KUKAW KUKAW!!!
FOOM
FOOOOSH!!
BA-BOOM!!
BOOM!!
HEH HEH... FUTILE!
AGH!
AGH!
KACHING!!
FWAP
FWAP
FWAP...
BA-BOOM...

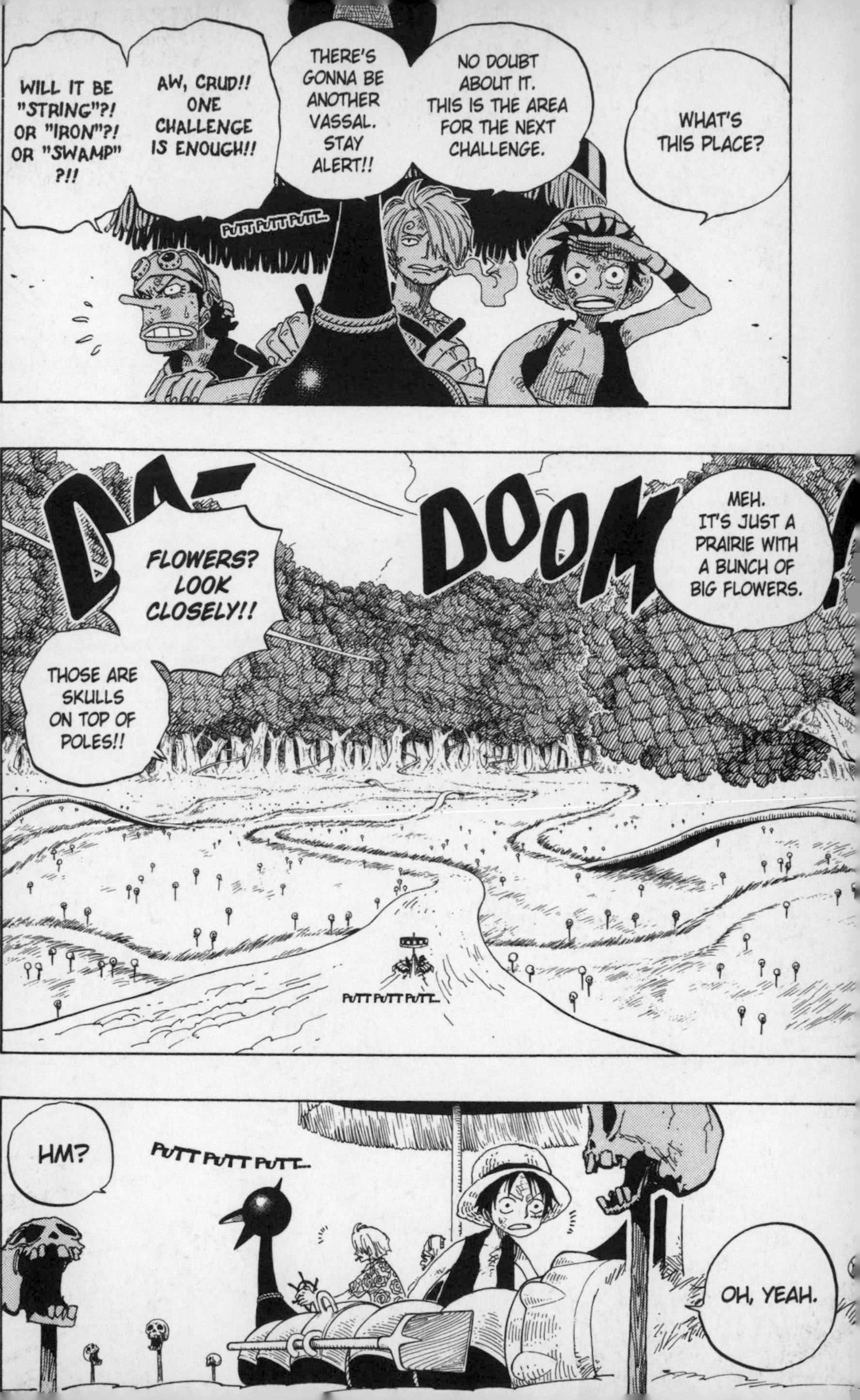
WHAT'S THIS PLACE?
NO DOUBT ABOUT IT. THIS IS THE AREA FOR THE NEXT CHALLENGE.
THERE'S GONNA BE ANOTHER VASSAL. STAY ALERT!!
AW, CRUD!! ONE CHALLENGE IS ENOUGH!!
WILL IT BE "STRING"?! OR "IRON"?! OR "SWAMP"?!!
PUTT PUTT PUTT...
DA-DOOM!
MEH. IT'S JUST A PRAIRIE WITH A BUNCH OF BIG FLOWERS.
FLOWERS? LOOK CLOSELY!!
THOSE ARE SKULLS ON TOP OF POLES!!
PUTT PUTT PUTT...
OH, YEAH.
PUTT PUTT PUTT...
HM?

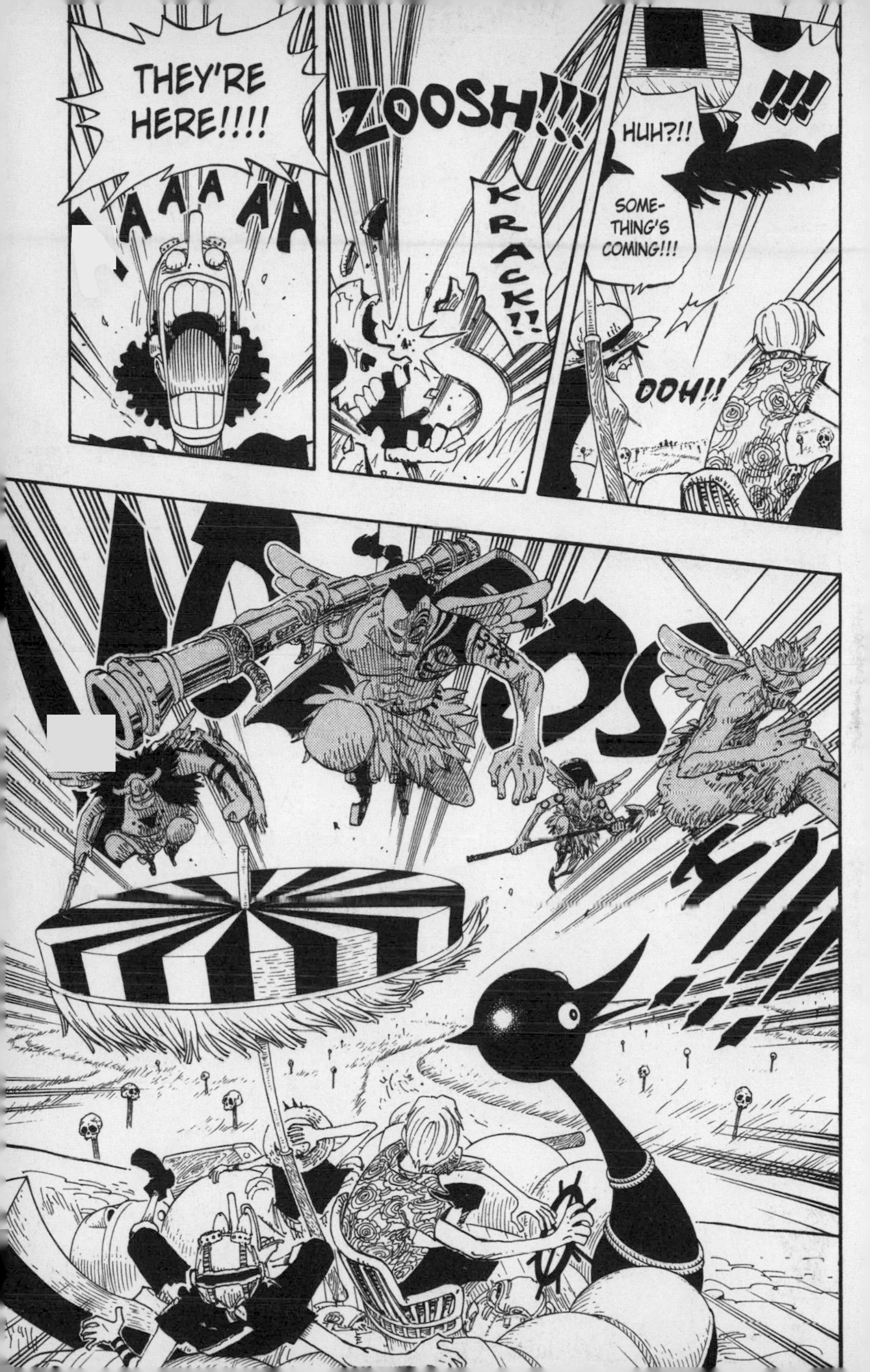
!!!
HUH?!!
SOME-
THING'S
COMING!!!
OOH!!
ZOOSH!!!
KRACK!!
THEY'RE
HERE!!!!
AAAA

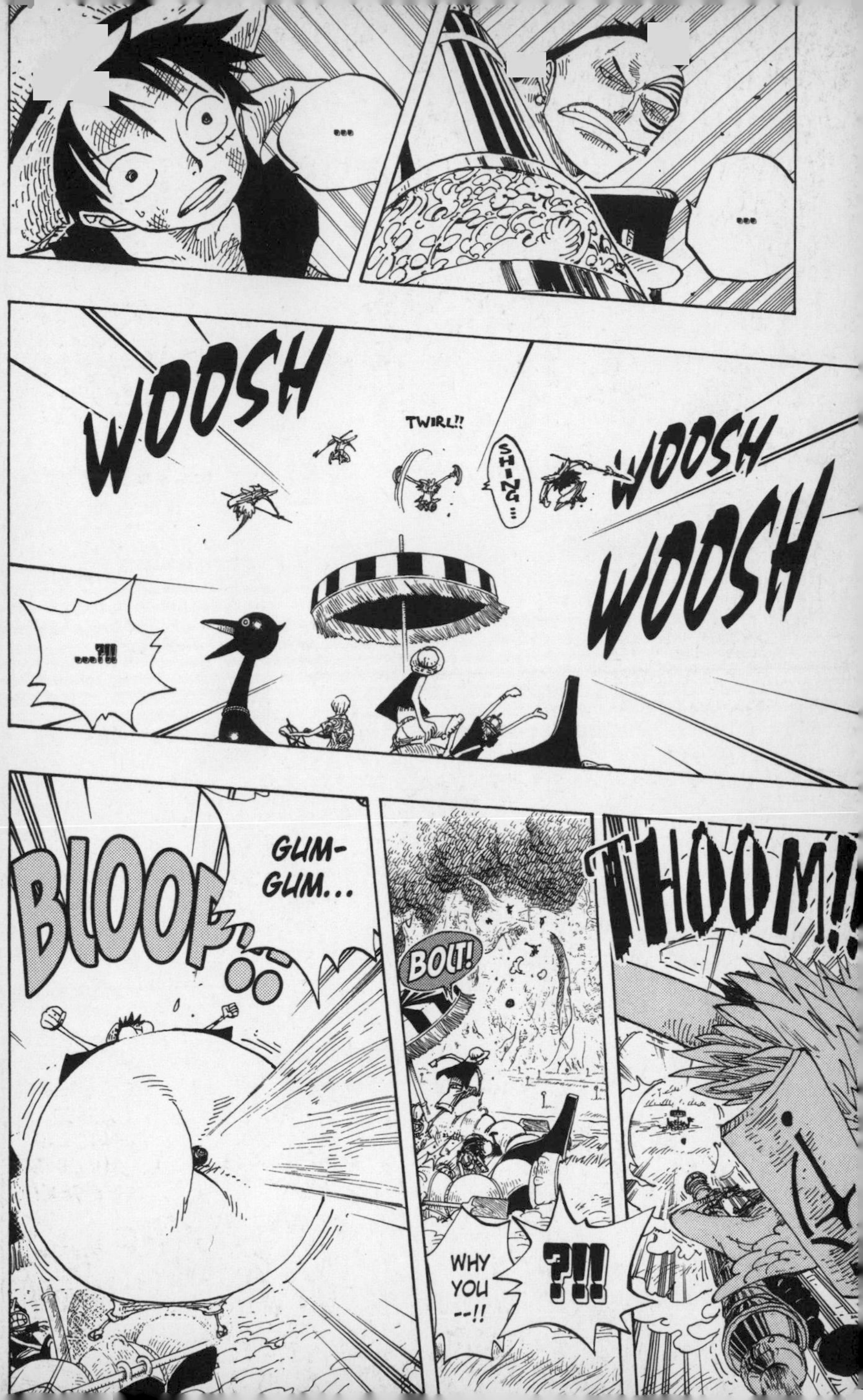
...
...
WOOSH
WOOSH
SHING...
TWIRL!!
WOOSH
...?!!
THOOM!!
BOLT!
?!!
WHY YOU --!!
GUM-GUM...
BLOOF...

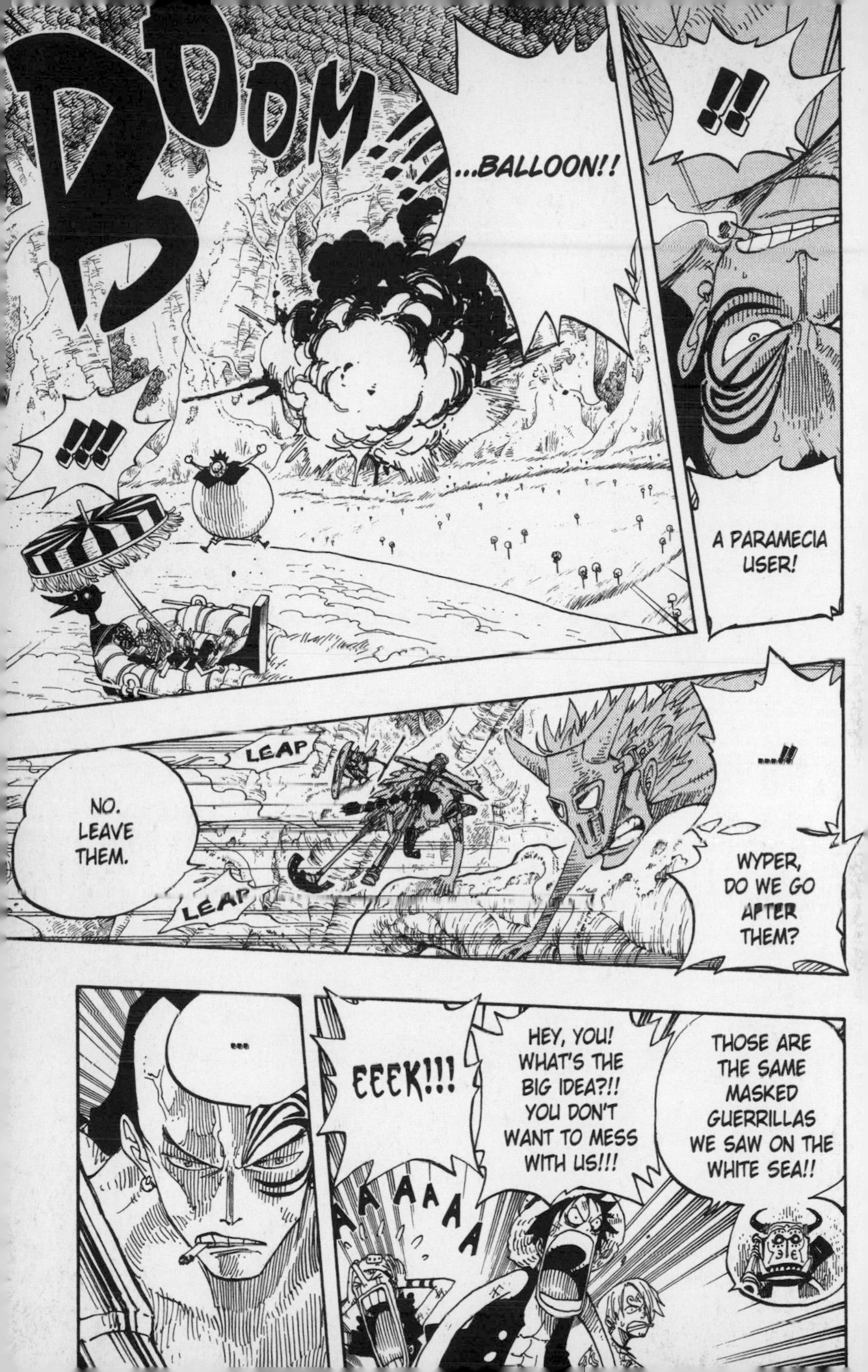
!!
A PARAMECIA USER!
BOOM!!
...BALLOON!!
!!!
...!!
WYPER, DO WE GO AFTER THEM?
LEAP
NO. LEAVE THEM.
LEAP
THOSE ARE THE SAME MASKED GUERRILLAS WE SAW ON THE WHITE SEA!!
HEY, YOU! WHAT'S THE BIG IDEA?!! YOU DON'T WANT TO MESS WITH US!!!
EEEK!!!
AAAAAA
...

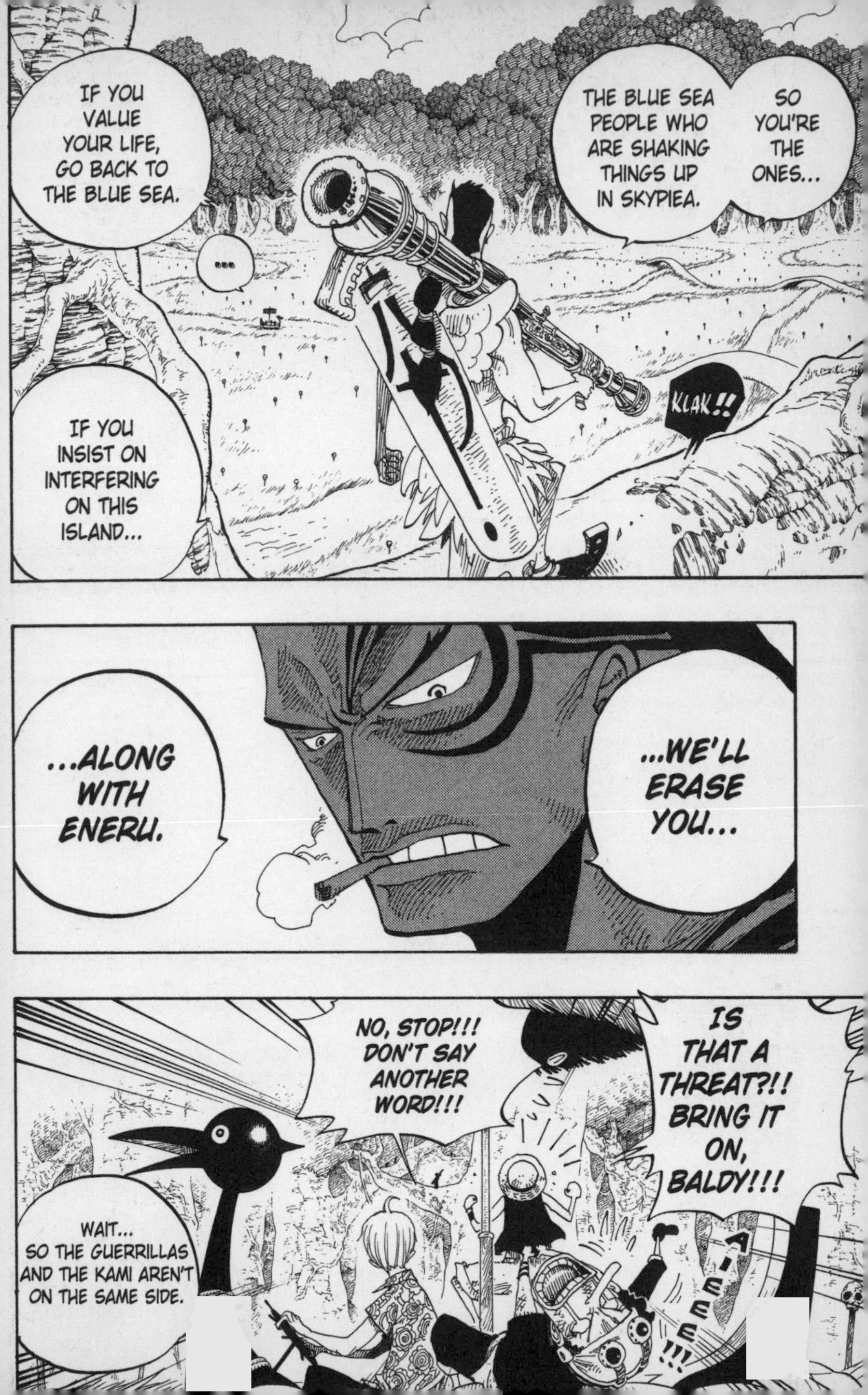
SO YOU'RE THE ONES...
THE BLUE SEA PEOPLE WHO ARE SHAKING THINGS UP IN SKYPIEA.
KLAK!!
...
IF YOU VALUE YOUR LIFE, GO BACK TO THE BLUE SEA.
IF YOU INSIST ON INTERFERING ON THIS ISLAND...
...WE'LL ERASE YOU...
...ALONG WITH ENERU.
IS THAT A THREAT?!! BRING IT ON, BALDY!!!
NO, STOP!!! DON'T SAY ANOTHER WORD!!!
AIEEE!!!
WAIT... SO THE GUERRILLAS AND THE KAMI AREN'T ON THE SAME SIDE.

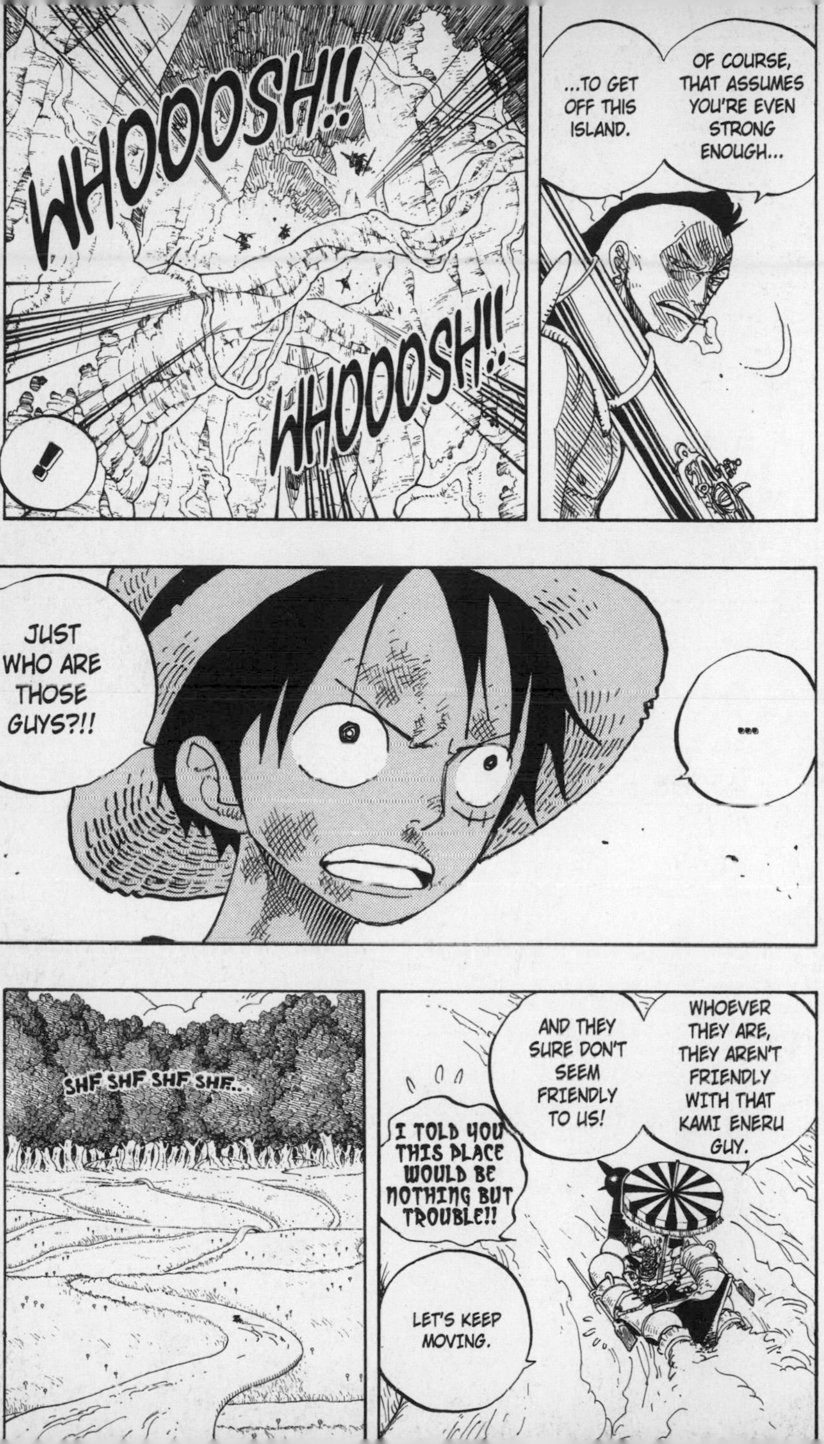
OF COURSE, THAT ASSUMES YOU'RE EVEN STRONG ENOUGH...
...TO GET OFF THIS ISLAND.
WHOOOSH!!
WHOOOSH!!
!
...
JUST WHO ARE THOSE GUYS?!!
WHOEVER THEY ARE, THEY AREN'T FRIENDLY WITH THAT KAMI ENERU GUY.
AND THEY SURE DON'T SEEM FRIENDLY TO US!
I TOLD YOU THIS PLACE WOULD BE NOTHING BUT TROUBLE!!
LET'S KEEP MOVING.
SHF SHF SHF SHF...

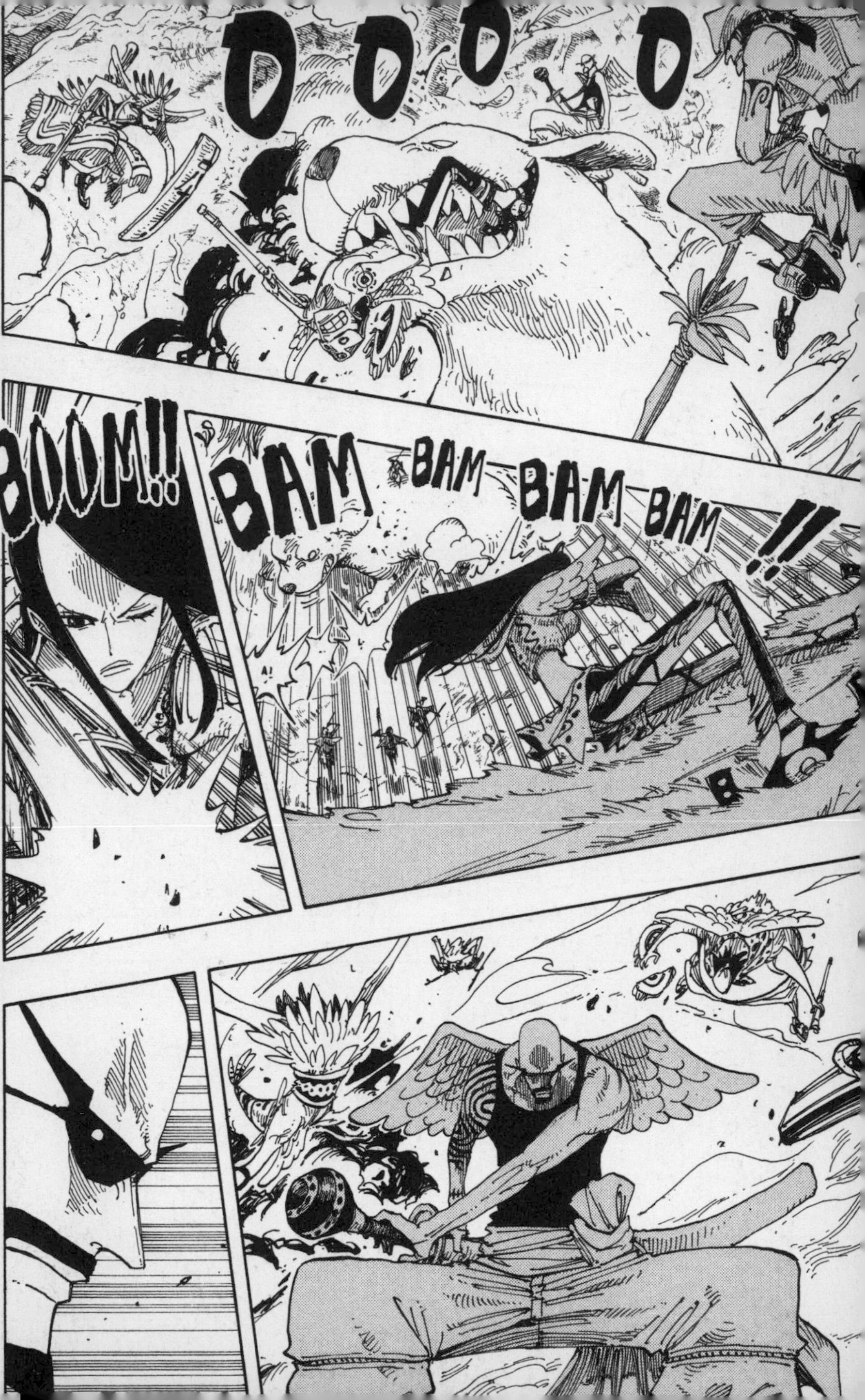

DDDD
BAM BAM BAM BAM!!
BOOM!!

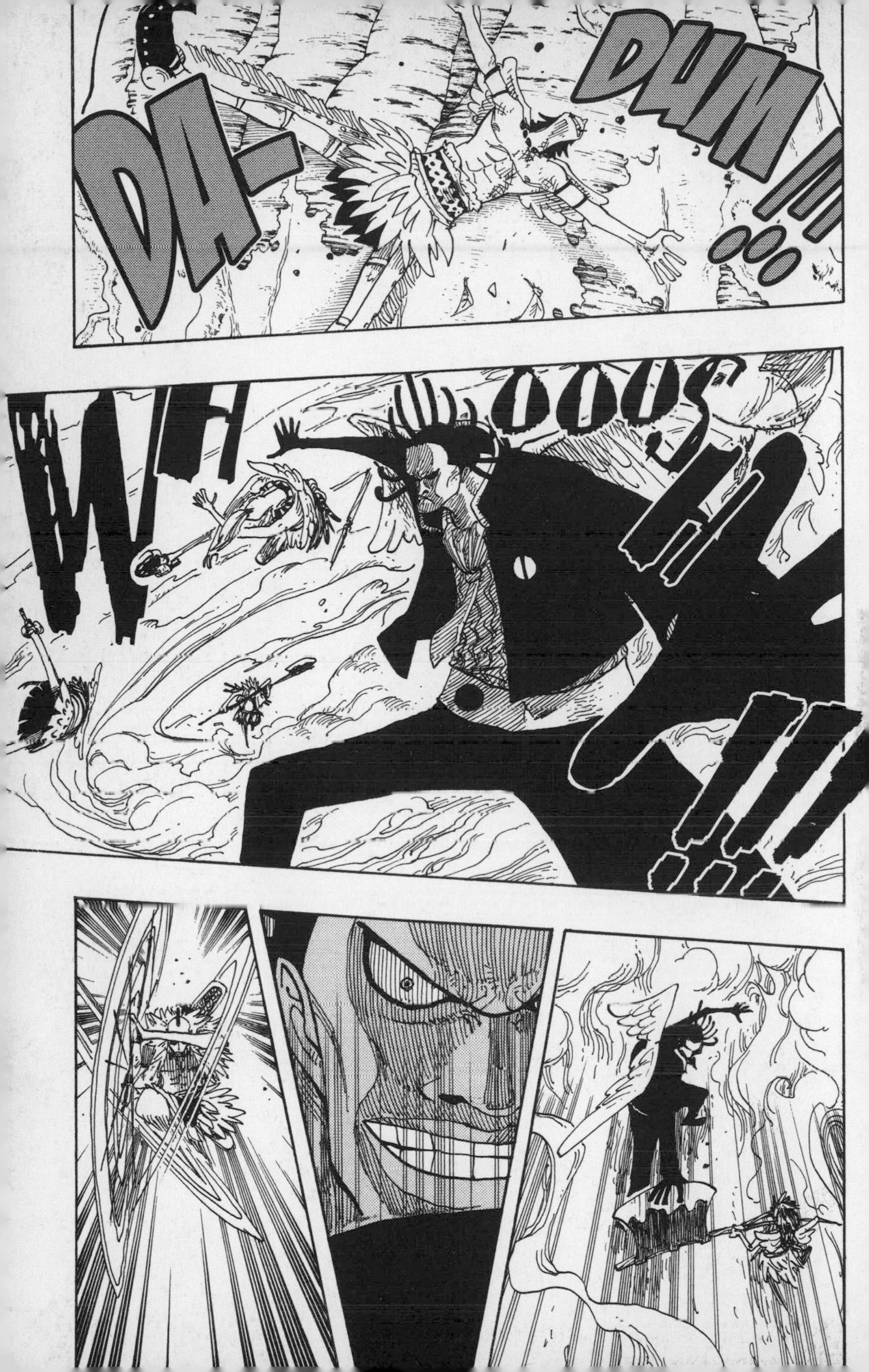
DA-DUM!!...
WHOOOSH!!!...

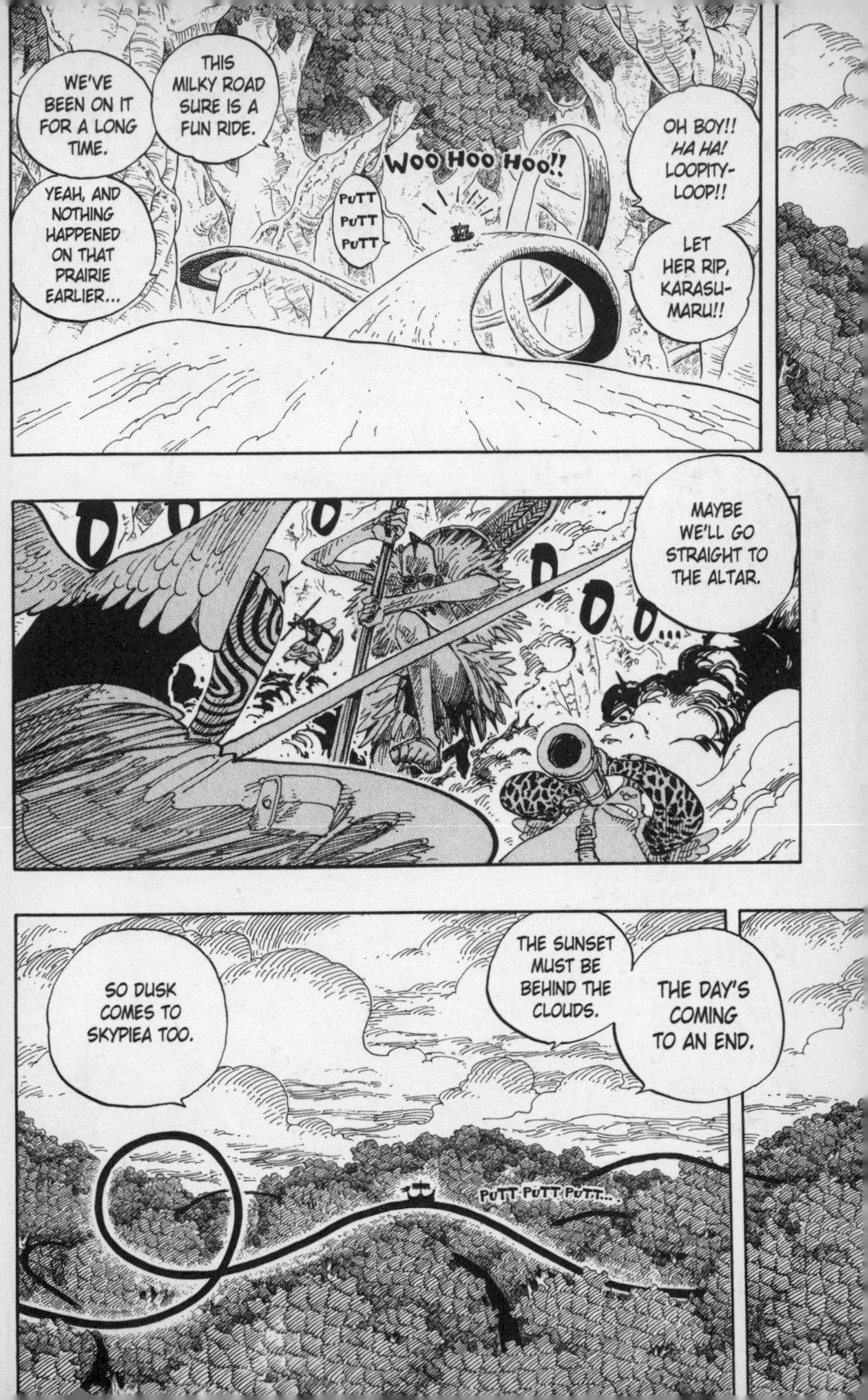
OH BOY!! HA HA! LOOPITY-LOOP!!
LET HER RIP, KARASU-MARU!!
WOO HOO HOO!!
THIS MILKY ROAD SURE IS A FUN RIDE.
PUTT PUTT PUTT
WE'VE BEEN ON IT FOR A LONG TIME.
YEAH, AND NOTHING HAPPENED ON THAT PRAIRIE EARLIER...
MAYBE WE'LL GO STRAIGHT TO THE ALTAR.
DOO...
THE DAY'S COMING TO AN END.
THE SUNSET MUST BE BEHIND THE CLOUDS.
SO DUSK COMES TO SKYPIEA TOO.
PUTT PUTT PUTT...

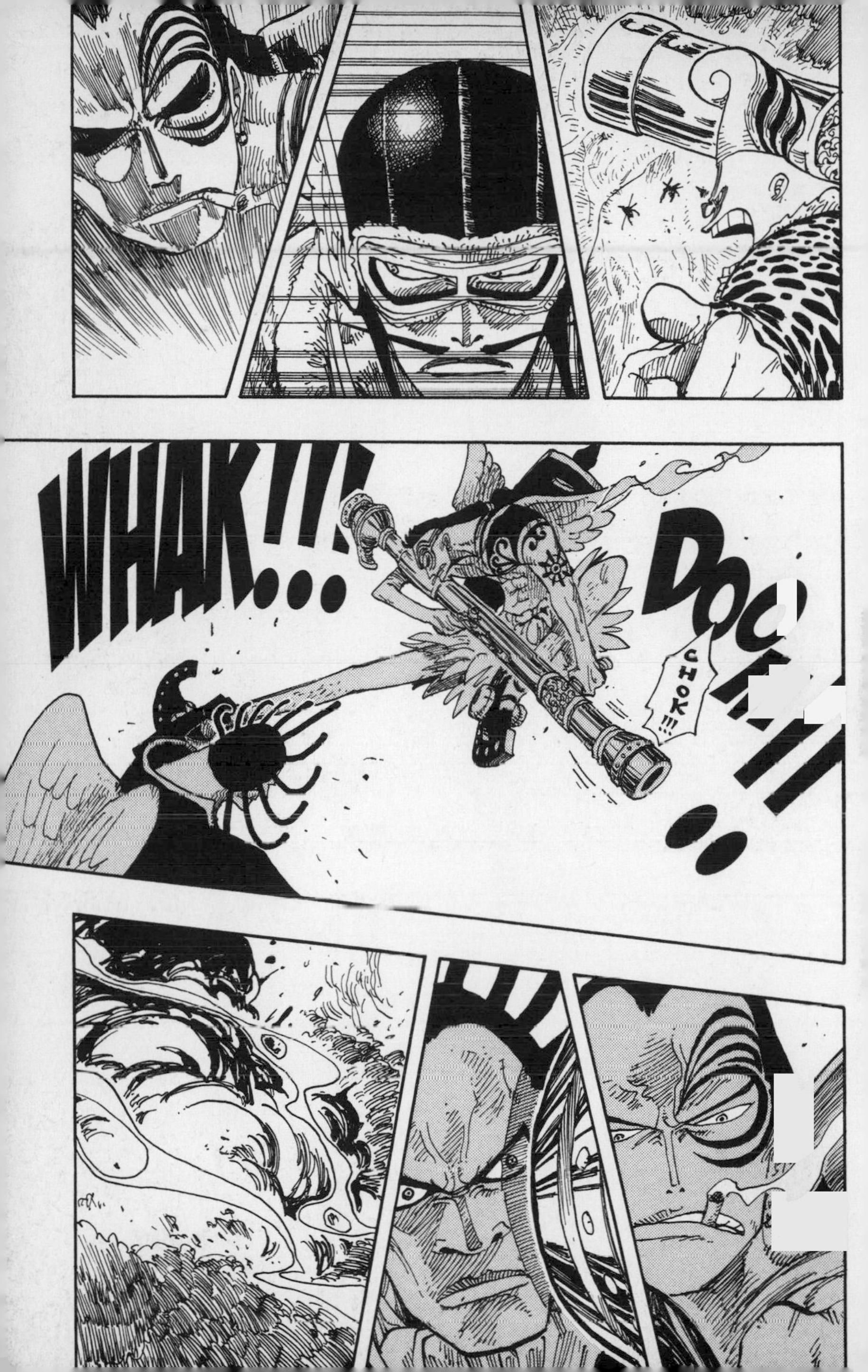
DOOM!!
CHOK!!!
WHAK!!!...

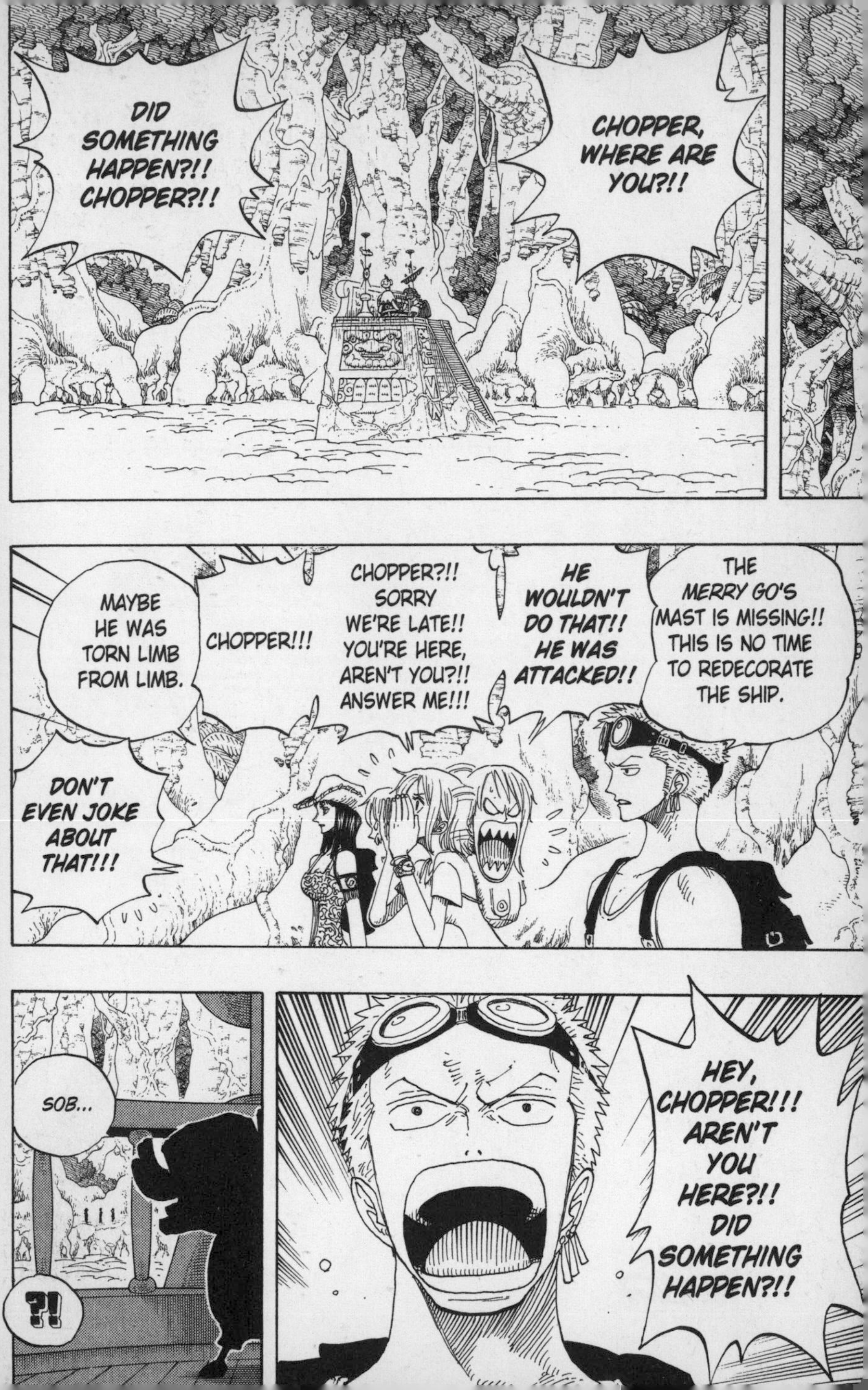
CHOPPER, WHERE ARE YOU?!!
DID SOMETHING HAPPEN?!! CHOPPER?!!
THE MERRY GO'S MAST IS MISSING!! THIS IS NO TIME TO REDECORATE THE SHIP.
HE WOULDN'T DO THAT!! HE WAS ATTACKED!!
CHOPPER?!! SORRY WE'RE LATE!! YOU'RE HERE, AREN'T YOU?!! ANSWER ME!!!
CHOPPER!!!
MAYBE HE WAS TORN LIMB FROM LIMB.
DON'T EVEN JOKE ABOUT THAT!!!
HEY, CHOPPER!!! AREN'T YOU HERE?!! DID SOMETHING HAPPEN?!!
SOB...
?!

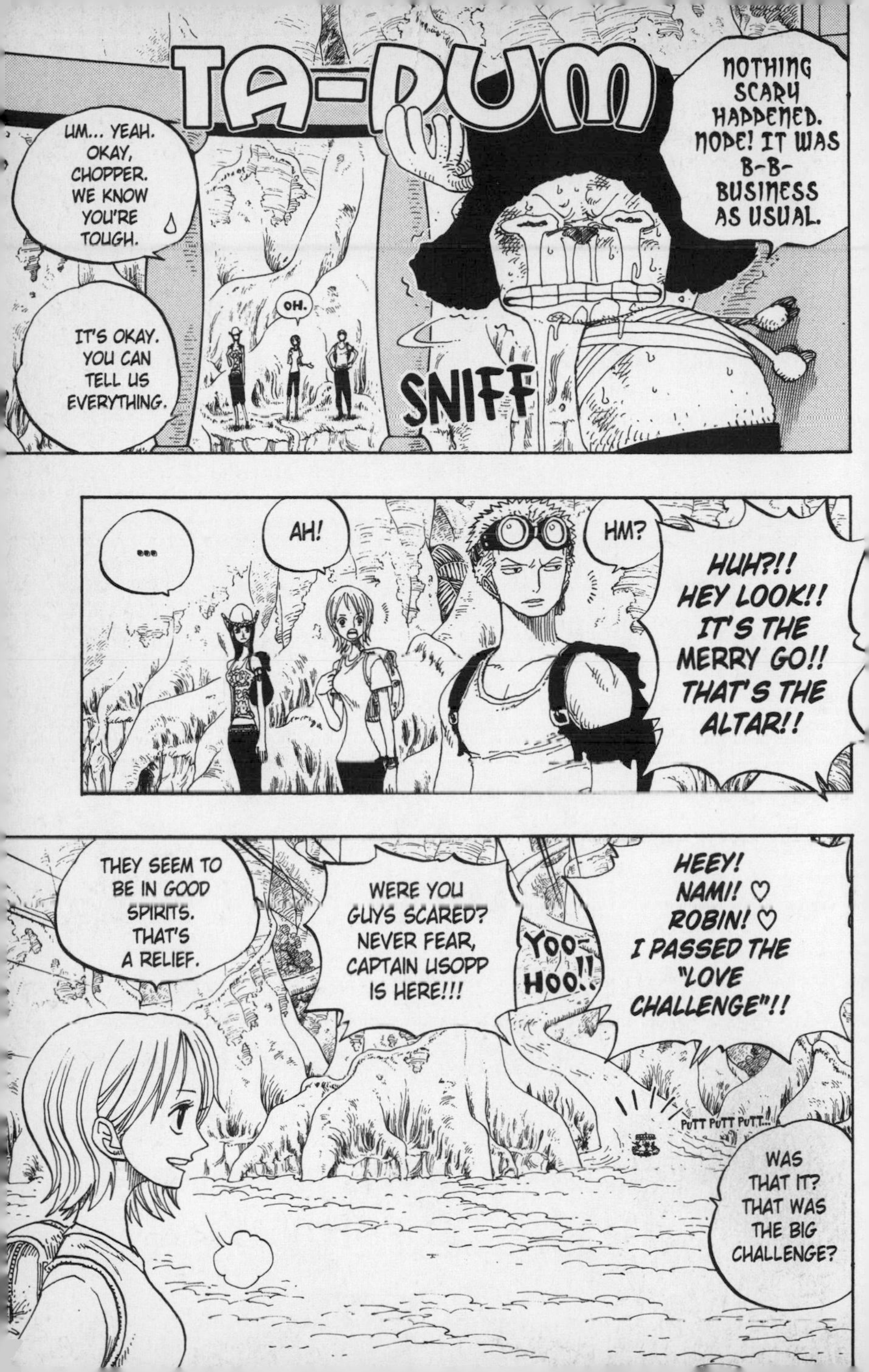
TA-DUM
NOTHING SCARY HAPPENED. NOPE! IT WAS B-B-BUSINESS AS USUAL.
SNIFF
UM... YEAH. OKAY, CHOPPER. WE KNOW YOU'RE TOUGH.
OH.
IT'S OKAY. YOU CAN TELL US EVERYTHING.
HUH?!! HEY LOOK!! IT'S THE MERRY GO!! THAT'S THE ALTAR!!
HM?
AH!
...
HEEY! NAMI! ♡ ROBIN! ♡ I PASSED THE "LOVE CHALLENGE"!!
YOO-HOO!!
WERE YOU GUYS SCARED? NEVER FEAR, CAPTAIN USOPP IS HERE!!!
THEY SEEM TO BE IN GOOD SPIRITS. THAT'S A RELIEF.
PUTT PUTT PUTT...
WAS THAT IT? THAT WAS THE BIG CHALLENGE?

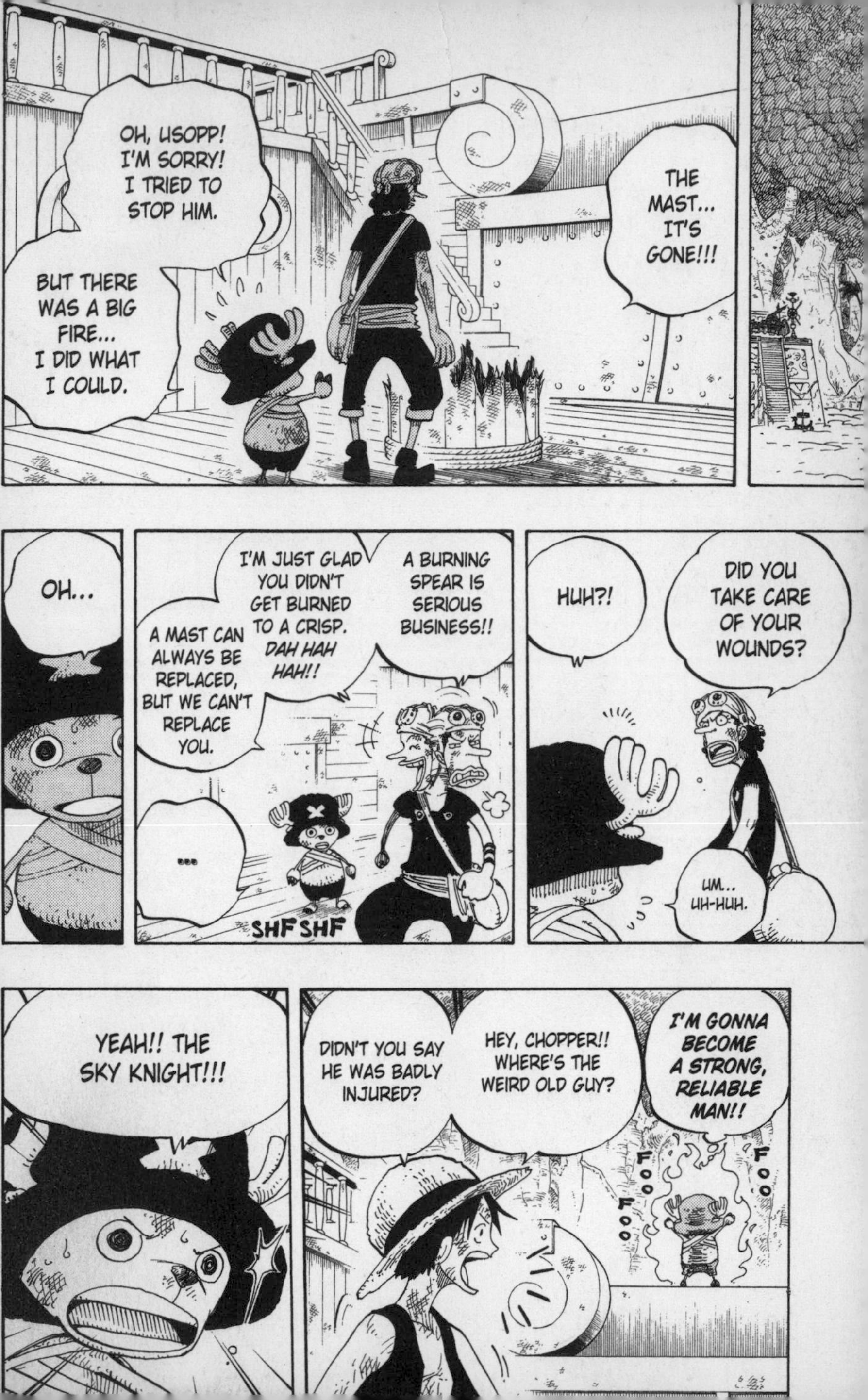
THE MAST... IT'S GONE!!!
OH, USOPP! I'M SORRY! I TRIED TO STOP HIM.
BUT THERE WAS A BIG FIRE... I DID WHAT I COULD.
DID YOU TAKE CARE OF YOUR WOUNDS?
HUH?!
UM... UH-HUH.
A BURNING SPEAR IS SERIOUS BUSINESS!!
I'M JUST GLAD YOU DIDN'T GET BURNED TO A CRISP. DAH HAH HAH!!
A MAST CAN ALWAYS BE REPLACED, BUT WE CAN'T REPLACE YOU.
...
SHF SHF
OH...
I'M GONNA BECOME A STRONG, RELIABLE MAN!!
FOO
FOO
FOO
FOO
HEY, CHOPPER!! WHERE'S THE WEIRD OLD GUY?
DIDN'T YOU SAY HE WAS BADLY INJURED?
YEAH!! THE SKY KNIGHT!!!

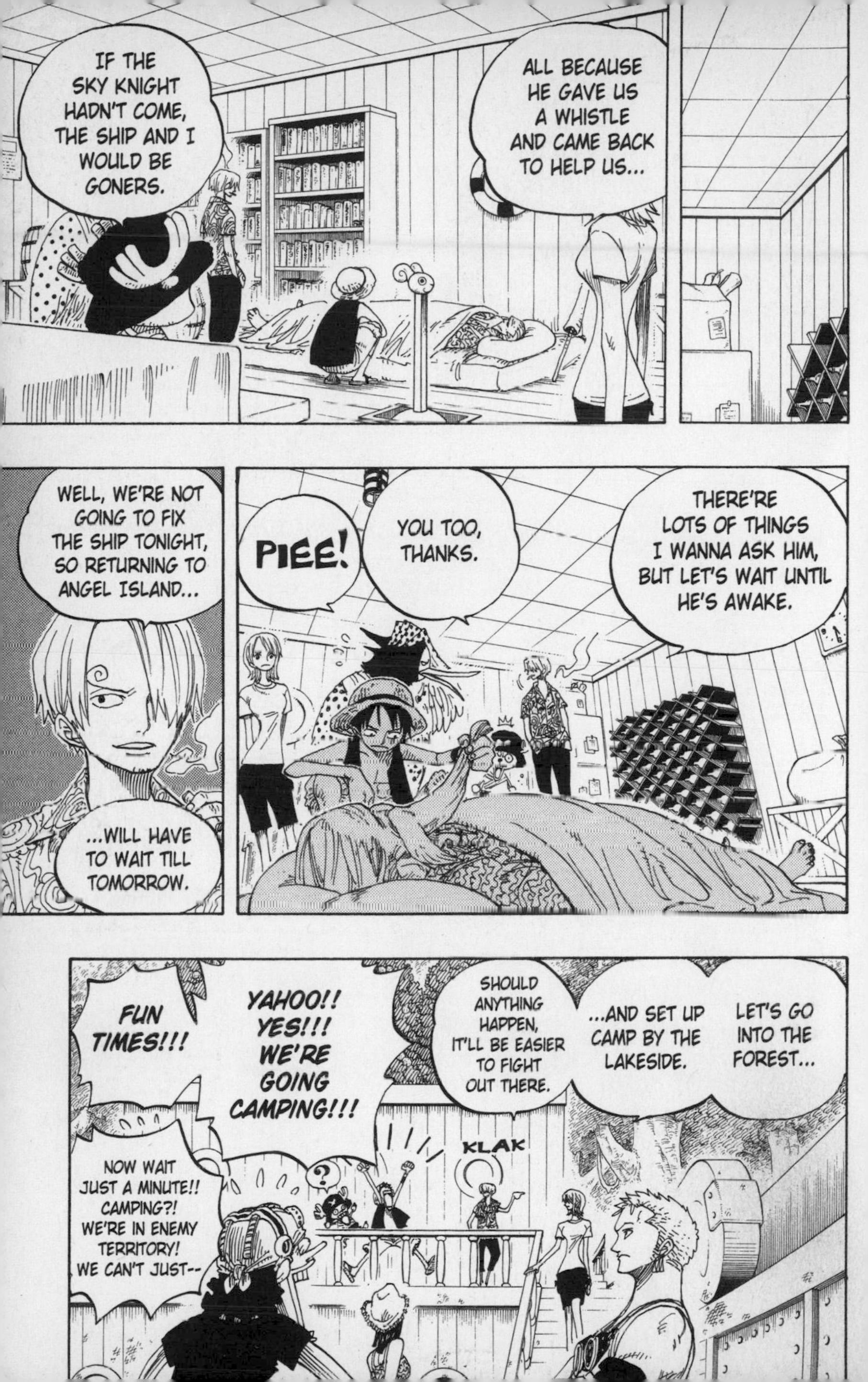
ALL BECAUSE HE GAVE US A WHISTLE AND CAME BACK TO HELP US...
IF THE SKY KNIGHT HADN'T COME, THE SHIP AND I WOULD BE GONERS.
THERE'RE LOTS OF THINGS I WANNA ASK HIM, BUT LET'S WAIT UNTIL HE'S AWAKE.
YOU TOO, THANKS.
PIEE!
WELL, WE'RE NOT GOING TO FIX THE SHIP TONIGHT, SO RETURNING TO ANGEL ISLAND...
...WILL HAVE TO WAIT TILL TOMORROW.
LET'S GO INTO THE FOREST...
...AND SET UP CAMP BY THE LAKESIDE.
SHOULD ANYTHING HAPPEN, IT'LL BE EASIER TO FIGHT OUT THERE.
KLAK
YAHOO!! YES!!! WE'RE GOING CAMPING!!!
FUN TIMES!!!
NOW WAIT JUST A MINUTE!! CAMPING?! WE'RE IN ENEMY TERRITORY! WE CAN'T JUST--

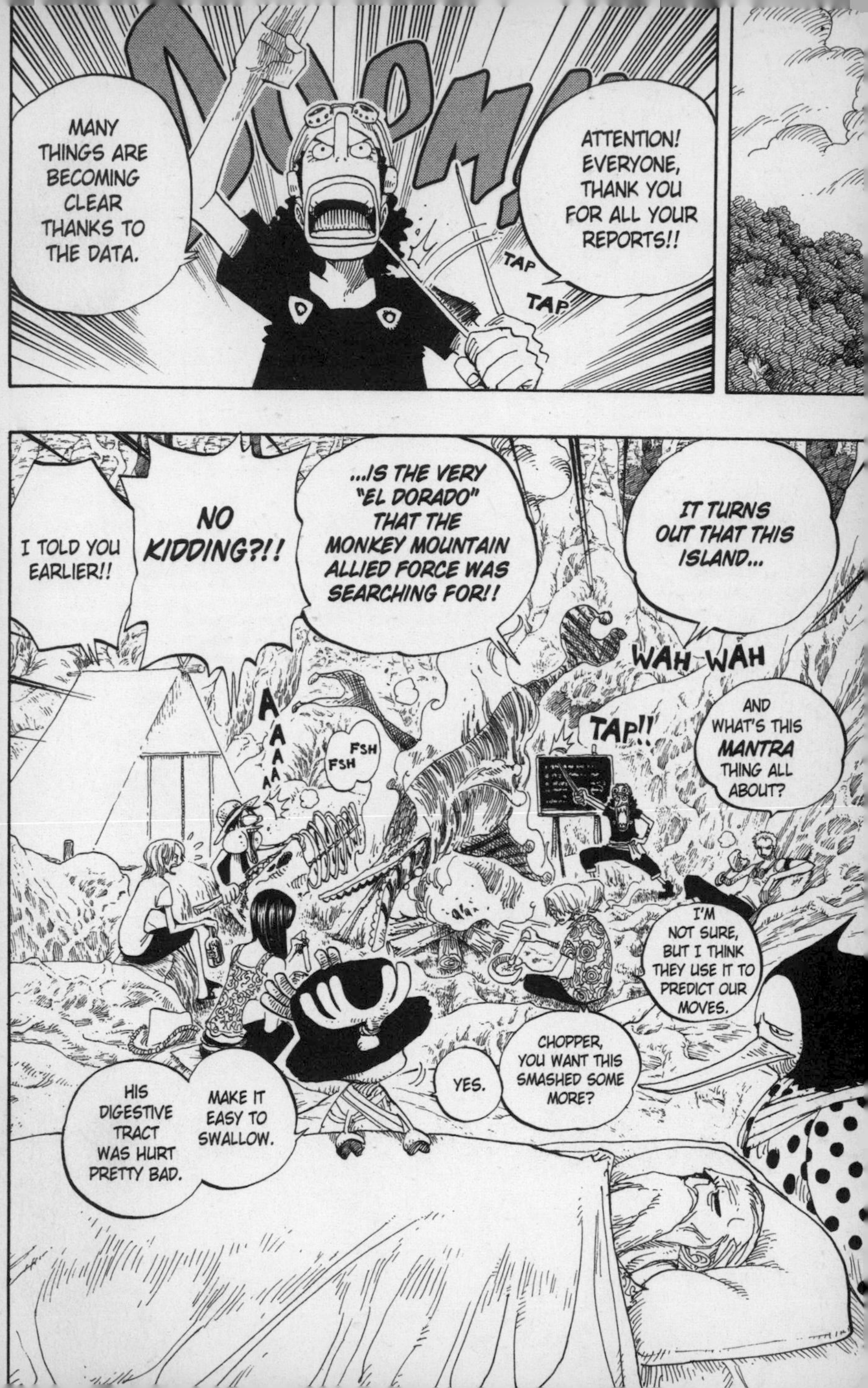
ATTENTION! EVERYONE, THANK YOU FOR ALL YOUR REPORTS!!
TAP
TAP
MANY THINGS ARE BECOMING CLEAR THANKS TO THE DATA.
IT TURNS OUT THAT THIS ISLAND...
...IS THE VERY "EL DORADO" THAT THE MONKEY MOUNTAIN ALLIED FORCE WAS SEARCHING FOR!!
NO KIDDING?!!
I TOLD YOU EARLIER!!
WAH WAH
AND WHAT'S THIS MANTRA THING ALL ABOUT?
TAP!!
FSH FSH
AAAAA
I'M NOT SURE, BUT I THINK THEY USE IT TO PREDICT OUR MOVES.
CHOPPER, YOU WANT THIS SMASHED SOME MORE?
YES.
MAKE IT EASY TO SWALLOW.
HIS DIGESTIVE TRACT WAS HURT PRETTY BAD.

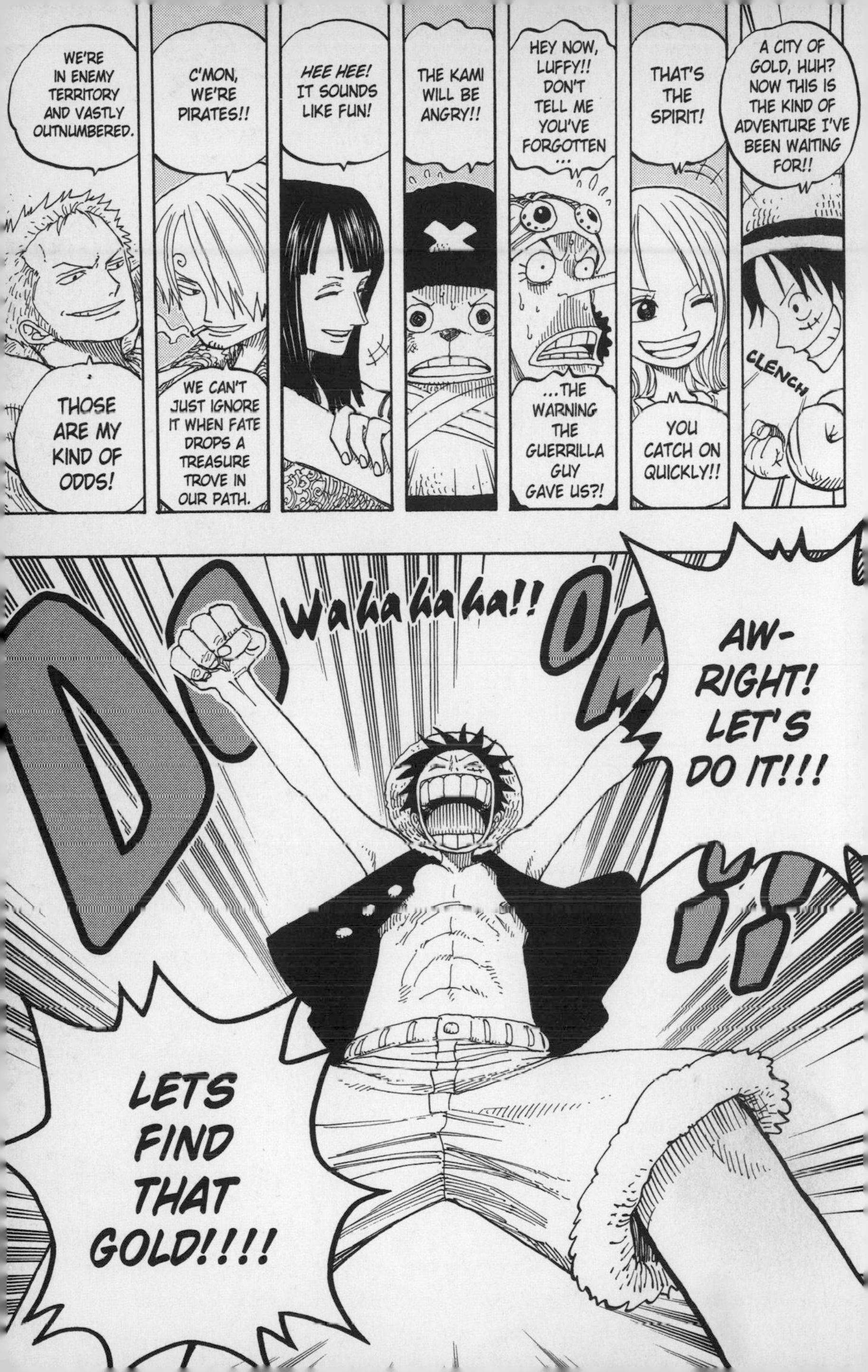
A CITY OF GOLD, HUH? NOW THIS IS THE KIND OF ADVENTURE I'VE BEEN WAITING FOR!!
CLENCH
THAT'S THE SPIRIT!
YOU CATCH ON QUICKLY!!
HEY NOW, LUFFY!! DON'T TELL ME YOU'VE FORGOTTEN ...
...THE WARNING THE GUERRILLA GUY GAVE US?!
THE KAMI WILL BE ANGRY!!
HEE HEE! IT SOUNDS LIKE FUN!
C'MON, WE'RE PIRATES!!
WE CAN'T JUST IGNORE IT WHEN FATE DROPS A TREASURE TROVE IN OUR PATH.
WE'RE IN ENEMY TERRITORY AND VASTLY OUTNUMBERED.
THOSE ARE MY KIND OF ODDS!
AW-RIGHT! LET'S DO IT!!!
Wahahaha!!
LETS FIND THAT GOLD!!!!

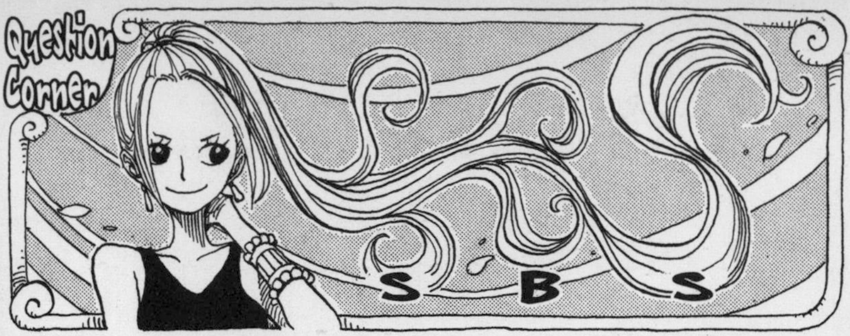
Question Corner
SBS

Q: Hello. I'm a great fan of Nami. And here's a question! The bracelet that Nami is wearing in volume 23 must be very valuable since she wears it even when she's bathing!! I checked through the whole volume and she's had it on since she left Coco Village. And before that, it looks like Nojiko was wearing it! Did Nojiko give it to Nami when she left Coco Village? Surely there's a tearful tale of sisterly love here…? (sob sob) Please tell me the truth behind this!!

--Bon-chan

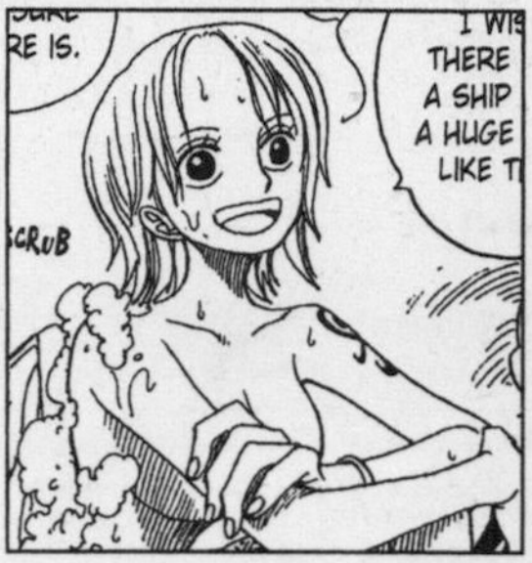
SCRUB

A: Yes. The bracelet. On the morning of their parting (volume 11), it was no longer on Nojiko's wrist. And on her shoulder are the tattoos that represent her foster parents, tangerines for Belle-Mère and a pinwheel for Genzo. And on her left wrist is the bracelet from her big sister. Although they aren't related by blood, Nami's family is always close, even across the great blue deep.

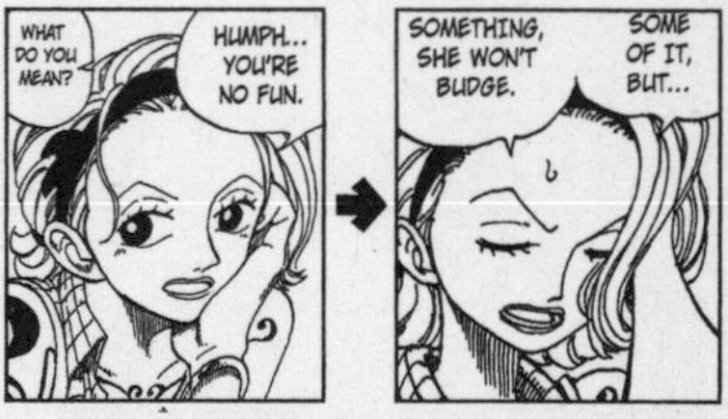
HUMPH... YOU'RE NO FUN.
WHAT DO YOU MEAN?
SOME OF IT, BUT...
SOMETHING, SHE WON'T BUDGE.

Q: This is out of blue, but I love coloring. Oda Sensei, please do more coloring pages of the seven main characters! (Lots and lots please!)

--Mitchi the sophomore

A: Oh! You like to color? Coloring is fun, isn't it? Speaking of which, we haven't had a coloring page lately. I'll add one--it's on page 166. And about that, the black parts on the image have already been filled in. Sorry but that's just how the file was created. If you have any requests for illustrations, please let me know. Until the next Question Corner

Chapter 253: VARSE

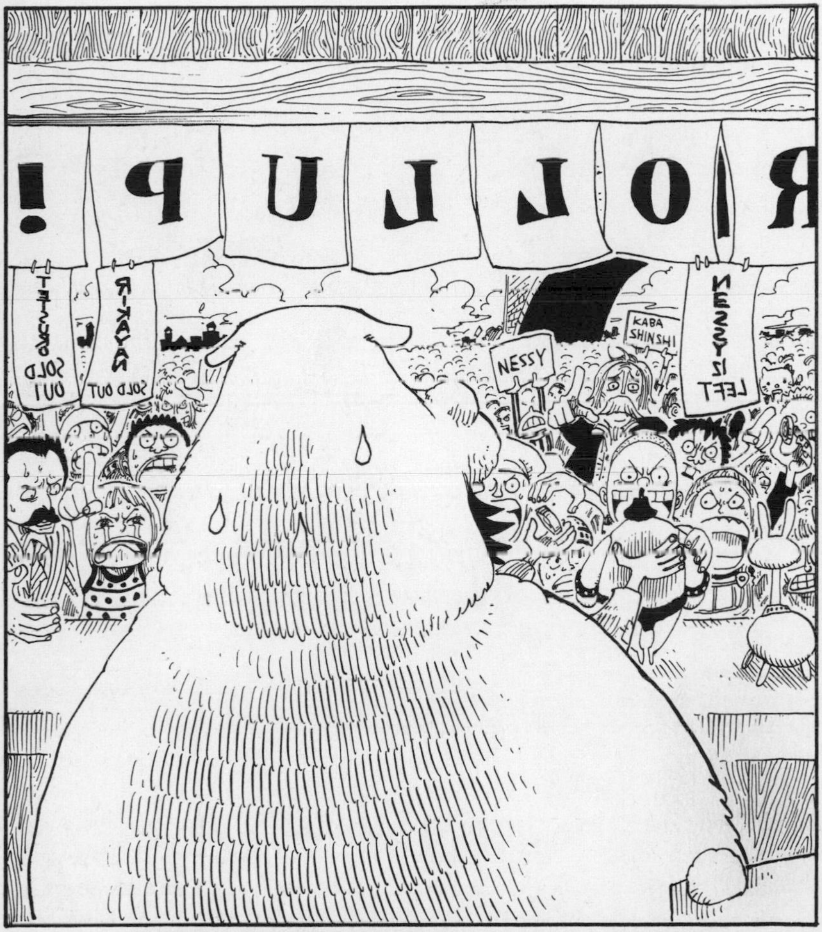
KABA SHINSHI
NESSY

WAPOL'S OMNIVOROUS RAMPAGE, VOL. 16:
"ALL OF A SUDDEN, BUSINESS IS BOOMING!"

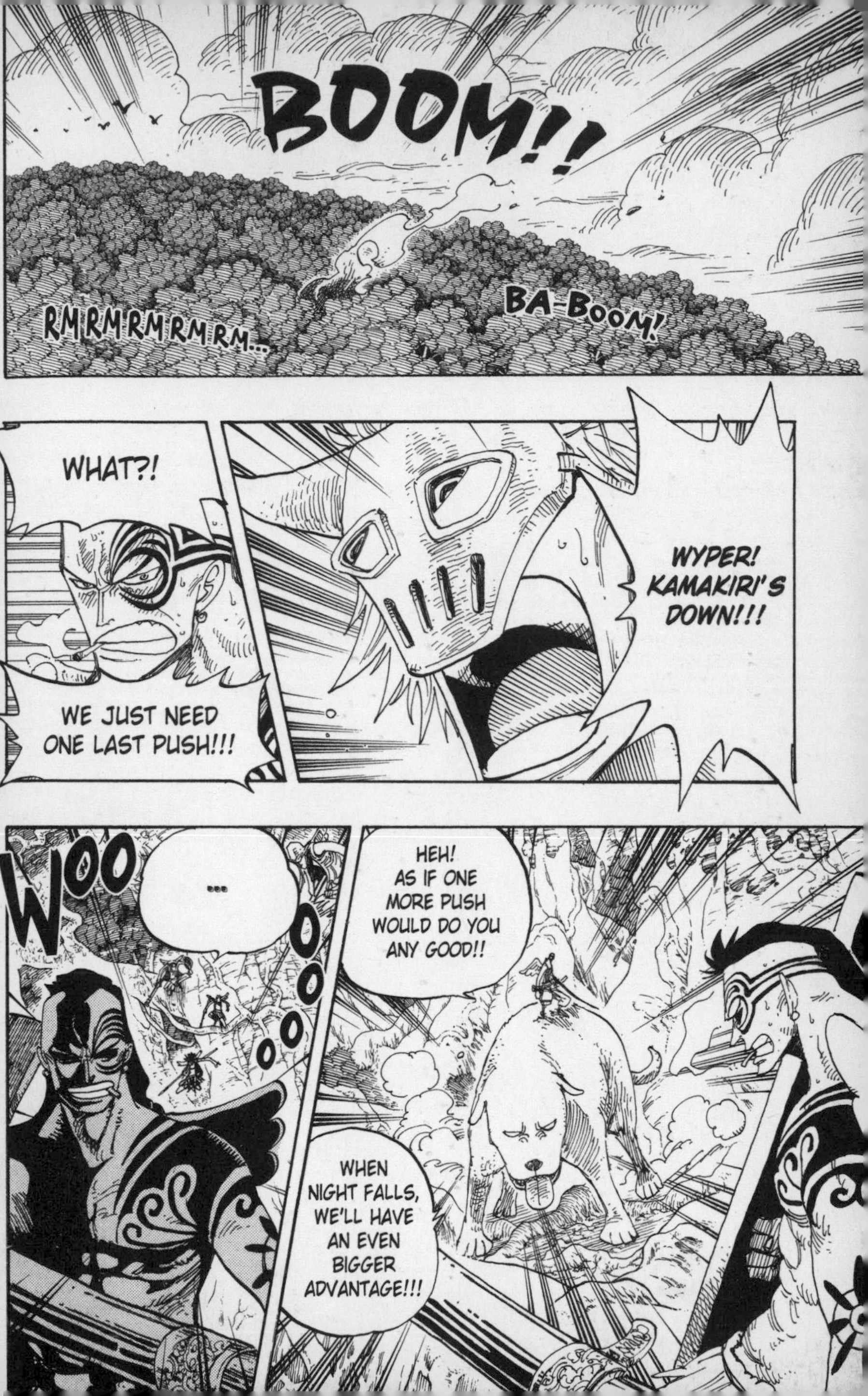
BOOM!!
BA-BOOM!
RM RM RM RM RM...
WYPER! KAMAKIRI'S DOWN!!!
WHAT?!
WE JUST NEED ONE LAST PUSH!!!
HEH! AS IF ONE MORE PUSH WOULD DO YOU ANY GOOD!!
WHEN NIGHT FALLS, WE'LL HAVE AN EVEN BIGGER ADVANTAGE!!!
...
WOOOOOOO

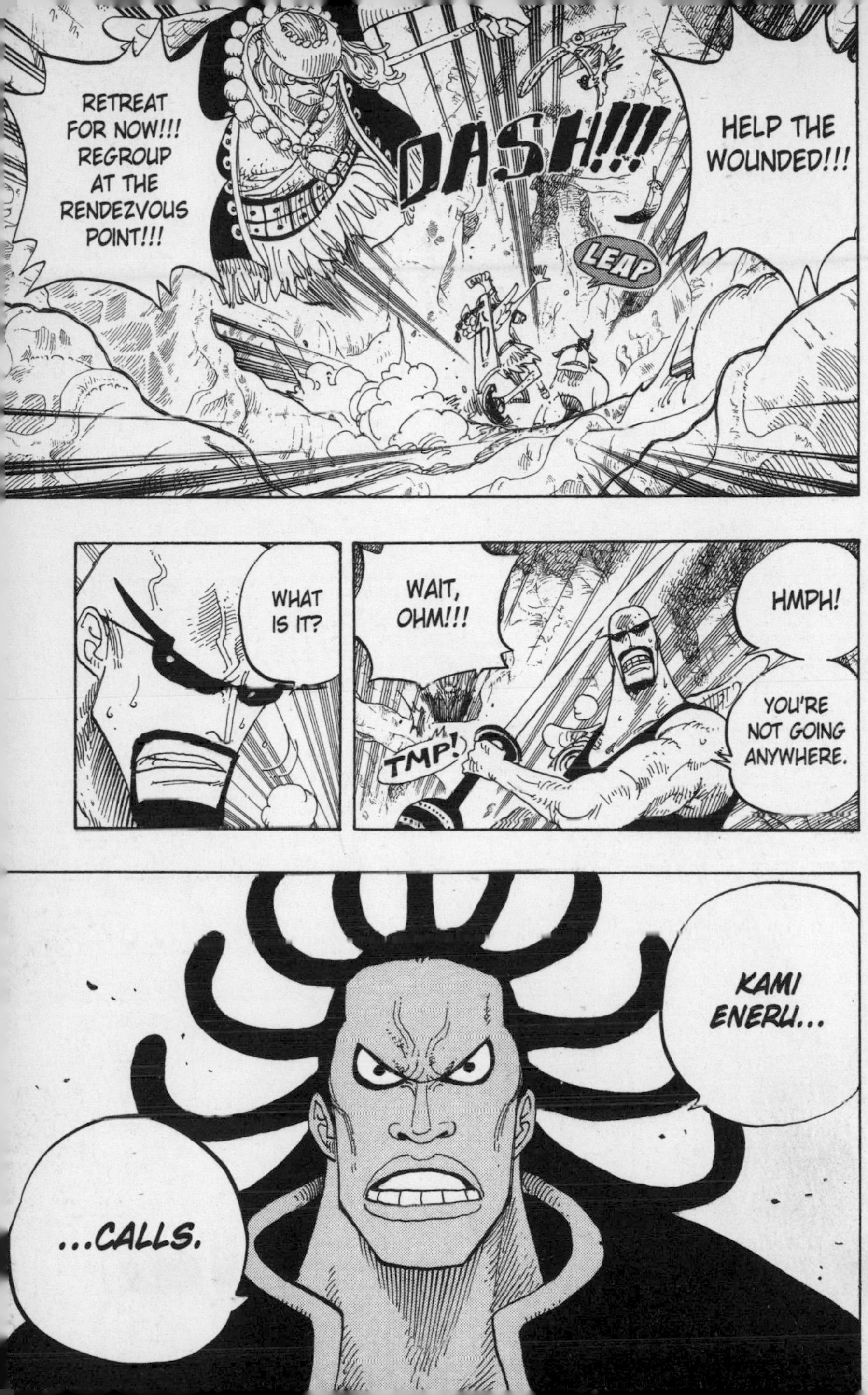
HELP THE WOUNDED!!!
DASH!!!!
LEAP
RETREAT FOR NOW!!! REGROUP AT THE RENDEZVOUS POINT!!!
HMPH!
WAIT, OHM!!!
YOU'RE NOT GOING ANYWHERE.
TMP!
WHAT IS IT?
KAMI ENERU...
...CALLS.

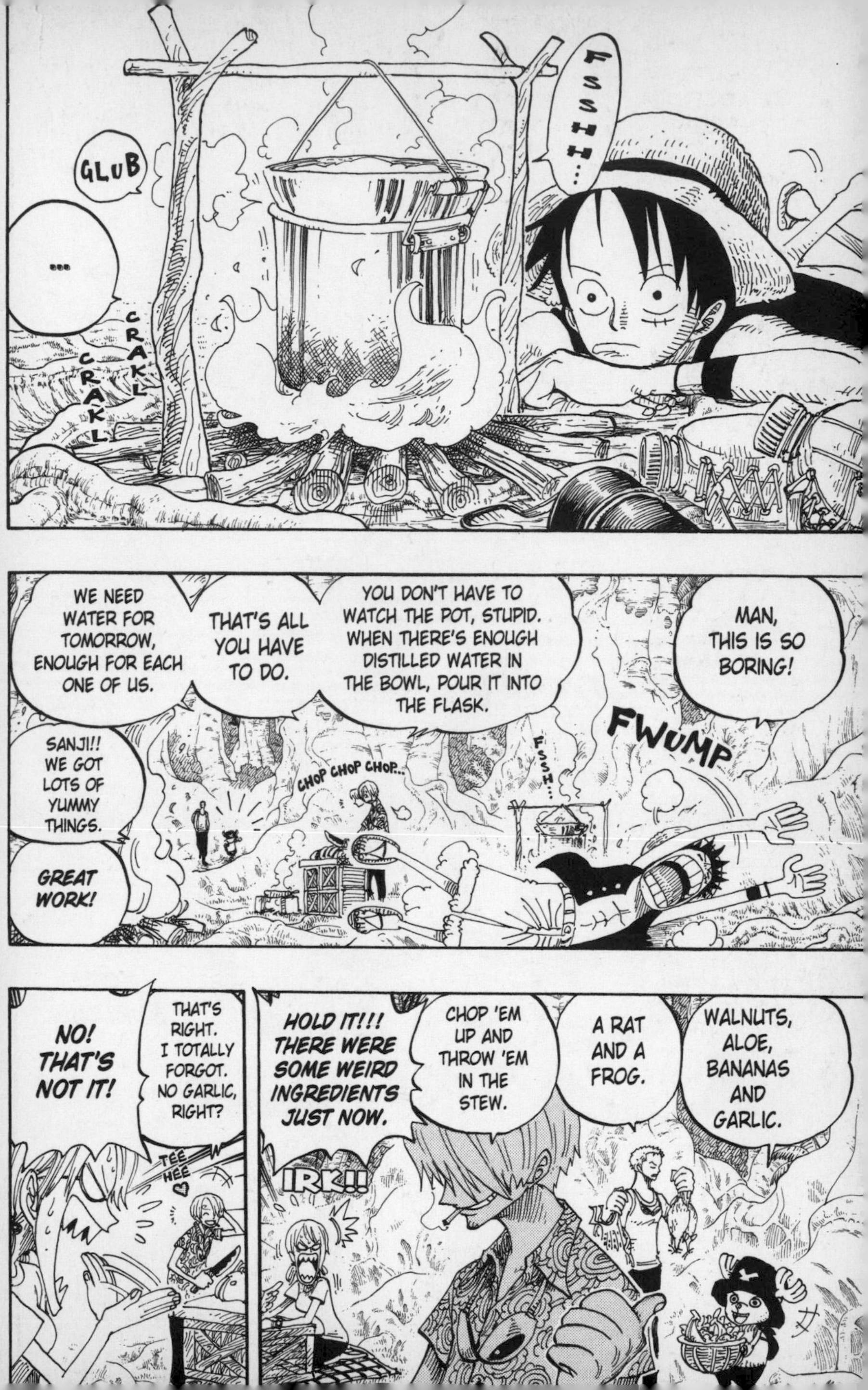
FSSHH...
GLUB
...
CRAKL
CRAKL
MAN, THIS IS SO BORING!
FWUMP
YOU DON'T HAVE TO WATCH THE POT, STUPID. WHEN THERE'S ENOUGH DISTILLED WATER IN THE BOWL, POUR IT INTO THE FLASK.
THAT'S ALL YOU HAVE TO DO.
WE NEED WATER FOR TOMORROW, ENOUGH FOR EACH ONE OF US.
FSSSH...
CHOP CHOP CHOP...
SANJI!! WE GOT LOTS OF YUMMY THINGS.
GREAT WORK!
WALNUTS, ALOE, BANANAS AND GARLIC.
A RAT AND A FROG.
CHOP 'EM UP AND THROW 'EM IN THE STEW.
HOLD IT!!! THERE WERE SOME WEIRD INGREDIENTS JUST NOW.
IRK!!
THAT'S RIGHT. I TOTALLY FORGOT. NO GARLIC, RIGHT?
NO! THAT'S NOT IT!
TEE HEE

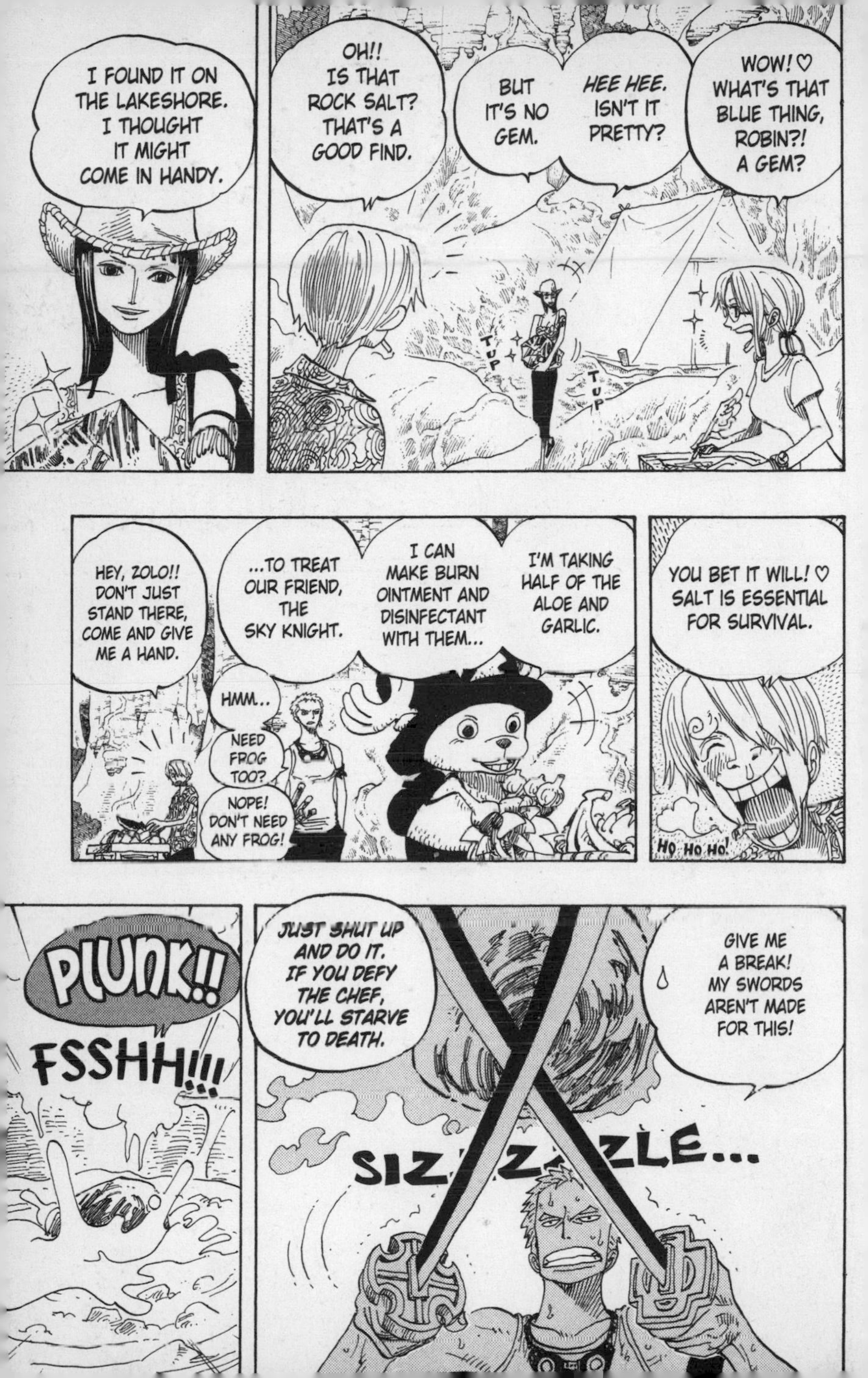
WOW! ♡ WHAT'S THAT BLUE THING, ROBIN?! A GEM?
HEE HEE. ISN'T IT PRETTY?
BUT IT'S NO GEM.
OH!! IS THAT ROCK SALT? THAT'S A GOOD FIND.
TUP
TUP
I FOUND IT ON THE LAKESHORE. I THOUGHT IT MIGHT COME IN HANDY.
YOU BET IT WILL! ♡ SALT IS ESSENTIAL FOR SURVIVAL.
HO HO HO!
I'M TAKING HALF OF THE ALOE AND GARLIC.
I CAN MAKE BURN OINTMENT AND DISINFECTANT WITH THEM...
...TO TREAT OUR FRIEND, THE SKY KNIGHT.
HEY, ZOLO!! DON'T JUST STAND THERE, COME AND GIVE ME A HAND.
HMM...
NEED FROG TOO?
NOPE! DON'T NEED ANY FROG!
GIVE ME A BREAK! MY SWORDS AREN'T MADE FOR THIS!
JUST SHUT UP AND DO IT. IF YOU DEFY THE CHEF, YOU'LL STARVE TO DEATH.
SIZZZZLE...
PLUNK!!
FSSHH!!!

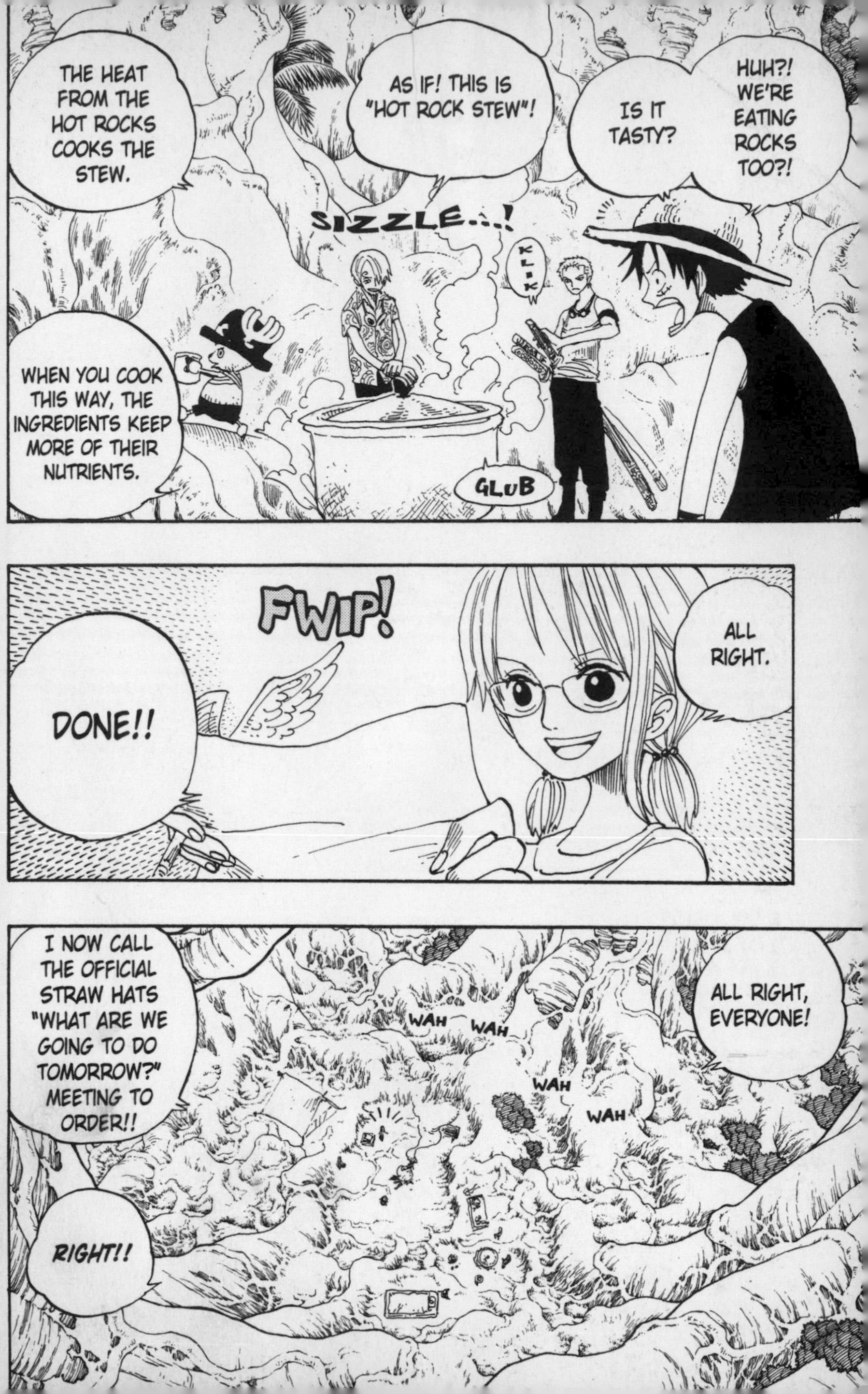
HUH?! WE'RE EATING ROCKS TOO?!
IS IT TASTY?
AS IF! THIS IS "HOT ROCK STEW"!
THE HEAT FROM THE HOT ROCKS COOKS THE STEW.
SIZZLE...!
KLIK
WHEN YOU COOK THIS WAY, THE INGREDIENTS KEEP MORE OF THEIR NUTRIENTS.
GLUB
ALL RIGHT.
FWIP!
DONE!!
ALL RIGHT, EVERYONE!
I NOW CALL THE OFFICIAL STRAW HATS "WHAT ARE WE GOING TO DO TOMORROW?" MEETING TO ORDER!!
WAH WAH
WAH WAH
RIGHT!!

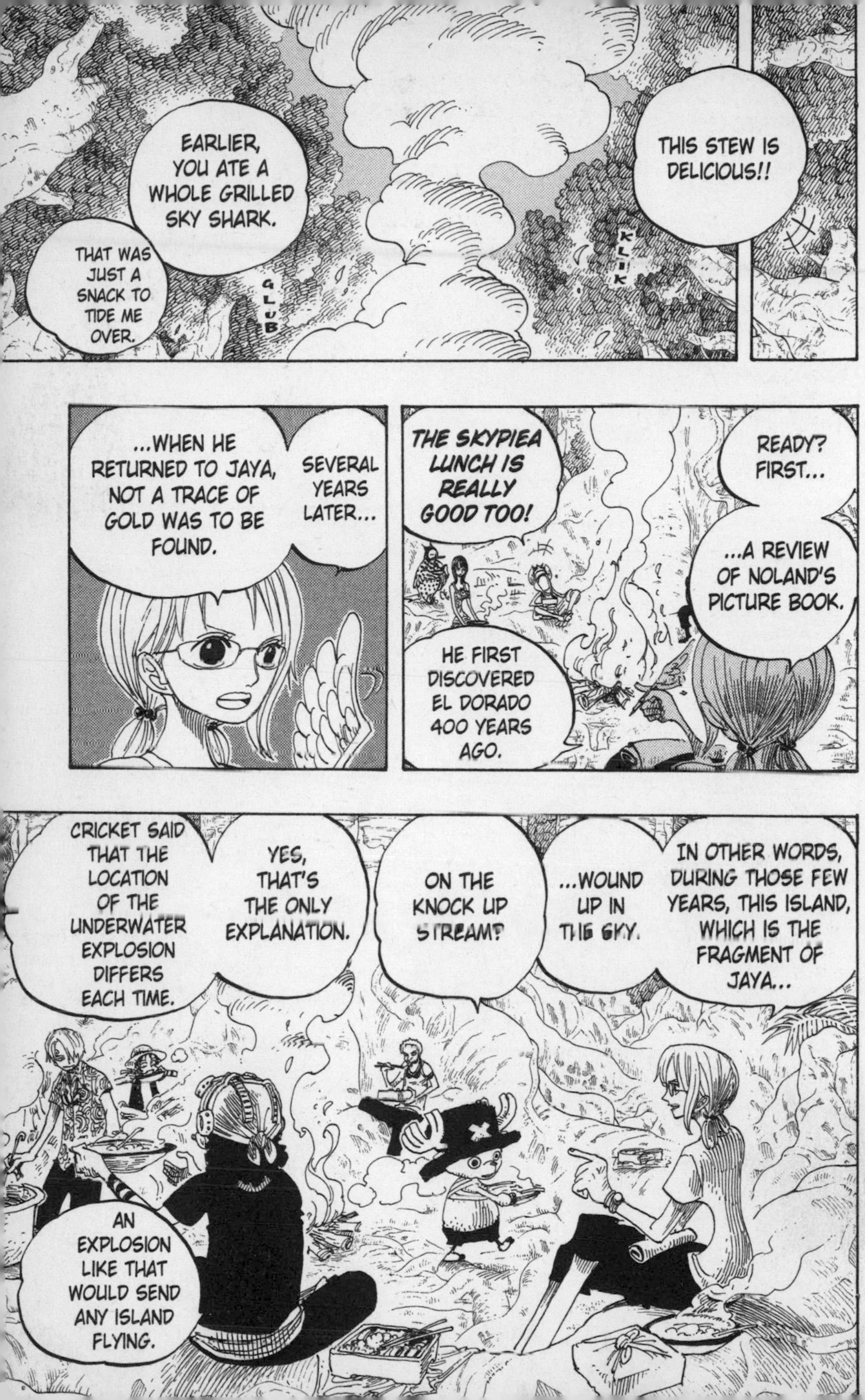
THIS STEW IS DELICIOUS!!
KLIK
EARLIER, YOU ATE A WHOLE GRILLED SKY SHARK.
GLUB
THAT WAS JUST A SNACK TO TIDE ME OVER.
READY? FIRST...
...A REVIEW OF NOLAND'S PICTURE BOOK.
THE SKYPIEA LUNCH IS REALLY GOOD TOO!
HE FIRST DISCOVERED EL DORADO 400 YEARS AGO.
SEVERAL YEARS LATER...
...WHEN HE RETURNED TO JAYA, NOT A TRACE OF GOLD WAS TO BE FOUND.
IN OTHER WORDS, DURING THOSE FEW YEARS, THIS ISLAND, WHICH IS THE FRAGMENT OF JAYA...
...WOUND UP IN THE SKY.
ON THE KNOCK UP STREAM?
YES, THAT'S THE ONLY EXPLANATION.
CRICKET SAID THAT THE LOCATION OF THE UNDERWATER EXPLOSION DIFFERS EACH TIME.
AN EXPLOSION LIKE THAT WOULD SEND ANY ISLAND FLYING.

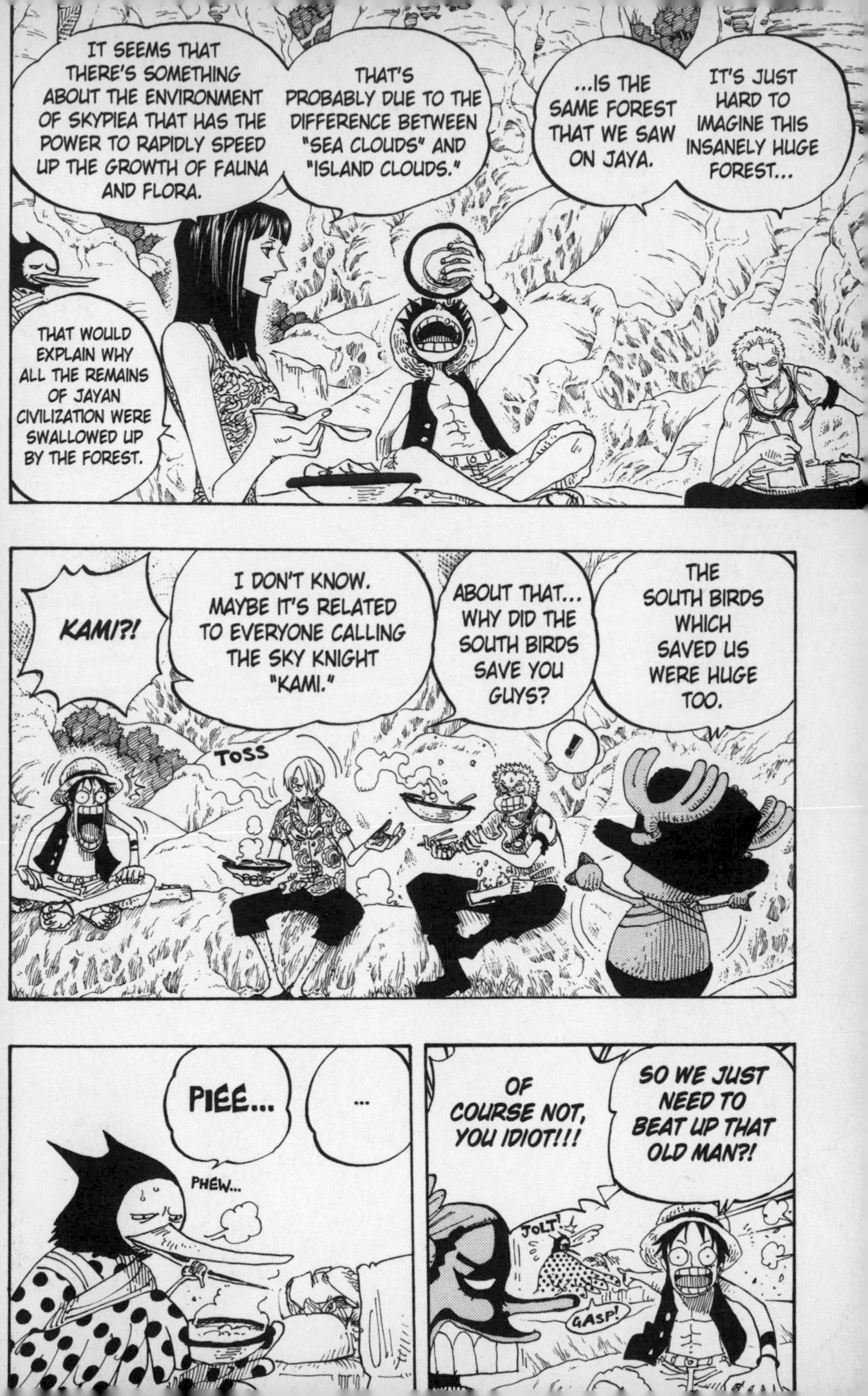
IT'S JUST HARD TO IMAGINE THIS INSANELY HUGE FOREST...
...IS THE SAME FOREST THAT WE SAW ON JAYA.
THAT'S PROBABLY DUE TO THE DIFFERENCE BETWEEN "SEA CLOUDS" AND "ISLAND CLOUDS."
IT SEEMS THAT THERE'S SOMETHING ABOUT THE ENVIRONMENT OF SKYPIEA THAT HAS THE POWER TO RAPIDLY SPEED UP THE GROWTH OF FAUNA AND FLORA.
THAT WOULD EXPLAIN WHY ALL THE REMAINS OF JAYAN CIVILIZATION WERE SWALLOWED UP BY THE FOREST.
THE SOUTH BIRDS WHICH SAVED US WERE HUGE TOO.
!
ABOUT THAT... WHY DID THE SOUTH BIRDS SAVE YOU GUYS?
I DON'T KNOW. MAYBE IT'S RELATED TO EVERYONE CALLING THE SKY KNIGHT "KAMI."
TOSS
KAMI?!
SO WE JUST NEED TO BEAT UP THAT OLD MAN?!
OF COURSE NOT, YOU IDIOT!!!
JOLT!
GASP!
...
PIEE...
PHEW...

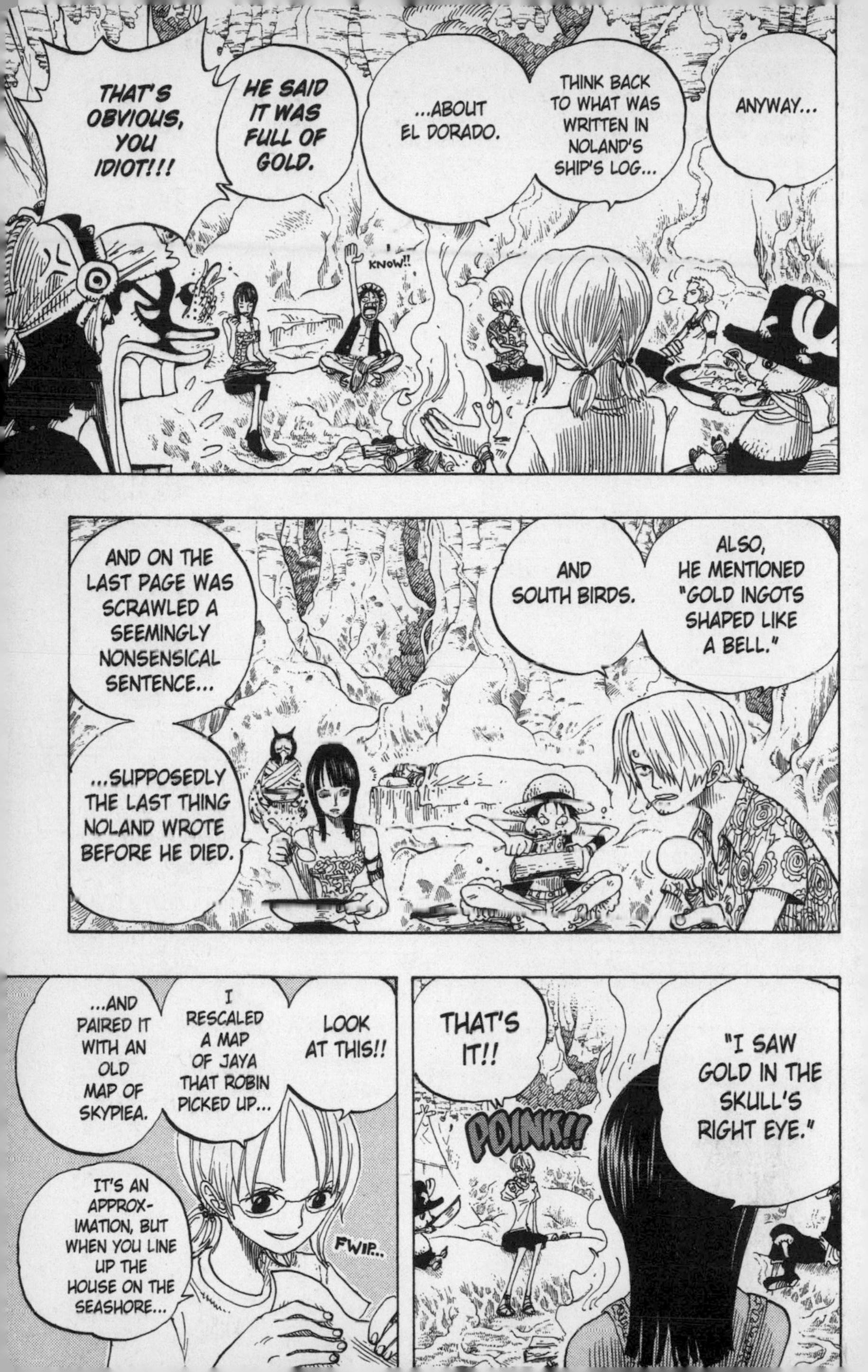
ANYWAY...
THINK BACK TO WHAT WAS WRITTEN IN NOLAND'S SHIP'S LOG...
...ABOUT EL DORADO.
HE SAID IT WAS FULL OF GOLD.
I KNOW!!
THAT'S OBVIOUS, YOU IDIOT!!!
ALSO, HE MENTIONED "GOLD INGOTS SHAPED LIKE A BELL."
AND SOUTH BIRDS.
AND ON THE LAST PAGE WAS SCRAWLED A SEEMINGLY NONSENSICAL SENTENCE...
...SUPPOSEDLY THE LAST THING NOLAND WROTE BEFORE HE DIED.
"I SAW GOLD IN THE SKULL'S RIGHT EYE."
THAT'S IT!!
POINK!!
LOOK AT THIS!!
I RESCALED A MAP OF JAYA THAT ROBIN PICKED UP...
...AND PAIRED IT WITH AN OLD MAP OF SKYPIEA.
FWIP...
IT'S AN APPROX-IMATION, BUT WHEN YOU LINE UP THE HOUSE ON THE SEASHORE...

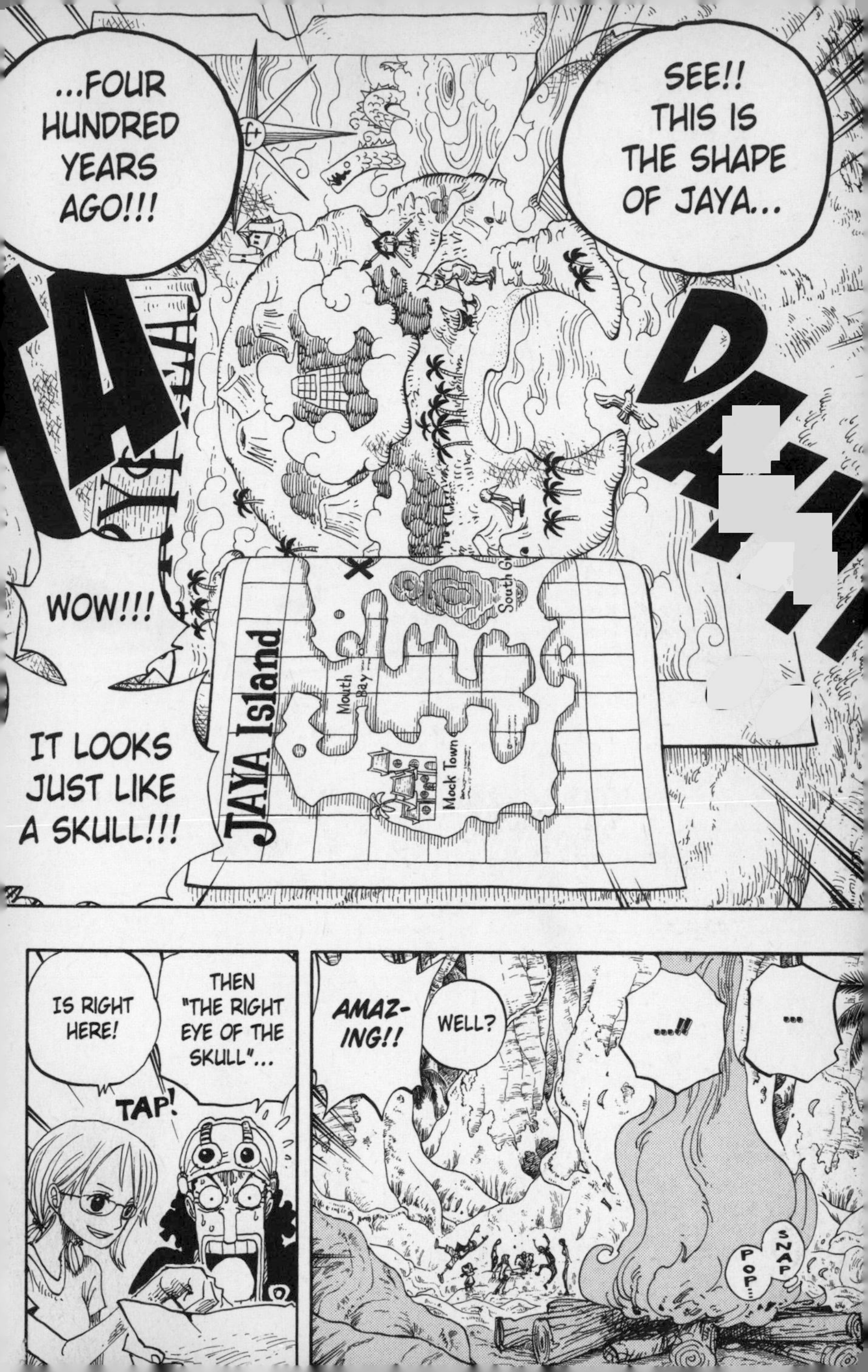
SEE!! THIS IS THE SHAPE OF JAYA...
...FOUR HUNDRED YEARS AGO!!!
JAYA Island
Mouth Bay
Mock Town
WOW!!!
IT LOOKS JUST LIKE A SKULL!!!
...
...!!
WELL?
AMAZ-ING!!
SNAP
POP...
THEN "THE RIGHT EYE OF THE SKULL"...
IS RIGHT HERE!
TAP!

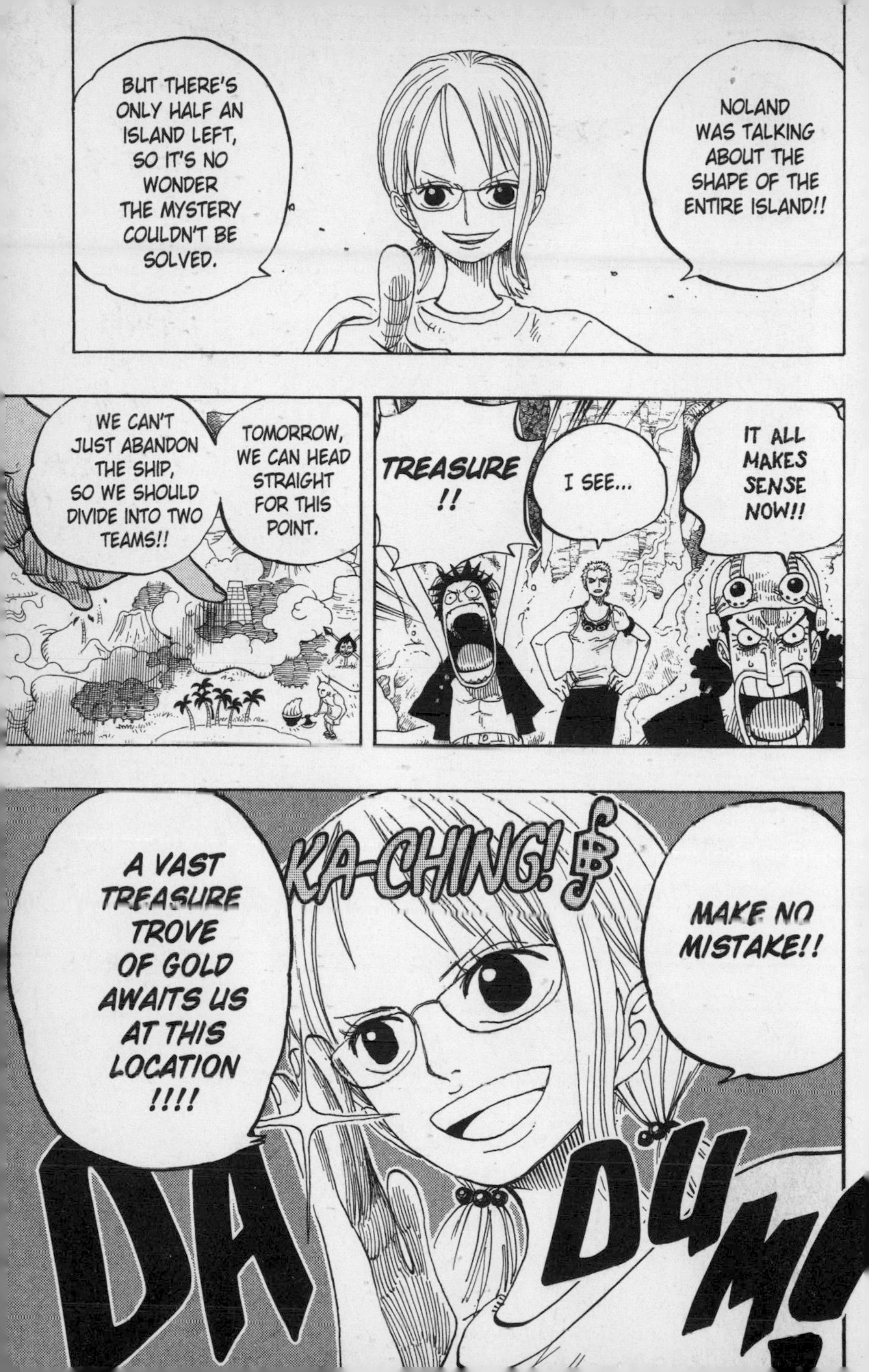
NOLAND WAS TALKING ABOUT THE SHAPE OF THE ENTIRE ISLAND!!
BUT THERE'S ONLY HALF AN ISLAND LEFT, SO IT'S NO WONDER THE MYSTERY COULDN'T BE SOLVED.
IT ALL MAKES SENSE NOW!!
I SEE...
TREASURE !!
TOMORROW, WE CAN HEAD STRAIGHT FOR THIS POINT.
WE CAN'T JUST ABANDON THE SHIP, SO WE SHOULD DIVIDE INTO TWO TEAMS!!
MAKE NO MISTAKE!!
KA-CHING!
A VAST TREASURE TROVE OF GOLD AWAITS US AT THIS LOCATION !!!!
DA DUM!

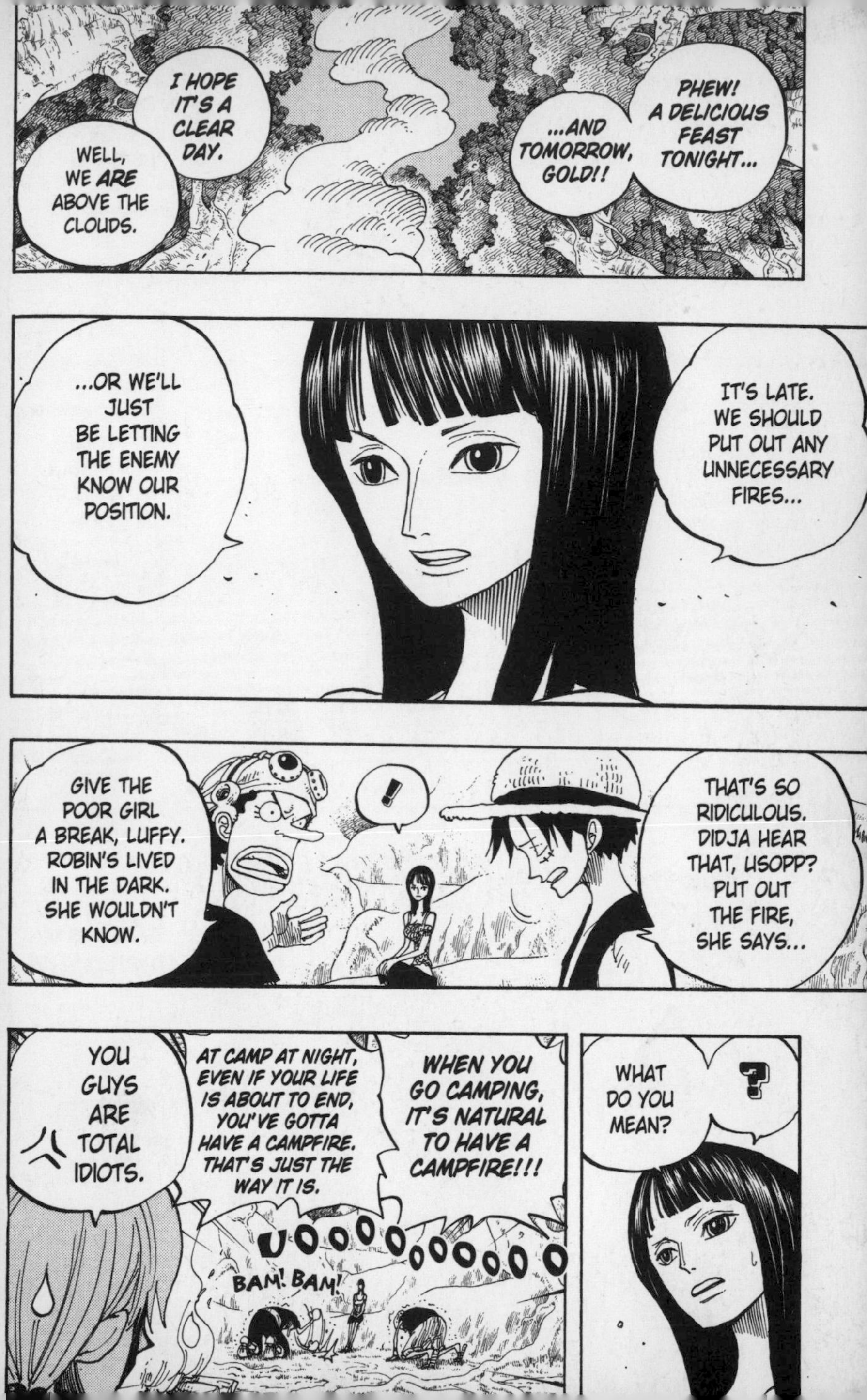
PHEW! A DELICIOUS FEAST TONIGHT...
...AND TOMORROW, GOLD!!
I HOPE IT'S A CLEAR DAY.
WELL, WE *ARE* ABOVE THE CLOUDS.
IT'S LATE. WE SHOULD PUT OUT ANY UNNECESSARY FIRES...
...OR WE'LL JUST BE LETTING THE ENEMY KNOW OUR POSITION.
THAT'S SO RIDICULOUS. DIDJA HEAR THAT, USOPP? PUT OUT THE FIRE, SHE SAYS...
!
GIVE THE POOR GIRL A BREAK, LUFFY. ROBIN'S LIVED IN THE DARK. SHE WOULDN'T KNOW.
WHAT DO YOU MEAN?
?
WHEN YOU GO CAMPING, IT'S NATURAL TO HAVE A CAMPFIRE!!!
AT CAMP AT NIGHT, EVEN IF YOUR LIFE IS ABOUT TO END, YOU'VE GOTTA HAVE A CAMPFIRE. THAT'S JUST THE WAY IT IS.
YOU GUYS ARE TOTAL IDIOTS.
UOOOOOOOOOOOO
BAM! BAM!

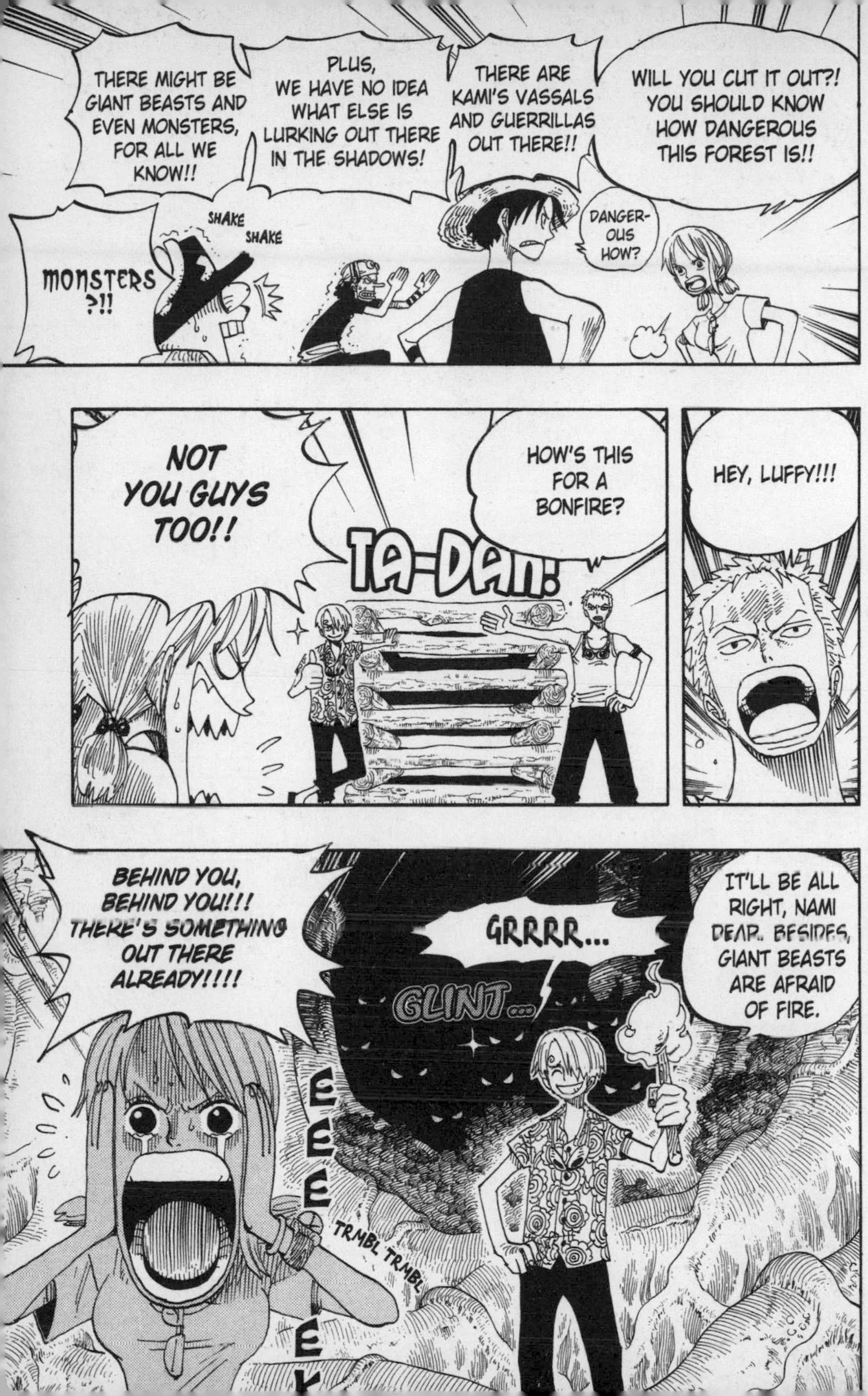

WILL YOU CUT IT OUT?! YOU SHOULD KNOW HOW DANGEROUS THIS FOREST IS!!
THERE ARE KAMI'S VASSALS AND GUERRILLAS OUT THERE!!
PLUS, WE HAVE NO IDEA WHAT ELSE IS LURKING OUT THERE IN THE SHADOWS!
THERE MIGHT BE GIANT BEASTS AND EVEN MONSTERS, FOR ALL WE KNOW!!
DANGER-OUS HOW?
SHAKE SHAKE
MONSTERS ?!!
HEY, LUFFY!!!
HOW'S THIS FOR A BONFIRE?
NOT YOU GUYS TOO!!
TA-DAN!
IT'LL BE ALL RIGHT, NAMI DEAR. BESIDES, GIANT BEASTS ARE AFRAID OF FIRE.
GRRRR...
BEHIND YOU, BEHIND YOU!!! THERE'S SOMETHING OUT THERE ALREADY!!!!
GLINT...
EEEE
TRMBL TRMBL

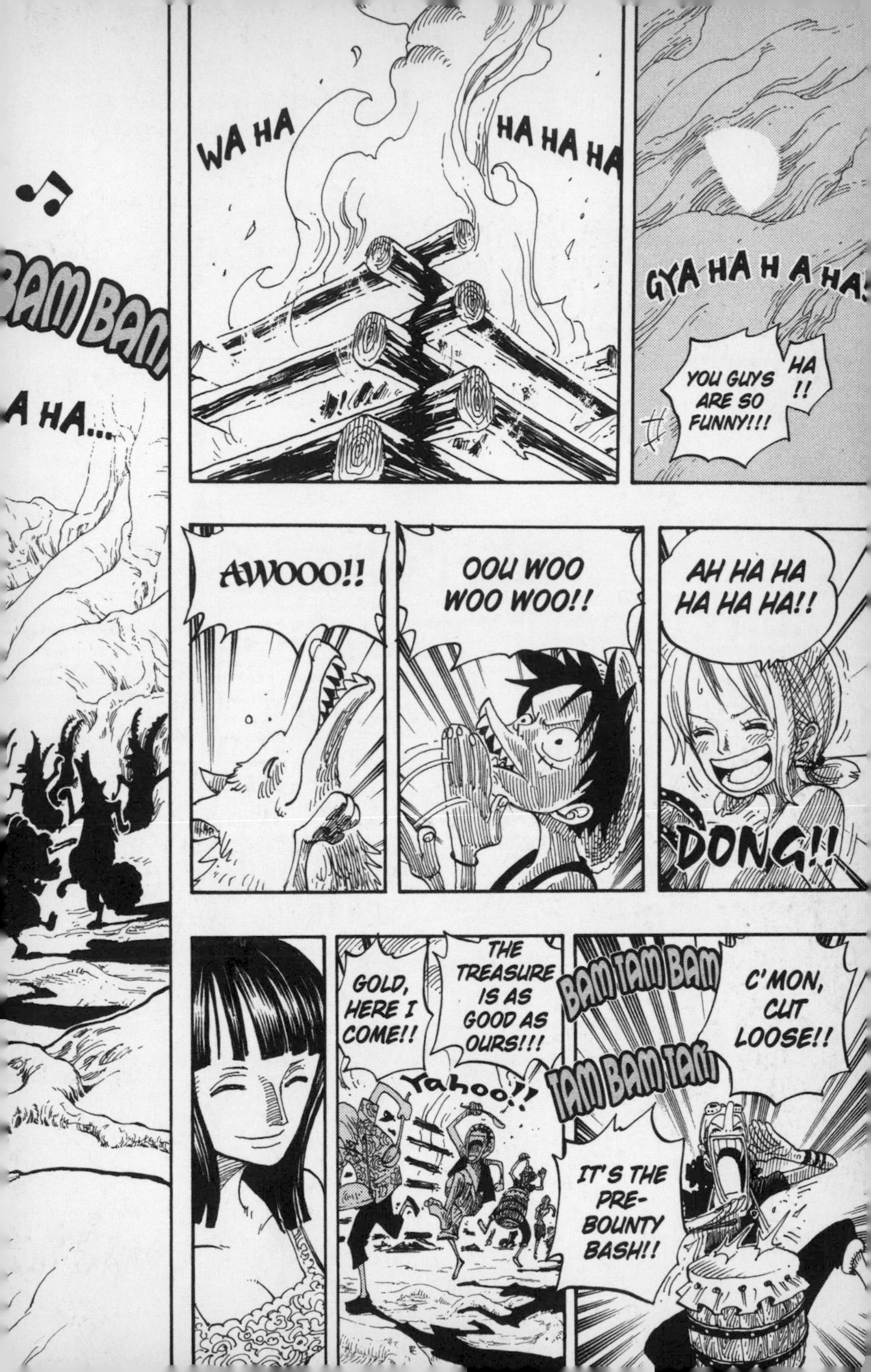
GYA HA H A HA!
YOU GUYS ARE SO FUNNY!!!
HA !!
WA HA
HA HA HA
AH HA HA HA HA HA!!
DONG!!
OOU WOO WOO WOO!!
AWOOO!!
C'MON, CUT LOOSE!!
BAM TAM BAM
TAM BAM TAM
IT'S THE PRE-BOUNTY BASH!!
THE TREASURE IS AS GOOD AS OURS!!!
GOLD, HERE I COME!!
Yahoo!!
BAM BAM
A HA....

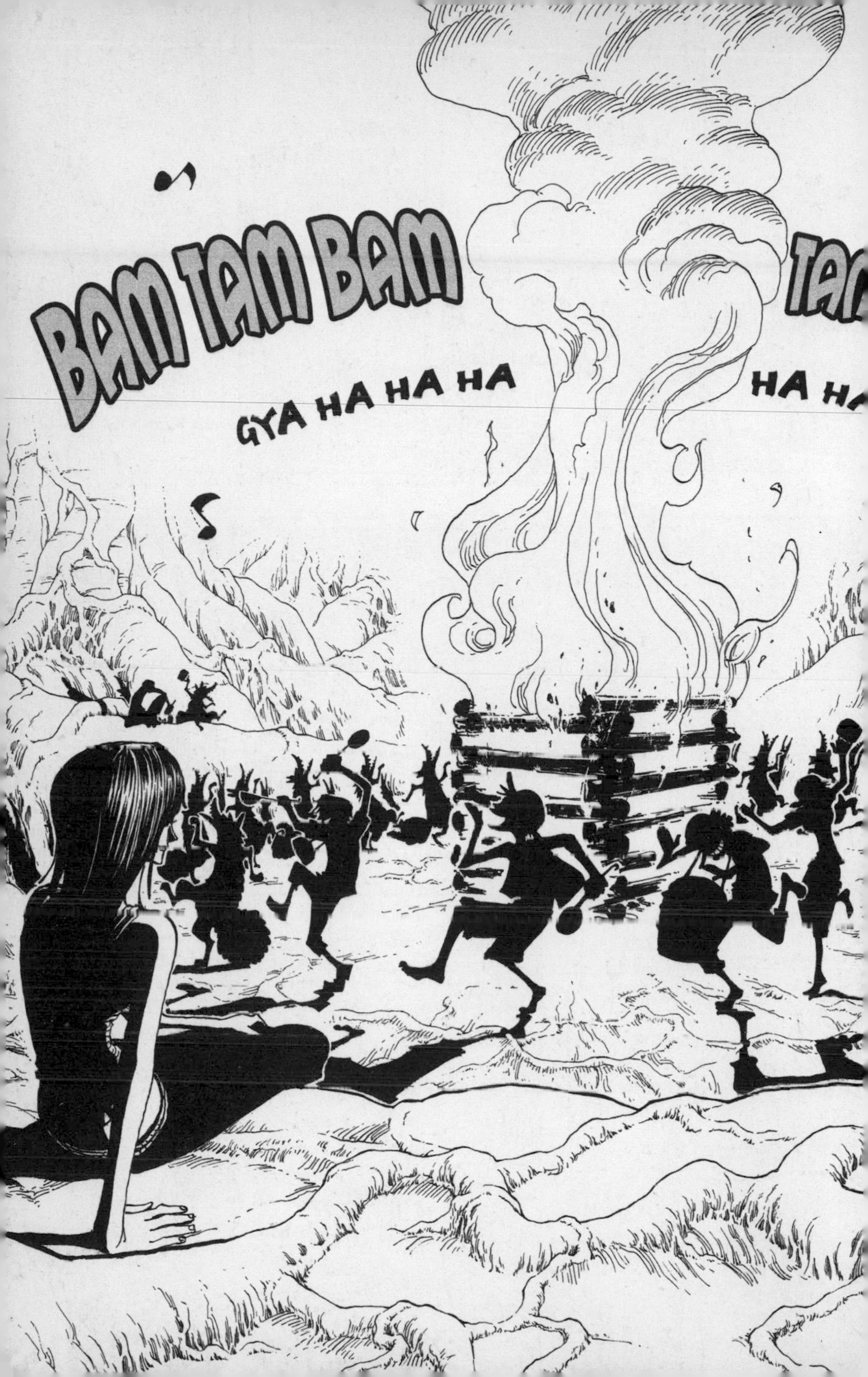
BAM TAM BAM
GYA HA HA HA
TAM
HA HA

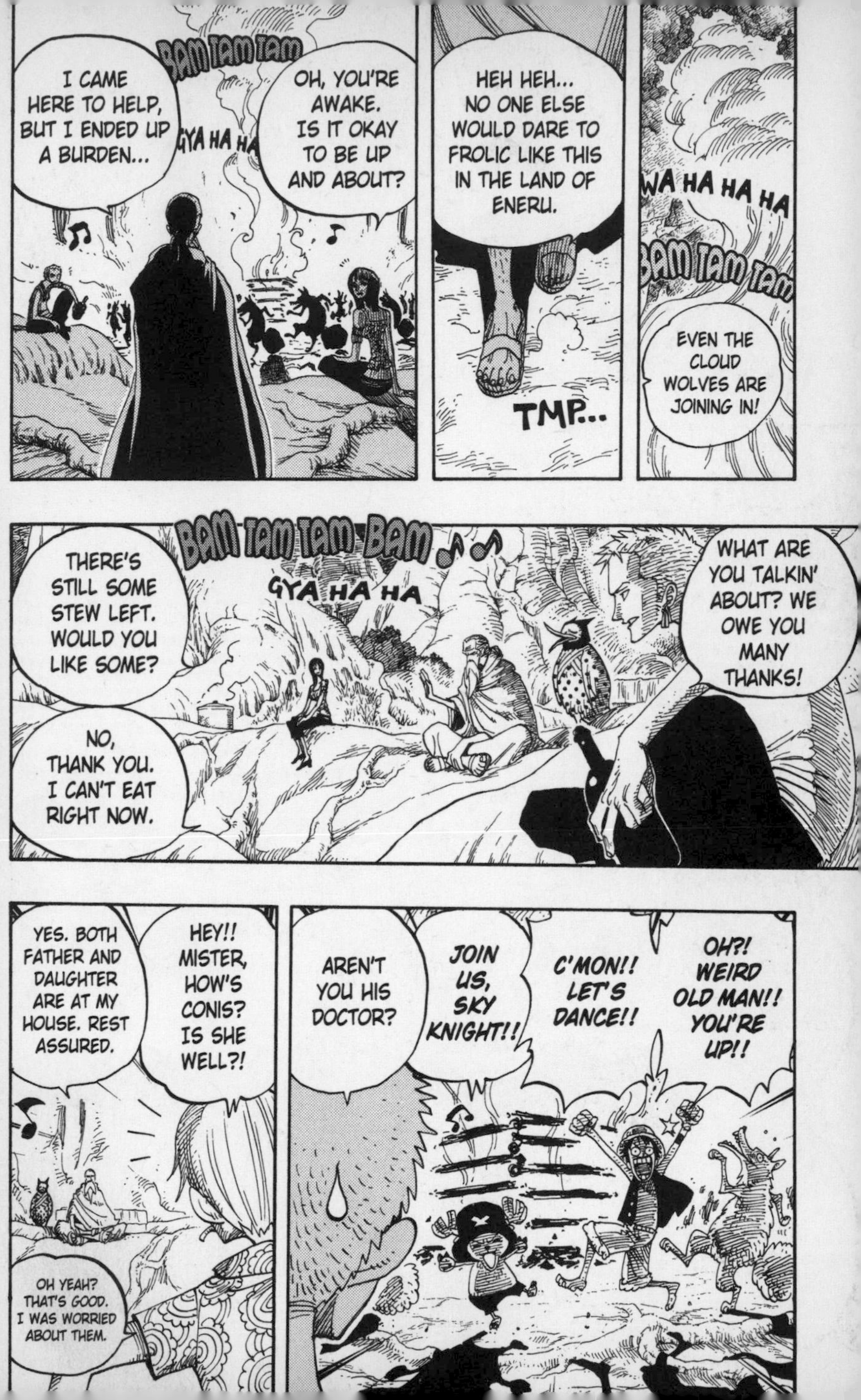
WA HA HA HA
BAM TAM TAM
EVEN THE CLOUD WOLVES ARE JOINING IN!
HEH HEH... NO ONE ELSE WOULD DARE TO FROLIC LIKE THIS IN THE LAND OF ENERU.
TMP...
BAM TAM TAM
OH, YOU'RE AWAKE. IS IT OKAY TO BE UP AND ABOUT?
GYA HA HA
I CAME HERE TO HELP, BUT I ENDED UP A BURDEN...
BAM TAM TAM BAM
WHAT ARE YOU TALKIN' ABOUT? WE OWE YOU MANY THANKS!
GYA HA HA
THERE'S STILL SOME STEW LEFT. WOULD YOU LIKE SOME?
NO, THANK YOU. I CAN'T EAT RIGHT NOW.
OH?! WEIRD OLD MAN!! YOU'RE UP!!
C'MON!! LET'S DANCE!!
JOIN US, SKY KNIGHT!!
AREN'T YOU HIS DOCTOR?
HEY!! MISTER, HOW'S CONIS? IS SHE WELL?!
YES. BOTH FATHER AND DAUGHTER ARE AT MY HOUSE. REST ASSURED.
OH YEAH? THAT'S GOOD. I WAS WORRIED ABOUT THEM.

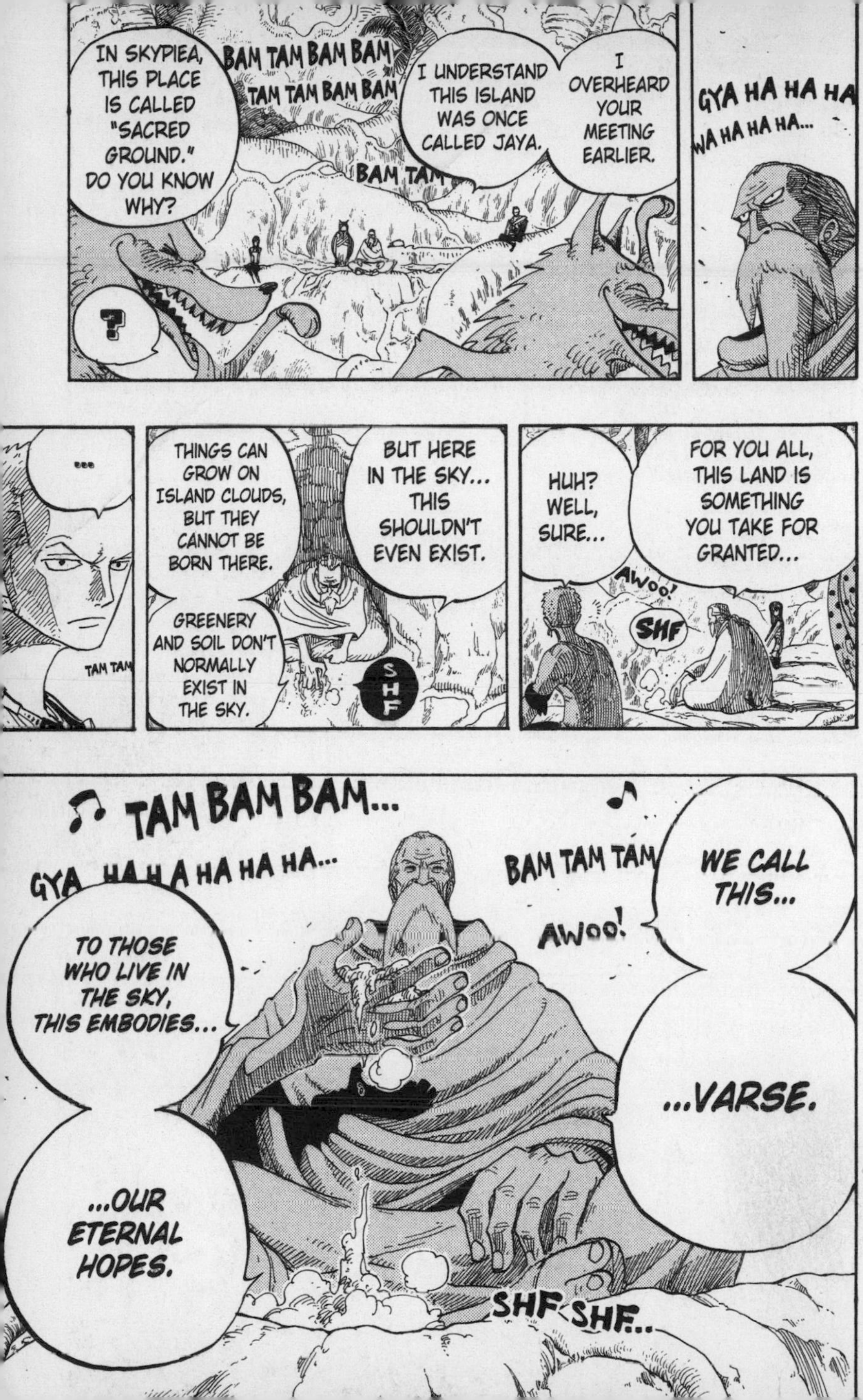
GYA HA HA HA
WA HA HA HA...
I OVERHEARD YOUR MEETING EARLIER.
I UNDERSTAND THIS ISLAND WAS ONCE CALLED JAYA.
BAM TAM BAM BAM
TAM TAM BAM BAM
IN SKYPIEA, THIS PLACE IS CALLED "SACRED GROUND." DO YOU KNOW WHY?
BAM TAM
?
FOR YOU ALL, THIS LAND IS SOMETHING YOU TAKE FOR GRANTED...
HUH? WELL, SURE...
AWOO!
SHF
BUT HERE IN THE SKY... THIS SHOULDN'T EVEN EXIST.
THINGS CAN GROW ON ISLAND CLOUDS, BUT THEY CANNOT BE BORN THERE.
GREENERY AND SOIL DON'T NORMALLY EXIST IN THE SKY.
SHF
...
TAM TAM
WE CALL THIS...
BAM TAM TAM
TAM BAM BAM...
GYA HA HA HA HA HA...
AWOO!
TO THOSE WHO LIVE IN THE SKY, THIS EMBODIES...
...VARSE.
...OUR ETERNAL HOPES.
SHF SHF...

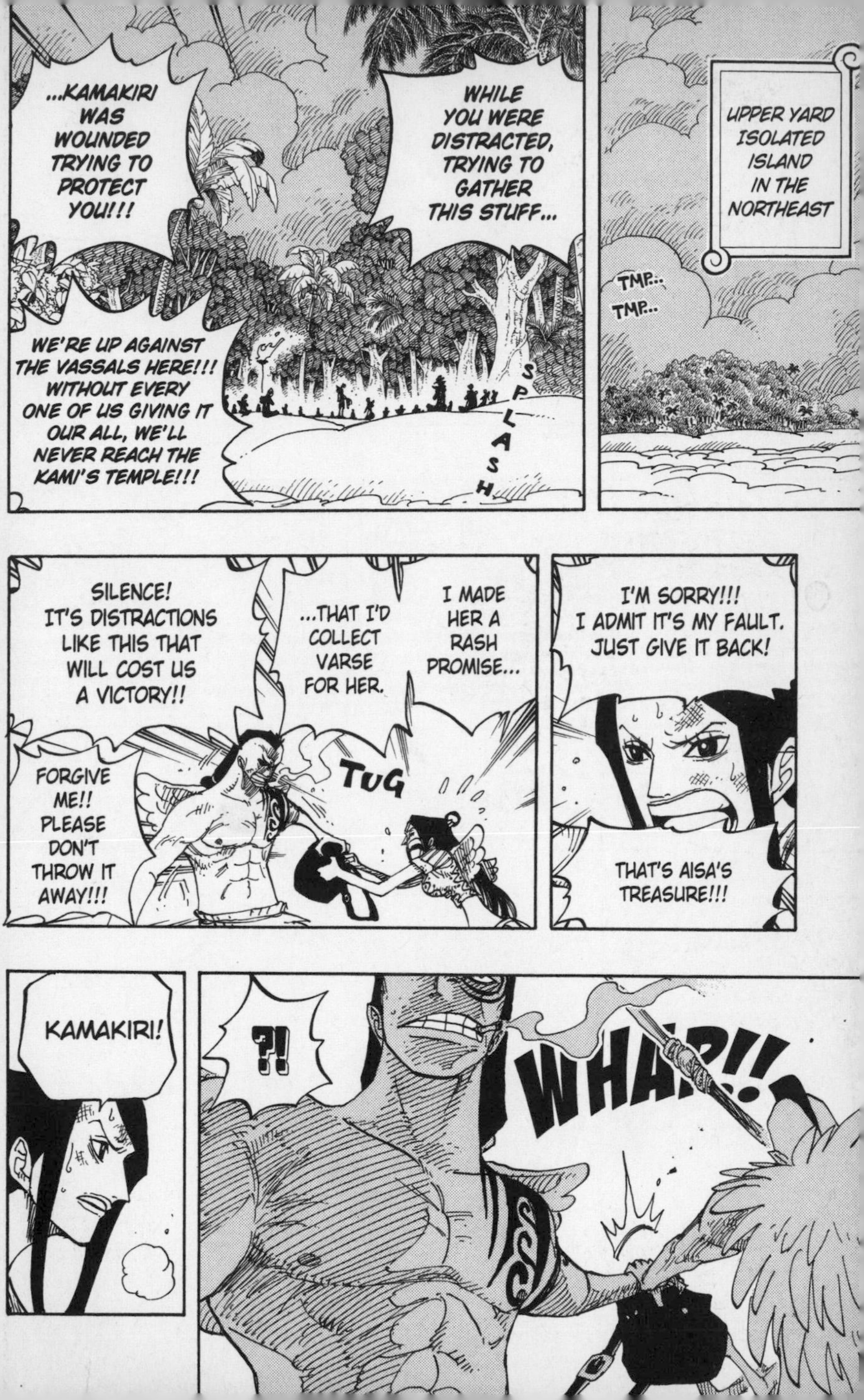
UPPER YARD ISOLATED ISLAND IN THE NORTHEAST
TMP... TMP...
WHILE YOU WERE DISTRACTED, TRYING TO GATHER THIS STUFF...
...KAMAKIRI WAS WOUNDED TRYING TO PROTECT YOU!!!
SPLASH
WE'RE UP AGAINST THE VASSALS HERE!!! WITHOUT EVERY ONE OF US GIVING IT OUR ALL, WE'LL NEVER REACH THE KAMI'S TEMPLE!!!
I'M SORRY!!! I ADMIT IT'S MY FAULT. JUST GIVE IT BACK!
THAT'S AISA'S TREASURE!!!
I MADE HER A RASH PROMISE...
...THAT I'D COLLECT VARSE FOR HER.
SILENCE! IT'S DISTRACTIONS LIKE THIS THAT WILL COST US A VICTORY!!
TUG
FORGIVE ME!! PLEASE DON'T THROW IT AWAY!!!
?!
WHAP!!
KAMAKIRI!

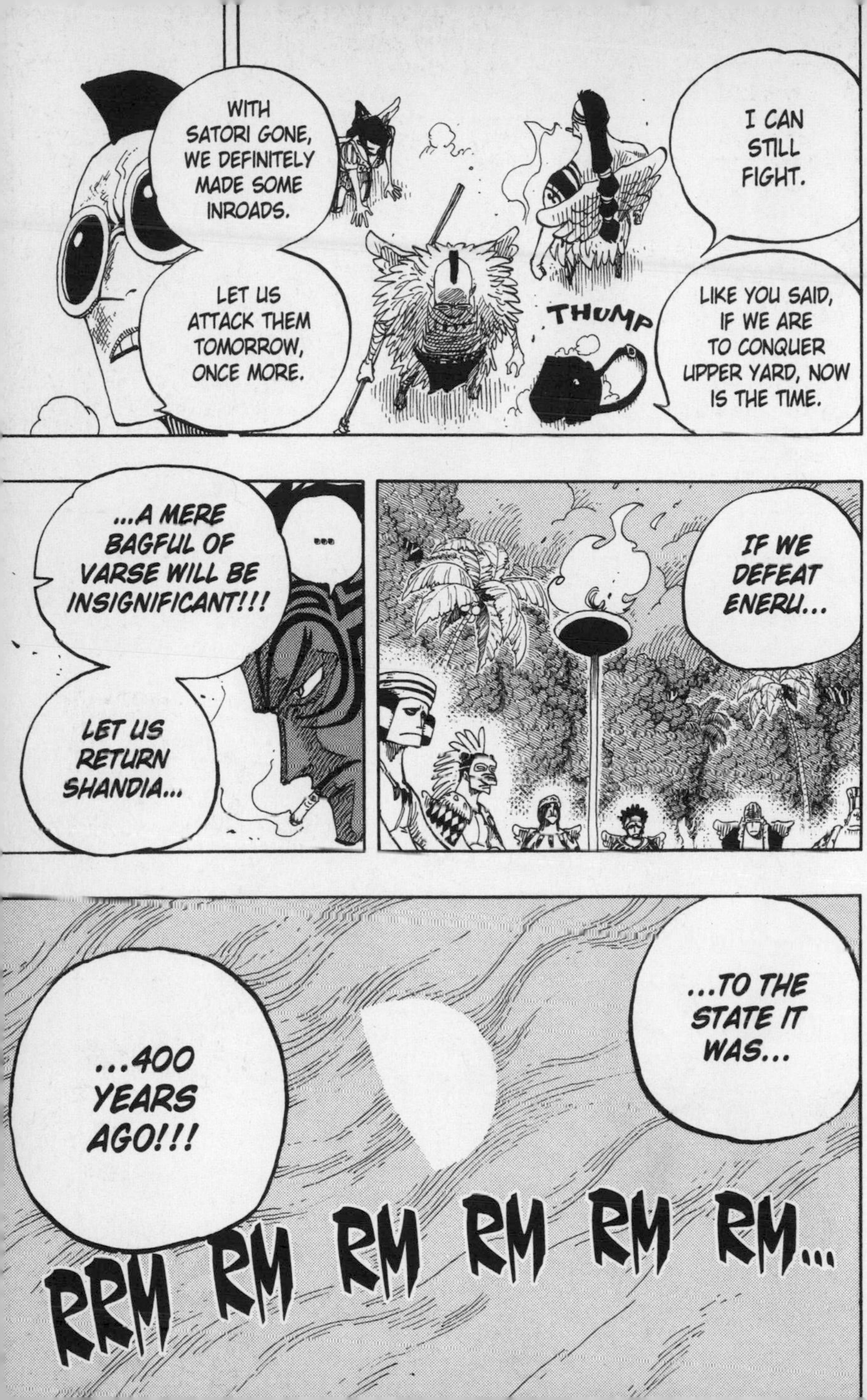
I CAN STILL FIGHT.
LIKE YOU SAID, IF WE ARE TO CONQUER UPPER YARD, NOW IS THE TIME.
THUMP
WITH SATORI GONE, WE DEFINITELY MADE SOME INROADS.
LET US ATTACK THEM TOMORROW, ONCE MORE.
IF WE DEFEAT ENERU...
...A MERE BAGFUL OF VARSE WILL BE INSIGNIFICANT!!!
...
LET US RETURN SHANDIA...
...TO THE STATE IT WAS...
...400 YEARS AGO!!!
RRM RM RM RM RM RM...

Chapter 254: AUBADE

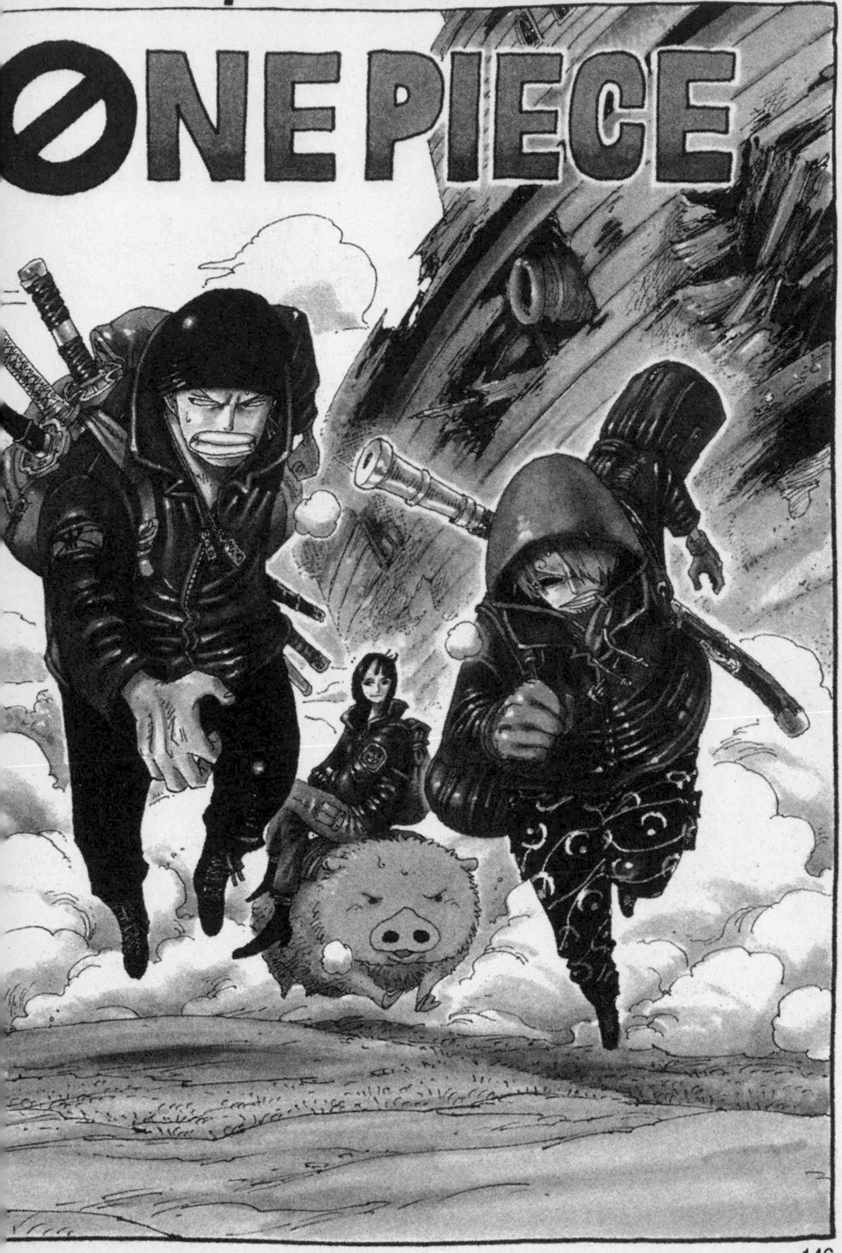
ONE PIECE

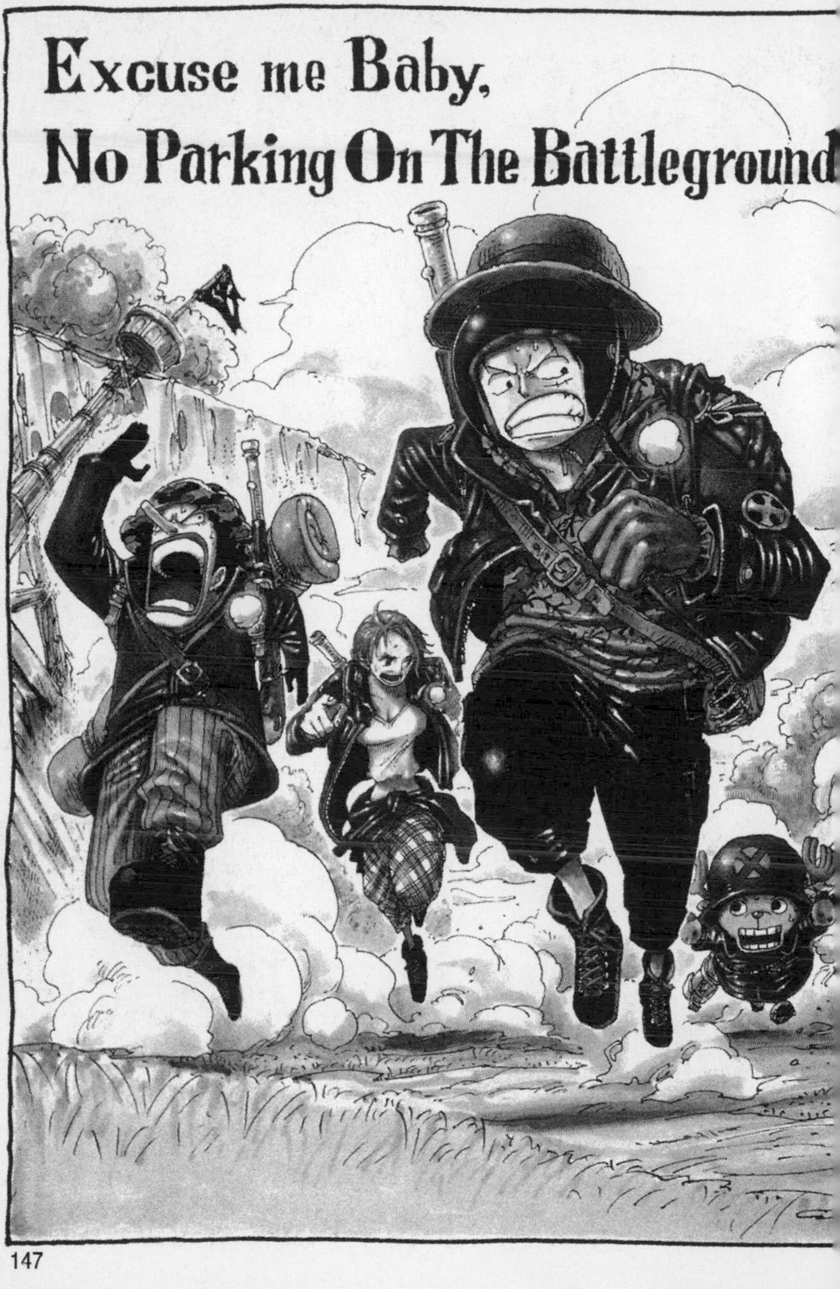
Excuse me Baby,
No Parking On The Battleground

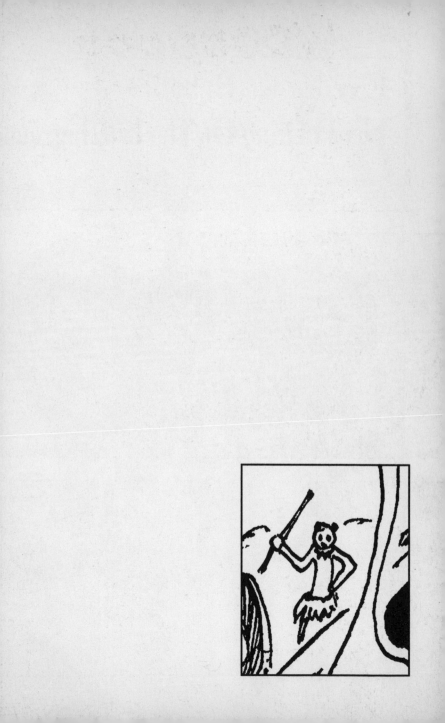

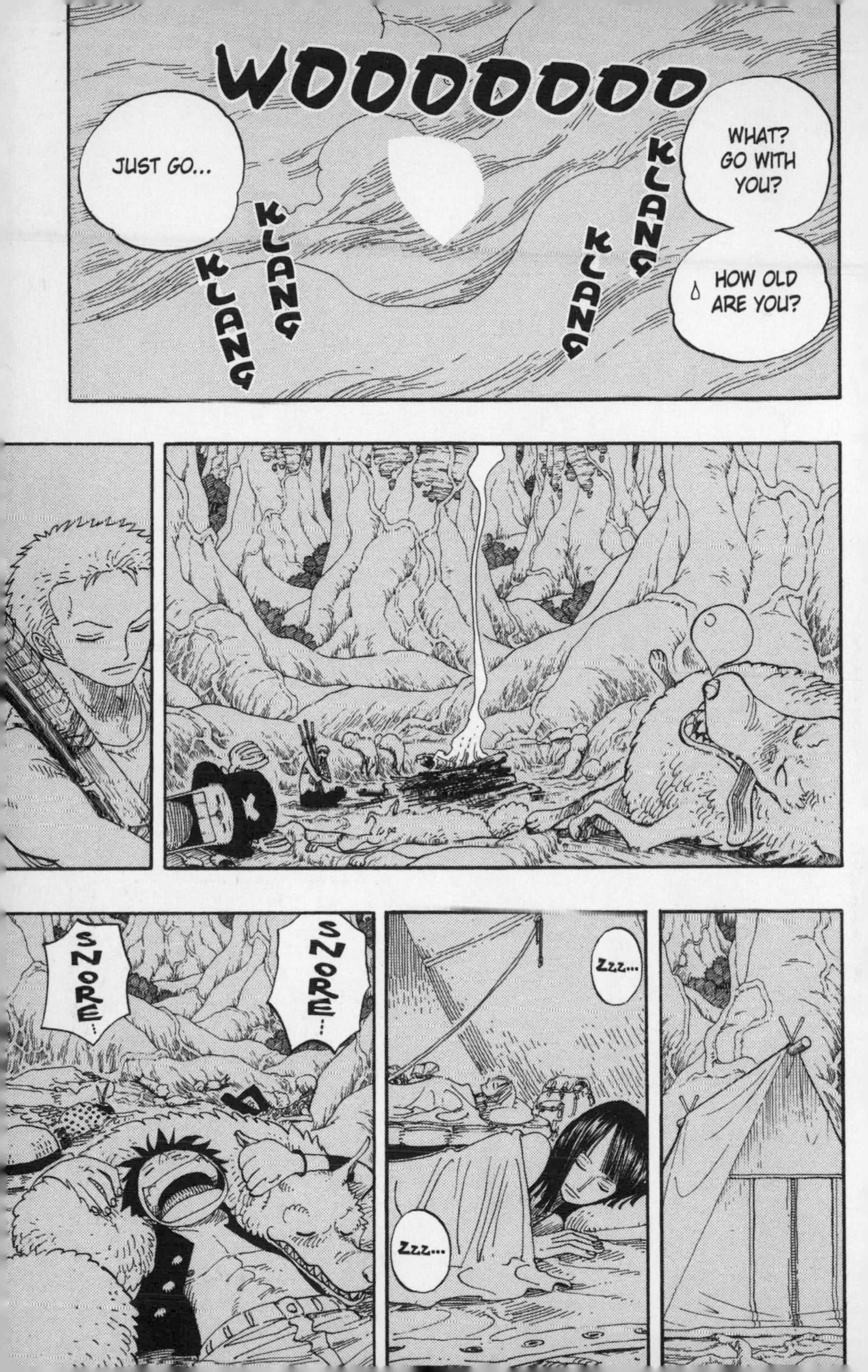
WOOOOOOOO
WHAT? GO WITH YOU?
HOW OLD ARE YOU?
KLANG
KLANG
KLANG
KLANG
JUST GO...
Zzz...
Zzz...
SNORE...
SNORE...

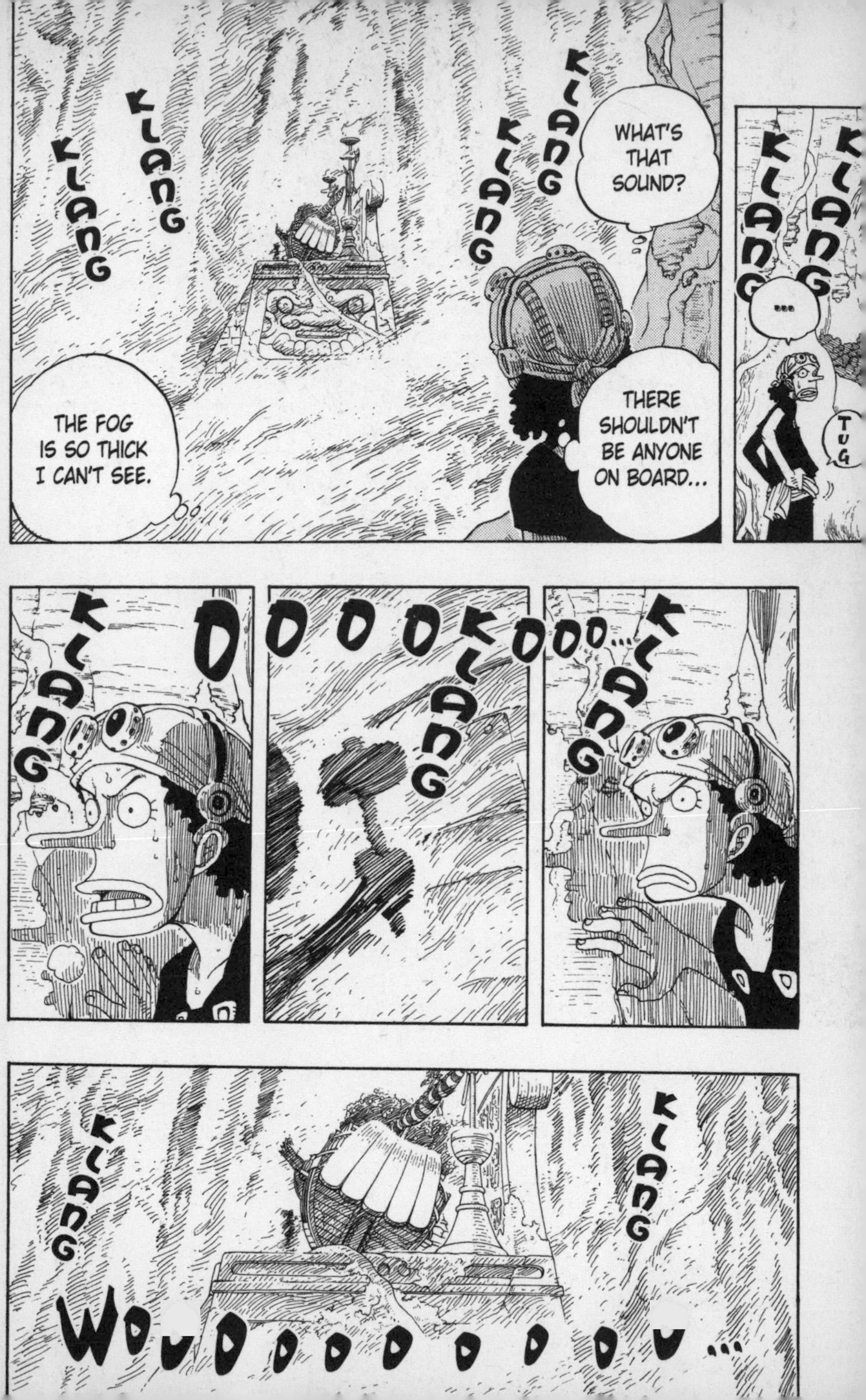
KLANG
KLANG
...
TUG
KLANG
KLANG
WHAT'S THAT SOUND?
THERE SHOULDN'T BE ANYONE ON BOARD...
KLANG
KLANG
THE FOG IS SO THICK I CAN'T SEE.
KLANG
DOOOOOO...
KLANG
KLANG
KLANG
KLANG
WOOOOOOOOOOO...

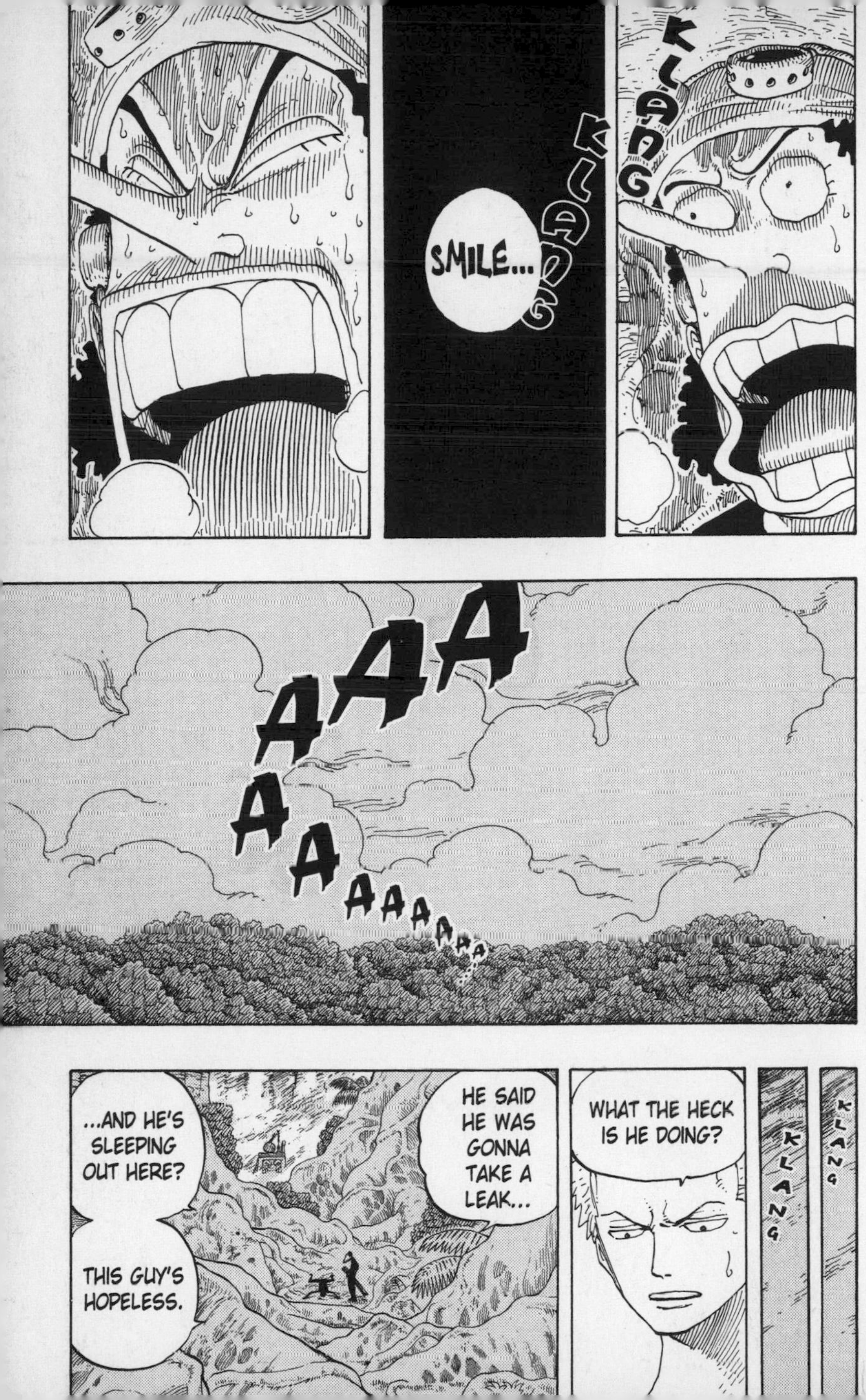
KLANG
KLANG
SMILE...
AAAAAAAAAAA
KLANG
KLANG
WHAT THE HECK IS HE DOING?
HE SAID HE WAS GONNA TAKE A LEAK...
...AND HE'S SLEEPING OUT HERE?
THIS GUY'S HOPELESS.

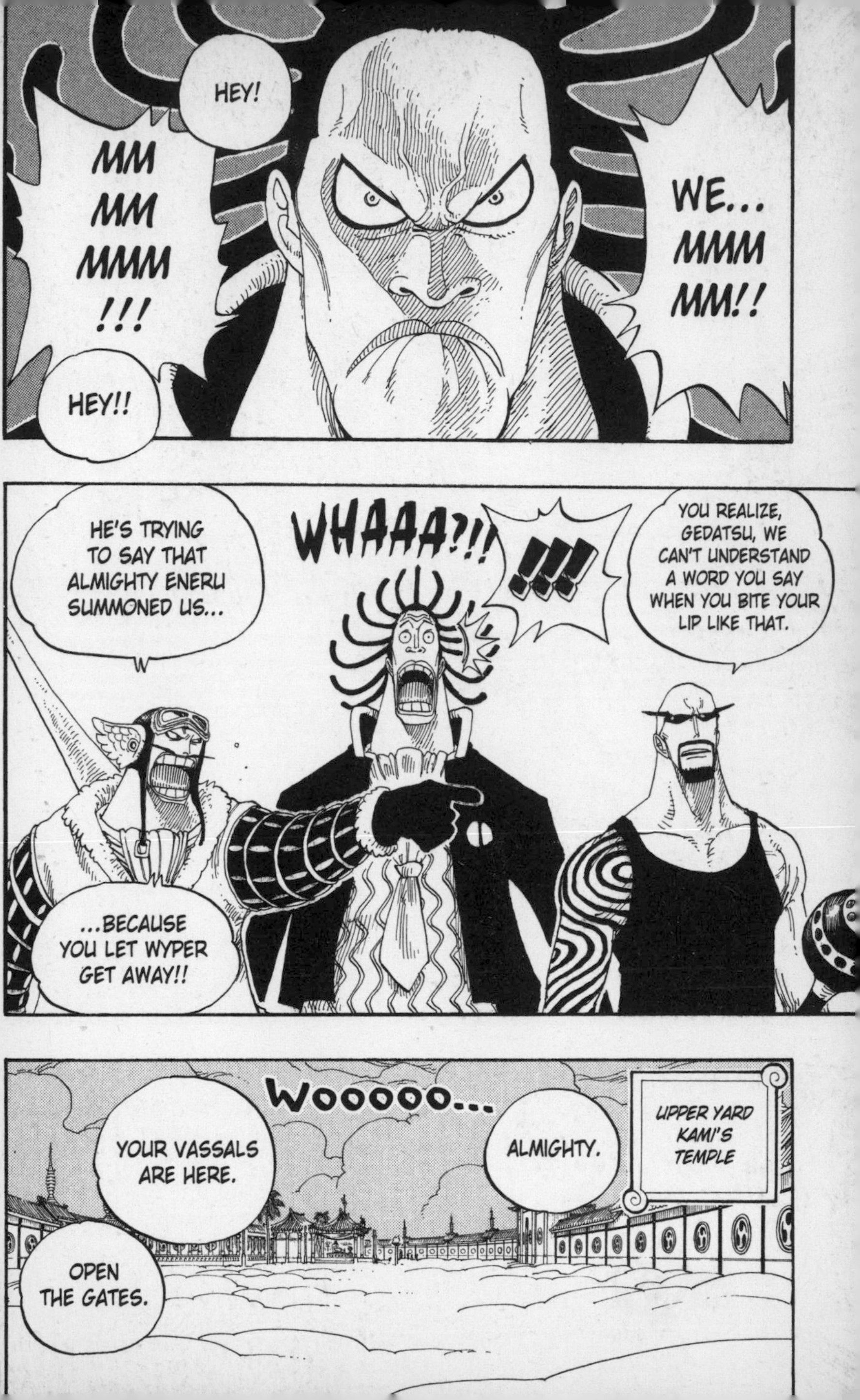
HEY!
WE... MMM MM!!
MM MM MMM !!!
HEY!!
YOU REALIZE, GEDATSU, WE CAN'T UNDERSTAND A WORD YOU SAY WHEN YOU BITE YOUR LIP LIKE THAT.
!!!
WHAAA?!!
HE'S TRYING TO SAY THAT ALMIGHTY ENERU SUMMONED US...
...BECAUSE YOU LET WYPER GET AWAY!!
UPPER YARD KAMI'S TEMPLE
ALMIGHTY.
WOOOOO...
YOUR VASSALS ARE HERE.
OPEN THE GATES.

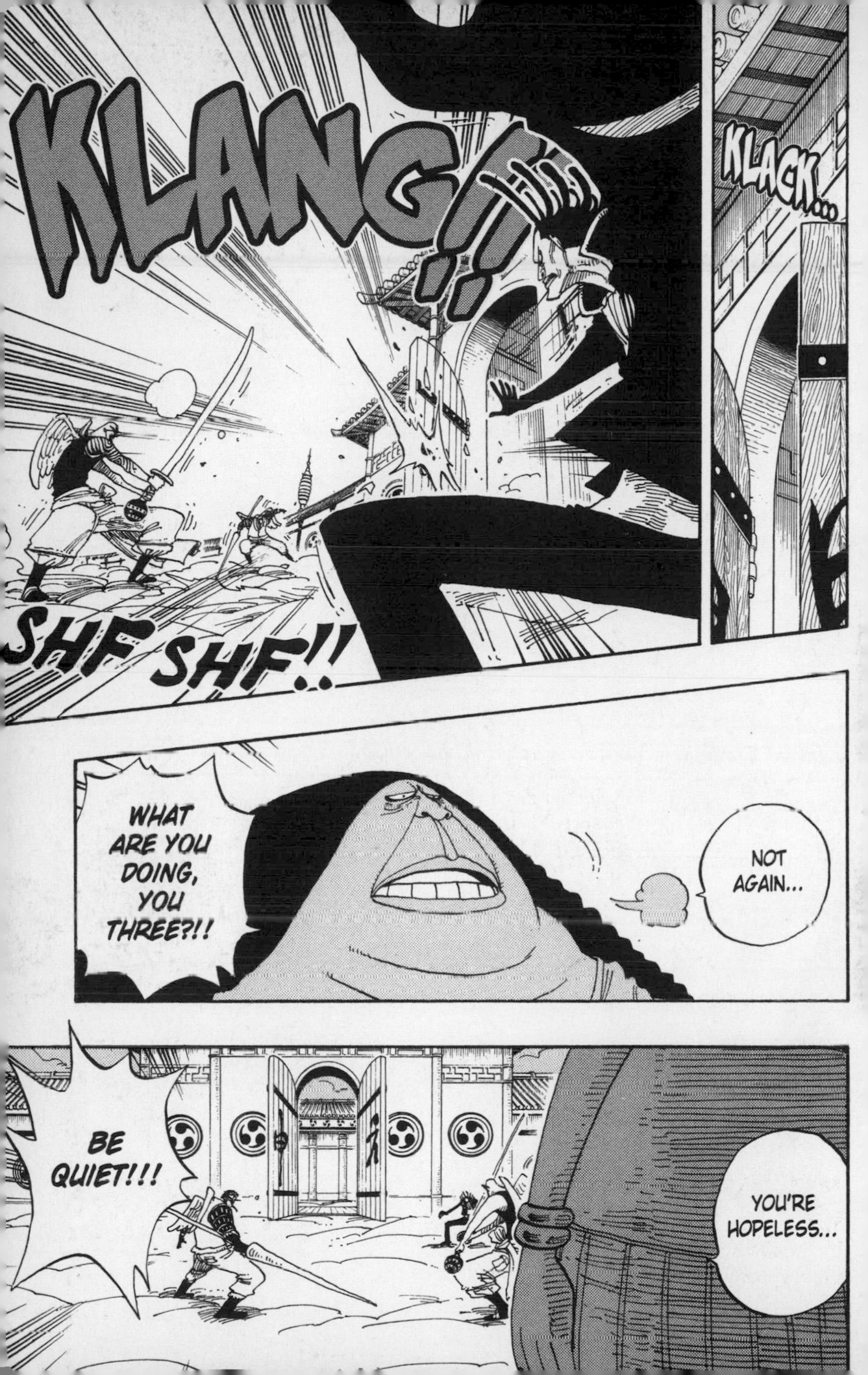
KLACK...
KLANG!!
SHF SHF!!
NOT AGAIN...
WHAT ARE YOU DOING, YOU THREE?!!
YOU'RE HOPELESS...
BE QUIET!!!

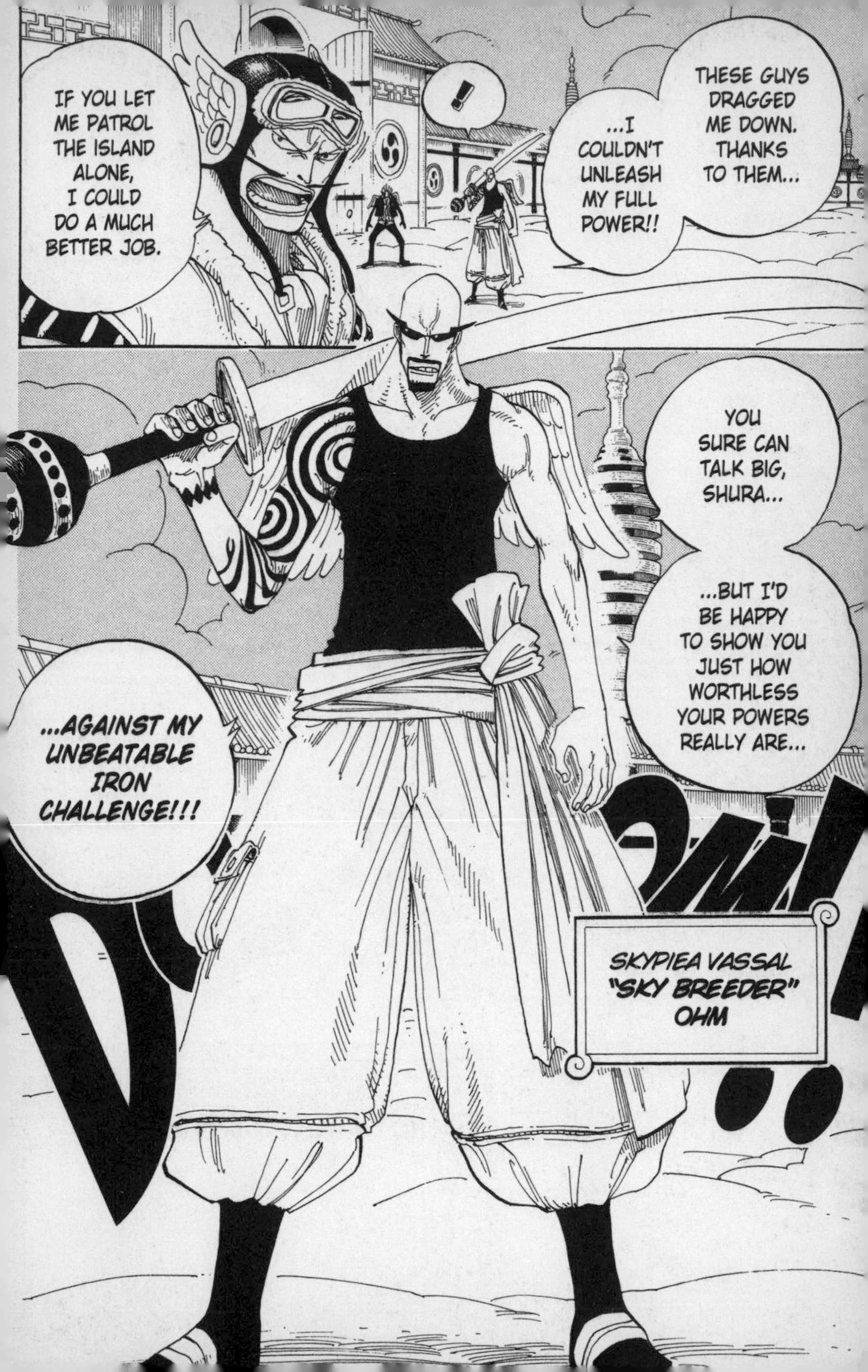
THESE GUYS DRAGGED ME DOWN. THANKS TO THEM...
...I COULDN'T UNLEASH MY FULL POWER!!
!
IF YOU LET ME PATROL THE ISLAND ALONE, I COULD DO A MUCH BETTER JOB.
YOU SURE CAN TALK BIG, SHURA...
...BUT I'D BE HAPPY TO SHOW YOU JUST HOW WORTHLESS YOUR POWERS REALLY ARE...
...AGAINST MY UNBEATABLE IRON CHALLENGE!!!
SKYPIEA VASSAL "SKY BREEDER" OHM

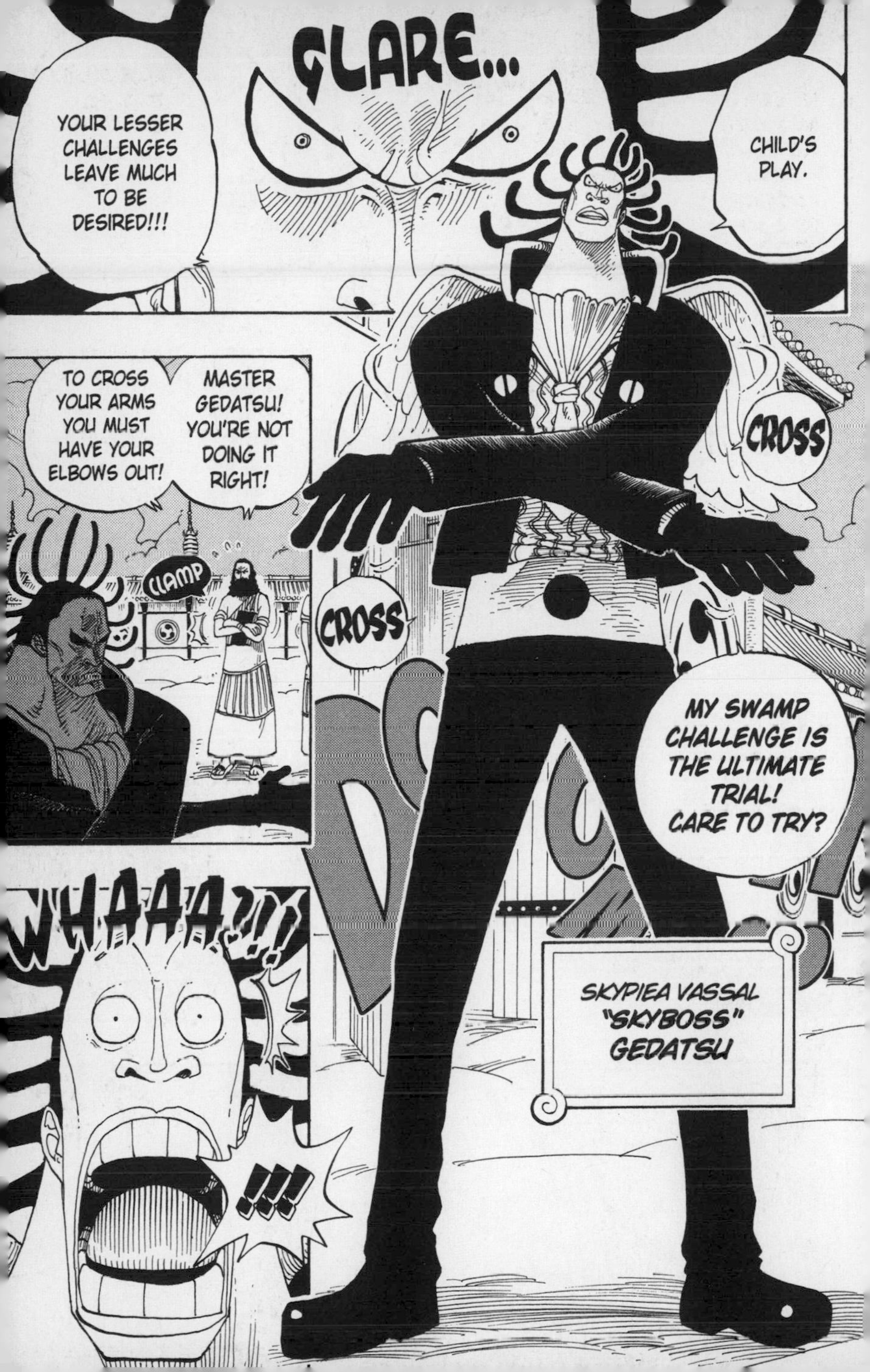
CHILD'S PLAY.
GLARE...
YOUR LESSER CHALLENGES LEAVE MUCH TO BE DESIRED!!!
CROSS
CROSS
MY SWAMP CHALLENGE IS THE ULTIMATE TRIAL! CARE TO TRY?
SKYPIEA VASSAL "SKYBOSS" GEDATSU
MASTER GEDATSU! YOU'RE NOT DOING IT RIGHT!
TO CROSS YOUR ARMS YOU MUST HAVE YOUR ELBOWS OUT!
CLAMP
WHAAA?!!
!!!

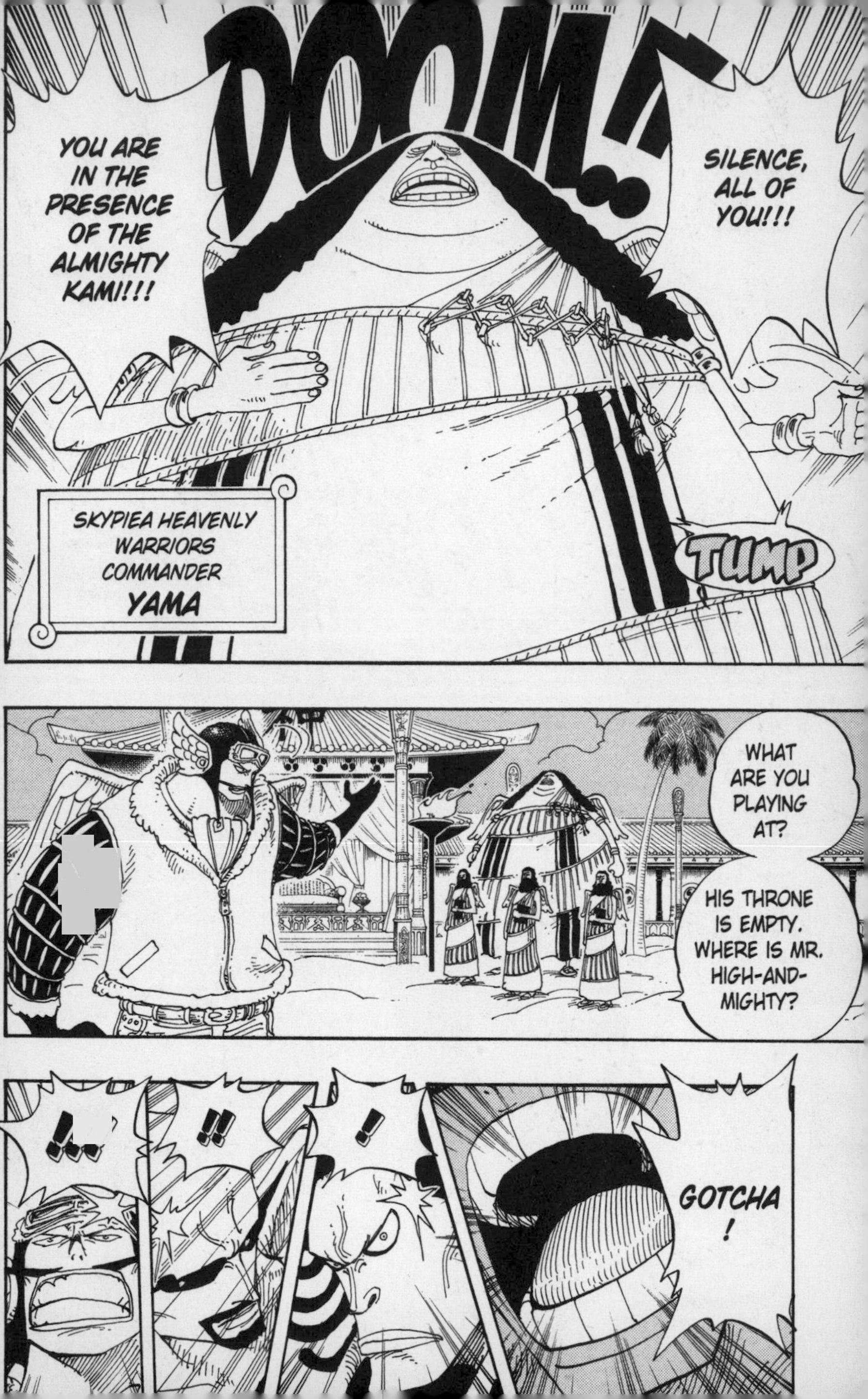
DOOM...
SILENCE, ALL OF YOU!!!
YOU ARE IN THE PRESENCE OF THE ALMIGHTY KAMI!!!
TUMP
SKYPIEA HEAVENLY WARRIORS COMMANDER YAMA
WHAT ARE YOU PLAYING AT?
HIS THRONE IS EMPTY. WHERE IS MR. HIGH-AND-MIGHTY?
GOTCHA !
!
!!
!!

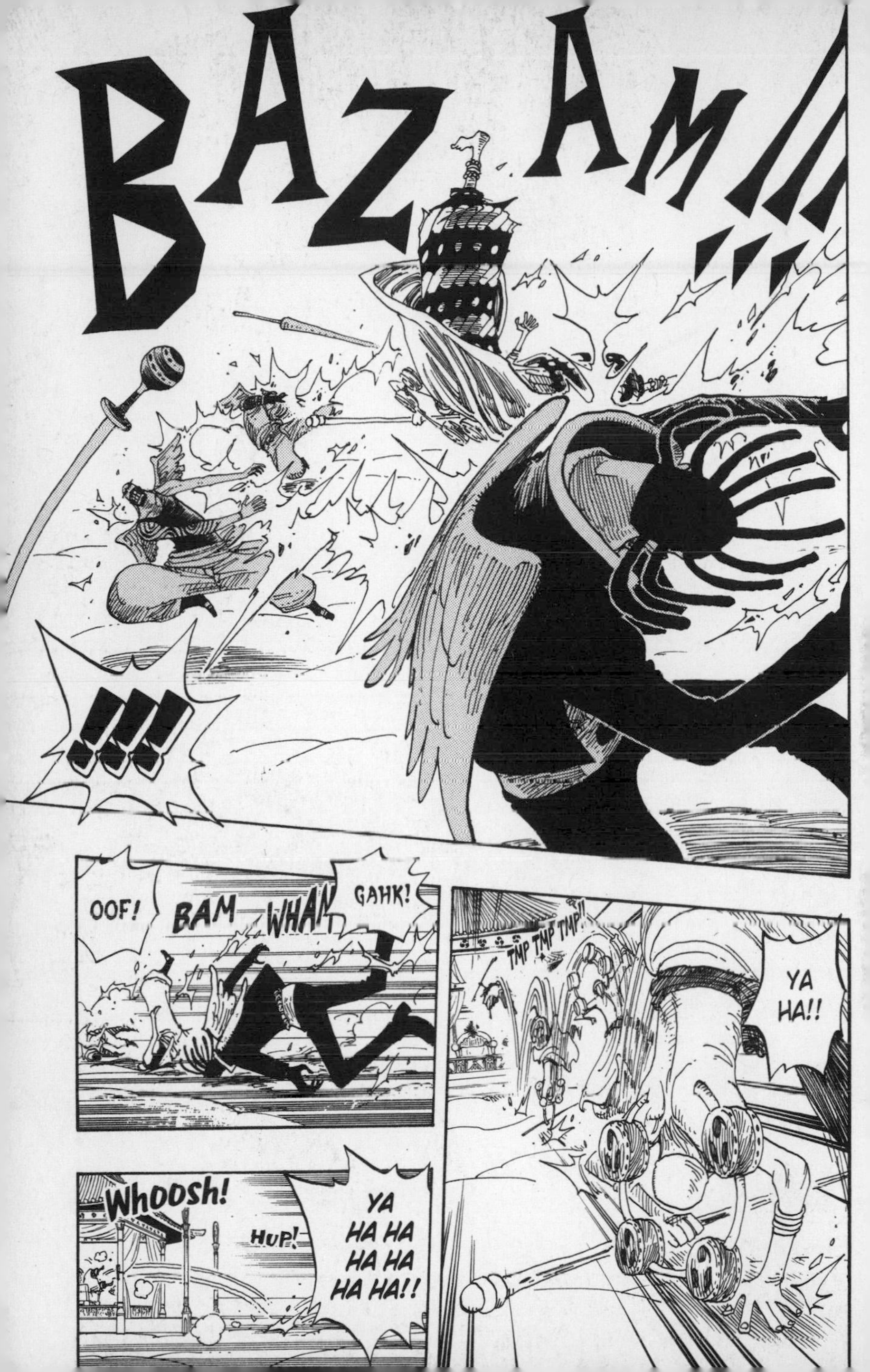
BAZAM!!!!
!!!
TMP TMP TMP!!
YA HA!!
GAHK!
WHAM
BAM
OOF!
YA HA HA HA HA HA HA!!
HUP!
Whoosh!

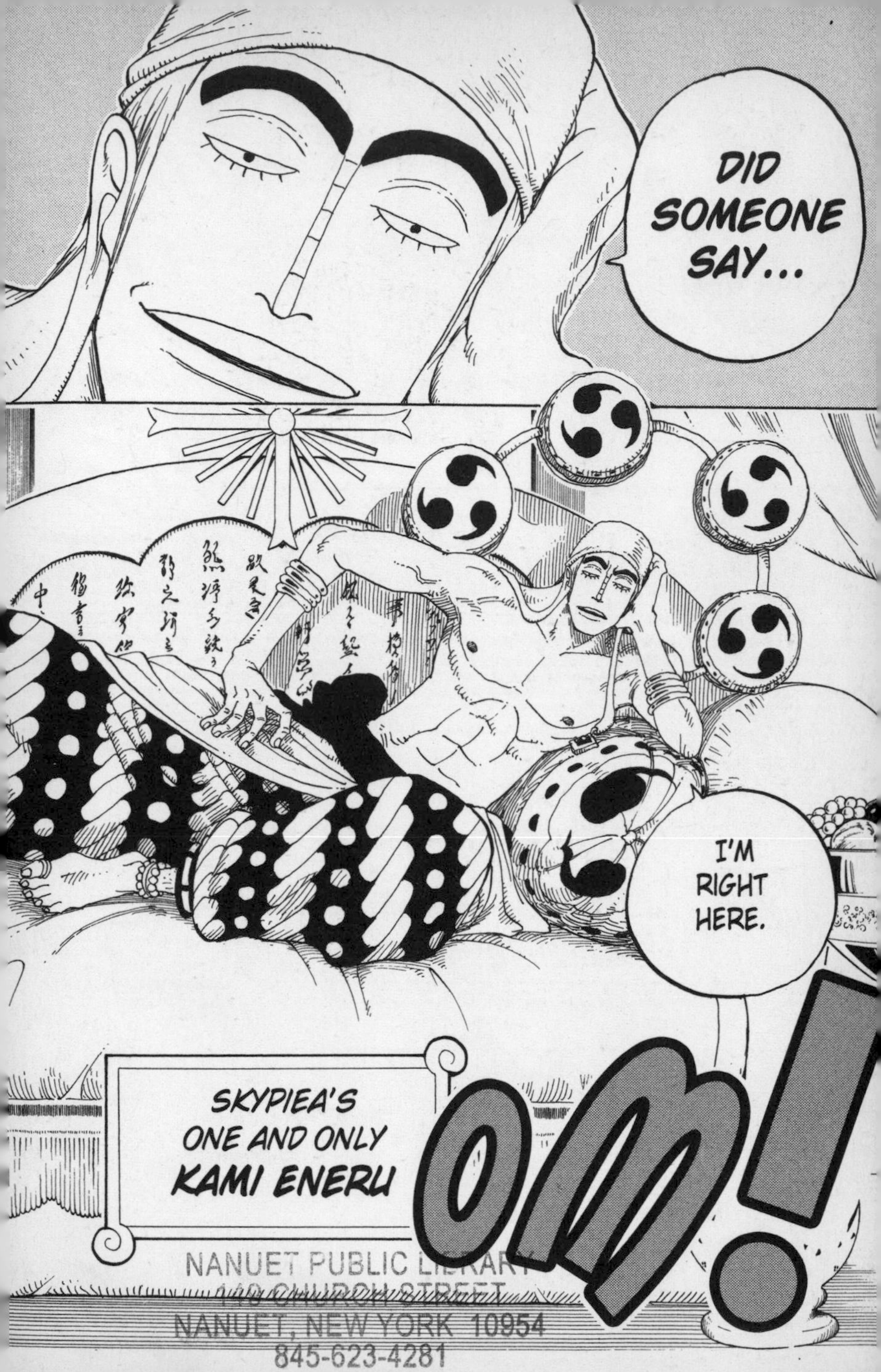
DID SOMEONE SAY...
I'M RIGHT HERE.
SKYPIEA'S ONE AND ONLY KAMI ENERU
OM!

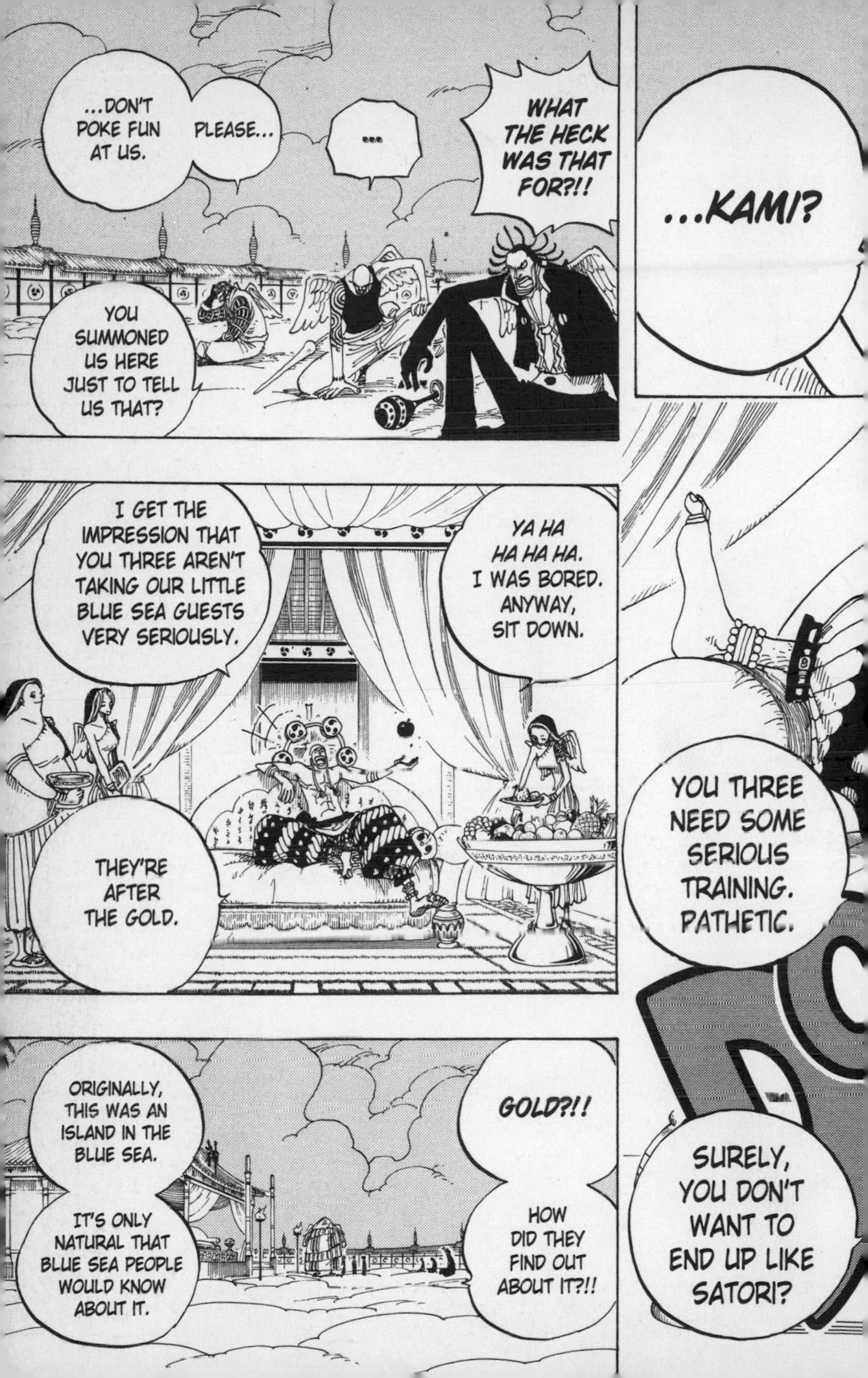
...KAMI?
YOU THREE NEED SOME SERIOUS TRAINING. PATHETIC.
SURELY, YOU DON'T WANT TO END UP LIKE SATORI?
WHAT THE HECK WAS THAT FOR?!!
...
PLEASE...
...DON'T POKE FUN AT US.
YOU SUMMONED US HERE JUST TO TELL US THAT?
YA HA HA HA HA. I WAS BORED. ANYWAY, SIT DOWN.
I GET THE IMPRESSION THAT YOU THREE AREN'T TAKING OUR LITTLE BLUE SEA GUESTS VERY SERIOUSLY.
THEY'RE AFTER THE GOLD.
GOLD?!!
HOW DID THEY FIND OUT ABOUT IT?!!
ORIGINALLY, THIS WAS AN ISLAND IN THE BLUE SEA.
IT'S ONLY NATURAL THAT BLUE SEA PEOPLE WOULD KNOW ABOUT IT.

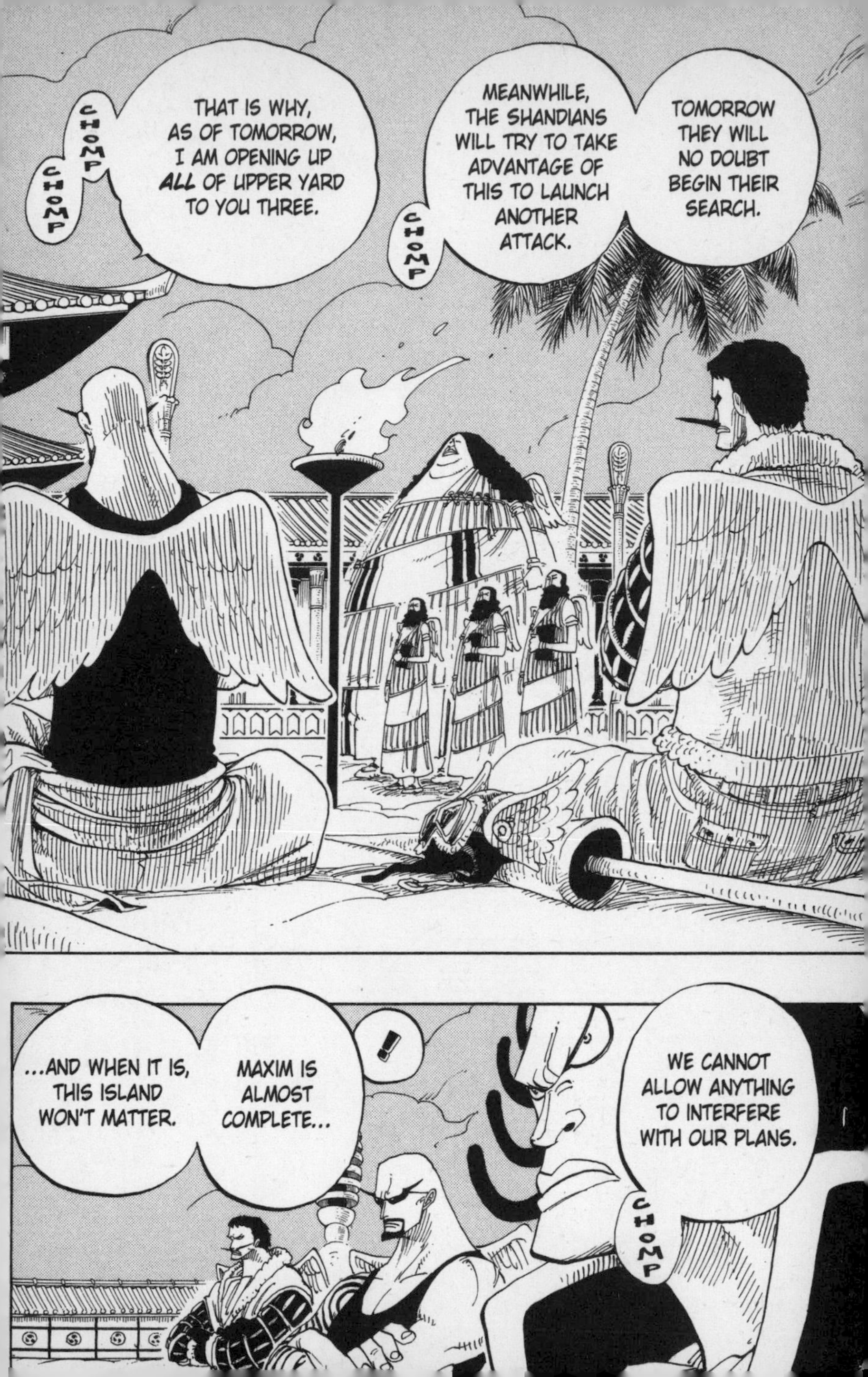
TOMORROW THEY WILL NO DOUBT BEGIN THEIR SEARCH.
MEANWHILE, THE SHANDIANS WILL TRY TO TAKE ADVANTAGE OF THIS TO LAUNCH ANOTHER ATTACK.
CHOMP
THAT IS WHY, AS OF TOMORROW, I AM OPENING UP ALL OF UPPER YARD TO YOU THREE.
CHOMP
CHOMP
WE CANNOT ALLOW ANYTHING TO INTERFERE WITH OUR PLANS.
CHOMP
!
MAXIM IS ALMOST COMPLETE...
...AND WHEN IT IS, THIS ISLAND WON'T MATTER.

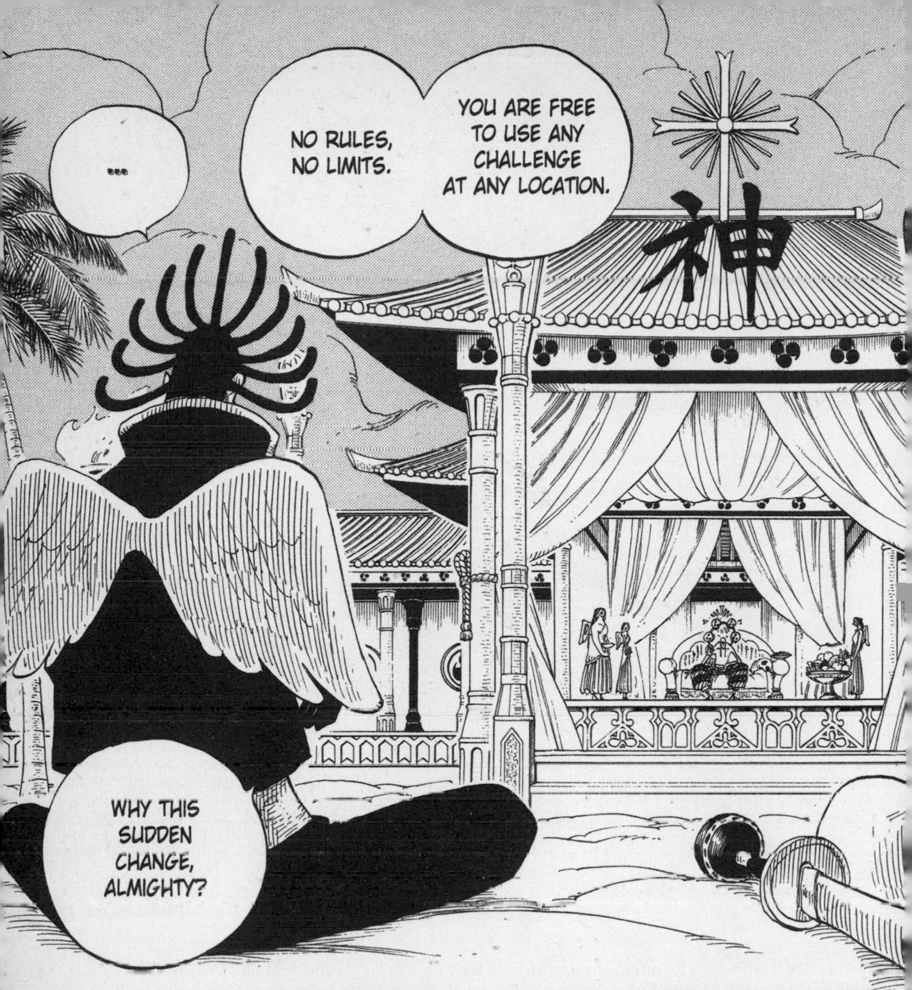
YOU ARE FREE TO USE ANY CHALLENGE AT ANY LOCATION.
NO RULES, NO LIMITS.
...
WHY THIS SUDDEN CHANGE, ALMIGHTY?

KANJI ON ROOF SAYS "KAMI" --ED

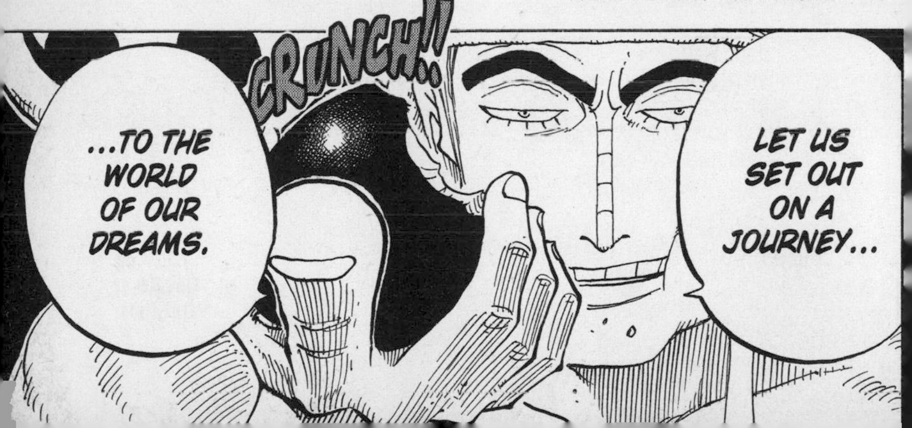
LET US SET OUT ON A JOURNEY...
CRUNCH!!
...TO THE WORLD OF OUR DREAMS.

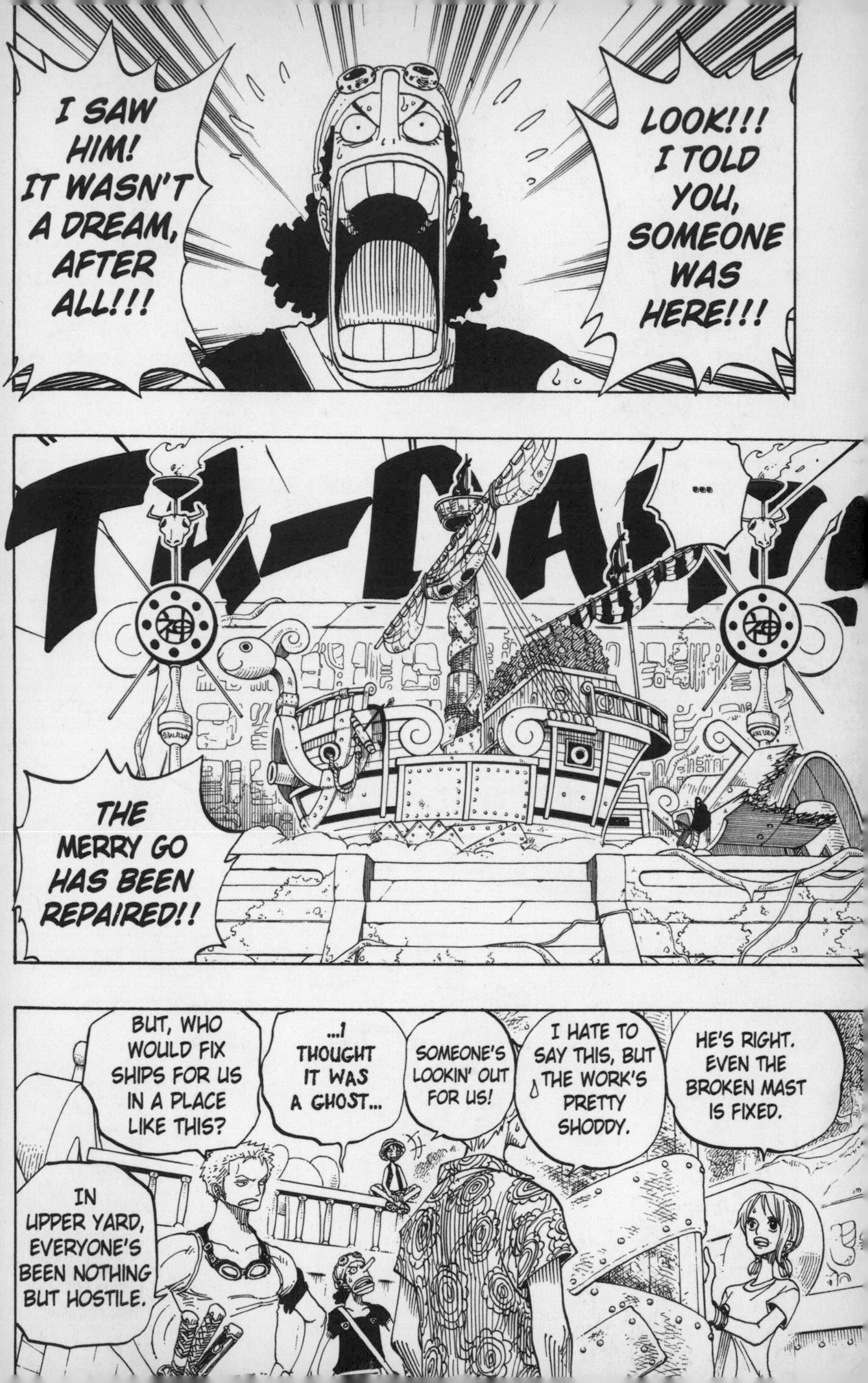
LOOK!!! I TOLD YOU, SOMEONE WAS HERE!!!
I SAW HIM! IT WASN'T A DREAM, AFTER ALL!!!
THE MERRY GO HAS BEEN REPAIRED!!
HE'S RIGHT. EVEN THE BROKEN MAST IS FIXED.
I HATE TO SAY THIS, BUT THE WORK'S PRETTY SHODDY.
SOMEONE'S LOOKIN' OUT FOR US!
...I THOUGHT IT WAS A GHOST...
BUT, WHO WOULD FIX SHIPS FOR US IN A PLACE LIKE THIS?
IN UPPER YARD, EVERYONE'S BEEN NOTHING BUT HOSTILE.

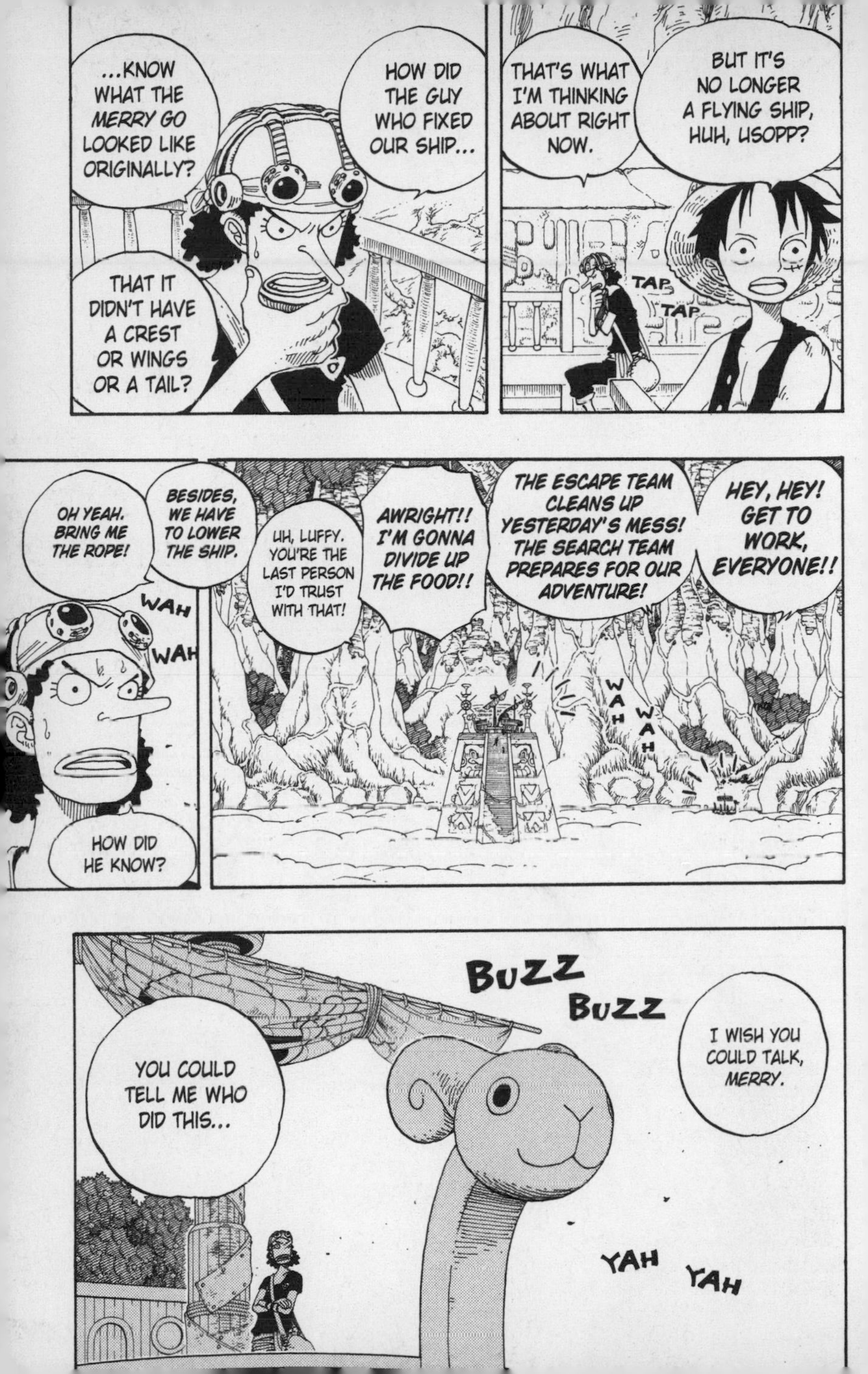
BUT IT'S NO LONGER A FLYING SHIP, HUH, USOPP?
THAT'S WHAT I'M THINKING ABOUT RIGHT NOW.
TAP
TAP
HOW DID THE GUY WHO FIXED OUR SHIP...
...KNOW WHAT THE MERRY GO LOOKED LIKE ORIGINALLY?
THAT IT DIDN'T HAVE A CREST OR WINGS OR A TAIL?
HEY, HEY! GET TO WORK, EVERYONE!!
THE ESCAPE TEAM CLEANS UP YESTERDAY'S MESS! THE SEARCH TEAM PREPARES FOR OUR ADVENTURE!
AWRIGHT!! I'M GONNA DIVIDE UP THE FOOD!!
UH, LUFFY. YOU'RE THE LAST PERSON I'D TRUST WITH THAT!
WAH
WAH
BESIDES, WE HAVE TO LOWER THE SHIP.
OH YEAH. BRING ME THE ROPE!
WAH
WAH
HOW DID HE KNOW?
BUZZ
BUZZ
I WISH YOU COULD TALK, MERRY.
YOU COULD TELL ME WHO DID THIS...
YAH
YAH

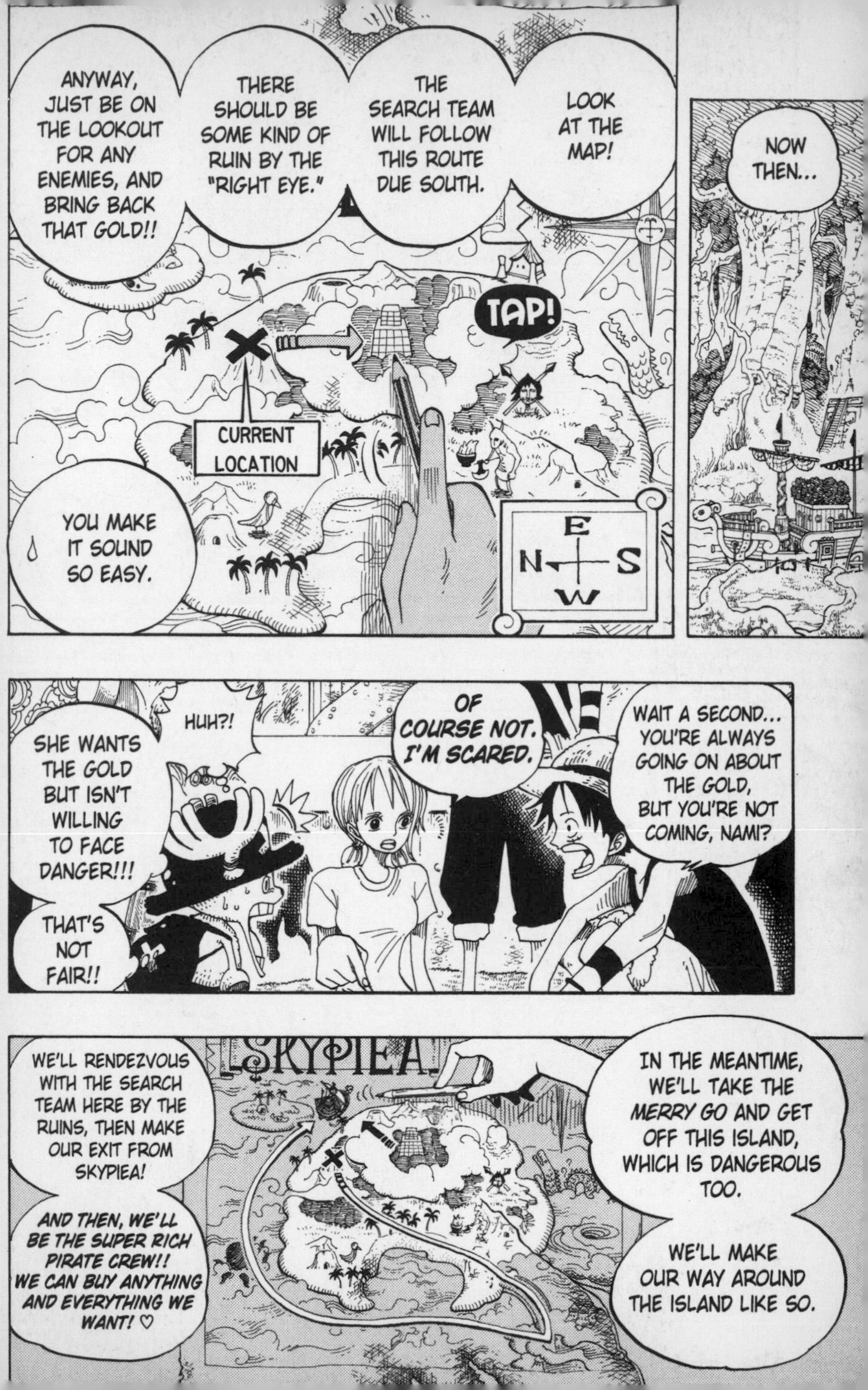
NOW THEN...
LOOK AT THE MAP!
THE SEARCH TEAM WILL FOLLOW THIS ROUTE DUE SOUTH.
THERE SHOULD BE SOME KIND OF RUIN BY THE "RIGHT EYE."
ANYWAY, JUST BE ON THE LOOKOUT FOR ANY ENEMIES, AND BRING BACK THAT GOLD!!
TAP!
CURRENT LOCATION
E
N
S
W
YOU MAKE IT SOUND SO EASY.
WAIT A SECOND... YOU'RE ALWAYS GOING ON ABOUT THE GOLD, BUT YOU'RE NOT COMING, NAMI?
OF COURSE NOT. I'M SCARED.
HUH?!
SHE WANTS THE GOLD BUT ISN'T WILLING TO FACE DANGER!!!
THAT'S NOT FAIR!!
IN THE MEANTIME, WE'LL TAKE THE MERRY GO AND GET OFF THIS ISLAND, WHICH IS DANGEROUS TOO.
WE'LL MAKE OUR WAY AROUND THE ISLAND LIKE SO.
SKYPIEA
WE'LL RENDEZVOUS WITH THE SEARCH TEAM HERE BY THE RUINS, THEN MAKE OUR EXIT FROM SKYPIEA!
AND THEN, WE'LL BE THE SUPER RICH PIRATE CREW!! WE CAN BUY ANYTHING AND EVERYTHING WE WANT! ♡

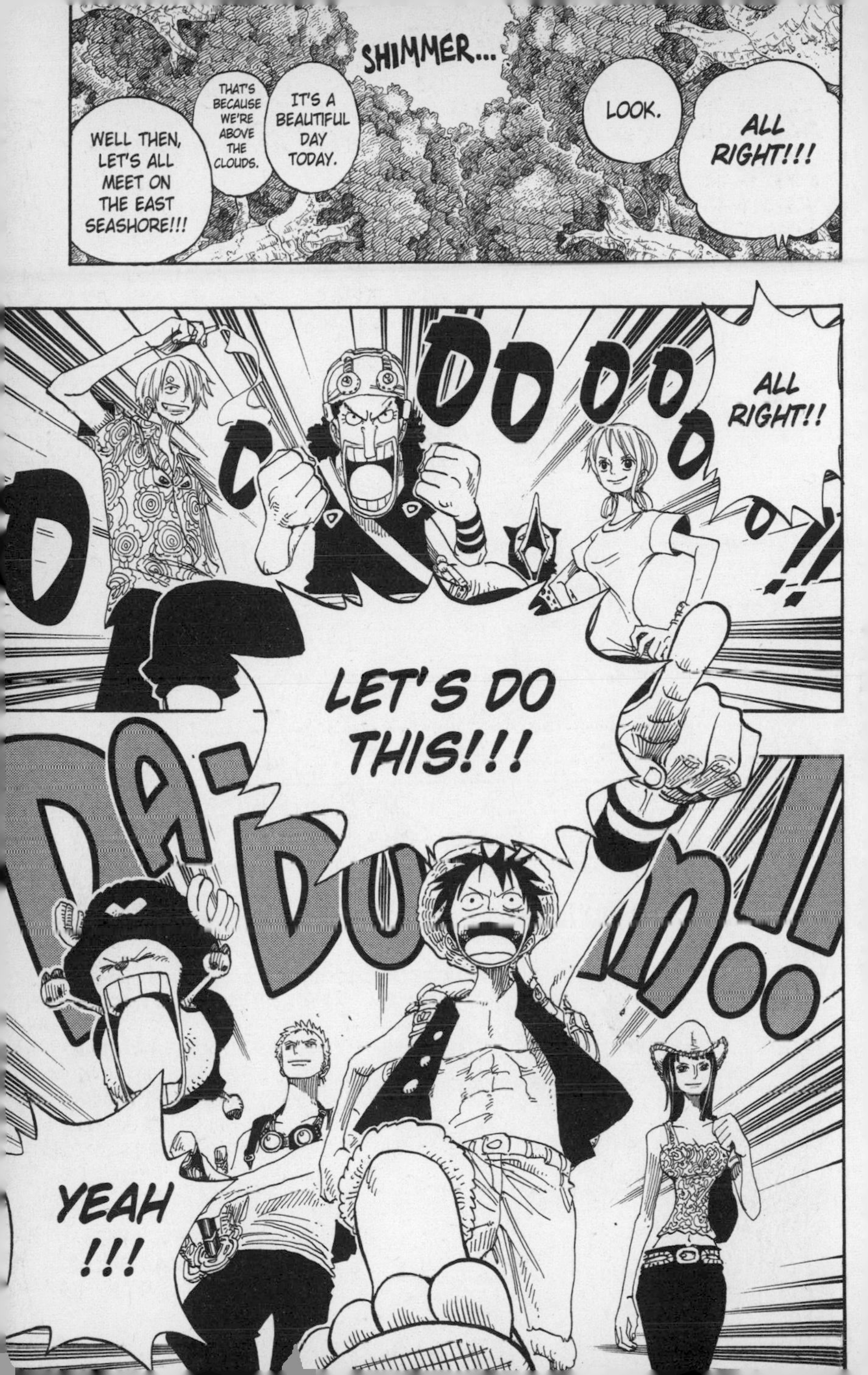
ALL RIGHT!!!
LOOK.
SHIMMER...
IT'S A BEAUTIFUL DAY TODAY.
THAT'S BECAUSE WE'RE ABOVE THE CLOUDS.
WELL THEN, LET'S ALL MEET ON THE EAST SEASHORE!!!
ALL RIGHT!!
LET'S DO THIS!!!
DA-DUN!!
YEAH!!!

COLORING PAGE

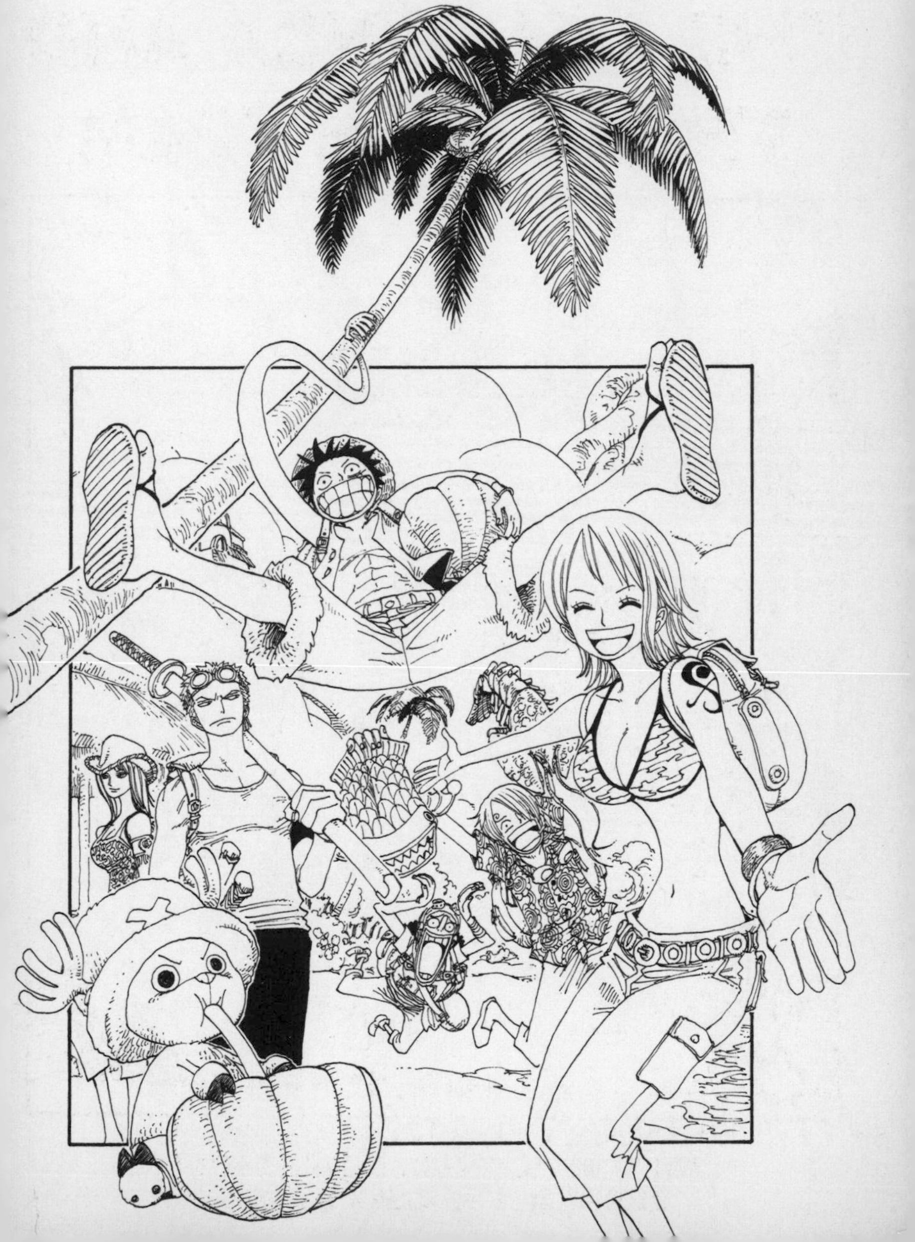

Chapter 255:

THE ANACONDA AND THE SEARCH TEAM

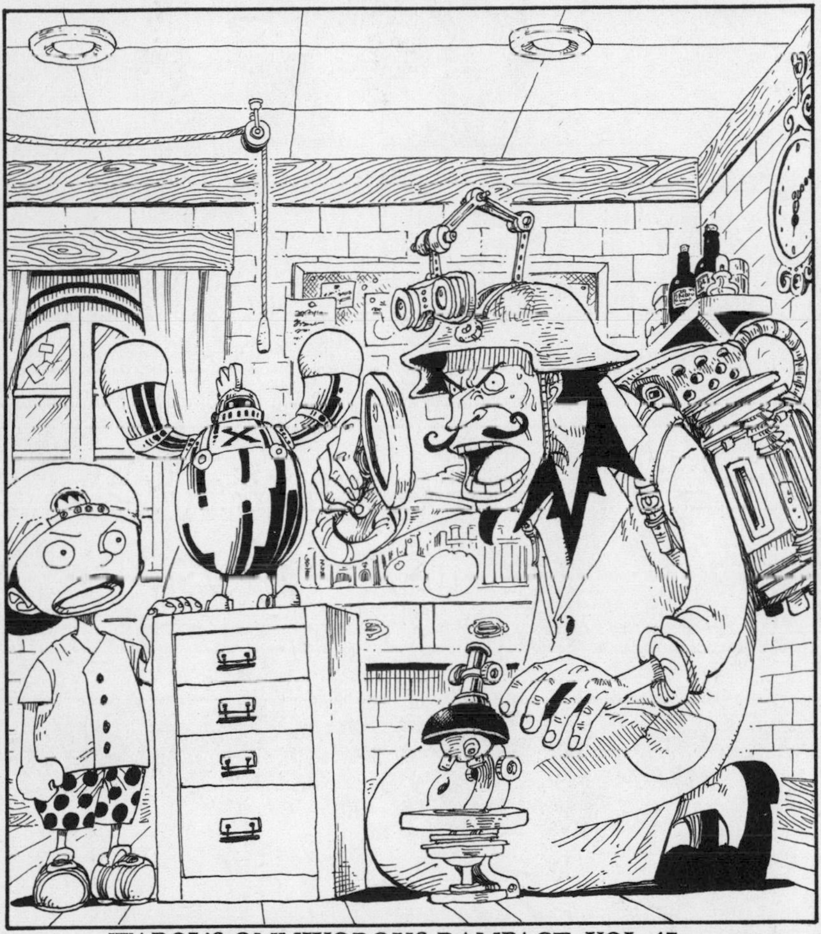

WAPOL'S OMNIVOROUS RAMPAGE, VOL. 17:
"THE TOWN SCIENTIST SEARCHES FOR THE SECRET OF WAPOL'S TOYS"

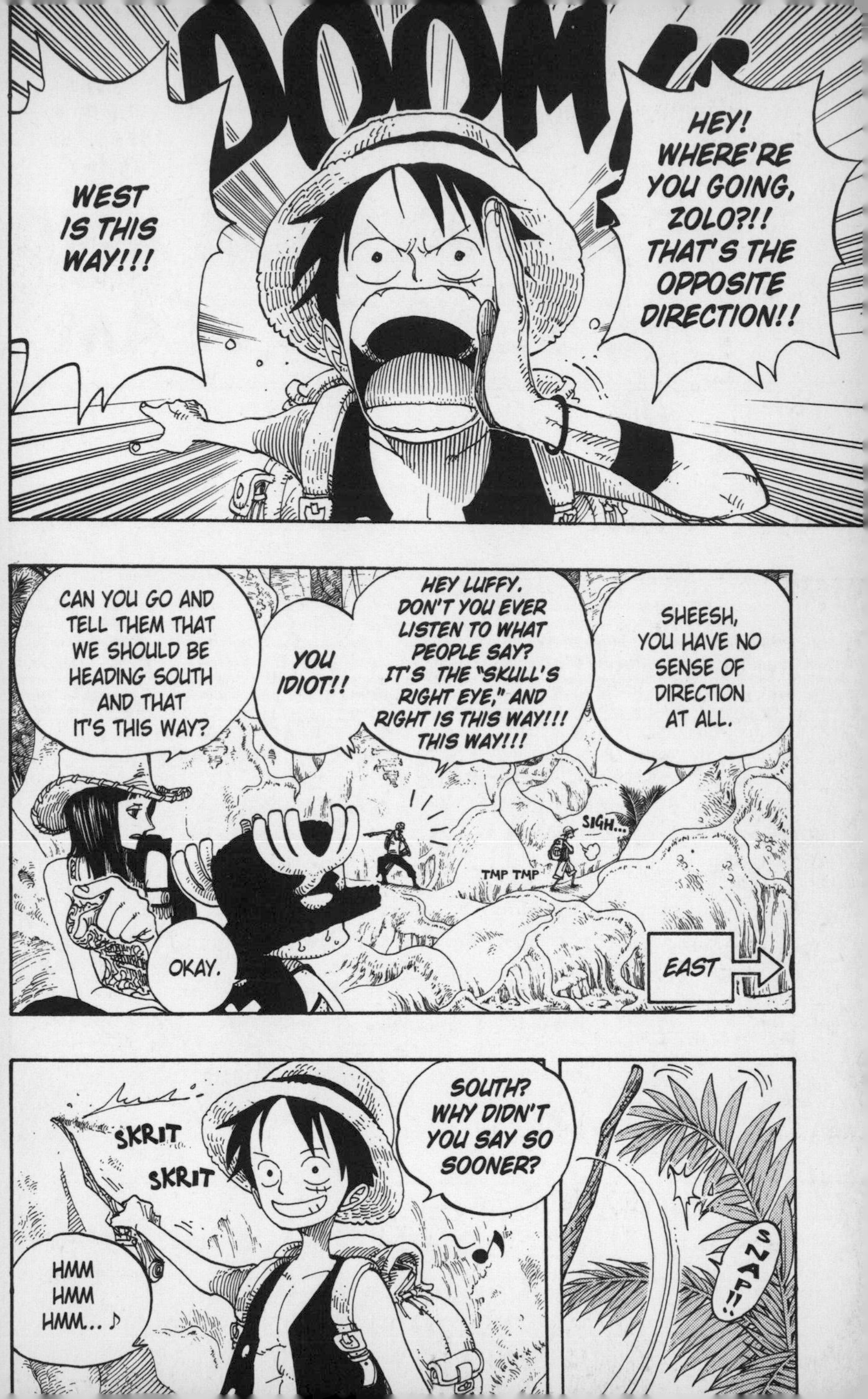
DOOM
HEY! WHERE'RE YOU GOING, ZOLO?!! THAT'S THE OPPOSITE DIRECTION!!
WEST IS THIS WAY!!!
SHEESH, YOU HAVE NO SENSE OF DIRECTION AT ALL.
HEY LUFFY. DON'T YOU EVER LISTEN TO WHAT PEOPLE SAY? IT'S THE "SKULL'S RIGHT EYE," AND RIGHT IS THIS WAY!!! THIS WAY!!!
YOU IDIOT!!
CAN YOU GO AND TELL THEM THAT WE SHOULD BE HEADING SOUTH AND THAT IT'S THIS WAY?
SIGH...
TMP TMP
OKAY.
EAST
SNAP!!
SOUTH? WHY DIDN'T YOU SAY SO SOONER?
SKRIT
SKRIT
HMM HMM HMM...♪

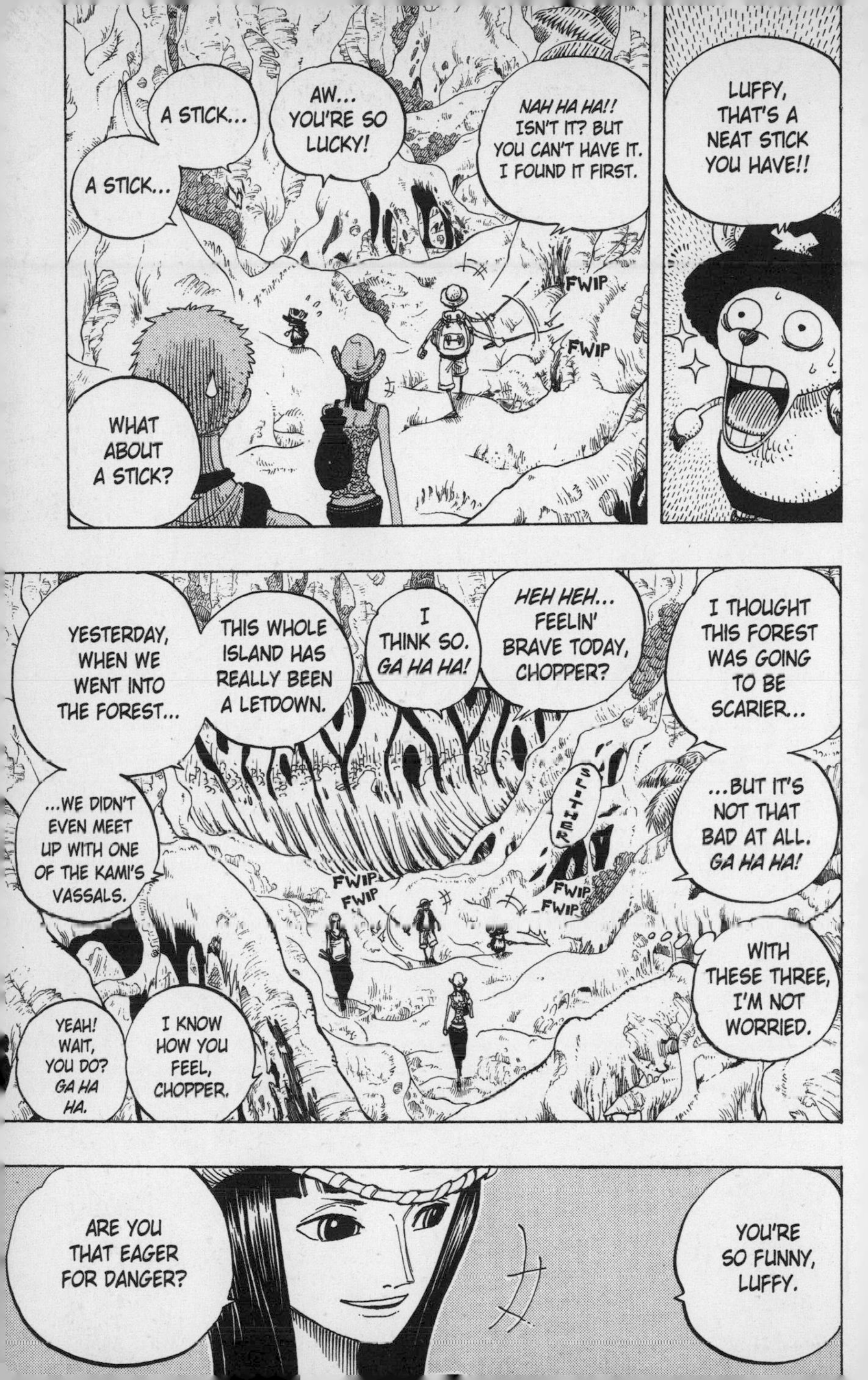
LUFFY, THAT'S A NEAT STICK YOU HAVE!!
NAH HA HA!! ISN'T IT? BUT YOU CAN'T HAVE IT. I FOUND IT FIRST.
AW... YOU'RE SO LUCKY!
A STICK...
A STICK...
FWIP
FWIP
WHAT ABOUT A STICK?
I THOUGHT THIS FOREST WAS GOING TO BE SCARIER...
...BUT IT'S NOT THAT BAD AT ALL. GA HA HA!
HEH HEH... FEELIN' BRAVE TODAY, CHOPPER?
I THINK SO. GA HA HA!
THIS WHOLE ISLAND HAS REALLY BEEN A LETDOWN.
YESTERDAY, WHEN WE WENT INTO THE FOREST...
SLITHER
...WE DIDN'T EVEN MEET UP WITH ONE OF THE KAMI'S VASSALS.
FWIP FWIP
FWIP FWIP
WITH THESE THREE, I'M NOT WORRIED.
I KNOW HOW YOU FEEL, CHOPPER.
YEAH! WAIT, YOU DO? GA HA HA.
YOU'RE SO FUNNY, LUFFY.
ARE YOU THAT EAGER FOR DANGER?

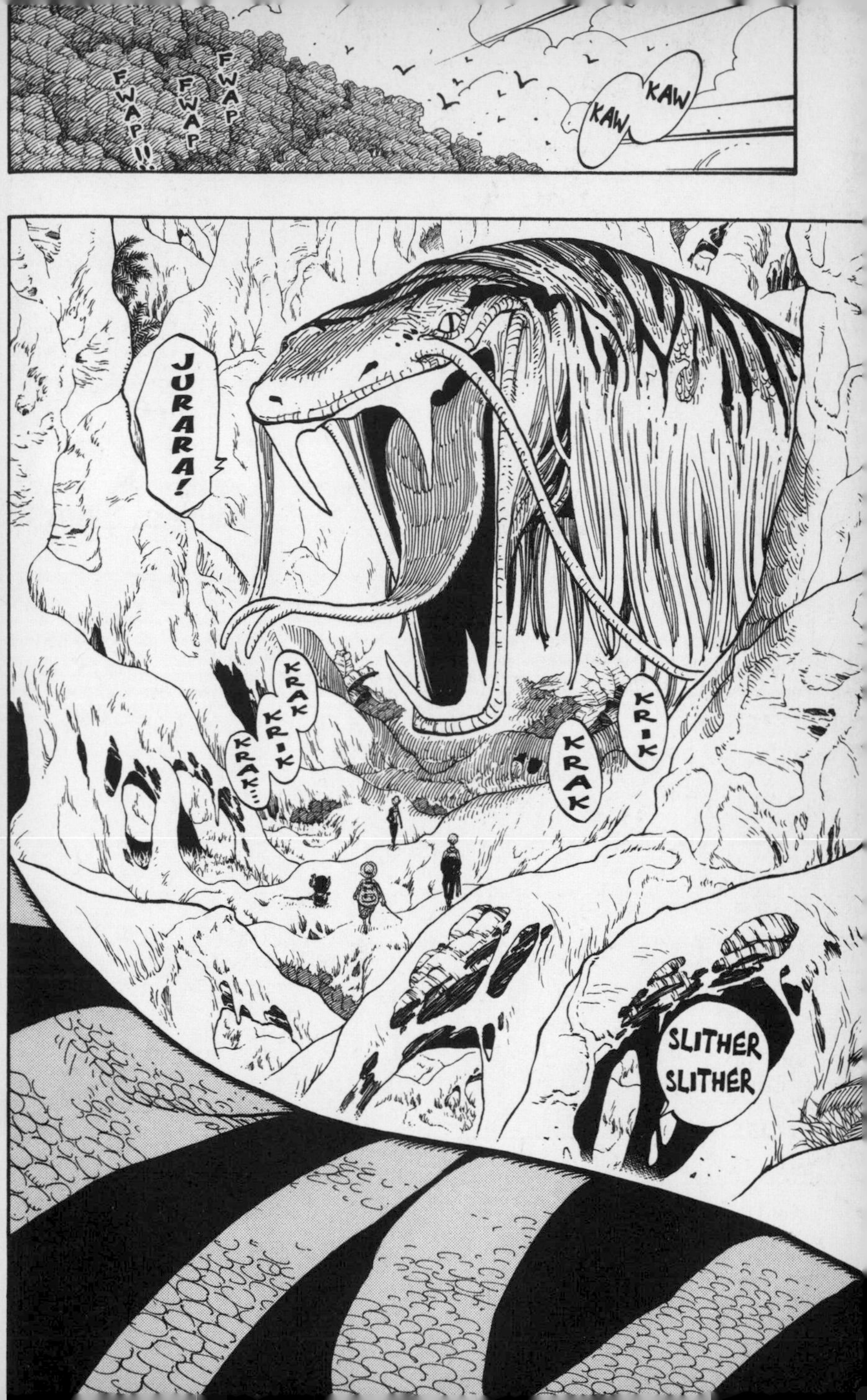
KAW
KAW
FWAP
FWAP
FWAP!!
JURARA!
KRIK
KRAK
KRAK
KRIK
KRAK...
SLITHER
SLITHER

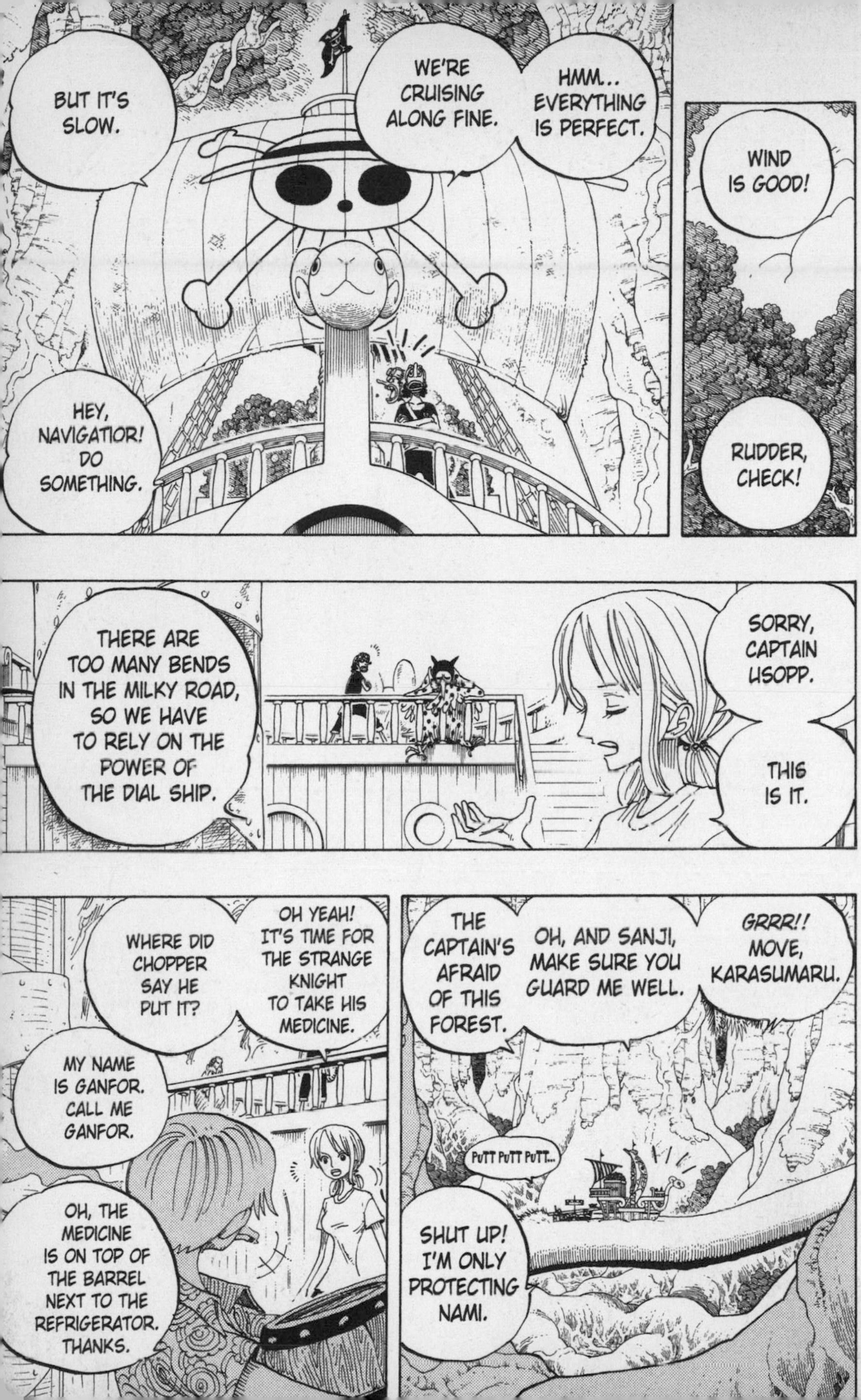
WIND IS GOOD!
RUDDER, CHECK!
HMM.. EVERYTHING IS PERFECT.
WE'RE CRUISING ALONG FINE.
BUT IT'S SLOW.
HEY, NAVIGATIOR! DO SOMETHING.
SORRY, CAPTAIN USOPP.
THIS IS IT.
THERE ARE TOO MANY BENDS IN THE MILKY ROAD, SO WE HAVE TO RELY ON THE POWER OF THE DIAL SHIP.
GRRR!! MOVE, KARASUMARU.
OH, AND SANJI, MAKE SURE YOU GUARD ME WELL.
THE CAPTAIN'S AFRAID OF THIS FOREST.
PUTT PUTT PUTT...
SHUT UP! I'M ONLY PROTECTING NAMI.
OH YEAH! IT'S TIME FOR THE STRANGE KNIGHT TO TAKE HIS MEDICINE.
WHERE DID CHOPPER SAY HE PUT IT?
MY NAME IS GANFOR. CALL ME GANFOR.
OH, THE MEDICINE IS ON TOP OF THE BARREL NEXT TO THE REFRIGERATOR. THANKS.

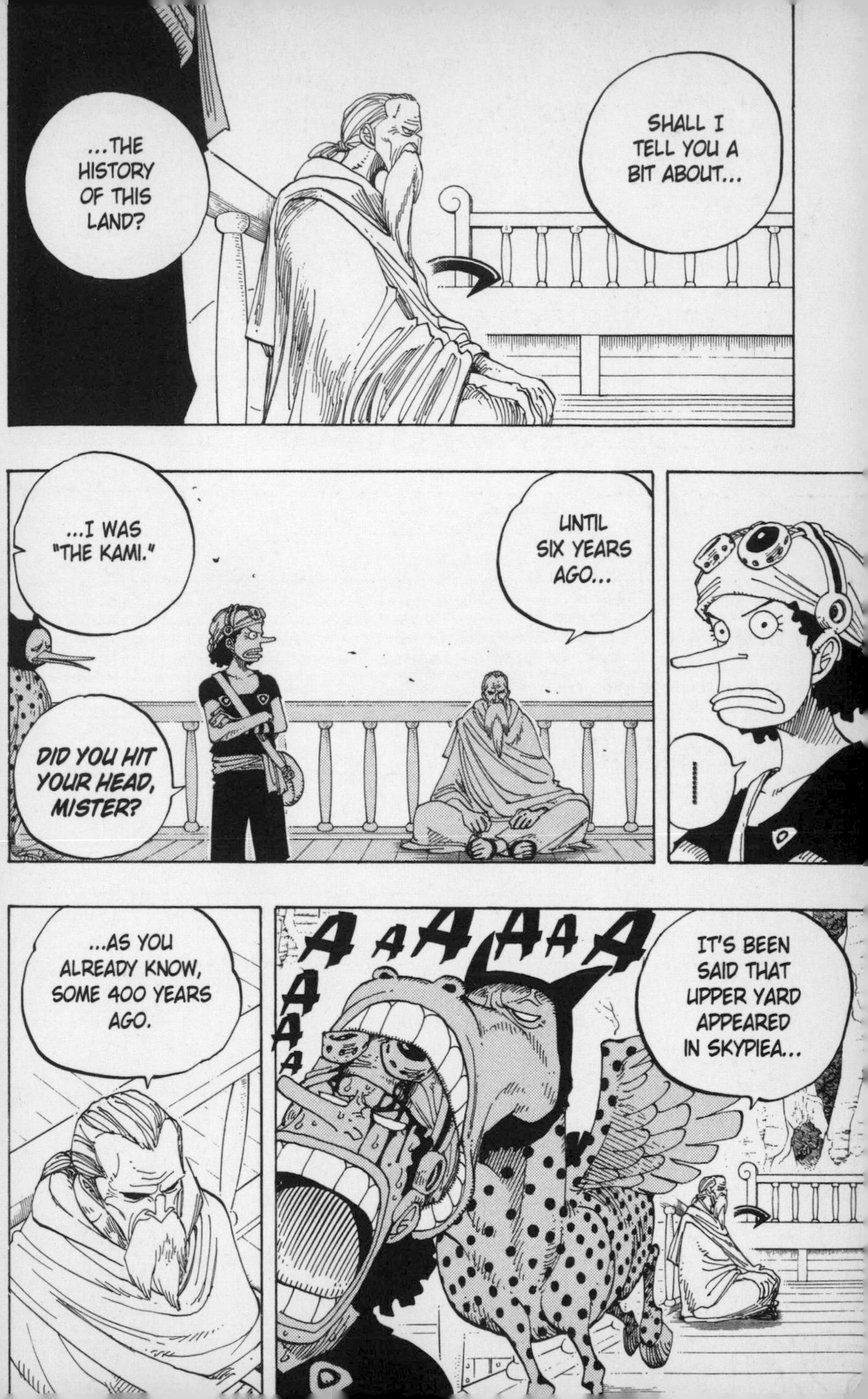
SHALL I TELL YOU A BIT ABOUT...
...THE HISTORY OF THIS LAND?
....
UNTIL SIX YEARS AGO...
...I WAS "THE KAMI."
DID YOU HIT YOUR HEAD, MISTER?
AAAAAAAAAAA
IT'S BEEN SAID THAT UPPER YARD APPEARED IN SKYPIEA...
...AS YOU ALREADY KNOW, SOME 400 YEARS AGO.

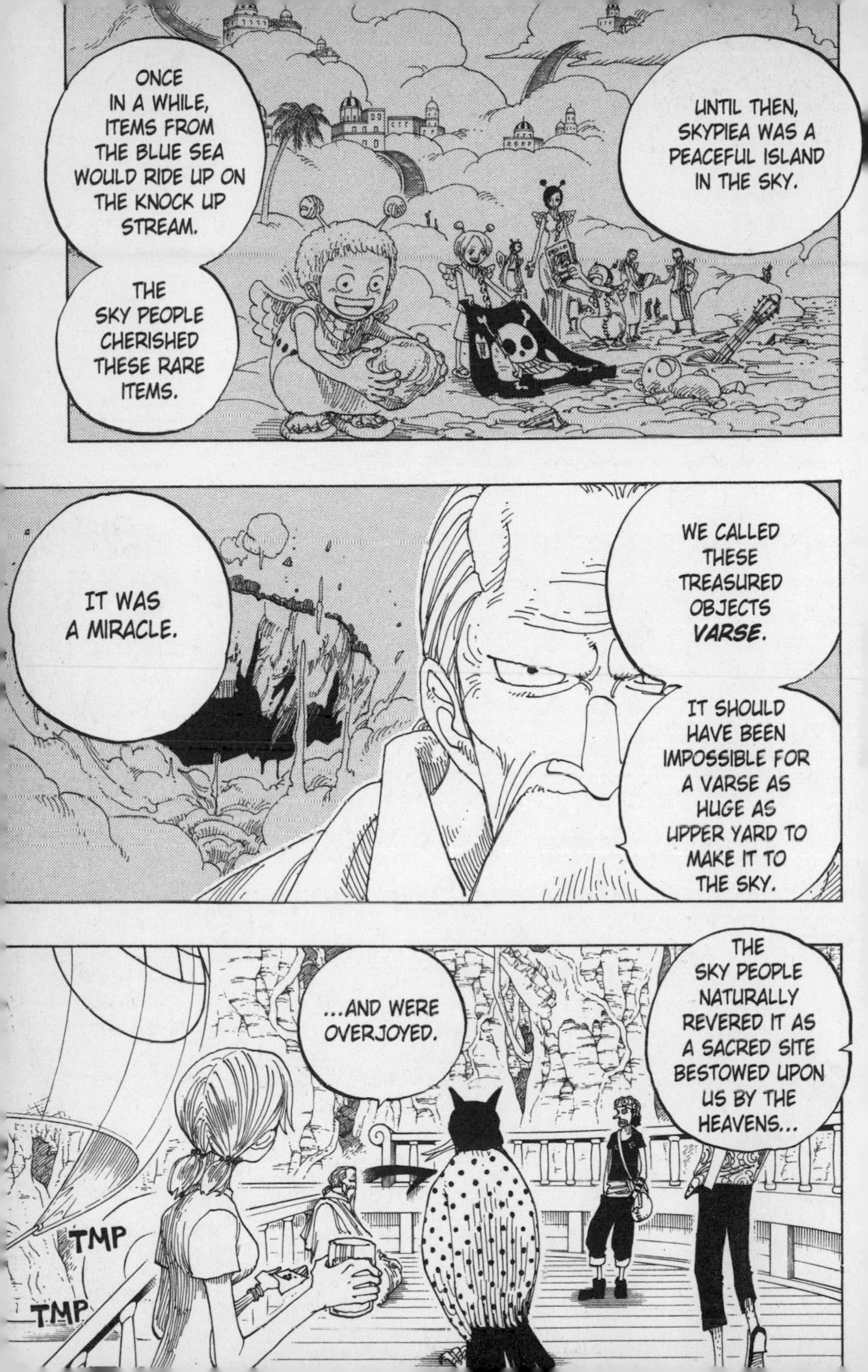
UNTIL THEN, SKYPIEA WAS A PEACEFUL ISLAND IN THE SKY.
ONCE IN A WHILE, ITEMS FROM THE BLUE SEA WOULD RIDE UP ON THE KNOCK UP STREAM.
THE SKY PEOPLE CHERISHED THESE RARE ITEMS.
WE CALLED THESE TREASURED OBJECTS *VARSE*.
IT SHOULD HAVE BEEN IMPOSSIBLE FOR A VARSE AS HUGE AS UPPER YARD TO MAKE IT TO THE SKY.
IT WAS A MIRACLE.
THE SKY PEOPLE NATURALLY REVERED IT AS A SACRED SITE BESTOWED UPON US BY THE HEAVENS...
...AND WERE OVERJOYED.
TMP
TMP

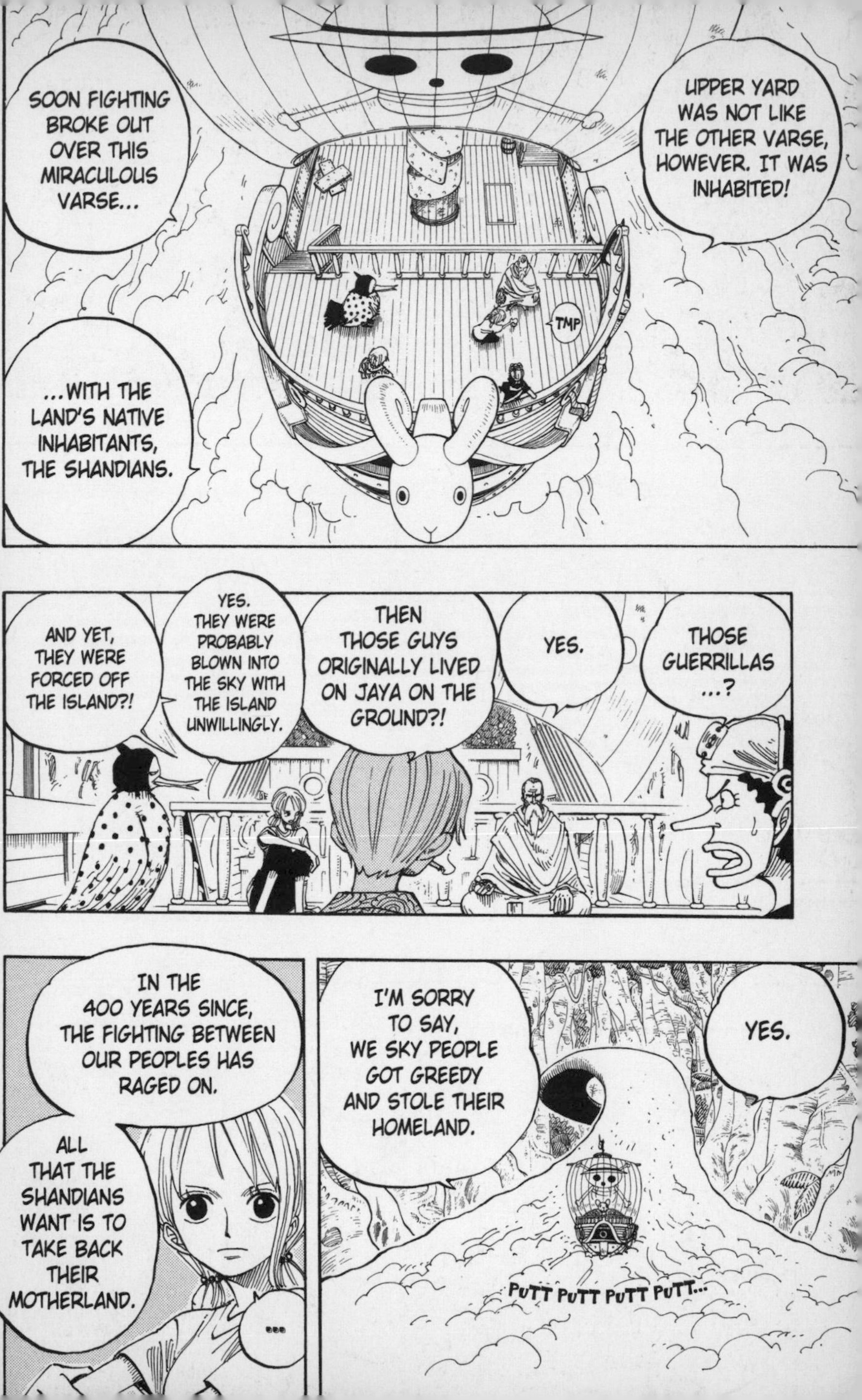
UPPER YARD WAS NOT LIKE THE OTHER VARSE, HOWEVER. IT WAS INHABITED!
SOON FIGHTING BROKE OUT OVER THIS MIRACULOUS VARSE...
TMP
...WITH THE LAND'S NATIVE INHABITANTS, THE SHANDIANS.
THOSE GUERRILLAS ...?
YES.
THEN THOSE GUYS ORIGINALLY LIVED ON JAYA ON THE GROUND?!
YES. THEY WERE PROBABLY BLOWN INTO THE SKY WITH THE ISLAND UNWILLINGLY.
AND YET, THEY WERE FORCED OFF THE ISLAND?!
YES.
I'M SORRY TO SAY, WE SKY PEOPLE GOT GREEDY AND STOLE THEIR HOMELAND.
PUTT PUTT PUTT PUTT...
IN THE 400 YEARS SINCE, THE FIGHTING BETWEEN OUR PEOPLES HAS RAGED ON.
ALL THAT THE SHANDIANS WANT IS TO TAKE BACK THEIR MOTHERLAND.
...

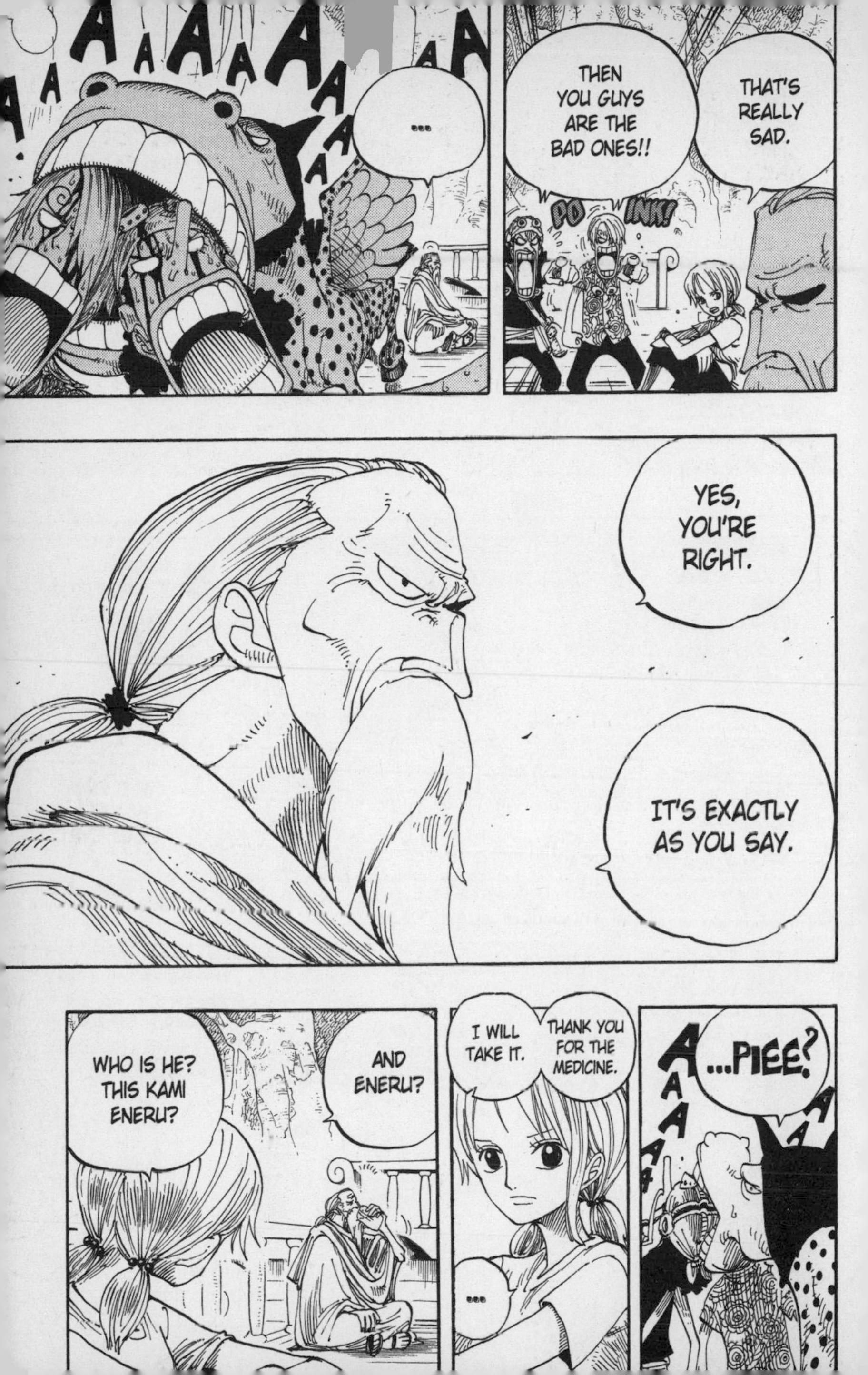
THAT'S REALLY SAD.
THEN YOU GUYS ARE THE BAD ONES!!
PO
INK!
...
AAAAAAAAAAAAA
YES, YOU'RE RIGHT.
IT'S EXACTLY AS YOU SAY.
...PIEE?
AAAAA
THANK YOU FOR THE MEDICINE.
I WILL TAKE IT.
...
AND ENERU?
WHO IS HE? THIS KAMI ENERU?

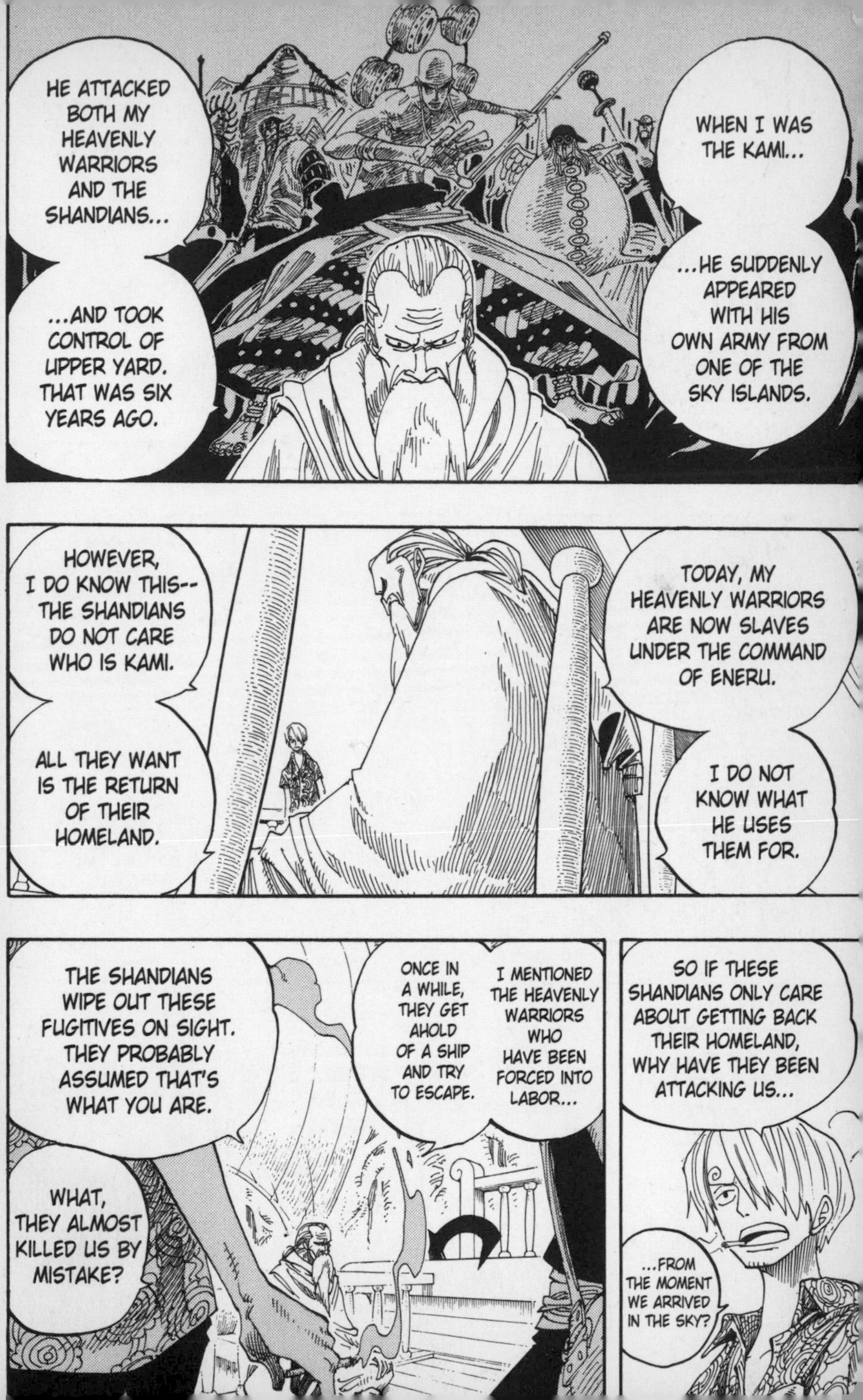
WHEN I WAS THE KAMI...
...HE SUDDENLY APPEARED WITH HIS OWN ARMY FROM ONE OF THE SKY ISLANDS.
HE ATTACKED BOTH MY HEAVENLY WARRIORS AND THE SHANDIANS...
...AND TOOK CONTROL OF UPPER YARD. THAT WAS SIX YEARS AGO.
TODAY, MY HEAVENLY WARRIORS ARE NOW SLAVES UNDER THE COMMAND OF ENERU.
I DO NOT KNOW WHAT HE USES THEM FOR.
HOWEVER, I DO KNOW THIS-- THE SHANDIANS DO NOT CARE WHO IS KAMI.
ALL THEY WANT IS THE RETURN OF THEIR HOMELAND.
SO IF THESE SHANDIANS ONLY CARE ABOUT GETTING BACK THEIR HOMELAND, WHY HAVE THEY BEEN ATTACKING US...
...FROM THE MOMENT WE ARRIVED IN THE SKY?
I MENTIONED THE HEAVENLY WARRIORS WHO HAVE BEEN FORCED INTO LABOR...
ONCE IN A WHILE, THEY GET AHOLD OF A SHIP AND TRY TO ESCAPE.
THE SHANDIANS WIPE OUT THESE FUGITIVES ON SIGHT. THEY PROBABLY ASSUMED THAT'S WHAT YOU ARE.
WHAT, THEY ALMOST KILLED US BY MISTAKE?

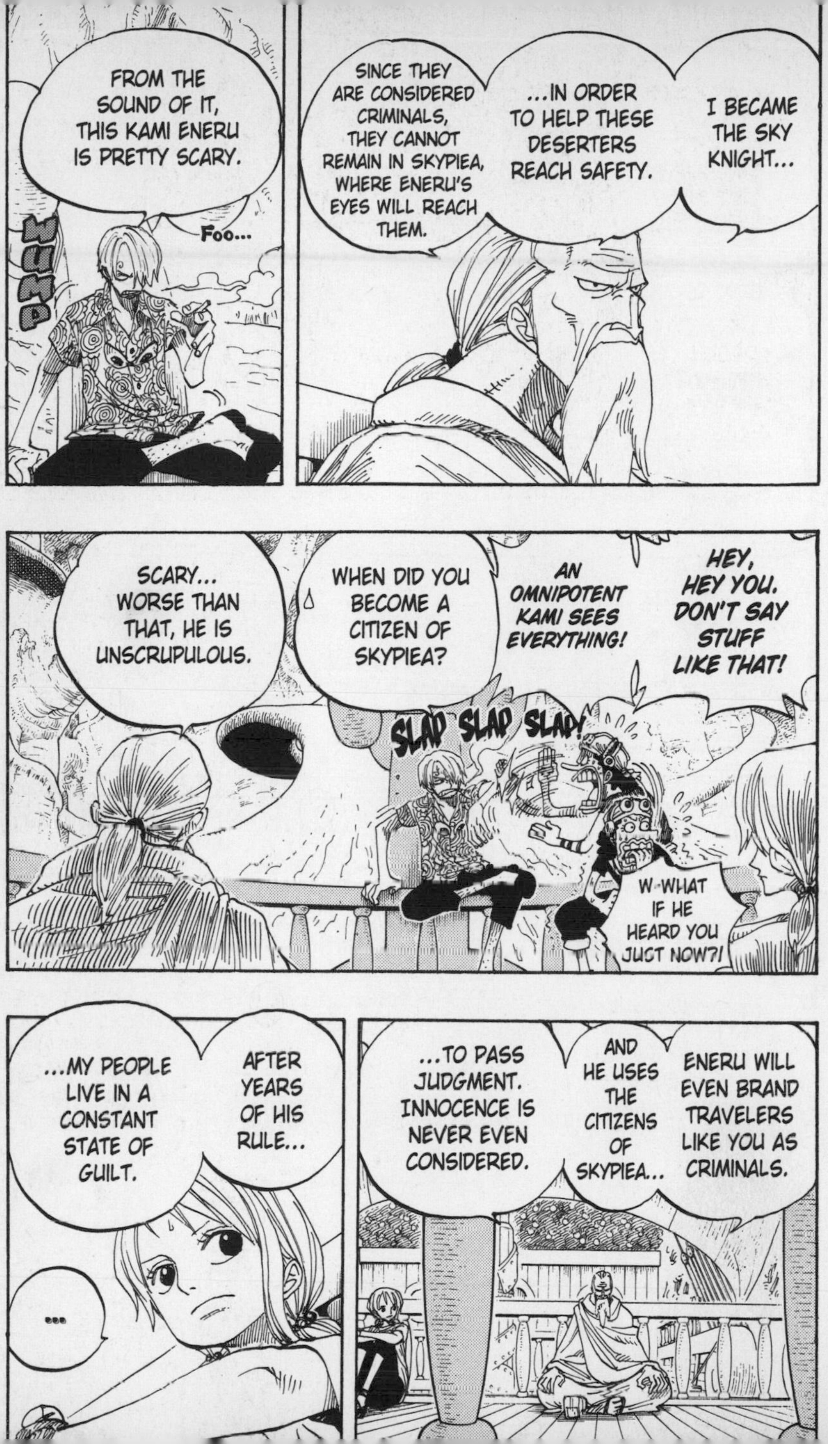
I BECAME THE SKY KNIGHT...
...IN ORDER TO HELP THESE DESERTERS REACH SAFETY.
SINCE THEY ARE CONSIDERED CRIMINALS, THEY CANNOT REMAIN IN SKYPIEA, WHERE ENERU'S EYES WILL REACH THEM.
FROM THE SOUND OF IT, THIS KAMI ENERU IS PRETTY SCARY.
Foo...
WUMP
HEY, HEY YOU. DON'T SAY STUFF LIKE THAT!
AN OMNIPOTENT KAMI SEES EVERYTHING!
WHEN DID YOU BECOME A CITIZEN OF SKYPIEA?
SLAP SLAP SLAP!
W-WHAT IF HE HEARD YOU JUST NOW?!
SCARY... WORSE THAN THAT, HE IS UNSCRUPULOUS.
ENERU WILL EVEN BRAND TRAVELERS LIKE YOU AS CRIMINALS.
AND HE USES THE CITIZENS OF SKYPIEA...
...TO PASS JUDGMENT. INNOCENCE IS NEVER EVEN CONSIDERED.
AFTER YEARS OF HIS RULE...
...MY PEOPLE LIVE IN A CONSTANT STATE OF GUILT.
...

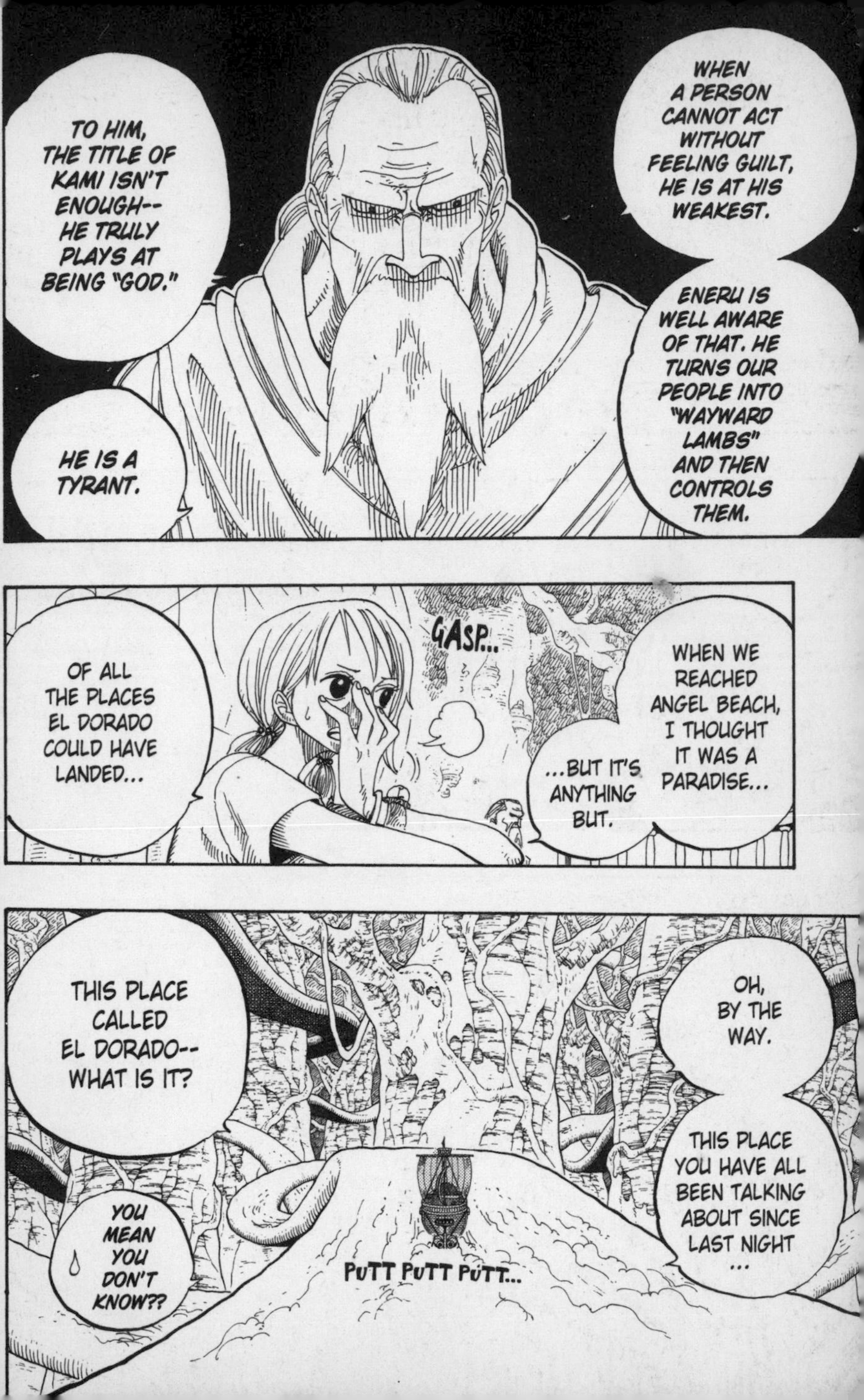
WHEN A PERSON CANNOT ACT WITHOUT FEELING GUILT, HE IS AT HIS WEAKEST.
ENERU IS WELL AWARE OF THAT. HE TURNS OUR PEOPLE INTO "WAYWARD LAMBS" AND THEN CONTROLS THEM.
TO HIM, THE TITLE OF KAMI ISN'T ENOUGH--HE TRULY PLAYS AT BEING "GOD."
HE IS A TYRANT.
WHEN WE REACHED ANGEL BEACH, I THOUGHT IT WAS A PARADISE...
...BUT IT'S ANYTHING BUT.
GASP...
OF ALL THE PLACES EL DORADO COULD HAVE LANDED...
OH, BY THE WAY.
THIS PLACE YOU HAVE ALL BEEN TALKING ABOUT SINCE LAST NIGHT...
THIS PLACE CALLED EL DORADO--WHAT IS IT?
PUTT PUTT PUTT...
YOU MEAN YOU DON'T KNOW??

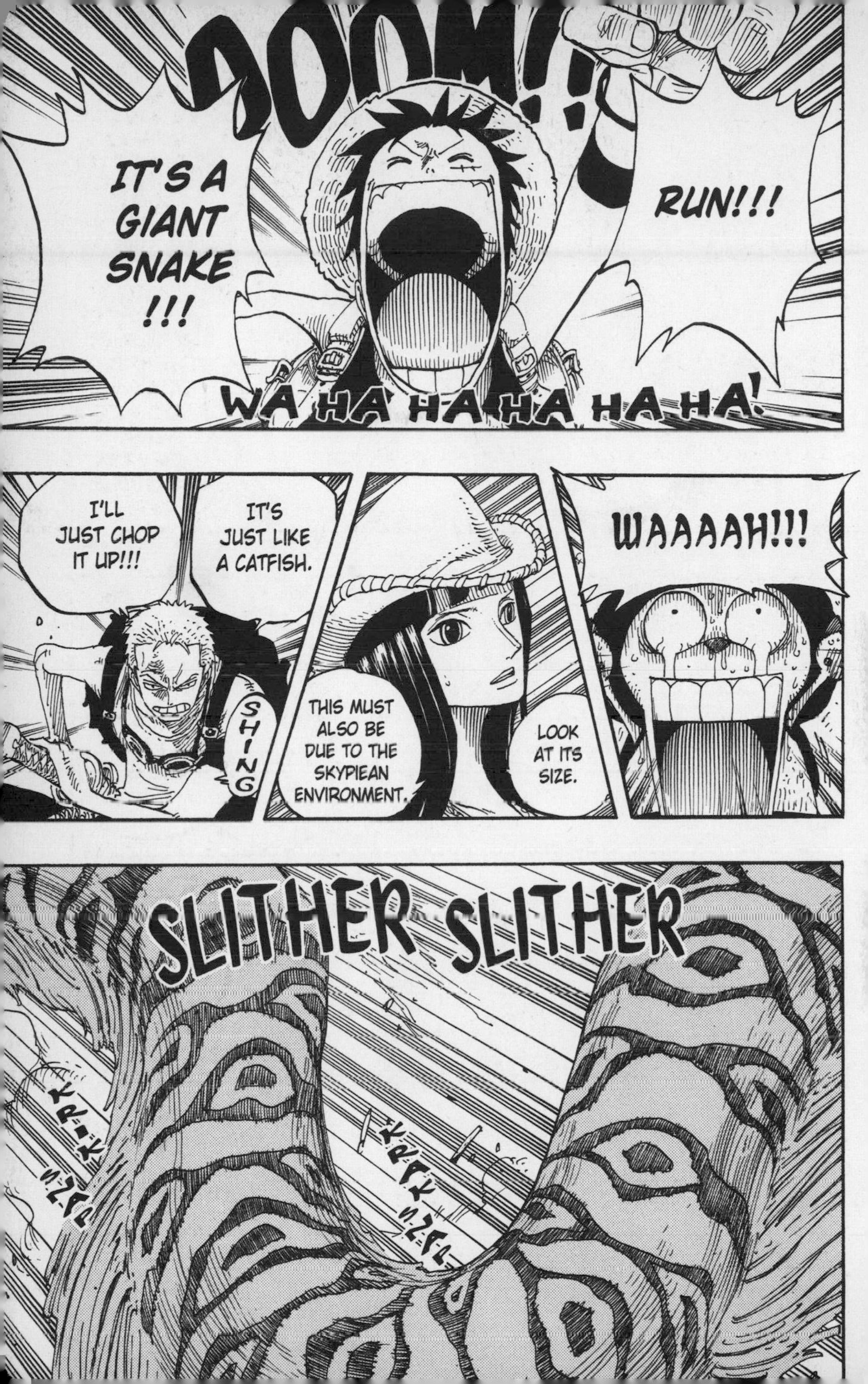
DOOM!!
RUN!!!
IT'S A GIANT SNAKE!!!
WA HA HA-HA HA HA-HA!
WAAAAH!!!
LOOK AT ITS SIZE.
THIS MUST ALSO BE DUE TO THE SKYPIEAN ENVIRONMENT.
IT'S JUST LIKE A CATFISH.
I'LL JUST CHOP IT UP!!!
SHING
SLITHER SLITHER
KRAK SNAP
KRIK SNAP

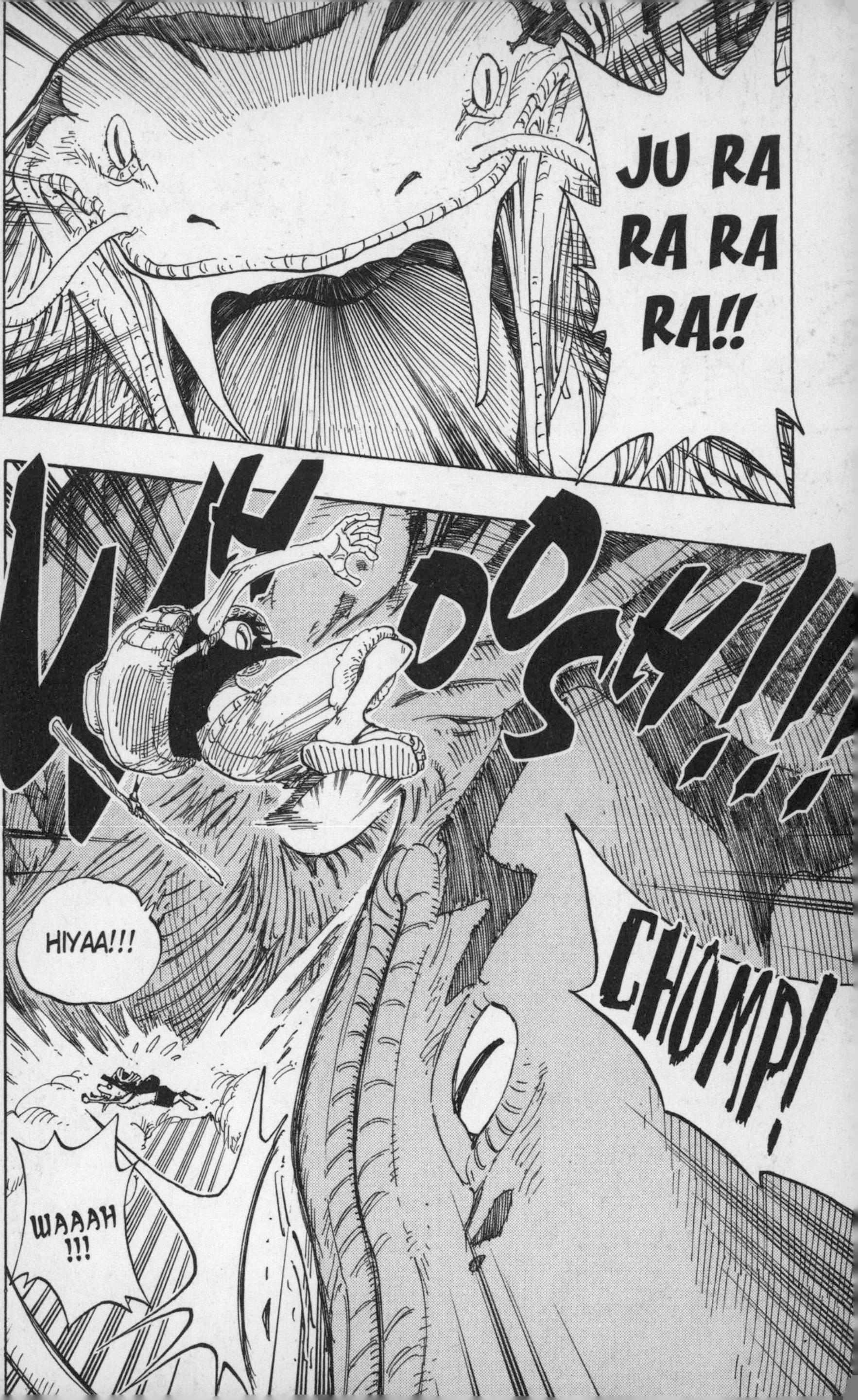
JU RA RA RA RA!!
DOSH!!!!
CHOMP!
HIYAA!!!
WAAAH !!!

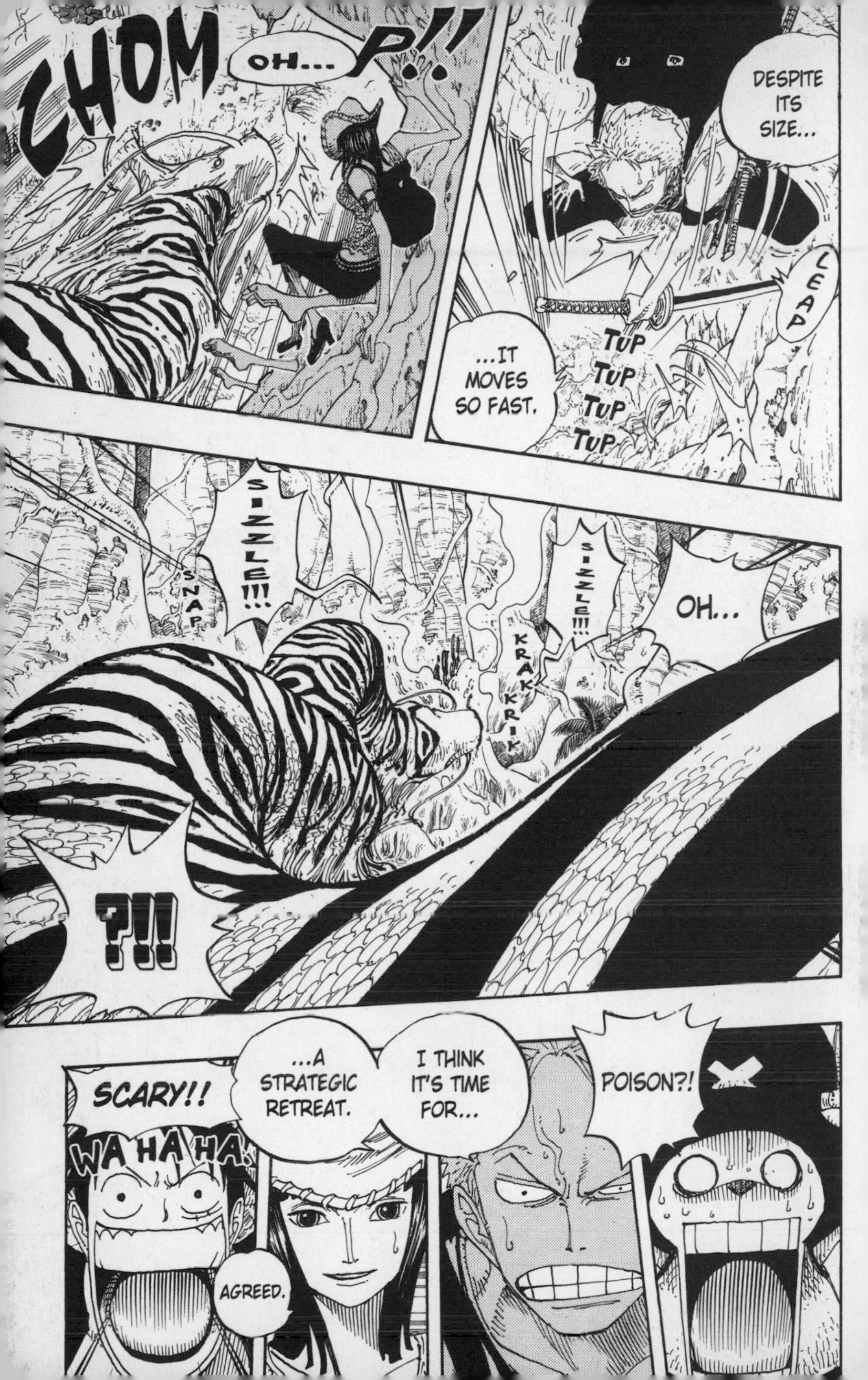
DESPITE ITS SIZE...
LEAP
TUP TUP TUP TUP
...IT MOVES SO FAST.
CHOM
OH...
P!!
OH...
SIZZLE!!!
KRAK KRIK
SIZZLE!!!
SNAP
?!!
POISON?!
I THINK IT'S TIME FOR...
...A STRATEGIC RETREAT.
AGREED.
SCARY!!
WA HA HA.

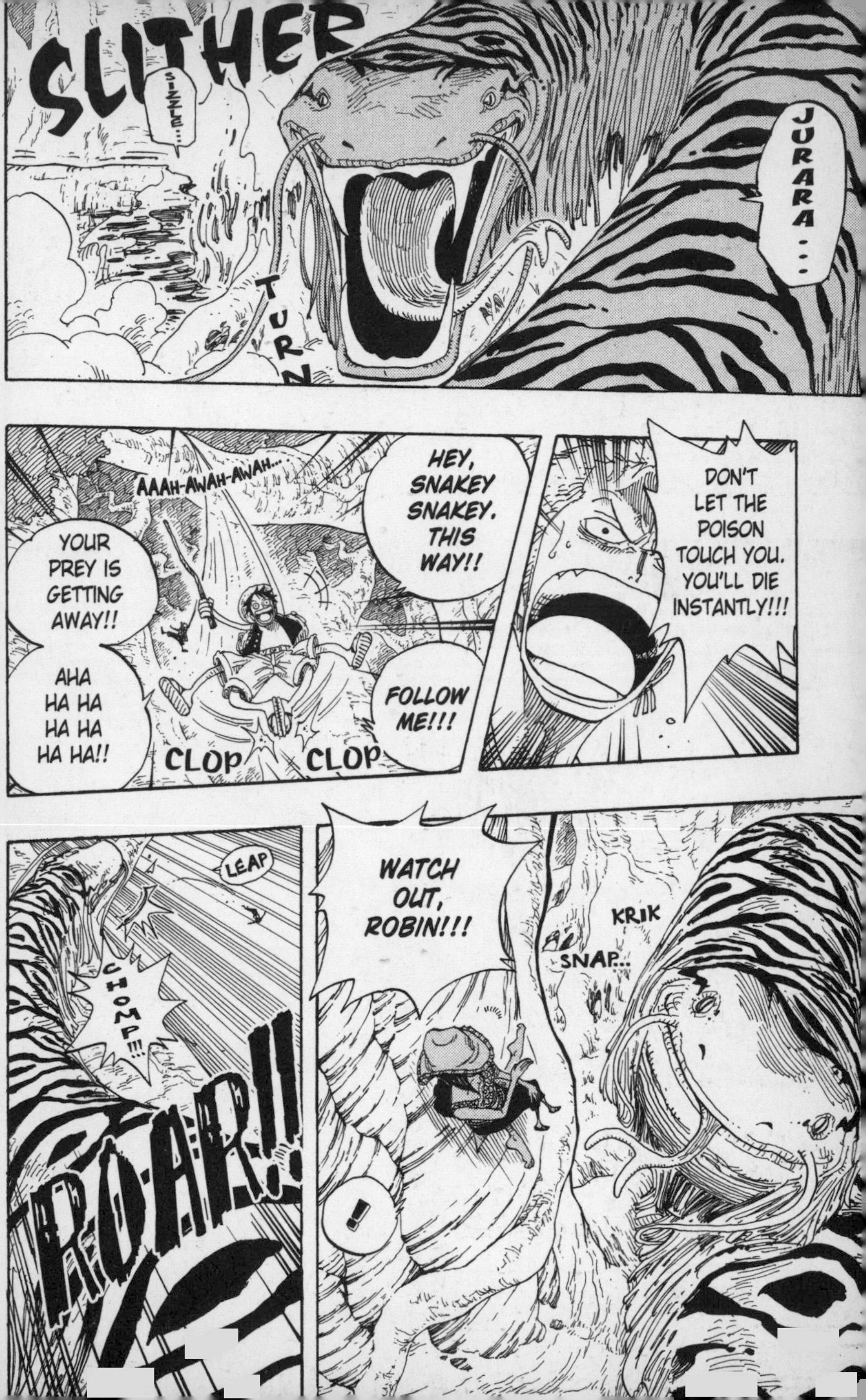
JURARA...
SLITHER
SIZZLE...
TURN
DON'T LET THE POISON TOUCH YOU. YOU'LL DIE INSTANTLY!!!
HEY, SNAKEY SNAKEY. THIS WAY!!
AAAH-AWAH-AWAH...
YOUR PREY IS GETTING AWAY!!
FOLLOW ME!!!
AHA HA HA HA HA HA HA!!
CLOP
CLOP
WATCH OUT, ROBIN!!!
KRIK
SNAP...
!
LEAP
CHOMP!!!
ROAR!!

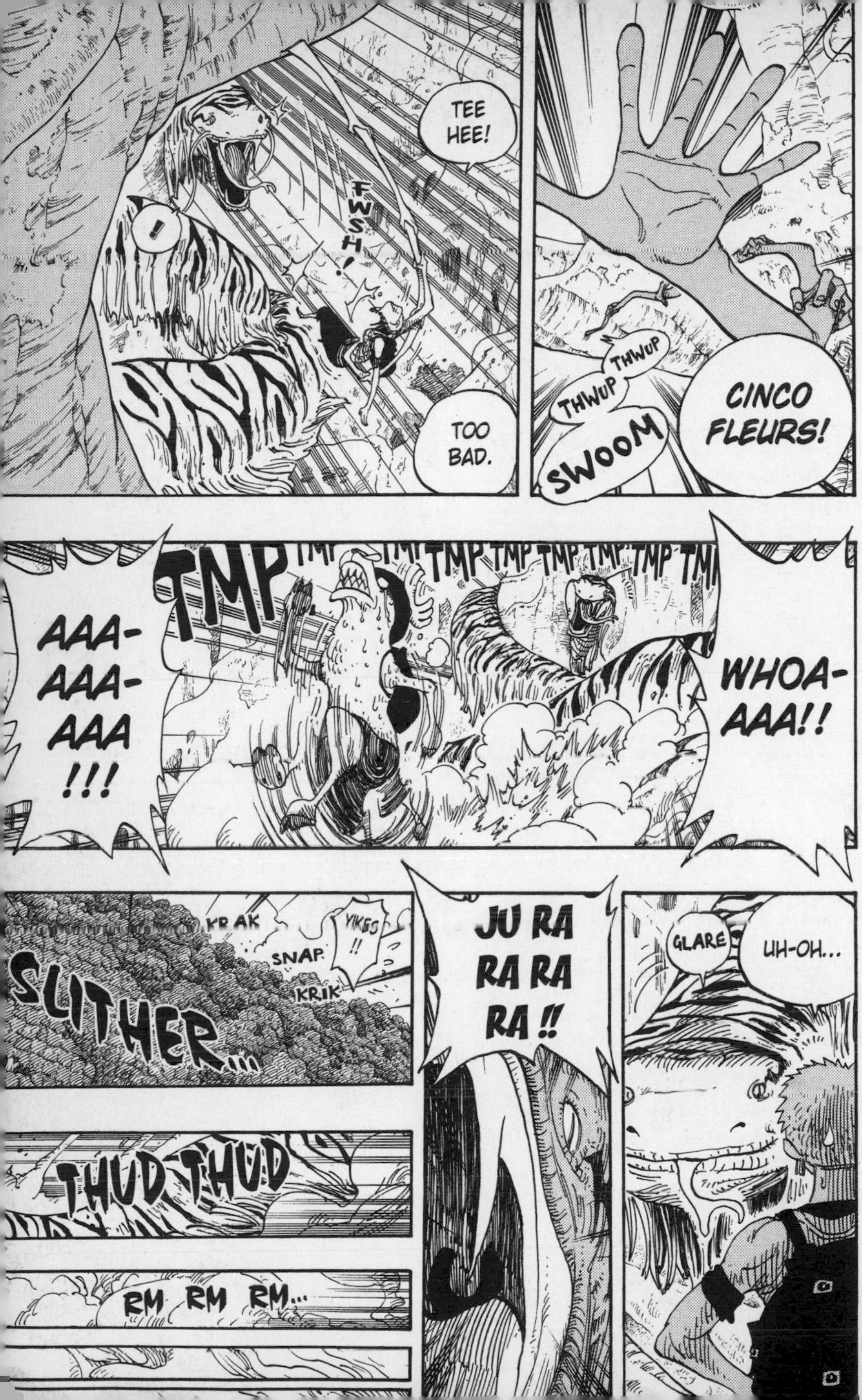
THWUP THWUP
CINCO FLEURS!
SWOOM
TEE HEE!
FWSH!
!
TOO BAD.
WHOA-AAA!!
TMP TMP TMP TMP TMP TMP TMP TMP TMP
AAA-AAA-AAA!!!
UH-OH...
GLARE
JU RA RA RA RA!!
YIKES!!
KRAK
SNAP
KRIK
SLITHER...
THUD THUD
RM RM RM...

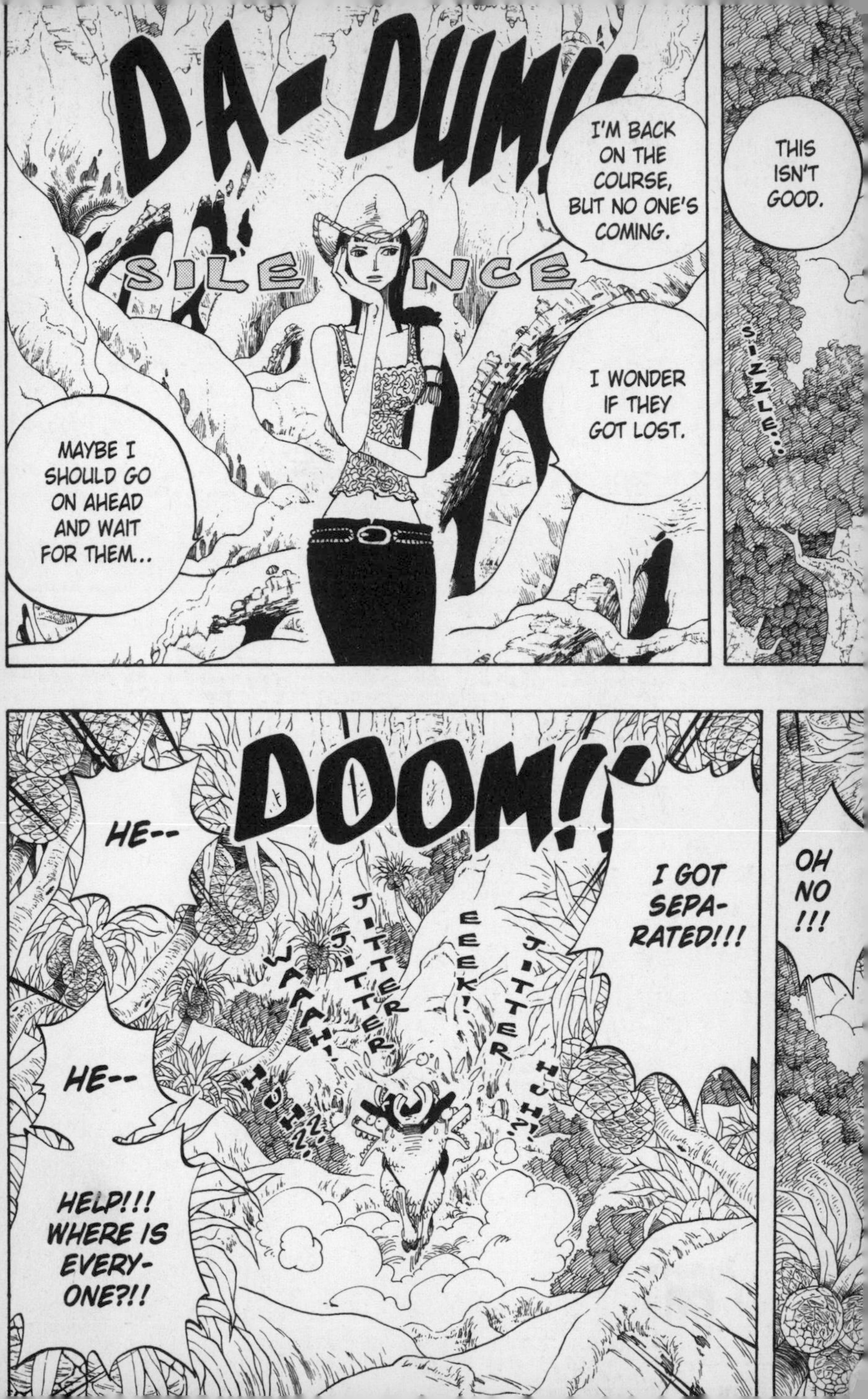
THIS ISN'T GOOD.
SIZZLE...
DA-DUM!!
I'M BACK ON THE COURSE, BUT NO ONE'S COMING.
SILENCE
I WONDER IF THEY GOT LOST.
MAYBE I SHOULD GO ON AHEAD AND WAIT FOR THEM...
OH NO!!!
DOOM!!
I GOT SEPARATED!!!
HE--
JITTER
EEEK!
JITTER JITTER
WAAAH!
HUH?!
HUH?!
HE--
HELP!!! WHERE IS EVERYONE?!!

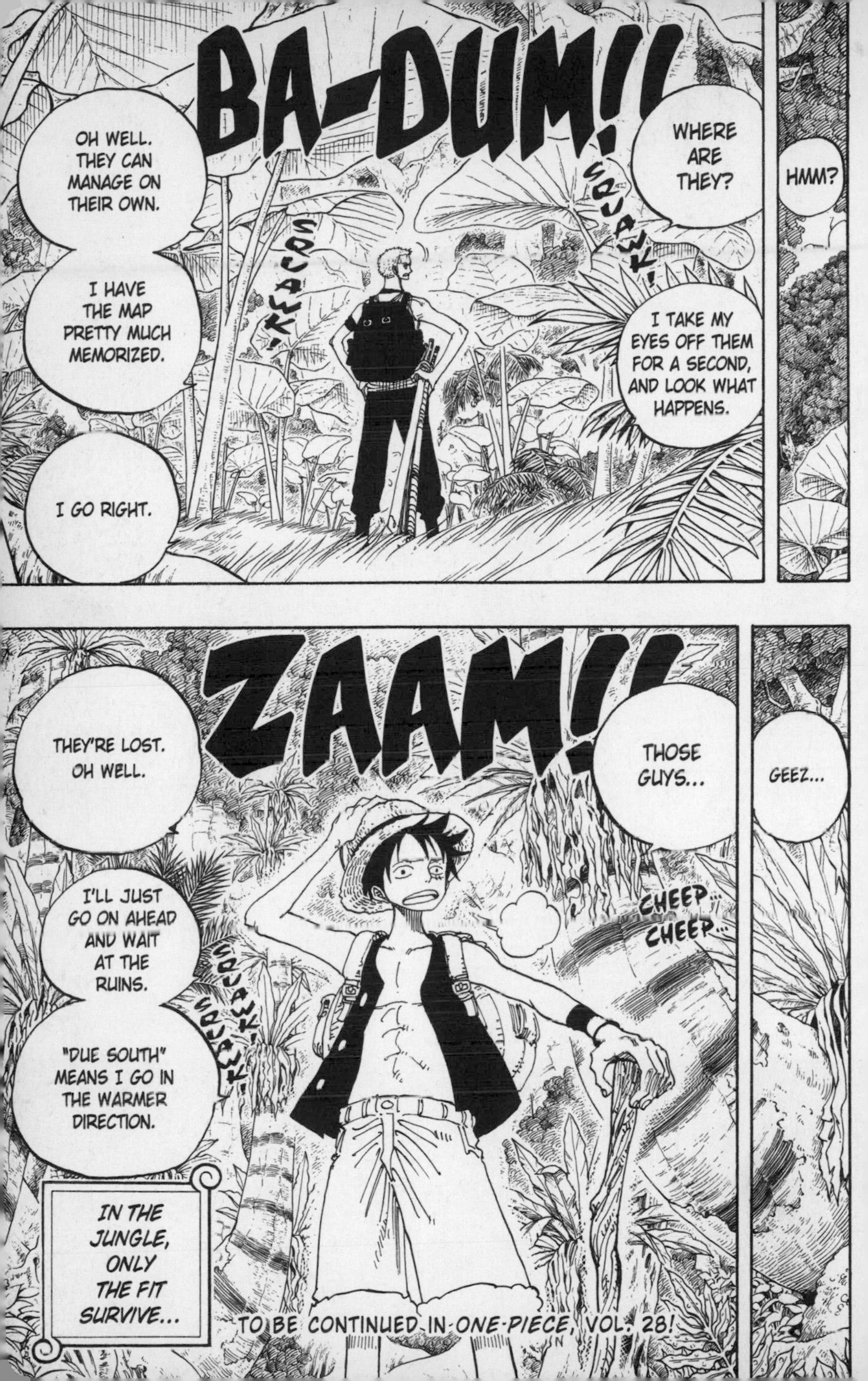
HMM?
WHERE ARE THEY?
BA-DUM!!
SQUAWK!
SQUAWK!
I TAKE MY EYES OFF THEM FOR A SECOND, AND LOOK WHAT HAPPENS.
OH WELL. THEY CAN MANAGE ON THEIR OWN.
I HAVE THE MAP PRETTY MUCH MEMORIZED.
I GO RIGHT.
GEEZ...
THOSE GUYS...
ZAAM!!
THEY'RE LOST. OH WELL.
CHEEP... CHEEP...
I'LL JUST GO ON AHEAD AND WAIT AT THE RUINS.
SQUAWK SQUAWK!
"DUE SOUTH" MEANS I GO IN THE WARMER DIRECTION.
IN THE JUNGLE, ONLY THE FIT SURVIVE...
TO BE CONTINUED IN ONE PIECE, VOL. 28!

COMING NEXT VOLUME:

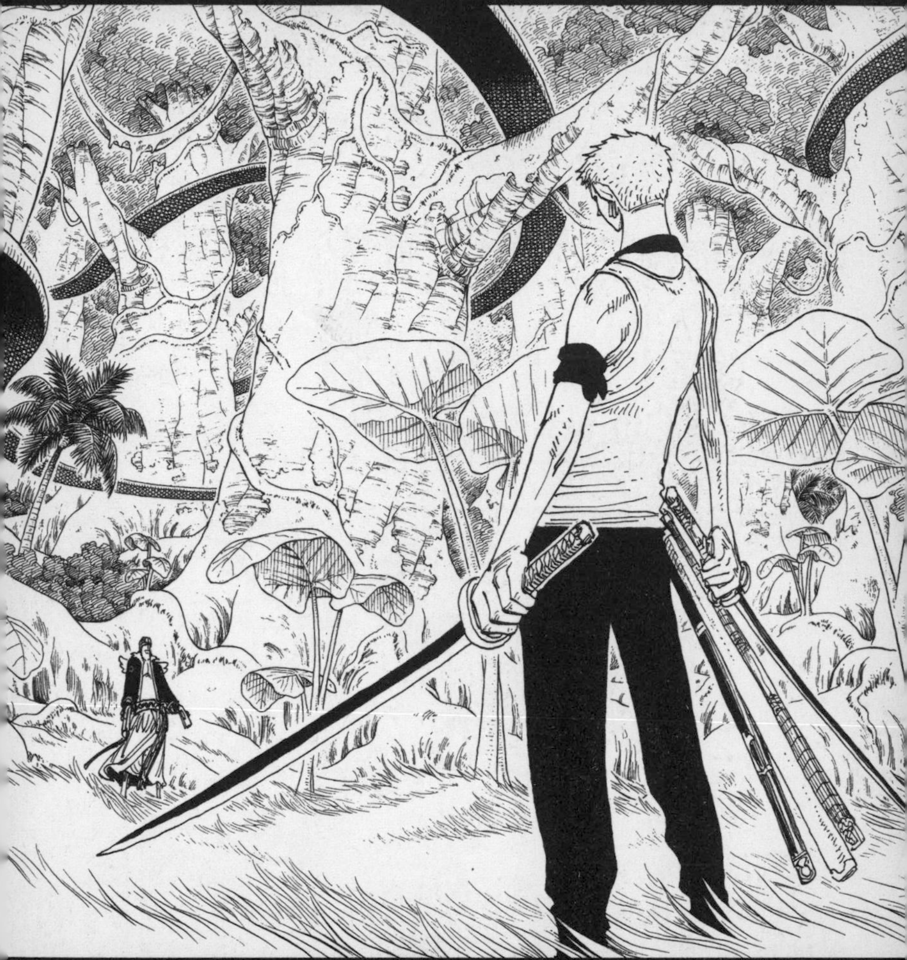

Luffy and crew are on the move to find the hidden gold in the Upper Yard but end up getting caught in the middle of a war between the Shandian guerrillas and the Kami's forces for Skypiea instead. Can the Straw Hats find the treasure before they get pulled into battle?

ON SALE NOW!

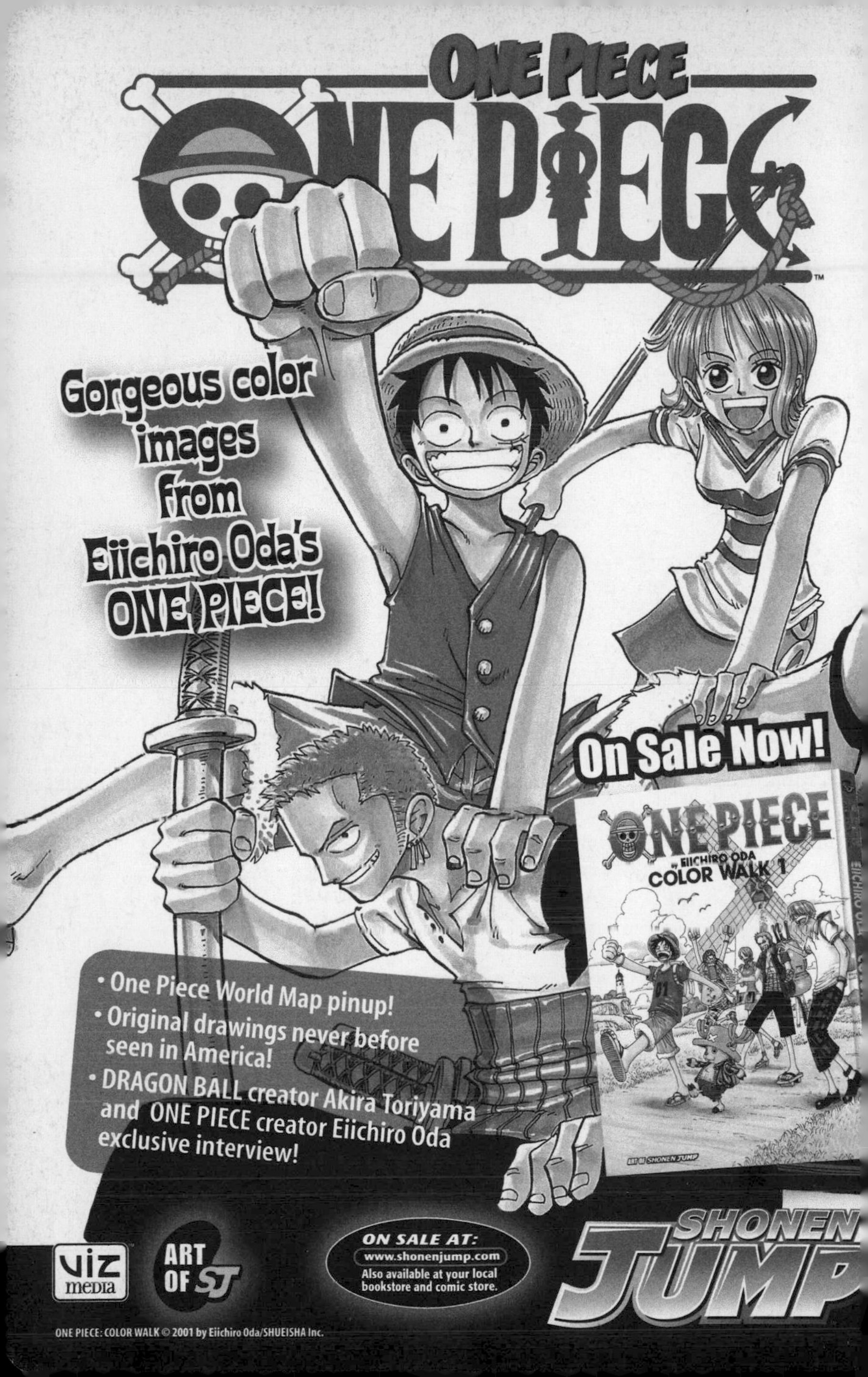
ONE PIECE
ONE PIECE™
Gorgeous color images from Eiichiro Oda's ONE PIECE!
On Sale Now!
ONE PIECE
by EIICHIRO ODA
COLOR WALK 1
• One Piece World Map pinup!
• Original drawings never before seen in America!
• DRAGON BALL creator Akira Toriyama and ONE PIECE creator Eiichiro Oda exclusive interview!
viz media
ART OF SJ
ON SALE AT:
www.shonenjump.com
Also available at your local bookstore and comic store.
SHONEN JUMP
ONE PIECE: COLOR WALK © 2001 by Eiichiro Oda/SHUEISHA Inc.

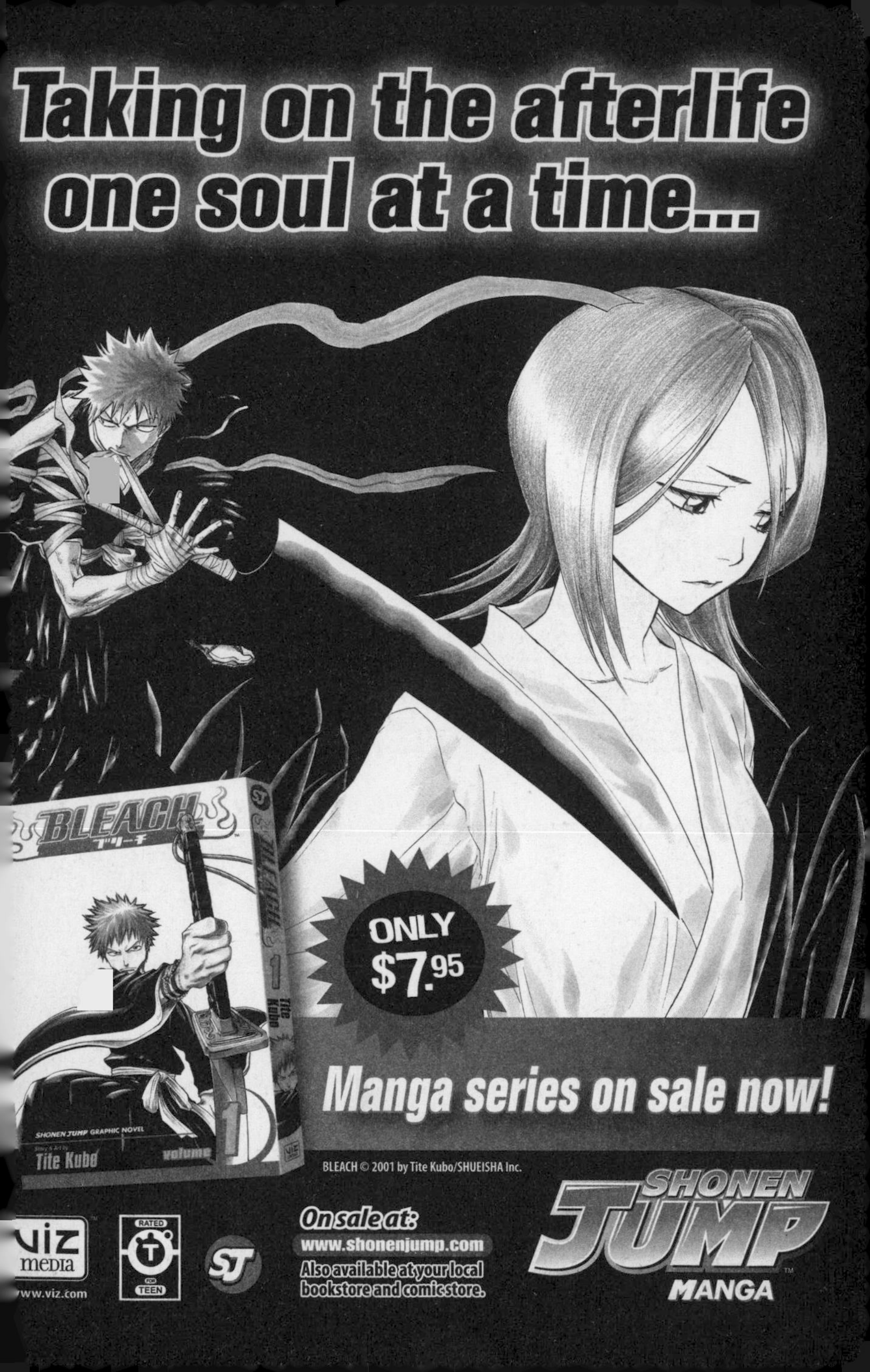
Taking on the afterlife one soul at a time...
BLEACH
SHONEN JUMP GRAPHIC NOVEL
Tite Kubo
volume
1
ONLY $7.95
Manga series on sale now!
BLEACH © 2001 by Tite Kubo/SHUEISHA Inc.
SHONEN JUMP MANGA
On sale at:
www.shonenjump.com
Also available at your local bookstore and comic store.
viz media
www.viz.com
RATED T FOR TEEN
SJ

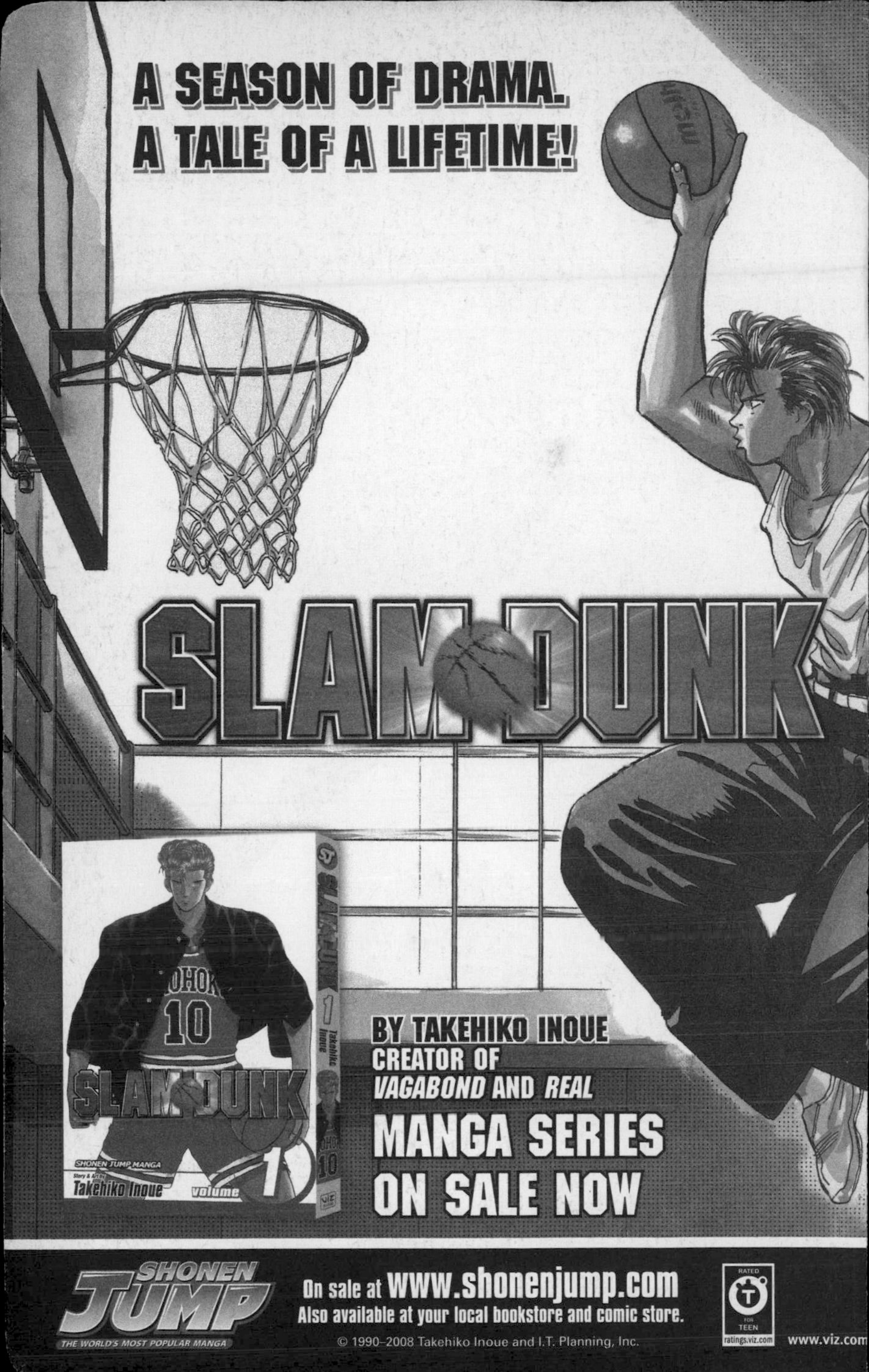
A SEASON OF DRAMA.
A TALE OF A LIFETIME!
SLAM DUNK
SHONEN JUMP MANGA
Story & Art by
Takehiko Inoue
volume 1
SLAM DUNK 1 Takehiko Inoue
BY TAKEHIKO INOUE
CREATOR OF
VAGABOND AND REAL
MANGA SERIES
ON SALE NOW
SHONEN JUMP
THE WORLD'S MOST POPULAR MANGA
On sale at www.shonenjump.com
Also available at your local bookstore and comic store.
© 1990–2008 Takehiko Inoue and I.T. Planning, Inc.
RATED T FOR TEEN
ratings.viz.com
www.viz.com